The Best American
Travel Writing 2001

The Best American
Travel Writing 2001

Edited and with an Introduction
by **Paul Theroux**

Jason Wilson, Series Editor

HOUGHTON MIFFLIN COMPANY

BOSTON · NEW YORK   2001

Visit our Web site: www.houghtonmifflinbooks.com.

ISSN 1530-1516
ISBN 0-618-11877-2
ISBN 0-618-11878-0 (pbk.)

Printed in the United States of America

DOC 10 9 8 7 6 5 4 3 2 1

118 - 5127

Contents

Foreword   xi

Introduction by Paul Theroux   xvii

SCOTT ANDERSON. *As Long As We Were Together, Nothing Bad Could Happen to Us*   1
from *Men's Journal*

RUSSELL BANKS. *Fox and Whale, Priest and Angel*   20
from *Esquire*

TIM CAHILL. *Volcano Alley Is Ticking*   29
from *Men's Journal*

PHILIP CAPUTO. *Among the Man-Eaters*   47
from *National Geographic Adventure*

ANDREW COCKBURN. *Iran: Are You Ready?*   75
from *Condé Nast Traveler*

GRETEL EHRLICH. *The Endless Hunt*   88
from *National Geographic Adventure*

MICHAEL FINKEL. *Desperate Passage*   105
from *The New York Times Magazine*

IAN FRAZIER. *Desert Hideaway*   125
from *The Atlantic Monthly*

PETER HESSLER. *View from the Bridge* 132
from *The New Yorker*

PICO IYER. *Why We Travel* 142
from *Salon Travel*

KATHLEEN LEE. *Into the Heart of the Middle Kingdom* 152
from *Condé Nast Traveler*

JANET MALCOLM. *Travels with Chekhov* 164
from *The New Yorker*

LAWRENCE MILLMAN. *Daughter of the Wind* 189
from *Islands*

SUSAN MINOT. *This We Came to Know Afterward* 199
from *McSweeney's*

SUSAN ORLEAN. *The Place to Disappear* 228
from *The New Yorker*

DAVID QUAMMEN. *The Post-Communist Wolf* 238
from *Outside*

SALMAN RUSHDIE. *A Dream of Glorious Return* 254
from *The New Yorker*

EDWARD W. SAID. *Paradise Lost* 276
from *Travel & Leisure*

BOB SHACOCHIS. *Something Wild in the Blood* 286
from *Men's Journal*

THOMAS SWICK. *Croatian Rock* 301
from *South Florida Sun-Sentinel*

PATRICK SYMMES. *Miraculous Fishing* 318
from *Harper's Magazine*

JEFFREY TAYLER. *Back in the USSR?* 341
from *Harper's Magazine*

MARCEL THEROUX. *The Very, Very, Very Big Chill* 361
from *Travel & Leisure*

Contents

BRAD WETZLER. *Is Just Like Amerika!* 366
from *Outside*

JASON WILSON. *Dining Out in Iceland* 380
from *The North American Review*

SIMON WINCHESTER. *Beyond Siberia* 401
from *Condé Nast Traveler*

Contributors' Notes 409
Notable Travel Writing of 2000 415

Foreword

I have been sent many odd promotional items by wrongheaded public relations people desperate for me to write about their clients. Nothing, however, has been more misguided than the Kwikpoint™ International Translator that I received a few years ago.

The Kwikpoint™ International Translator is a laminated, legal-sized card, folded three times, with full-color illustrations inside and out. On the front cover, the Kwikpoint™ International Translator proclaims: "Say It with Pictures!"; "Point to Pictures and Make Yourself Understood Anywhere in the World!" Above those proclamations is a cartoon drawing of a tourist, a man with a camera strapped around his neck, seated at a restaurant table. His ignored menu sits beside him on the table and in his hands is a trusty Kwikpoint™ International Translator. The man points at a simple illustration of a cup of coffee, while above him, inside his cartoon dialogue bubble, the same image of a cup of coffee is rendered. Meanwhile, the smiling waitress stands before him and dutifully writes down his order. In her cartoon thought bubble is the exact same image of a cup of coffee. The cartoon's message is clear: An international crisis has just been averted. Without ever having to learn that pesky foreign word for coffee, our tourist friend has successfully conveyed his beverage choice to the smiling waitress, who has understood him — even though she's made it very difficult for our friend by not speaking his language.

But coffee isn't the only image that the Kwikpoint™ International Translator provides. Open the thing up and there are hundreds of tiny pictures for the tourist to point at, and presumably resolve any situation that might arise. There are, of course, images for police, fire, hospital, pharmacy, currency exchange, hotel, train station, toothpaste, and the red-circle-with-a-slash international sign for "No." But there are also more advanced images for specific needs — massage, diving equipment, casino games, squat toilet, male and female contraceptives, jumper cables, pipe-smoking supplies, poached egg, frog legs, life preserver. By following the guide at the bottom of the page, you can create compound ideas. Pointing at a glass of ice cubes plus a cup of coffee would equal iced coffee, for instance. Pointing to the red-circle-with-a-slash plus a jar of mustard equals "No Mustard." Almost as an afterthought, in tiny letters, at the very bottom of the back page, the following advice is printed: "Learn a few key words in the local language: Yes, No, Hello, Goodbye, Thank You, Please, Love, Peace."

I believe that we have reached a very strange place in the evolution of travel when a product like the Kwikpoint™ International Translator appears. And I can't help but feel sorry for the person who feels compelled to tuck one of these into his fanny pack, next to his electronic currency converter, just in case he finds himself separated from the tour bus and suddenly in a place where no English is spoken.

I don't want to suggest that everyone who plans to travel should learn to speak a new language in order to do so. Nor do I want to get into another silly debate about what separates a "real traveler" from someone who's "simply a tourist" — I happen to agree with Paul Fussell, who, in his seminal book *Abroad*, wrote: "We are all tourists now, and there is no escape."

I bring up the Kwikpoint™ International Translator here because it strikes me as the antithesis of what travel is supposed to be. The person who uses this item is a person who, at worst, has an absolute, almost colonial, need to exert control over any people, place, or situation he encounters. The message: I can't understand a word you're saying, but it doesn't matter, because I can point to a picture of pancakes and syrup, and you will fetch it for me. At best, the person who uses the Kwikpoint™ International Translator is sadly incapable of leaving any part of his trip to serendipity. He deprives himself of the full experience that travel offers. "Strolling through the marketplace of travel opportunities, one cannot help but recognize that preparedness has become an obsession," writes Edwin Dobbs, observing the proliferation of travel guides and packaged tours in "Where the Good Begins," an essay published several years ago in *Harper's*. This obsession with preparedness is perhaps part of a larger obsession in our society: to eradicate fear, from every situation and at all costs. But fear and travel nearly always go hand in hand.

"Without fear, travel has no meaning," writes Keath Fraser in the introduction to the anthology *Bad Trips*. "In the finest travel writing the storyteller resolves his fears through the catharsis of narrative." Dobbs, in his essay, says that to travel well, "one must court difference." While certainly far from the only barometers of great travel writing, these are very good places to start. Most often, the fear is simply of the unknown. And since the unknown differs so wildly from person to person, it's one of the reasons why travel writing is a rich genre. An experienced adventurer like Scott Anderson may be at home in war zones and, as his humorous and poignant memoir in this collection shows, it may take the odd brush with a land mine for fear finally to rush in. But your bookish relative from a small town in Minnesota who has never been to Europe may also travel well — if he courts difference and embraces fear and allows the world to work its magic while observing intently.

Over thirty years ago, that relative — my father's cousin Bob, in this case — arrived in Lisbon without speaking any Portuguese. On his first night in town, he found himself in a restaurant, unable to read the menu. The waiter, finally exasperated with Bob's linguistic attempts, sat him at a table with a young, well-dressed Portuguese man, who spoke just enough English to help Bob order his dinner. Though the two men could barely communicate, they struck up a friendship, and continued to dine together for the next three nights. The young man took Bob to wonderful, hidden, traditional restaurants in the gothic streets of the Bairro Alto, where they both ate heartily and the young man never let Bob pay for his meals. The dinner conversation never got beyond the basics, but over several evenings Bob learned that the young man had once lived in Lisbon, but no longer did, and that these restaurants had once been his family's favorites. On their last night together, the man became very serious and teary, and tried to explain something important to Bob. But in the end, the language gap was too great.

Several months later, after Bob had returned home from his European tour, he received a letter, in Portuguese. He presumed it was from the young man he'd met, but the postmark was from South America. Unable to read the letter, he threw it in a drawer, and didn't pick it up again until many years later, when he found it and asked a Brazilian friend to translate.

The translation was heartbreaking. The letter had not, in fact, come from the young man, but instead from his wife. She explained that the young man had died soon after their dinners together. His wife went on to write that the young man had been diagnosed with a terminal illness, with only a few months to live. The man's family had been aristocrats of some kind, and lived in exile for many years. He had longed to return to Portugal once again before he died, above all to taste the food of his homeland. She expressed her gratitude to Bob for keeping her husband company during his emotional journey. Bob wept uncontrollably, and suddenly the strange encounter took on the power of a very personal myth.

Over dinner last year, Bob told my family this story. Thirty years later, the naive, chance event still brought him to tears at the dinner table. Perhaps it goes without saying that if Bob had been able to point to a picture of a lamb chop on his Kwikpoint™ International Translator, this encounter would never have occurred.

The wonderful stories that Paul Theroux has chosen for this year's *Best American Travel Writing* all deal on some level with fear and misadventure and serendipity. That, along with memorable storytelling, gives them power and significance over what generally passes for magazine travel writing — the "overedited, reader-friendly text bowdlerized by fact checkers, published with a layout of breathtaking photographs" that Theroux decries in his introduction. Among the stories inside: Salman Rushdie returns to India for the first time since Ayatollah Khomeini's fatwa. Gretel Ehrlich fights cold and hunger on a hunting trip with an Inuit family in Greenland. Susan Minot seeks the truth about the abducted children of Uganda. Philip Caputo treks Kenya's Tsavo National Park among its notorious "man-eating" lions. Andrew Cockburn enters an Iran that now welcomes visitors from America. Michael Finkel stows away on a Haitian refugee boat. Russell Banks confronts Aconcagua, the Andes' highest peak, as well as himself — and at a climactic moment in the story, he remembers this telling quotation from Rilke's *Duino Elegies:* "Every angel is terrifying."

While many of the stories here deal with serious and gripping topics, there is no lack of humor to be found in this collection. Peter Hessler is robbed in his Chinese hotel room in the first line of his story "View from the Bridge." Yet Hessler maintains his great sense of humor and wit throughout. "Li Peng gave me free food and drinks at the beer garden," he writes. "I had become a local celebrity — the Foreigner Who Broke His Finger Fighting the Thief." Ian Frazier searches out Charles Manson's desert hideaway after tiring of golf in Death Valley. Susan Orlean hangs with the international mélange of backpackers on Bangkok's funky Khao San Road.

I think it's safe to say that none of the writers in this collection would ever be caught dead with a Kwikpoint™ International Translator in his travel bag.

The stories included in this anthology are selected from among hundreds of stories in hundreds of diverse publications — from mainstream and specialty magazines to Sunday newspaper travel sections to literary journals to in-flight magazines. My eyes are far from perfect, but I have done my best to be fair and representative, and in my opinion the best one hundred travel stories from the year 2000 were forwarded to Paul Theroux, who made the final selections.

And so with this publication, I begin anew by reading the hundreds of stories published in 2001. I am once again asking editors and writers to submit the best of whatever it is they define as "travel writing." These submissions must be nonfiction, published in the United States during the 2001 calendar year. They must not be reprints of excerpts from published books. They must include the author's name, date of publication, and publication name, and must be submitted as tear sheets, a copy of the complete publication, or a clear photocopy of the piece as it originally appeared. I must receive all submissions by January 30, 2002, in order to ensure full consideration for the next collection. Further, publications that want to make certain their contributions will be considered for the next edition should make sure to include this anthology on their subscription list. Submissions or subscriptions should be sent to

Jason Wilson, *The Best American Travel Writing*, P.O. Box 260, Haddonfield, New Jersey 08033.

It was an honor to work with Paul Theroux, whose work I have long admired. I want to thank him, and would like to mention that much of the work for this collection happened as Paul was preparing to make a lengthy and difficult journey from Cairo to Cape Town. I enormously appreciate his efforts in the weeks preceding this trip. I would also like to thank Tammy Powley for her invaluable assistance on this year's anthology, as well as the people at Houghton Mifflin who helped put this anthology together: Deanne Urmy, Liz Duvall, Ryan Boyle, Don Hymans, and Janet Silver. But, of course, the writers included here deserve the greatest praise. *The Best American Travel Writing* is dedicated, as always, to them.

JASON WILSON

Introduction

It is not hyperbole to say there are no Edens anymore: we live on a violated planet. Travelers are witnesses to change and decay, and when they write we are entertained and sometimes enlightened. But the mode of expression, like the world, has changed.

In the past it was fairly easy to describe travel writing. An intrepid person — say, Isabella Bird or Sir Richard Burton — went on a long trip to a remote place and wrote about it. Bird produced nine books, her subjects ranging from Kurdistan to Hawaii. Burton traveled to this hemisphere and so did his compatriots Trollope and Dickens; American writers went in the opposite direction — Emerson, Twain, and James to Europe. Many others set sail. The books reflected the traveler's personality and literary style as much as the journey. *American Notes* is Dickensian, *English Hours* is Jamesian. Even Henry David Thoreau, who scorned foreign travel, wrote magazine pieces about his jaunts to Cape Cod and Maine. So much for the nineteenth century, a time when much of the prowled-upon world still awaited discovery.

Bridging the gap between these writers and those of the 1930s — the next great traveling era — is Kipling as well as the underrated traveler Somerset Maugham, notably in *The Gentleman in the Parlor*, about his trek through Southeast Asia. This in-between era also saw some subtle works of travel-exploration, such as Fridtjof Nansen's about the Arctic and Apsley Cherry-Garrard's about Antarctica. There were also curiosities by such accidental travelers as E. M. Forster and J. R. Ackerly, who like Kipling (d. 1936) lived on well into the twentieth century. Some critics assert (mistakenly, I think) that the thirties produced the best travel books. The rationale is that it was a time when, as Evelyn Waugh wrote, "the going was good." This implied exoticism, escapism, no passports necessary — unlimited access in Mexico, Asia, Africa, and elsewhere for Waugh, Peter Fleming, Graham Greene, Robert Byron, and others. Greene was seeing hidden Mexico, Waugh was observing deepest Abyssinia, Fleming was bushwhacking in Brazil and China — exuberant writers traveling off the map.

It is true that Waugh's *Remote People* and Byron's *Road to Oxiana* are marvelous books, but they are of their time. Every age offers its own peculiar destinations and modes of reaching them, the work of the travelers always reflecting that peculiarity. It goes almost without saying that Greene would not be walking through the anarchic and bloody hinterland of Liberia today with his young cousin Barbara. *Journey Without Maps,* difficult hike that it was, would be a nightmare now.

In postwar traveling, there has been more latitude and less luxury, but still a sense of adventure and high spirits — Rebecca West, Henry Miller, and Lawrence Durrell are transitional figures, not so lighthearted as their predecessors. More recently, other travelers (and in nearly every case they have also been novelists) have continued the tradition: V. S. Naipaul, Norman Lewis, Ted Hoagland, Peter Matthiessen, Bruce Chatwin, Redmond O'Hanlon, Jonathan Raban, yours truly. But, sad to say, even this recent writing will soon be history.

The world has turned, and these narratives are little help in understanding an age when just about the entire earth has been visited and revisited. Even the world I was peregrinating less than forty years ago I hardly recognize now. Am I a fogey, or has the world actually been transformed? The latter, I suspect — or maybe both.

This seismic change happened fast. For example, less than thirty years ago, Lago Agrio, a large, hideous oil boomtown in northeastern Ecuador, did not exist — not even the name. Texas drillers named it after a town back home called Sour Lake. Erosion and toxic waste and brothels and 30,000 interlopers have displaced the indigenous people who lived in a traditional way, fishing in the Aguarico River, watched over by shamans, with a rich dream life —

from peaceful slumber, from psychedelic drugs. Where there is blight now, there was rain forest, and among those trees there were jaguars. I am not saying that Lago Agrio is not a travel destination, but it is a different one from that other, tranquil, undrilled place, requiring a different sensibility and different expectations. The result of a trip to this hellish place will be different — travel writing of a sort, but I am not sure what.

Travel writing these days seems to be many things; but in my opinion it is not what usually passes for travel writing. It is not a first-class seat on an airplane, not a week of wine tasting on the Rhine, not a weekend in a luxury hotel. It is not a survey of expensive brunch menus, a search for the perfect margarita, or a roundup of the best health spas in the Southwest. In short, it is not about vacations or holidays, not an adjunct to the public relations industry. Travel writing is certainly not an overedited, reader-friendly text bowdlerized by fact checkers, published with a layout of breathtaking photographs — and, heretically, travel writing is not necessarily tasteful, perhaps not even factual, and seldom about pleasure. Come to think of it, the horrific town of Lago Agrio is perhaps a perfect subject.

Travel writing — a pair of words that makes me uneasy because it reminds me of a label on a cracker barrel, because it is a label for so many different sorts of narrative, serving so many purposes, some of them utterly bogus — as I was saying, travel writing at its best relates a journey of discovery that is frequently risky and sometimes grim and often pure horror, with a happy ending: to hell and back. The traveler ends up at home and seizes your wrist with his skinny hand and holds you with his glittering eye and relates his spellbinding tale.

This postmodern view of travel as adversity was well expressed by Martha Gellhorn, who, having been married for some years to Ernest Hemingway, knew a thing or two about adversity. (Among other traits, Ernest was unbelievably accident-prone, as conflicted people often are.) In "Credentials," an apt title for the preface to her account of her love of foreign places, *Travels with Myself and Another* (Ernest was "another"), she reflected on travel as a rewarding misery. She had taken a trip to Crete and found herself in a run-down village on a littered beach ("a sewer"): "I had the depressed feeling that I spent my life doing this sort of thing and might well end my days here. This is the traveler's deep dark night of the soul and can happen anywhere at any hour. I was reduced to a contemptible muck heap outside Kastelli. The future loomed coal black; nowhere to go that was worth going to. I might as well stop traveling." And then: "Stop traveling? Come, come. That was carrying despair to preposterous lengths. I'd been in much worse places than Kastelli. Furthermore, millions of other travelers set forth with high hopes and land symbolically between a water-logged shoe and a rusted potty. I was not unique, singled out for special misfortune." In the subsequent pep talk she gives herself, she says, "If you can't learn from experience at least you can use it. What have you done with your long rich experience of horror journeys?"

Any serious traveler can attest that horror journeys are the most memorable, the most valuable, the most instructive, and the most pleasurable to write about because invariably the horror is recollected in tranquillity. The traveler makes notes en route but writes the finished piece at home, in comfort: finishes the crossword puzzle over toast and marmalade and a lightly boiled egg in the bosom of the family and then nips upstairs to resume that episode about hunger and foul weather and hostile locals. This may account for the note of gloating self-congratulation in travel writing, since so much of it — these days especially — is about survival.

More recently, such writing has also become personal to the point of idiosyncrasy, quirkish in the extreme. I don't say this is a bad thing, but it is an obvious thing. In the past a traveler might casually jeer at the natives — Waugh did it, so did Naipaul, and even in the late seventies Martha Gellhorn was writing breezily of how her love for the natural world "did not extend to mankind in Africa or its differing ways of life." Incredibly, she did not see how offensive this attitude was, and how unrewarding.

There is greater penetration among recent travelers — socially, sexually. True, Sir Richard Burton hinted at sexual liaisons in his travels, but these days such episodes are likely to be elaborated upon. There is an insistence today, in all aspects of writing, on the confessional — and this includes travel confessions. But of course writing is invention, and approximation, and selection. So much is left out or edited out or skewed or spun, I sometimes think that everything is fiction and that travel is something that happens in your head.

Travel is an attitude, a state of mind. It is not residence, it is motion. A traveler to Hawaii in January would write of high surf and strong winds and think the place has been nailed down in that description. The traveler to Hawaii in July will describe lakelike seas mirroring unmoving palms and will believe that to be the truth of the islands. The traveler who gets mugged on the beach reports the destination to be villainous, while just a few feet away a snorkeling traveler is thinking: paradise!

What is the reality of a place? Think how just the notion of New York scares people, how it is the City of Dreadful Night for some and Fun City for others. Like any huge city, New York is many things: Babylon, Xanadu, a jungle, a horror, a pleasure, a snake pit, a nuisance. It depends on who is writing about it. Perhaps the only reality is the sum of all the travelers' tales.

Unless there is a strong sense of place there is no travel writing, but it need not come from topographical description; dialogue can also convey a sense of place. Even so, I insist, the traveler invents the place. Feeling compelled to comment on my travel books, people say to me, "I went there" — China, India, the Pacific, Albania — "and it wasn't like that." I say, "Because I am not you."

It seems paradoxical that in an age of accurate information there is so much opinionated travel writing — but of course there are also more travelers. Never before in history has the world been accessible to so many people. The conventional view is that the countries and the cultures are being evaluated, and in many cases this is demonstrably true, yet one of the dominant themes in the modern travel narrative is self-evaluation, not the country being described but rather the traveler. In many books and essays, travel writing is a form of autobiography. This is not to belittle it — and in this sense the modern tendency was prefigured by such books as Isabella Bird's *A Lady's Life in the Rocky Mountains* (1893). The travel narrative with the gloating theme "This is me having a terrible time in a foreign country" can also produce subtle results. And there are many other forms: the spell in the wilderness, the letter home from foreign parts, the dangerous adventure, the sentimental journey, the exposé, the shocking revelation, the eyewitness report, the ordeal, the quest. There is also the traveler as the bringer-home of news. It is the desire of all travelers to be able to say, with Othello (though Shakespeare cribbed the details from a travel book), that they have seen the Anthropophagi, and men whose heads do grow beneath their shoulders.

This collection represents many of these tendencies in travel, some of them modern; nothing in travel is older than the quest. I am puzzled by one tic in contemporary travel writing, a love of the present tense. What is it about this tense that turns travel writers' heads? I regard it as unfortunate — precious, self-regarding, a distraction — but there is nothing I can do except deplore it. There is a shared sensibility among travelers, though. "How very odd that one bends one's own twig and it stays bent," Martha Gellhorn wrote. "Who could have foreseen the effect of childhood journeys on streetcars?" How true. I grew up in a large family and began my travels to get out of the house.

The challenge for the serious traveler in the age of globalization is to prove that the word *globalization* is fairly meaningless. A traveler never really need leave home, in a virtual sense: You can go on a gorilla safari and still talk to your stockbroker on your cell phone ("Fax me in Kampala!"). Or, seeing this as a crock, you can take a leap in the dark to understand that some places are out of touch. And to understand them you need to *be* out of touch. The challenge lies in finding the independence and self-sufficiency to make discoveries. So much of the world is so well trodden that since few of us can find places that are truly off the map, we look for places that have changed, or places to visit in a new way. No one would want to go to the dangerous tropical slums of Port Moresby or Lagos, which might be the very reason they qualify for a traveler's attention.

After the camera crews and the reporters and the research teams move on, and the dust settles, then we need the independent eyewitness, the scarcely visible budget-conscious traveler who simply ambles along, becoming lost in the shuffle, lingering, making notes.

PAUL THEROUX

The Best American
Travel Writing 2001

SCOTT ANDERSON

As Long As We Were Together, Nothing Bad Could Happen to Us

FROM *Men's Journal*

JON SAW THE STACK of articles about the war in Chechnya on my coffee table and looked up at me appraisingly. "You thinking of going back?"

"Oh, I don't know," I said, glancing around my living room, "not really." But my older brother knew me too well to believe that. "I guess so."

As journalists who always seemed to cover dangerous places, Jon and I had both had some close calls over the years, but a high percentage of mine had come during a single three-week period in Chechnya in 1995, and I'd returned from there quite rattled. Now, in February 2000, the Russians and Chechens were at war again, it was at least as vicious as before, and for reasons that weren't clear even to me, I wanted to return.

"You think it's a bad idea?" I asked.

Jon pondered this. "Remember Sarajevo?" He saw the puzzled look on my face. "The land mine?"

I laughed. In the summer of 1996, I'd done an astonishingly stupid thing in Bosnia. The war had ended six months earlier, but there were still mines everywhere, and one day I'd gone hiking in the hills above Sarajevo. Walking down a dirt trail I didn't know, I'd nearly stepped on a partially exposed mine in the path. On trembling legs, I'd spent the next two hours gingerly making my way back up the trail. I'd told Jon about it as a kind of humorous, embarrassing anecdote.

"But that was just idiotic," I said. "I got careless."

"Yeah, but you almost got yourself killed in peacetime. Don't you think that's kind of an omen?"

By the time of that conversation in my living room, Jon and I had spent most of our adult lives writing about the worst people and places in the world. That month, I had recently returned from northern Albania, where I'd reported a story on blood vendettas, while Jon was about to head off for war-ruined Angola. When we got together — which, given our schedules, was only about every six months — we talked of where we had just been, where we were thinking of going next.

What we did not talk about — at least not directly — was how any of this affected us. Instead, we had developed a kind of verbal shorthand with each other, the sharing of anecdotes, like mine about the ill-advised hike in Bosnia, that had no real punch lines: "And then I walked back to the hotel," or, "For a while it looked like they were going to shoot us, but then they waved us on and we drove to the capital." We didn't need punch lines; we'd both had enough of these moments to know what the other had felt.

Yet the sharing of these oblique stories served a purpose. My brother and I had both become increasingly superstitious over the years, convinced that all the narrow escapes in our past made it less likely that we would escape in the future, and we relied on each other to tote up the odds. "Is this bet too risky?" "Do I walk away from this story now?" And the reason we sought this guidance from each other was because, in a peculiar way, our stakes were joined, rooted in a secret fear that had held us all our adult lives: that something would happen to the other when he was off in the world and alone, that one of us would die on the other's watch.

The seed of this, I believe, had been planted twenty-five years earlier, in the first great journey my brother and I shared. Whether coincidence or not, that journey also marked the first time we began to regard each other with anything more than contempt.

Summer afternoons are always brutally hot in Gainesville, Florida, but this one, in the middle of June 1975, had been downright perverse. I'd come home from soccer practice wanting nothing more than to lie in front of the air conditioner, only to find my parents huddled close together at the dining-room table. I was surprised to see my father there — my parents had recently divorced, and he came around less and less often — but then I noticed that they were poring over a postcard.

"It's from your brother," my mother said, handing me the card. "He's had a bad accident."

The photo showed some mangy-looking beach in Honduras. On the back, Jon had crammed about eight hundred tiny words — economical, perhaps, but mostly incomprehensible. Something about building a rock wall, collecting coconuts, meeting a witch doctor. The salient details were in the postscript: "P.S. Writing this from hospital. Accidentally kicked a machete and sliced open right foot. Swollen up to three times normal. Doctors say infected, maybe gangrenous, might have to amputate. Ah well, *c'est la vie.* Much love, Jon."

"Gee, that's a damned shame," I said, and faked a somber look for several seconds. "Well, gotta go take a shower."

While it was something our parents had refused to acknowledge, Jon and I were not close. If I really tried, I could dimly recall some pleasant moments in our early childhood, but not many. Much stronger was the memory of the day Jon decided to teach me how to catch by heaving a large rock at my head, leaving a jagged scar through my upper lip. I was six then, Jon eight, and it was a harbinger of the violence to come; from then on he beat me up almost daily. By the summer of 1975, though, I'd barely seen Jon for two years and was quite happy to keep it that way — and if he lost a foot, well, it might just even the playing field in our next fistfight.

But I also saw precisely where this little gathering in the dining room was headed, for on the table next to my father was a small pile of papers: plane tickets, a thin vinyl folder of traveler's checks, and, on top, a half sheet of thin paper that I recognized as a telex record. Somebody was being press-ganged into rescuing Jon in Honduras, and from the way my parents stared at me, I had a pretty good idea who.

This might require a bit of explaining about my family. My brother, my three sisters, and I had spent most of our childhoods being bounced from one Third World country to the next, the result of our father being a foreign-aid officer for the American government. That upbringing, combined with our parents' hands-off approach to child-rearing, had instilled in most of us a fiercely self-sufficient and adventurous streak. Jon, for example, had hitch-hiked across East Africa by himself at thirteen. Our oldest sister, Michelle, had solo-trekked the Kalahari Desert on horseback at seventeen. At fourteen, I had spent two months on my own in Bangkok.

The catch to all this freedom, though, came into play whenever something went awry with one of us kids. Rather than directly involving themselves in the problem, our parents felt far more comfortable casting another of their children into the fray, and it was with Jon that problems most consistently arose. The previous year, he had dropped out of high school and, after announcing that he was off to the Spanish Sahara to join the Polisario guerrillas in their independence war against Morocco, promptly vanished somewhere between England and North Africa. Our parents had dispatched Michelle, then twenty, to search for him, and she'd eventually found him in the Canary Islands, living on the beach as he tried to repair an old boat he was planning to sail to the war zone. She'd hauled him back to the States, but it hadn't been long before Jon had set out once more, this time to Honduras to help build a friend's house on the Caribbean coast. That's where he had been for the past six months, and now he was in trouble again.

"You're sending Michelle, right?" I asked hopefully, reaching for the telex slip. My parents shook their heads.

My father loved sending telexes. They were charged by the word, with a maximum of ten characters per word, and he could spend hours devising messages that gave him his money's worth. This one was addressed to the main post office in La Ceiba, the town in Honduras where Jon got his mail, and he'd obviously put a lot of effort into it: SCOTTCOMES TOHONDURAS TOMORROWPM. NOREPEATNO AMPUTATION BEFORETHEN LOVEMOMPOP.

This was irritating. My sophomore year in high school had ended a week earlier, and I had big plans for my summer vacation. It was more than that, though. I had always been the good son, the dutiful one, while Jon had always been the hellion, the one who'd started having run-ins with the law at age eleven. It was he who had introduced me to the fine art of shoplifting at eight, and, as he constantly reminded me, we never would have been caught if I hadn't started stealing expensive cigars to give to our father to assuage my guilt.

"Look," I said to my parents in the dining room, "Jon has been nothing but trouble to you people for years; did you stop to think that losing a foot might be just the thing to straighten him out?"

I think that for the briefest of moments my parents actually considered the idea. Then my father shook his head. "Let's not make a big deal out of this. All you have to do is go down there, get him out of the hospital, and put him on a plane home. You'll be back before you know it."

The Paris bar was one of the only places in La Ceiba with air conditioning, and it felt pleasingly arctic compared to outside. Jon and I sat at a window table, sipping from beers and staring out at the plaza. I was not in a good mood. An hour earlier, I'd been sitting on the front steps of the tiny airport terminal in La Ceiba, contemplating how to find the hospital, when a small, blue pickup truck raced up the driveway and came to a skidding, sideways stop. From out of the passenger seat leaped my brother. He was wearing a straw hat and had a sheathed machete dangling from one hip, and as he nimbly loped up the steps toward me, I couldn't help but notice that he still had both his feet. As it turned out, Jon had sent his fateful postcard nearly a month earlier, and, with the aid of penicillin injections, his foot was now fine.

"So why the hell didn't you call to say you were okay?" I asked.

"Well, I thought about it, but . . ." Jon shrugged lamely. After about a three-second pose of remorse, he grinned and gave a dismissive little backward flip of his hand — a new gesture. "Ah well," he said, "*c'est la vie*. Now that you're here, we'll just make the best of it. Come on, let's go into town."

I didn't have a lot of choice in the matter; the plane that had brought me had just taken off for the return to Miami, and there wouldn't be another one for two days. Angrily grabbing my rucksack, I followed Jon down to the pickup and climbed in for the ride to La Ceiba and the Paris bar.

Our conversation so far had been desultory, with lots of long silences and me staring fixedly out the window. Despite my bad mood, I was struck by how much my brother's appearance had changed in the six months since I'd last seen him: He was deeply tanned and muscular beneath his white T-shirt, and his blond hair had turned even blonder in the tropics. With his machete and his battered straw hat tilted to a rakish angle, he seemed like some Hollywood prototype of a jungle explorer. I fell to studying the machete, hanging from his belt to brush the floor.

"So, what's with the knife?" I asked.

He drew the machete, handed it to me by the black plastic handle. "Whacking things. Down here, you've always got to whack something."

It felt good, heavy, in the hand. The blade was nearly three feet long and razor-sharp. I tried a couple of short wrist-flick swings in the air before giving it back.

"You know," Jon said, sliding the machete into its sheath, "now that you're here, you should stay awhile. My job just ended, and we can knock around, have some fun."

Beyond the dirty plate-glass window was La Ceiba's main square, a bedraggled little plaza with some rusting statue in the middle. I hadn't seen anything in Honduras so far that resembled fun. "Maybe you've forgotten," I said, "but we don't really like each other."

He seemed surprised by this. "I always thought we got along pretty well. Oh, sure, we had our little spats every once in a while, but all brothers go through that. It's not like I gave you any permanent scars or anything."

I leaned over the table, pointed to the thin scar in my lip where Jon had hit me with the rock ten years before. Throughout growing up, I'd been rather self-conscious about the scar, a self-consciousness Jon had done his best to promote by constantly referring to it as "the harelip." He squinted to see where I was pointing. "Oh, Christ," he said, "are you still on about the harelip? I apologized for that years ago." He sat back in disgust, motioned to the waitress for two more beers. I returned to staring out the window.

"So how are things in Florida?" Jon asked after a while.

A hard question to answer. Our family had disintegrated exactly two years earlier. My father had taken me out of school, and we'd spent a year traveling together across Europe and the Middle East, but then he'd left me in Florida with my mother and taken to the road again. I'd spent the next six months there plotting my escape: hitchhiking to wherever my father might be, heading to the Yukon to pan for gold with a Scottish guy I'd met on a ship crossing the Atlantic. It had only been very recently that I'd tried to adjust and settle into a normal high school existence. At the Paris bar, I told Jon only about that part — about my friends, soccer, girls I was interested in — but I could tell he wasn't buying it. "It's not going to work, you know. Fitting in, becoming an American — it's not going to work. We started too late to belong anywhere. The only thing we'll ever belong to is this family, each other."

He looked out the window, his eyes darting over the plaza. It was late afternoon, and the streets of La Ceiba were gradually coming back to life, couples strolling through the plaza, lottery-ticket sellers calling for customers in strange, bullfrog voices. "And we're always going to end up in places like this."

I imagine that everyone's childhood, no matter how unconventional or exotic, seems absolutely normal while it's being lived. By the time I arrived in Honduras, I was only beginning to comprehend the downside of how we had grown up, the hidden cost that comes with not being from anywhere in particular. Jon, it seemed, had figured it out a little bit sooner. In the years ahead, we would both be caught up in a seemingly endless cycle of trying to fit in, failing, moving on. In a funny way, I think we both drew a certain comfort in the other's inability to settle down — proof that there was at least one more misfit in the family.

At least initially, it appeared that I was making a better go of things. By force of will, I'd actually managed to stick it out through high school and, pushing off college to some indistinct future, had taken a job with the federal government in 1977. By my nineteenth birthday, I was a full-fledged civil servant inching my way up the bureaucratic ladder, living with my fiancée in a nice Washington, D.C., apartment. Jon, by contrast, had continued his errant ways. Having dropped out of school at seventeen, he'd talked his way into the University of Florida for a couple of quarters, but then signed on as an instructor with some high-school-at-sea schooner and jumped ship in South America. When I next saw him, he was passing through Washington on his way to Nunivak Island off Alaska to make a fortune collecting musk-ox wool, and I could tell he viewed my well-ordered, conventional life with a mix of envy and reproach. When that enterprise failed — it seemed the musk ox were a lot quicker than he was — he'd headed back down to South America.

By 1982, though, our roles had come full circle. That winter, Jon moved to Washington with his Peruvian wife to take a cub-reporter job, wore a tie, and went to an office every day. By then, I had long since quit my engagement and my government job to spend three years drifting around the country while writing a bad novel. I was rootless, unmoored, so the day after Jon moved to Washington, so did I, becoming a bartender in Georgetown. Jon would occasionally come by to sit at my bar. It was a weird turn of events; now he was the one with the stable home life and a real job, while I was the wastrel, the one the others in the family worried about.

But I'd always been a bit suspicious of this new-and-improved Jon, and when he stopped by my bar one afternoon after work, his mask finally slipped. After staring darkly out at the shoppers on Wisconsin Avenue, he suddenly pointed to my tie, pointed to his own.

"Look at us," he said with disgust. "Look at what we've become." He violently wrenched off his tie and slapped it on the bar: "This is not the way we're supposed to live."

Most people probably wouldn't have understood the source of his discontent, but I did. One thing our upbringing had bestowed on us was a powerful sense of entitlement, a belief that we did not have to live by the rules — college, careers — of most everyone else.

Jon's solution was to head off for the civil wars of Central America. Mine was a five-month ramble across Europe and then to the free-fire zone of Beirut. For both of us, these were our first experiences in war zones, and in them we saw a way to have the lives we wanted, that we were "supposed" to have. We would be writers, together and apart, exploring the darker corners of the earth.

"The Mosquito Coast, man — think of it!" I had already been light-headed when we left the Paris, but now I could barely focus on the small, tattered map of Honduras that Jon spread on the table of the dockside bar. He kept jabbing his finger at the top-right corner, a vast stretch of green broken only by the spindly blue lines of rivers, the names of a few towns, and, across its breadth, the single word MOSQUITIA.

"The last great jungle in Central America," my brother went on. "No roads, no telephones. People have gone in there and never been heard from again. We have to go!"

Our stroll to the La Ceiba docks had seemed innocuous enough at first, but I soon discerned a pattern to the people Jon was engaging in conversation: sailors coming off the boats, the captains up in the pilothouses. There'd been at least a half dozen of these little chats before we came to *El Platanero*, a crude wooden coastal hauler of about thirty feet. Upon learning that it was leaving that very night for Brewers Lagoon, a town in the middle of the Mosquito Coast, Jon had grabbed hold of my arm, gazed at the string of ramshackle bars lining the waterfront, and marched me in their direction.

Now, with more beers before us, he was pulling out all the stops to convince me that sailing off on *El Platanero* was not just a good idea, but a kind of destiny. "So we get to Brewers," he said, "take a steamer upriver until we hit this highway, take a bus over to the capital, and then fly back to Florida. We're talking a week — ten days tops." He looked to me. "What do you say?"

This was a pattern that had been established over our lifetimes. Jon was the confident one who never saw obstacles until he came to them. I was the doubter, the questioner — and in his breezy imagining of our path through the Mosquitia, there was a lot to question. It was interesting, for example, how the forty-mile path out of the jungle had become a "highway" in Jon's telling, when the map indicated that a dotted black line meant "foot trail."

But for some reason — perhaps it was the cozy somnolence of the tropics, perhaps it was all that beer — I found I was reluctant to assume my traditional role. I was tired of being the cautious one.

And maybe something more. Sitting in the bar on the La Ceiba docks, I realized Jon was trying to establish a bond between us that had never existed before. I thought back to what he had said at the Paris, that all we would ever belong to was the family, each other. I wasn't convinced this was true, but on that evening it suddenly seemed a risky thing to chance.

"Okay," I said. "Let's do it."

With a great grin, Jon ordered more beers, then rose from the table and announced that he had to run a few errands. In his absence, I slid the map over and fell to staring at the great green void of the Mosquitia. I was in a happy mood, a happiness that deepened the longer I studied the map and fully grasped what a remarkably bad idea this was. When Jon returned, he was carrying a long,

narrow object wrapped in newspaper — a present, he explained. I
tore off the paper. It was a machete in a carved-leather sheath,
some goofy tassels hanging off the bottom. I slid it out, tested its
feel in my hand.

"I also let Mom and Dad know there's been a change in plans,"
he said, taking a folded sheet of paper from his back pocket. It was
a copy of a telex message. Jon had clearly inherited our father's
telex-writing style, if not his brevity:

MOMANDPOP: SCOTTWANTS GOMOSQUITO. METHINKS
SOMEKINDOF ADOLESCENT SELFESTEEM DEALSOMAY BENE-
FITALL INLONGRUN. BACKHOMEIN ELEVENDAYS 1MONTH-
TOPS. PSFOOTFINE.

Beyond the condescending tone, I was irked by how this had suddenly become my idea.

"Come on," my brother shrugged. "You're the sensible one. If
they thought I was behind it, they'd just worry."

Jon came slowly down the rotting wooden dock at Brewers Lagoon,
rubbing the back of his neck and staring at the ground as if stupe-
fied. This was a gesture I recognized, and it had a twofold meaning.
First, something was amiss. Second, it was not Jon's fault in any way;
whatever misfortune had befallen us was completely unavoidable, a
simple act of fate.

"Well," he said, "it appears there might be a problem."

Indeed. Rather than the constant flow of traffic up the Patuca
that Jon had envisioned, there was precisely one boat, a motorized
dugout canoe, that made the run, and it had left just that morning.
It wouldn't be back in Brewers for a week, which, funnily enough,
was right around the time that *El Platanero* — now a mere dot at the
far end of the vast lagoon — would return.

I looked at the Brewers Lagoon waterfront. It consisted of about
two dozen outhouses built on stilts over the mud flats, each
reached by its own little gangway, and my main source of entertainment while waiting for Jon had been watching the Brewers residents trooping back and forth to perform their bodily functions.

Jon continued to rub his neck. "I found a room we can stay in for
two dollars a night. It's got a couple of hammocks, and the woman
will cook for us." He followed my gaze over the sprawl of outhouses.
"Anyway, I'm sure there's a lot of interesting things to do around
here."

This, too, was in error. Rather, Brewers Lagoon was a collection of rude shanties in mosquito-infested swampland, its torpor broken only by the daily 3:00 rain. We passed the days examining ourselves for ticks and reading — then rereading — the paperback novels we had brought. When we heard that the dugout canoe was finally back in town, I practically cried tears of gratitude.

It was a surprisingly long boat, with an outboard motor in back and room for four or five passengers in its hollowed hull. We set off early in the morning, the two boatmen slowly poling their way through the dense jungle marshes at the far end of the lagoon, charting a course through the maze of water hyacinths and mangrove trees. After a couple of hours, the trees and vines suddenly separated, and before us was the wide, muddy expanse of the Patuca. The captain fired up the outboard and we began to race up the brown, barely moving river.

I watched the riverbanks as we passed. There were no towns, no other boats on the river, but every once in a while I glimpsed a crude wooden shack amid the jungle, a wisp of wood smoke above the trees.

"Miskito Indians," Jon said. "They're the only ones who live in here."

Our destination that first day was the trading town of Awas. According to Jon's interpretation of the map, it was a fairly large town and probably the best place to cash some traveler's checks and stock up on supplies before continuing our journey upriver to the jungle "highway." Of course, it wasn't as if we'd made any actual inquiries in this regard.

By late afternoon, the Patuca had narrowed to just fifty or sixty feet across, and it had been a very long time since we'd seen any signs of settlement. At last, we rounded a bend in the river, and there on the riverbank before us were several Miskito women washing clothes, a couple of crude rafts hauled up onto the mud. The captain killed the outboard as we coasted toward shore.

"Awas," he announced.

"I guess the commercial center is inland," Jon said, trying to sound confident.

For some time, we stood on the Awas riverbank, unable to fully grasp our predicament, a source of amusement for the Miskito women washing clothes on the river rocks. The "commercial center" of Awas, we had quickly discovered, consisted of a single trading-post store, a tiny wooden hut built on stilts at the edge of town. What's more, the river above Awas was studded with rapids, so no boats went any farther. The two little rafts pulled up on the riverbank had been built by upland Miskitos to bring their goods to the Awas trading post and then abandoned, their builders walking home through the jungle.

At first, all this seemed a mere logistical glitch to Jon — his new idea was to emulate the Indians and trek overland — but there was now a practical problem standing in the way of lunacy: money. Between us, we had about six dollars in Honduran lempiras; all the rest of our money was in traveler's checks, and despite Jon's painstaking tutorial on the workings of international finance, the trading-post owner simply stared at the brightly colored slips of paper in confusion. Finally accepting that we had no choice but to take the dugout back to Brewers, we returned to the riverbank, only to learn the boat had left fifteen minutes before.

"But don't worry," an old man said upon seeing our consternation. "It should be back in a few days — two weeks at most."

I tried to imagine spending that much time waiting in Awas, cadging off the Miskitos for food and a place to stay. Given the poverty of the place, and our own stupidity in getting stranded, that seemed indecent, the shame of those long, slow days intolerable. Then my gaze fell on the rafts. They were clearly built for short-term use, rough-cut balsa logs lashed together with jungle vines. One sported a cute little shed, about three feet wide and four feet deep, with its own thatched roof, like a miniature house. The beginning of an idea came to me.

Considering that we had made the trip up to Awas in six or seven hours, I estimated that we were about ninety miles from Brewers; without a motor, drifting along on the Patuca's scant current, our return could take days. I tried to envision a voyage down the river, what dangers might lie along the way, how we would ever know where to turn into the mangrove swamp before we reached the open sea, whether the raft would even hold together that long.

I think most of all, I wanted to impress Jon. So far on this journey, we had played out our traditional roles: he the creator of plans, the pursuer of adventure, me the cautious one, the follower.

I think I wanted to show him, for the first time, that I, too, could come up with truly bad ideas.

I pointed to the raft with the miniature hut. "Let's float down."

For both Jon and myself, getting out of tight spots has always been largely a matter of dumb luck. Of course, that's not quite the way we see it; before going to report on a war, for example, we can spend weeks trying to calculate the odds of something bad happening. It's a strange exercise — superstition, really — because the chief characteristic of such places is that their hazards can't be calculated, and all is random. But underlying our superstitions is something a bit more complex, something rooted in our experience in the Mosquitia and reinforced by our subsequent travels together: the belief that, so long as we are together, nothing bad can happen to us.

In the mid-1980s, Jon and I teamed up to write a book about the World Anti-Communist League, an international right-wing terrorist organization. For two years, we investigated death squads in Central America and Nazi war criminals living in the United States and Europe, tracking their trails of murder around the globe. After that, we set off to compile an oral history of modern war, spending a year going from one battlefield to the next across five continents. The journey was exciting, it felt important, but it also came at a high personal cost: for Jon, his marriage; for me, a three-year relationship. By the end of that year, we were like an old married couple, keenly attuned to each other's moods and silences, and there was the sense that, in our rootlessness, in our twin predicaments of having no one or nowhere to go back to, we were more joined than ever.

Afterward, we continued on our own: Jon headed out to do a book on guerrilla groups worldwide, while I investigated a murderous religious cult in the American Southwest and the underworld of organized crime in Northern Ireland and New York. In phone calls from Pakistan and Belfast and Burma, we kept each other posted on our progress, our setbacks, and, in the cryptic, half-spoken way we had cultivated, our close calls. And there was no getting around the fact that for both of us, these incidents were becoming more frequent. In Afghanistan, a Russian tank fired on Jon's jeep, missing it by a few yards. In Burma, he scrambled across a battlefield to interview a shellshocked Karen guerrilla commander who refused to leave a position that was about to be overrun by government troops. In one four-day span in Chechnya, I was confronted by firing squads from both sides and barely managed to negotiate my way out. By the time of our get-together in Brooklyn this past February, we had probably been to twenty-five wars between us and, if I truly did have nine lives, I calculated I'd now pissed away six of them. Now, when I thought back to that trip in the Mosquitia, our innocence and incompetence there, the simplicity of the hazards we faced, it was with a kind of longing.

While I spread banana leaves over the raft floor, Jon went back to the trading post with our last twenty lempiras to buy food — "provisions," he insisted on calling it — for the journey. He returned with two plastic bags and proudly displayed the contents: three bottles of Colonial rum, one tiny can of Vienna sausages, a kilo of beans, and another of cornmeal. He noticed me wincing.

"What, you think you could have done better?"

"No, it's fine," I said. "I just figured you'd get things we could actually eat." I thought of explaining to him that beans and cornmeal had to be cooked, but decided against it; after all, we were going to be stuck together on this raft for the next two or three days, so harmony was going to be pretty essential.

Evidently, word had spread through Awas of the folly being planned down on the riverbank, so that by the time we poled away, a good two hundred Miskitos had gathered on the bluff to see us off. It occurred to me that we were probably one of the strangest sights they had ever seen in their televisionless lives, these two white teenagers showing up one day, having journeyed all the way up from the coast just to take one of their rafts and float back down again. They waved goodbye to us as if we were sailing off into the abyss, and I suppose, from their perspective, we were.

It was a three-day voyage, endless hours of imperceptible progress along great looping bends, nothing but the sky and the brown water and the dark jungle around us. The Vienna sausages lasted only that first night, the rum not much longer, and after that we were kept alive with the help of the few Miskitos who lived along the river. In the strange way that news travels in the jungle, the Indians seemed to know of us ahead of time. One man, noticing we had only sticks and the bamboo rudder with which to steer, threw us his hand-carved oar as we passed. Others paddled out in their dugouts to give us tortillas or motioned us ashore to share a meal of beans and grilled monkey. These encounters were infrequent, though; there were no other boats on the river, no real settlements along the way. Leery of what animals might lurk along the banks, we poled through the nights, dozing in shifts in the little hut.

Along with the tedium were moments of crisis. On the first day, a sudden burst of wind tore the thatched roof off the hut and squarely into me, knocking me into the water; for what seemed a very long time, I struggled to free myself from the vines pulling me down into the murk. A few hours later, a low-hanging branch got caught on our rudder housing and sheared it away. And throughout was the slow-motion crisis we could do nothing about, the knowledge that we were gradually sinking, the balsa logs becoming steadily more saturated, the brown water sloshing ever higher.

But there was one moment, late in the afternoon on the second day, that stood out. Rounding a bend in the Patuca, we saw a patch of white water ahead and, amidst it, a newly fallen tree, its leaves still green, stretched across nearly to the far shore. We'd already been snared by at least a half dozen fallen trees and expended a lot of energy getting free, but this time, with an actual current pushing us, getting out might be impossible. Excited to finally have something to do, Jon and I got to our feet, took up our long poles, and began levering off the river bottom, steering toward the narrow passage the tree had left. We were doing well, nearly in position, when I felt a shudder pass through the raft, heard a small splash behind me. I turned, and for a moment I couldn't make sense of what I saw. On the far side of the raft, Jon was sitting, his left leg stretched out before him; he was using his arms to hoist himself up a few inches, then back down, as if performing some odd calisthenic.

"What the hell are you doing?"

He looked to me then, and I saw that his face was pale. "I'm stuck."

I hurried over. The spread of banana leaves had obscured a narrow gap between two of the balsa logs. Jon's right leg had found the gap and gone through; it was now wedged in tight, clamped just above the knee. I glanced downriver. We were almost to the rapids. "You've got to get out," I said pointlessly.

Jon tried again, his arms trembling with the exertion, pulling so hard that the skin around his knee came off in a broad swath. The logs held him fast.

I looked downstream again and now saw that the fallen tree didn't end where we had thought, but rather extended on across the river just beneath the surface; the raft would clear it, but Jon's pinioned leg wouldn't.

"You've fucking got to get out," I shouted.

"I can't!" he yelled back, still trying, his knee now covered in blood.

I had one of those moments in which the mind seems to skip over to a different plane, one that is less about conscious thought than simple instinctive clarity. I knew exactly what was going to happen if Jon didn't get free. Not the specifics — I didn't know whether the tree was going to break his leg, or slice it open, or take it off completely — but I did know that we were all alone on this river, and I understood the Mosquitia well enough by now to know that once things started going bad out here they just kept getting worse. In the remnants of the shed I spotted my machete. I scrambled over to it, pulled it from its sheath.

The raft consisted of eleven logs lashed together in front and back. Jon had fallen between the fourth and fifth logs on the right side, and I went to the bow and began furiously hacking through the vine roping. We were already in the rapids now, but it took only a few seconds, the last vine producing a snapping sound when it broke. The outer four logs immediately started to part, and Jon swung his leg out and got to his feet. When we scraped over the fallen tree a moment later, the half-separated logs caught on a branch and the force of the current ripped them away. I tried to imagine that force being directed against my brother's leg, and then I didn't want to think about it anymore.

Afterward, the Patuca returned to its usual brown calm, and I poled to keep us out of the shallows while Jon sat and examined his cuts. His leg was red from the knee to the ankle, but I couldn't tell if it was mostly blood or water.

"Just little scrapes, it looks like," he said after a while. He looked up at me. "Quick thinking; thanks."

I shrugged. "Sure."

On that day in February when Jon found the Chechnya articles on my coffee table, we had dinner at a little place in my Brooklyn neighborhood. He was leaving in the morning for his home in Spain, and from there would go on to Angola; I probably wouldn't see him again for four or five months.

"So, if you don't go to Chechnya," he asked, "what'll you do?"

"I don't know. Maybe start on the micro-nation story."

Jon scowled. "That's such a dumb idea. I can't believe anyone wants that."

I shrugged, tried to mask my smile. For years now, we had maintained a competition of who had been to the most foreign countries, updating our lists whenever we got together. Jon had always managed to stay about six countries ahead, and even though my total was now in the high sixties, his was in the mid-seventies, and Angola would give him one more. To keep his gloating to a minimum, I'd recently told him that a magazine wanted me to do a comprehensive report on the micro-nations of the world, a project that not only would mean traveling throughout the South Pacific and the Caribbean, but would add another thirty or so countries to my list. Jon found this prospect so disturbing that he now tended to avoid the country-competition topic altogether. On that night, I saw no reason to tell him it was a joke.

Over the course of the evening, we eventually ended up talking about that summer in Honduras. "Can you believe it's been almost twenty-five years?" Jon said. He shook his head. "Jesus, we were such idiots."

We had, of course, eventually made it back to Brewers Lagoon, and the raft trip proved to be only the first of our misadventures as we wandered through Central America that summer. A few weeks later, there was the near knife fight in a bar in El Salvador when Jon decided that a group of four *campesinos* were disrespecting us and drew out his machete; I quickly followed suit, but so did the *campesinos,* and when it occurred to us that we were about to be sliced to pieces, we backed out of the bar like characters in a spaghetti western. Then there was the volcano in Guatemala that had begun erupting so violently that the area had been evacuated — reason enough, in Jon's opinion, for us to climb to the rim for a closer look. When the vapor cloud suddenly shifted direction and came over us, the sulfur dioxide knocked me out, and Jon had to drag me to safety. Thirteen weeks later — or about twelve and a half weeks after I'd originally planned to get back to Florida — we turned up, filthy and penniless, at our grandmother's house in California. After that came our years of wandering, of trying to settle into some place or some job and giving up, of heading off to the wars of the world.

But whatever else was drawing us to this life — the adrenaline rush of danger, morbid curiosity, some poorly conceived notions of the power of journalism — I'd come to suspect that at least part of it was a desire to recapture the sensation we'd had floating down the Patuca, that peculiar mix of excitement and dread we'd felt, the sheer exuberant, innocent naiveté of it all. The problem was, we were no longer innocent or naive. We'd been scared — and scarred — by what we'd seen out there. We didn't trust in dumb luck anymore. My brother had remarried, he had three little kids now, and even though he was away from his family a great deal, he had a compelling reason to get home, to play it safer. For me, it was maybe more cerebral and selfish. I had a number of snapshot images floating around in my head from places I'd been, unpleasant ones, and I wasn't sure how many more I could or should take.

In the Brooklyn restaurant, Jon brought the conversation back to my talk of returning to Chechnya. "Look," he said, "you've had a good run — we both have — but our luck can't hold forever. It's already turned, don't you think?"

I stared at him. I remembered my first time in Chechnya, the land mine outside Sarajevo. I nodded.

"So don't go back," Jon said.

So I didn't.

A few days later, after Jon had left for Spain and Angola, I found myself pondering why I had so willingly accepted his advice. I suddenly realized that part of the reason was rooted in the Mosquitia, in my most distinct memory of that voyage down the Patuca. It was from our second night on the raft, maybe 3:00 or 4:00 in the morning, during my turn as captain.

For two hours, a lone bat had been my companion, endlessly flitting within inches of my head, and from the surrounding blackness came the sounds of birds, the light rustle of wind in the trees. It was both frightening and thrilling to be on that river in the darkness, and I looked down to see Jon sleeping in the remnants of our little wind-shattered hut. His bare legs were stretched over the logs, and in the faint moonlight I saw the scrapes and dried blood around his right knee.

What would he have done without me? I thought. *He would die out here without me.*

For the first time I saw that my brother was just as lost and helpless and alone as I was on that black river, and that for as long as I stood at the helm and let him sleep, I was his only protector. And in a short time, whenever I imagined that my three-hour shift was up — because, of course, we didn't have a watch either — I would wake him and we would switch places, and then it would be my turn to lie down and sleep on this slow-sinking raft somewhere in the jungle, his turn to stand over me, to carry me down the river.

RUSSELL BANKS

Fox and Whale, Priest and Angel

FROM *Esquire*

ON THE TENTH DAY of our climb, the wind rose, the temperature dropped, and light snow began to fall. Two days before, under a cobalt blue sky, we'd hauled ourselves and our gear over slurry talus and scree from the base camp at Plaza Argentina across the rock-scabbed skin of the Glaciar de Relinchos here to Camp One, at 16,170 feet. On a broad ledge where the glacier squeezed between one of Aconcagua's uplifted, sedimented skirts and rubble tumbled from the side of her slightly lower sister peak, Ameghino, we pitched our tents.

We double-poled them and lashed them to large rocks with nylon rope, then hauled ice from an exposed slab of the glacier to melt for drinking, cooking, and cleaning, and got the stoves fired up.

We were nine men, six moderately experienced climbers and three guides, scaling Aconcagua, the top of the Andes and, at 22,834 feet, the highest mountain in the world outside the Himalayas. With more than 6,000 feet still to go, we were exhausted, and one of us, Chris Zanger, the youngest and possibly the fittest, was showing early signs of altitude sickness: a viselike headache, nausea, and disorientation. It had been our toughest day so far. The trail had switchbacked over moraines and alongside deep crevasses where glacier melt splashed over room-sized boulders to the broad Valle de las Vacas thousands of feet below, the slowly ascending valley we'd hiked a week earlier, twenty-seven miles in from the road that runs between Mendoza, Argentina, and the Chile-Argentina border.

Early in the day, I had glanced off to my left and had spotted, trotting along the edge of the crevasse between us, a large red fox. For a long time, the fox over on its side of the crevasse kept wary pace with us on ours while we slogged along, the weight of our packs steadily increasing, it seemed. With each turn in the zigzag trail, our breathing became more labored. One breath per step; then, after a while, two; then, as the day wore on, three. I stopped and studied the fox. It stopped and looked across at me. In this extreme Andean glacial world, the sight of a red fox trotting watchfully across a page of a large-print geological history of the planet was like a hallucination. The fox is an animal I have long honored — a personal totem, practically. It's situated at the etymological base of my first name; its image is tattooed on my left arm. It was as if I had spotted across the crevasse a cousin or a neighbor from home. What the hell are *you* doing here? I almost said. Then it darted behind a boulder and was gone — an omen or a charm, I couldn't tell which. I asked the man next to me, my friend David Young, if he had seen the fox.

"Missed it," he said and kept climbing.

By the time we'd finished supper and cleaned up, the wind was gusting at fifty miles per hour. Snow was falling in tiny pellets. We retreated, three men to a tent. David and I shared a tent with Michael Zanger, one of head guide Alex Van Steen's two assistants and father of Chris Zanger, the young man suffering from altitude sickness. The eldest members of the group — I was about to turn sixty, Michael was right behind me, and David was in his early fifties — we'd taken to calling our tent the Assisted Living Facility. Nights we read poetry and listed favorite bebop musicians.

None of us wanted to hang around outside, as we had every evening so far, and watch the sky transform itself into the celestial universe of the Incas, a darkened theater of the old sky god's birth, death, and resurrection. We were too tired, and, moreover, it was too cold, even with parkas on, and the wind was howling now, up to seventy miles per hour and sustained, making it difficult to talk normally. We'd begun to shout to one another. Mostly it was Van Steen shouting, making sure that we were prepared for a tough night — he'd attempted Everest twice and knew what to expect. Check the ropes again! Make sure your packs are weighted down with rocks on top! For Van Steen, this was a military-style expedi-

tion, and his role was that of the war-weary lieutenant, whose first
responsibility was to get his men not safely up the mountain but
safely down. We did as told, then withdrew to the darkness of our
tents, curled up inside our sleeping bags, and waited for sleep.

The sound of a sustained seventy-mile-an-hour wind is like no
other, especially when a thin nylon skin is all that separates you
from it. It howls like a herd of maddened prehistoric animals for
ten or fifteen minutes straight, just long enough for you to think
that you've grown used to the roaring and can sleep in spite of it,
because it's steady and the volume does not vary. So you close your
eyes and unclench your hands and drift toward a dream of home,
and suddenly it stops. Black silence. No one in the tent speaks. You
can hear the others breathing rapidly in the thin air. You blink your
eyes open and wait, counting off the seconds, ten, eleven, twelve . . .
when the howl returns at full volume. The tent fabric slaps against
itself like the sails of a galleon in a hurricane, and you pray that the
ropes and the double poles hold, because if the tent starts to tear
anywhere, the whole thing will be shredded in minutes, and you
will die of exposure. The trap you're in protects you, but barely. It
can also kill you.

There were three consecutive nights and two days like this. We
melted snow, cooked, ate, pissed, and washed in our tents, leaving
only when absolutely necessary, to shit behind a rock. Day and
night merged. Time stopped. We feared wasting our headlamp batteries, so we rationed our reading and sought a semihibernated
consciousness. Sleep we treated with suspicion. At this altitude,
when you fall asleep, you neglect to breathe rapidly to compensate
for the thin air, and periodically you lurch awake, gasping, light-
headed and disoriented, as if you're suffocating. You *are* suffocating; you may even be suffering from cerebral edema, which can be
cured only by descending the mountain, a thing we could not do.
In the middle of the second night, David, who slept next to me, sat
up suddenly, moaned, and mumbled incoherently. Talking in his
sleep or altitude sickness? I shook him and gave him the only diag-
nostic test I could think of: "Say something witty, David."

After a few seconds, he answered, "When we landed at the Lima
airport, the moneychangers and taxi drivers outside were like grizzlies at a salmon run." Then, "Don't worry, man, it's only a panic
attack."

The wind took on a personality: It became a monstrous god with a malignant will, like Melville's whale, and it was difficult not to take its punishing power personally. I ran down the list of my recent and ancient sins of omission and commission, hoping that, if I could find a crime that warranted my execution, I could somehow claim extenuating circumstances, and the wind would stop. For the first time since beginning this climb, I saw that I had put my life at risk. And, unexpectedly, I was ashamed. I thought of my wife, my children, and my grandchild: If I die here, they will have every right to remember me with only anger.

On the morning of the third day, the whale swam away and the wind stopped, leaving behind a wake of playful gusts, as if to remind us that it was merely absent, not weakened. The sky cleared, and the temperature rose into the twenties. We stumbled from our tents, blinking and grinning like inmates granted last-minute pardons by the governor, and proceeded to change out of our funky clothing and air out our stinking sleeping bags by draping them over rocks and tent lines. After breakfast, we began the climb to Camp Two, 18,900 feet, at the base of the Polish Glacier. The bearlike, affable Michael Zanger, David's and my personal guide, as we thought of him, would not be with us, however. His son, Chris, whose altitude sickness had worsened, needed to descend at once, and Michael would take him.

On an expedition climb like this, you ascend the mountain twice. You climb high and sleep low at each camp, dividing your supplies and gear into two hauls, so that you can carry the load you don't need immediately to the next higher camp, stash it, and return to the lower camp for a second night. Three days earlier, on our first ascent from Camp One to Two, before the windstorm hit, as we chugged steadily uphill, the highest peaks of the Andes — gigantic, snow-covered, serrated blades of uplifted rock — had unfolded below us all the way to the horizon, a literally breathtaking sight, and I had caught the first glimmers of a fantasy evolving into a hallucination, and it had eased my climb considerably. Now, on our second ascent, it returned unbidden and full-blown, no longer a fantasy. I was a coca-chewing Inca priest in vicuña-cloth vestments, and instead of carrying a fifty-pound pack on my back, I was carrying a young girl, perhaps ten years old. She was drugged against the cold and the effects of altitude, and I had been en-

trusted by her family and the people of her village with the responsibility and honor of carrying her to the top of the Inca world, to
Aconcagua, the Quechuan Sentinel of Stone, to give her over to
the god of the Incas, who, in gratitude, would bless the coming
year's crops and keep the village from famine. She was not heavy,
though she wore gold amulets on her wrists and ankles and a brilliantly colored dress woven of wool spun from the hair of baby llamas. It was as if her body were made of feathers or as if she were inhabited by a bird, a condor, fluttering its wings and half lifting me
from the tilted ground as I climbed up and up and the mountains
slipped from above to below me.

At one point, while we were slumped on the ground taking one
of our hourly rest breaks, I leaned in to David and in a low voice
told him who I was and what I was doing here. He would understand, I knew.

He nodded and looked at the girl. "Do you know her name?" he
asked.

"She has no name," I said. "She left it in the village for another
to use."

"You're very lucky," he said as he stood unsteadily and, grunting
from the effort, wrestled his pack onto his back.

There was for me and David a dense, complex context for this
trek, one created inadvertently by the week we had spent earlier in
Peru, hiking the grassy ridges and pre-Columbian terraces outside
Cuzco, gazing on the remnants of the Inca walls in the ancient city,
and wandering awestruck across the plazas and through the magnificent stone temples of Machu Picchu. David is from Toronto, a
playwright and screenwriter and a longtime friend. Our fevered
imaginations tend to fuel each other, and in Peru, we had given
ourselves over to wild speculations and intellectually reckless intu-
itions regarding the history and sensibility of the ancient Incas. In
our minds, this landscape was connected seamlessly to the Inca ruins and their sacred art. So, for us, climbing Aconcagua was a pilgrimage, and not merely an assault on one of the so-called Seven
Summits.

On the sixteenth day, we made it from Camp Two to High Camp,
19,350 feet, the last stop before the summit attempt. Our two
backup summit days had been used when we were socked in below
by the wind, so either we made the top tomorrow or we'd have to
try again another year.

The plan was to wake at 3:30 A.M. and, weather permitting, get to the top by 3:00 P.M. and return to High Camp by dark. The wind was steady but not gale force, the sky was dark, and hard flecks of snow pecked our cheeks. It did not look good.

We were up and more or less ready to leave camp in the predawn dark as scheduled, but Van Steen was worried about the wind and held us back until, finally — as the sky in the east turned milky white and the stars overhead blinked out one by one — he gave the word, and we bucked into the wind and headed uphill. The craggy top of Aconcagua glowered in the rising sun thirty-five hundred vertical feet above us. The trail switchbacked and curled partly over open scree and partly over snow, passing through fields of *neve penitentes,* or "snow nuns," as they're called, head-high columns of white ice left as residue by the melting glacier, and along narrow, windswept ridges with thousand-foot drops on both sides. Barely a month ago, four young Argentinean climbers had fallen to their deaths here. We were using crampons and ice axes, moving carefully because of the tricky surface and slowly because of the altitude.

David was working hard, too hard, it seemed: His face was gray and pinched, and his usual running repartee and sly jokes were noticeably absent. I was struggling, too, fighting exhaustion and the cold and the treacherous footing and the altitude. The Inca child was still on my back, but she had grown heavy, as if she had woken from her drugged sleep and was now afraid of her fate and wanted to go down from the mountain, back to her mother and father in the village far, far below. The condor had released her. She struggled against the straps that held her to my back and tossed her head from side to side, throwing me off balance several times, causing me to trip and nearly fall.

At around 2:30 P.M., less than an hour before our turnaround time, we were climbing the Canaleta, the maddeningly loose, rock-studded collar of the summit, when David stopped, all but collapsing in Van Steen's arms, and sat down heavily in the snow and quietly said, "Fuck it. I'm sick." He couldn't go on. "Now I know," he gasped, "what it's like . . . when the tank is empty." His head felt stuck with needles, his stomach and bowels were roiling, and his mind was wobbling on its axis. He said that he was afraid he was going to shit his pants.

Van Steen told us to go on; he would stay below with David.

"Turn around at 3:30, no matter how close you are to the top," he said.

"You going to be okay?" I asked David.

"Yeah, sure. You go on." His breathing was labored and shallow.

With grave reluctance, I put him out of my mind and joined the others making their slow, arduous way up the narrow path toward the top, looming barely two stone's-throws above our heads. I think I'm going to be able to do this, I said to myself. But then two things happened. About three hundred feet from the summit, Ed Chiasson, a cardiologist and the largest man in our group, walking just in front of me, stumbled from exhaustion. He swung around off balance to face me, and the gleaming blade of his ice ax slashed the air between us, grazing my chest as it passed. "Jesus, Ed! Watch it!" A house call from Doctor Death, I thought, and I felt the blood drain from my face. Ed's face was expressionless, blank: He hadn't heard me. I doubt he even saw me. He turned and resumed walking: one step, three breaths; another step, three breaths more; and on, nearer and nearer to the top.

I followed for a few feet, and then — this is the second thing that happened — I pictured David below us, sick and maybe getting sicker by the minute, while he waited with Van Steen for our triumphant return from the summit. I had utter faith in Van Steen's judgment and knew that he would take David down at once if he got worse. But what if that happens while I go on ahead without him? What if David's brain starts to swell and bleed, what if his lungs fill with water, what if he has begun to *die*, while I stagger on with the others just to tag the summit? And what if the next time Ed stumbles, his ice ax tears through my parka into my chest? And, yes, what if I stop climbing now, here, a few hundred feet from the top, while I still seem to have the strength to get there but might not have enough left to get down? If I stop now, what will happen? What will it *mean*?

It was a Zen decision, which is to say, no decision. I simply stopped in my tracks, turned, and descended to where David and Van Steen huddled, waiting on the trail, and joined them there, relieved to find that David was okay — still sick but not worse — and sure to improve as soon as we started down. I didn't regret turning back so close to the summit, but I didn't quite understand it, either. An hour later, the others rejoined us, exultant, grinning — except for Ed, who clearly had emptied his tank and had kept going none-theless — mission accomplished. Van Steen roped us together in a line, with Ed, utterly depleted, in the middle, so that if he fell as we traversed the windblown Cresta del Viento, the treacherously nar-row, snow-covered ridge from the Canaleta to the Independencia *refugio* with the darkened Gran Acarreo yawning below, we'd be able to stop his fall with our ice axes.

Once we made Independencia, a wind-blocking knob with a small, one-man, plywood A-frame beside it, we collapsed in a scat-tered heap in the lee of the knob to regather strength for the rest of the descent to High Camp. We were slightly behind schedule, and light was fading fast. I lay on the ground a short way apart from the others and sank into myself, wondering morosely if I had failed to accomplish what I had set out to do — a thing that I had trained to do for a full year and on which I had spent thousands of dollars. I wanted to know, at bottom, how to regard myself. For in the end, wasn't that the point of a venture like this, to learn better how to re-gard oneself? One does not climb a mountain because it is there; one doesn't climb a mountain to conquer it. Perhaps, I thought, one climbs a mountain for the same reason one enters a monas-tery: to pray.

My thoughts were broken by the appearance of a stranger next to me, a climber with a backpack and parka, crampons and an ice ax, just like us, but a young woman and, most strange, alone. She seemed to have come up the mountain rather than down — but why would someone be ascending at this time of day? She sat down beside me and unwrapped a fruit bar and shared it with me. She was a lovely dark-haired woman, in her mid-thirties perhaps, with an easy smile. I asked her why she was here, and in a soft Balkan or Eastern European accent she answered that she was meeting a friend.

"Are you alone, then?"

"Yes. I've been here for several days," she said. "Waiting for my friend."

I asked her where she was from, and she said Slovenia. *Slovenia?* I checked my companions a few feet away: They were gazing wonder-struck in her direction. She was evidently not a hallucination — unless we were all having the same vision.

"Did you make it to the top of the mountain?" she asked me.

I shook my head sadly, no.

She smiled. "That doesn't matter. Beyond the mountains there are more mountains. And the journey is always more important than the arrival."

I smiled back, comforted by these familiar bits of ancient wisdom. For the first time in my life, I actually believed them. She asked if she could take my picture with her camera. I said certainly. She stood, snapped off a photo with a disposable drugstore camera, calmly turned, and left the way she had come.

I felt then an inexpressible peacefulness and remembered Rilke's line from the *Duino Elegies:* "Every angel is terrifying." But a true angel is a balm to a conflicted mind. They're terrifying only when we don't *believe* in them, I thought. A few moments later, my companions and I, without mentioning the mysterious Slovenian visitor — or visitation, as I thought of her — continued our descent to High Camp. Over the next few days, as we made our way down the side of the mountain to the Plaza de Mulas and out along the Valle de los Horcones, I spoke with David of the woman I'd met up there at twenty-two thousand feet, and with the others, too. Yes, they had all seen her and had been as startled by her appearance as I. But no one, other than David, seemed to know that she belonged solely and wholly to the mountain and that she was still up there, waiting at the *refugio* for her friend.

TIM CAHILL

Volcano Alley Is Ticking

FROM *Men's Journal*

I. Powder Keg

IT WAS RAINING fiercely along the equator the day the protesters blocked the Pan-American Highway with barricades of burning tires. We had left Quito, Ecuador — where a volcano looming over the city, Guagua Pichincha, was in a state of near constant eruption — and were driving south toward Baños, where another volcano, Tungurahua, was booming and roaring, spitting up great blocks of burning rock, flows of lava, and copious clouds of ash and steam. Baños, a town of 18,000 people situated at the foot of that bad-boy volcano, had been evacuated by the government. About two-thirds of the townsfolk had already left, and those who had chosen to remain had been given two periods of daylight to evacuate, because the danger of a catastrophic eruption was great and imminent, or so said the government after listening to the advice of various volcanologists, who ought to know.

We were slaloming along the narrow, two-lane highway, dodging the potholes and dead dogs that littered the wet road.

"There are," I told photographer Rob Howard, "no old dogs on the Pan-American Highway."

A truck passed closely and I had to swerve to avoid a fresh canine corpse.

"There's another one that's not going to get any older," Rob said.

"Poor son of a bitch."

For several days we had been dashing madly between the active

volcanoes — back and forth, back and forth — because our impression was that either of them could blow big, and at any moment. Naturally, we needed to be there when it happened.

Some people are drawn to snakes, or to hurricanes, or to lions,
or to tornadoes. With me, it's volcanoes. Twenty years ago next
month, I was in Cougar, Washington, for the eruption of Mount St.
Helens, when she blew with a force estimated to have been five
hundred times that of the blast that leveled Hiroshima. Scores of
people died, some of them needlessly. One was Harry Truman, a
tough-talking eighty-three-year-old who refused to leave his lodge
near Spirit Lake, on the upper slopes of the mountain, though authorities had evacuated and closed the area. Harry said, in effect,
that he lived there, by God, and he just wouldn't go. Another casu-
alty was a young photographer I'd met while covering the story.
Reid Blackburn had made it through the roadblocks and was right
where he should have been for a great shot of the eruption when it
happened, which is to say, well inside the evacuation zone.

I sort of understood why Harry Truman, a man set in his ways,
might not want to leave his home no matter what some damned
expert said. But I knew exactly why Reid Blackburn was there. You
say you're a journalist, you say it's your job, you say it's your beat.
Like the moth mindlessly circling a flickering candle, you have no
choice. And although you may not be brave as a matter of course,
you advance into the flame with a kind of terror-struck courage.
You are, in short, a moron.

The Pan-American Highway was not without its own terror. The
truck ahead of me hit its brakes hard, and when I pulled around to
pass, we saw black smoke rising from the roadway and a solid wall of
flames ten or fifteen feet high fiercely burning against a pewter
gray sky. Trucks and buses and cars were pulled over willy-nilly, and
I thought we were approaching the scene of some hideous accident. Then I noticed dozens of demonstrators, most of them young
and well dressed, standing four or five deep across the roadway in
the rain. They were singing and shaking their fists and shouting slogans. The Pan-American behind them was piled high with giant
truck tires, which had been doused in kerosene and set afire.

We parked and walked over to talk to the demonstrators. They
were mostly students from the nearby city of Latacunga, but there
was also a smattering of rugged-looking, older men representing

various local labor unions. As in the United States, it is rare for these disparate groups to join one another in a demonstration, and that fact alone suggested a unanimity of anger and purpose.

Two of the students, an attractive couple in their early twenties named Luis and Monica, said that working folks and students had come together to protest the lack of jobs and the high cost of living: Inflation was running at about 60 percent, the highest rate in all of Latin America, and only a third of the working-age population was fully employed. Corruption was rampant and flaunted at the highest (and lowest) levels of government. Anger was focused on Jamil Mahuad, the president, who was said to be not only corrupt but incompetent.

Luis had no idea how long the demonstration might last. The fact that there were two live volcanoes — one threatening Quito, the capital city, and the other spitting ash all over Baños, one of the country's premier tourist destinations — seemed to be of little matter. There was always some volcano spewing out great ashfalls and burping up poisonous gases.

Indeed, when Alexander von Humboldt passed through Ecuador in 1802, traveling what would become the Pan-American Highway, he called the path the "Avenue of the Volcanoes." Currently, the two most obstreperous of the mountains — Pichincha and Tungurahua — were vomiting up gas, ash, and lava simultaneously. They were both on a vague schedule: Pichincha became active every three hundred years or so, while Tungurahua erupted about once a century. It was inevitable that sooner or later the two mountains would become active at about the same time.

In fact, the Quechua-speaking indigenous population — various groups of Indians with remarkably varied cultures — was in agreement on one thing: When Guagua (meaning "baby") Pichincha cries, Mama Tungurahua wakes up and Daddy Cotopaxi roars. As yet, snowcapped Cotopaxi, at 19,347 feet the world's highest continually active volcano, was dozing fitfully, but it seldom remained quiet for more than fifteen years and might roar soon. It rose just north of us, obscured now by the rain, which was falling in biblical torrents.

Luis and Monica said that if we were interested, they could show us a way around the barricade. And so the very people who had been blocking our way ten minutes earlier got into the car and directed us back the way we had come. We were soon stopped by a line of police wearing gray camouflage gear, which stood out starkly against the grassy green hillsides.

The police, it seemed, were determined not to be provocative. They had established their lines out of sight of the demonstration and were just waiting for it to be over. My impression was that the cops sympathized with the demonstrators and that Mahuad — who, after just sixteen months, had also managed to alienate the indigenous people and the military — wasn't long for the office of the president.

It occurred to me that there along the Pan-American Highway, amid the dead dogs and burning tires, I was watching the rumblings of some serious social unrest, and the words *powder* and *keg* kept clanging together in my mind.

Luis and Monica directed us down a series of gravel roads that emptied back onto the highway just south of the barricade. The students said goodbye and walked off to rejoin their cohorts in protest.

Just southeast of Ambato, on the outskirts of a small town called Pelileo, the police had barricaded the road to Baños. We convinced the officers that we were world-famous journalists, here to cover the evacuation of Baños and the eruption of Tungurahua. They let us through, and we plowed down a steep grade in the general direction of the Amazon jungle. About five miles later, we encountered another barricade, this one manned by the military, professional soldiers who, it seemed, didn't care if we were famous international journalists, movie stars, or astronauts. No one was allowed past the checkpoint.

But we had permission from the Geophysical Institute in Quito to visit with the two American scientists studying the mountain: Patty Mothes and Peter Hall.

"Ah, well," the soldiers said, "you moronic little turds," or words to that effect. Then they informed us that we'd passed the house where the scientists were staying. It was up the hill and down a gravel road that forked many times, in many directions.

In the end, we piled a pair of soldiers into the back seat and they escorted us to the house, just as the students had directed us around their own barricade. The seismological observatory where Mothes and Hall worked had been donated to the Geophysical In-

stitute by a prominent chicken farmer and was a long, white building with a red-tiled roof and large picture windows. Each of the
windows was taped with a big yellow X, which the soldiers said was a
protection against the window-shattering vibrations of an eruption.
Tungurahua, they said, was about seven miles away. We could actually hear the mountain, a series of avalanches rumbling faintly in
the distance.

There were soldiers camped outside the observatory in a large
green canvas tent. A Sergeant Jorge Aedo escorted us into the
house, where Mothes was talking with a group of people who had
been evacuated from Baños. Most were staying with friends or relatives in other cities, though about twenty-five hundred people were
living in a makeshift refugee camp.

The group at the observatory was well dressed and polite. They
were speaking with Colonel Rodrigo Yepes, who prefaced many of
his statements about the possibility of an imminent eruption of
Tungurahua with the words: "Please believe me . . ." Because apparently the people didn't believe him.

The delegation from Baños wanted to return to their town, if
only for a few hours. They had been evacuated nearly two months
earlier. The people wanted to have a High Mass and a solemn parade. They wanted to do it on Sunday, five days from today. It would
be a symbolic homecoming.

Patty Mothes admitted that, of late, the mountain had been seismically quiet. Sunday was a possibility. The colonel, after consult-
ing with General Carlos Moncayo, reluctantly approved the five-
hour return to Baños. When the meeting was over we explained to
the officer that we were world-famous journalists and would need
to accompany the people to their evacuated home. The colonel,
who exuded Latin graciousness, told us there would be provisions
made for the press, but the underlying message was that, frankly,
he didn't give a rat's ass who we were.

No matter. We were going to Baños on Sunday and that was that.

II. The Geophysical Stomp

The next day I was jumping up and down on solid rock at about
14,000 feet, just below the glaciers of Ecuador's highest mountain, Chimborazo, an inactive volcano that rises to an elevation of

20,702 feet. Buried beneath my feet were a couple of geophones, sensitive devices designed to measure the movement of the rock and convert that trembling into an electronic signal. At 210 pounds, I was the heaviest in our party and the man most likely to advance the cause of science in this case.

Rob Howard and I had accompanied Peter Hall and his Ecuadorean associate, Vinicio "Feny" Cáceres, to the middle slopes of Chimborazo to make some adjustments to one of the more important seismic stations in South America. We imagined that if we made ourselves helpful to the scientists, they would use their influence to ensure that the military allowed us into Baños with the returning evacuees.

The radio receiver in Peter's hand hummed a single tone, like a mezzo-soprano holding a note.

"Okay, now jump again," Peter instructed me, and I did.

The note wavered.

"Keep jumping."

The sound coming from the receiver was now like that of a mezzo-soprano holding a note on horseback at a full gallop.

"We bring these receivers up the active volcanoes," Peter said. "When they make this wavering, waffling sound, we know the rocks below are moving and it's time to get down quick."

"Those guys who died on Pichincha," I said, "didn't they have one of those receivers?"

"They shouldn't have been there anyway," Peter said as the note continued to flutter long after my last jump.

"Weren't they researchers of yours?"

"Yes," Peter said. "It was in March of ninety-three."

"What happened?"

"We're interested," Rob said, "because we're going up there on Friday."

"And we don't want to die," I added, rather unnecessarily.

"We'd miss Baños," Rob said.

"Where we don't want to die, either."

"They were told not to go," Peter said.

He looked up to where the glaciers started less than 1,000 feet above. The seismic station was set on a ledge at about 14,000 feet, on the northwest slope of the mountain. Below us the rock face gave way to what is called the *puna*, a steeply sloping grassland that looks rather like the moors of Scotland, minus the heather.

Overhead, one of the last one hundred condors in the northern Andes cut lazy circles through a dismal sky. A dozen or so vicuñas, slender and elegant, passed about fifty yards away. Vicuñas are related to llamas in the way that Fred Astaire is related to Ernest Borgnine.

Our cars were parked on a muddy dirt road about seven hundred feet below. It had been a stiff hour's climb for Peter and Feny, because they had both been carrying thirty-pound car batteries in awkward external-frame packs modified for the purpose. Feny had refused any help with the batteries, as had Peter, who has lived in Ecuador for twenty-eight years. (And people make machismo out to be a bad thing.) They had struggled through marshland to the rocks, then scrambled up another several hundred feet, gasping and bent double under the weight of the cruel batteries.

"My wife, Patty, had been in the crater the day before," Peter continued. "She went back to Quito and said, 'Hey, there's something happening in Pichincha.' One of the researchers, Victor, said, 'Oh, we should go up there and get some samples.' Patty said it was too dangerous. But Victor rounded up another researcher and they went up there early the next morning."

Drawn to the flame, I thought.

A dense fog drifted in from the north, and our world became a single shade of gray. Peter shook his head.

"Victor called down on the radio about ten-thirty that morning. Said he was up there. About eleven forty-five, the seismographs at the Institute registered an explosion on Pichincha."

"From a station like this one here?" I asked.

"Exactly. There are several of them up there."

The seismic station where we stood consisted of a fifty-five-gallon drum buried in the ground and covered over with a solar panel. It read a signal from geophones buried deeper in the ground and sent that signal to the Institute from an antenna set on an outcropping fifty feet above us. The station was powered by the car batteries, which were charged by the solar panel. The batteries had to be replaced about once a year — which was why we were there, standing on the ledge, waiting for Peter to tell us how the students died on Pichincha.

"We were concerned about Victor," Peter said. "And then we couldn't reach him on the radio.

"They didn't come out that afternoon, so the next morning I

went up to the summit with another fellow. We walked halfway down into the crater, and that's when I saw them. Two bodies covered in ash."

"What killed them?" I asked. "Ash? Poison gas?"

"No, they got impacted in the chest and face by rocks, big blocks . . ."

Rob and I thought about this for a moment. Pichincha, for obvious reasons, was closed to casual hiking, but after much discussion and many visits to several offices we'd obtained permission from both the Institute and the military.

"Who are you going up with?" Peter asked.

"Nine-one-one," I said. This is Quito's emergency response squad as well as its search-and-rescue organization.

"They'll be in radio contact with the Institute," Peter said. "So do what they tell you."

Well, that's good thinking there, Peter, I thought, as a sudden, stiff wind ripped the fog to shreds and the condor wheeled above.

"Could you jump again?" Peter asked. "We're checking the telemetry here. How the radio signal travels to the Institute." There was no cellular-phone link at Chimborazo, so Peter was speaking on a hand-held radio to a person about thirty miles away, who simultaneously phoned each jump in to the Institute at Quito, where my hard-rock trampoline act was being recorded digitally. Quito called back and said, in effect, that the fat guy was coming in loud and clear.

"Exactly how sensitive is this station?" I asked, more than a little breathless. "I mean, is it just for Chimborazo?"

"Oh no," Peter said. "On good massive rock like this — and if an earthquake or eruption is big enough — we can pick up events from anywhere in South America. This is a vitally important station, especially if the event is at Tungurahua."

There were many other seismic stations along von Humboldt's Avenue of the Volcanoes in Ecuador, the most problematic being the one on Cotopaxi, which von Humboldt had declared unclimbable. The Institute had sent teams of strong, young researchers with technical climbing experience up into the snowfields and glaciers, but they'd failed to reach the station three times running.

"Don't you have a lot of world-class climbers coming to Ecuador?" I asked. "I bet you could get some good people to volunteer their help."

"Well no," Peter said. "I've asked. No one wants to do it."

"Why not?"

"Because a car battery," he said, "is an intensely objectionable object to carry up a mountain."

Feny, meanwhile, was about to solder a resistor into the electronic guts of the station, which would cause the geophones not to overreact to a vibration. He looked up from his work. "I need the oscilloscope now," he said.

Peter looked at the gear spread out around the station and didn't like what he saw. A great sorrow clouded his face. "I thought *you* brought it," he said.

And then we looked down to the cars, seven hundred vertical feet below. They appeared to be about the size of a pair of cockroaches. Feny and Peter both turned toward Rob, the youngest and strongest in our party.

"The oscilloscope," Peter said, "is in our car, in the back seat. It's a big yellow gadget with an LCD window near the top. It's about the size of a long loaf of bread."

"Only a lot heavier," I said, heartlessly. I was the jumper; Rob was the gofer. We were making ourselves useful to the scientists, as planned.

Twenty or thirty minutes later, Rob was splashing through the marshland and only about five minutes from the oscilloscope. He had made good time.

"Geez," Peter said mildly, "I really hope I didn't lock the car."

III. Eruption

We had a date with Pichincha early the next day, and so we raced back north, along the Avenue of Dead Dogs, to Quito, where the volcano, looking mostly green and devoid of snow, loomed over the city. The radio news said there was increased unrest among the indigenous people, who were gaining political strength by the day.

The next morning Marcelo Redin, a man who worked with 911, picked us up in a well-maintained Chevy truck tricked out with winches and special lights. It was 4:00 in the morning, and we sped through the sleeping city. There were only a few pedestrians wandering the streets. Many wore painter's masks and goggles, indicating that it was already a bad day for ashfall. Pichincha was definitely acting up.

On the way out of the city, we picked up Yvan, a 911 officer, and Gireya, a young woman from Lloa, a village high on the slopes of Pichincha. She was learning about the volcano in order to inform her village of its many dangers.

At the military checkpoint on the road to the summit, we met our escort, a sergeant of the Tiger commandos ("We are always ready") who introduced himself as "John Baez, mountain guide." He carried radios, along with rescue gear and a full first-aid kit.

By now there were seven people in the truck, and Marcelo threw the Chevy into four-wheel drive as we careened over the muddy path in the dark. He knew the road, which was fortunate because the headlights were backscattering badly due to a light ashfall.

We parked just below the summit at the *refugio,* a shelter for hikers. A sign on the wall suggested that trekkers refrain from going down into the crater itself. DANGER, the sign read. YOU COULD LOSE YOUR LIFE AS A RESULT OF AN EXPLOSIVE ERUPTION DUE TO THE EJECTED FRAGMENTS OF ROCKS, DUE TO POISONOUS GASES . . . And so on. There were a lot of ways to die in the crater.

In the spectral light of false dawn, we began trudging up the long, ash-covered talus to the rim of the crater and arrived just before sunrise. We could see a dark cloud rising above — evidence of an eruption — and it was raining small particles of ash. There was no sound, no explosion, no rumbling, only the steady howl of the wind.

A winding trail led down into the abyss, where white fumes of vaporous steam from various fumaroles rose straight up out of the lumpy, ash-covered soil. The cloud was swelling up out of the earth from somewhere else much farther back in the crater.

It was now 6:40 A.M., and Yvan called down to the Institute, reporting the cloud of ash and steam that was rising about a mile and a half over our heads. Sergeant John Baez described it as a fairly significant eruption.

It looked like a big goddamned eruption to me.

Happily, we were standing on the east rim of the crater, and the wind was at our backs, blowing the ash off over the virtually uninhabited areas to the west of the mountain.

The lip of the crater was 14,800 feet high, according to my altimeter, and the sky above was a pale blue, interspersed with a few puffy white clouds. The ash billowed up in eerie silence. As the sun rose, the ash cloud — previously dark and malevolent — began to show its true colors. It was a subtle shade of salmon pink, a combination of steam and pulverized rock. The eruption continued unabated for several minutes, and the cloud grew, billowing out at the edges near the top. Heavier bits of rock and cooling steam began to fall along the sides of the column, which was now mushroom-shaped. It was well over a mile wide at our position, and four or five times that at its peak.

I looked to the south and saw that we had climbed above the clouds, which lay at about 10,000 feet, a perfectly flat layer of glittering white that took on the colors of the rising sun. The world below looked like a watercolor titled *Abstract in Pastels.*

And rising up out of the clouds on all sides were the volcanoes of Ecuador. I could see Cotopaxi, which looked like the archetype of all volcanoes, perfectly shaped and snowcapped. Chimborazo rose to the west, and Tungurahua — east of Chimborazo, south of Cotopaxi — was spitting out a column of foul black ash. The world consisted solely of volcanoes.

Yvan, who was still talking to the Institute, said that they were getting some very ominous readings from our position and that we should be prepared to evacuate.

"How do we do that?" I asked John Baez, "Tiger commando" and mountain guide.

"Run for your life," he advised.

Just because you've seen and survived one eruption does not necessarily mean things are hunky-dory and that there won't be another one following immediately. In fact, eruptions tend to be sequential: *boom, boom boom,* like that. The process starts at least sixty miles below the surface of the earth, where temperatures are hot enough to melt rock. Cracks in the earth's crust allow these superheated materials, called magma, to rise. As the magma moves toward the surface, expanding carbon and sulfur gases contained in the magma push the molten rock upward with even greater force.

An eruption, like the one we were watching, is essentially one big steam explosion. I glanced up at the cloud blooming overhead and felt the same steady tug I'd felt at Mount St. Helens.

"Can we go up there?" I asked, pointing to the highest point on the lip of the crater. It was about three hundred feet above us.

"If we hurry," said the sergeant.

We hustled right up past at least three seismic stations of the type we'd seen on Chimborazo. I was tempted to jump up and down over the buried geophones. See if I could force the evacuation of Quito, a town of 1.4 million souls.

"But that would be wrong," Rob advised me gravely.

I think he sensed it too, that giddy and imprudent foolishness I'd felt twenty years ago. We were, I thought, in a world of trouble, which is to say we were right where we should have been for great shots of the eruption.

Scrambling breathlessly, we reached the summit, where a plaque said we were standing at 4,781 meters, or 15,686 feet. The eruption began to subside and I could see down into the crater, which looked like a great ashy basin studded with various gray hillocks. The volcano, we had been told, was "building domes," six of them to date, and we could see them down there, piles of whiter rock pushed up out of the earth like so many pimples.

The crater wall was not perfectly formed but fell away sharply to the west in the way that a river cuts a wide canyon out of a rock wall. From the air, the entire crater must have looked rather like a cup tipped precipitously to the west.

Quito lay to the east, protected by the high wall of the crater, and by another mountain, Rucu Pichincha (which is actually part of the same volcanic massif as Guagua Pichincha), a volcanic peak that is currently inactive. What all this meant was that if Pichincha really blew, Quito would be largely protected. The brunt of the explosion would be directed off to the mostly uninhabited west.

From the summit, it was also possible to see the drainage patterns, which fell off to the west as well. That meant that rivers of lava would be directed away from the city, and so would the deadly pyroclastic flows — great heavy clouds of pulverized rocks, vapor, and poisonous gases that can pour down steep slopes at more than one hundred miles per hour. Some experts believe that this is probably what happened at Pompeii, when Mount Vesuvius blew in A.D. 79. The people were killed by pyroclastic flows, then buried in ash.

But Quito was essentially safe. In a big eruption, a stiff wind might carry heavy ash over the city, and a number of buildings might collapse. Pichincha's last major eruption, in 1660, had showered the city with a foot of ash. If the ash were hot enough this time around, there could be serious fires. But it wouldn't be Pompeii, or anything like it.

As I was contemplating the fate of Quito, a low, ominous rumbling rose up out of the crater, getting louder and louder. The receiver Yvan carried began making that wavering, waffling sound.

"What's going on?" I asked Sergeant Baez.

"Avalanche, I think." Either the west wall of the crater was further eroding, or one of the domes was pushing up a little higher. The rumbling began to sound like a jet plane taking off, and then the Institute called up to Yvan and suggested we evacuate the area in an orderly manner.

The roaring reverberated off the crater walls, but it stopped after a minute or so. As we scrambled down from the summit, another salmon-colored cloud billowed up out of the crater and painted the entire sky an ashy pink. By the time we reached the shelter, cooling gray ash was falling like light snow all around. Marcelo piled everyone into his truck and we took off like so many bats out of hell.

IV. To Live and Die in Baños

The next day's newspapers all had front-page pictures of the eruption of Pichincha. There had been two of them. The first, at 6:40 A.M., was of course the one we had seen from the rim of the crater. According to the newspaper *Hoy*, it produced an ash cloud that rose to three kilometers and was powerful enough that the mayor of Quito, Roque Sevilla, saw fit that morning to declare a combination orange and yellow alert. There were four stages of alert: White was "Inform yourself and report unusual volcanic activity"; yellow was "Maintain alert"; orange was "Prepare to evacuate"; and red meant, essentially, "Run for your life."

Later that day, there had been another and much more powerful eruption. The newspaper *El Comercio* said, "The second eruption was very big and produced a column of ash and gas higher than 10 kilometers." That one must have been a doozy. Twenty-four hours after our visit, part of the rim of the crater where we'd been standing utterly collapsed. The evacuation warning we'd gotten from the Institute had been precisely on the money.

This gave me a great deal of confidence in the expertise of the people at the Institute but did not settle my mind much, because the next day we were finally going into Baños, which those same scientists thought severely threatened. That night, I sat in my room at the aptly named Volcano View Lodge near Pelileo and watched Tungurahua spit fire. It was throwing up incandescent blocks big enough to be seen from the lodge, ten miles away. The summit itself was rimmed with glowing lava. Tungurahua — the name means "throat of fire" in Quechua — did not seem very seismically silent to me.

This perception was still on my mind the next morning as Rob and I arrived at the military barricade where we'd been turned back by the soldiers several days before. The evacuees, we'd been told, were just up the road from the barricade, and they were all packed inside buses — twenty-two of them — waiting for the military to escort them down the road to Baños, where the Amazon jungle meets the mountains.

Sergeant Aedo, who we'd met at the observatory, was along to help. He'd been living in the military tent for two months, working with Patty Mothes some of the time, and had come to understand a little about volcanoes, a subject that had never much entertained his interest previously.

While we were on Pichincha, for instance, he had been six thousand feet up the slopes of Tungurahua, helping Patty place tiltmeters used to measure the bulging of the earth. "The ground," he said, "was trembling under my feet."

"Were you scared?"

"Of course I was scared," Sergeant Aedo said.

We couldn't see Tungurahua from the checkpoint, but we could hear it. There was a faint rumbling, like the one at Pichincha, and it sounded, once again, like a jet plane not so very far away. The avalanches continued for more than thirty seconds. And then, in the sudden silence, there came the sound of honking horns and shouting, happy voices. The convoy of buses was moving slowly down the road, headed toward us. People were hanging out of the windows and sitting on the tops of the buses, all of them waving little white flags and shouting, "Long live Baños."

Sergeant Aedo talked Rob and me onto one of the buses and we were off to Baños, amid a crowd of singing people. I sat next to Daniel, a young guide who specialized in climbing and rafting. "Our city," he said, "waits for us."

There was a large banner hanging down behind the driver of the bus that said, I LIVE AND SHALL ALWAYS LIVE IN BAÑOS. The bus's public address system was playing a cassette of songs about Baños. The lyrics went something like, "Baños is the paradise where the jungle meets the mountains" and "In Baños life is beautiful" and "I live and shall always live in Baños."

People sang along with the music and waved the small white flags, most of which were emblazoned with words that echoed the songs, though some seemed to refer to this or that little bit of corruption: "Of the 10,000 American dollars, not 1,000 has arrived." They had heard for months that the International Monetary Fund was supposed to give Ecuador millions in direct aid to help resolve its massive banking crisis, but of course none of that money was ever likely to reach the country's poor.

We emerged from a canyon, and I could see Baños far below, spread out on a flat bench of land just above the Pastaza River. Across the river, rising abruptly, were the steep slopes of Tungurahua. It was spitting out a steady stream of ash that combined with the clouds in the sky, and the clouds, black and heavy-bellied, hung over the pretty city of Baños.

Ominously, I could also see the crater, and it was tipped off in one direction, like the one on Pichincha. Except that on Tungurahua, the town was basically situated at the foot of the mountain. In a major eruption, pyroclastic flows would hit the town almost immediately. The lava, according to scientists, could follow in as little as fifteen minutes.

We stopped at a bridge as several soldiers uncoiled the razor wire strung across the span, and we continued on into the abandoned city. There were some graceful colonial buildings, and flowers grew wild everywhere. It was a place, as the song goes, where the jungle meets the mountains, and one of the loveliest little towns I've ever seen.

Consequently it was more than strange to see such a place with no one on the streets, no one in the houses, no one anywhere. All the businesses along the empty streets — the pharmacy, the travel agencies, the restaurants, the hotels — were locked and shuttered.

The buses parked in front of the great basilica of Baños, an imposing gray building constructed entirely of stones from the nearby mountains. People stood in the square in front of the church, laughing and singing and embracing one another, as lines of soldiers blocked every side street in an attempt to funnel people into the basilica to hear the Mass.

Inside, a stern, gaunt-looking man stood at a lectern just under the altar and sang. He had a soaring voice, and his song opened up the floodgates so that most of the people standing in the pews began to weep openly. Behind him, a phalanx of women was placing flowers on the altar. A statue of the Virgin, holding the baby Jesus, was carried in on a pallet and placed up high to the left of the altar.

All along the side walls of the basilica, there were large oil paintings, each about ten feet wide by six feet high. I studied one of them while an elderly priest chanted a prayer to the Virgin. The painting showed Tungurahua erupting, spitting fire, with clouds of smoke and ash above. The river was pink with the reflection of the fire in the sky. Below, there were two or three huts, and what appeared to be a church. Several men — farmers as well as businessmen in suits — were carrying a statue of the Virgin and the baby Jesus out of the church. In the distance, people were running for their lives along a dirt path. The runners were depicted comically, with their legs spread too far apart, their arms stretched out in front of them, and their hats flying off their heads as in a cartoon.

Underneath, there was a great deal of writing, painted by hand. It said that the people of Baños have always protected the Virgin during eruptions of Tungurahua. On February 4, in the year 1773, the inscription read, Tungurahua erupted violently but Baños was spared major damage, while towns farther from the mountain were all but destroyed. There were other, even more miraculous events described, right up to the last serious eruptions, which lasted from 1916 to 1918. Baños had never been completely destroyed by an eruption of Tungurahua because Baños always protected the Virgin, who, presumably, returned the favor.

Presently, several men — some probably farmers, some probably businessmen — lifted up the statue of the Virgin and led the congregation out into the streets. The procession moved over the cobbled streets of the locked and shuttered city.

People walked shoulder to shoulder, well over two thousand of them, and they filled the street, from sidewalk to sidewalk, for more than two blocks. In some of the buildings, behind the taped windows, we saw starving cats. People who had brought sandwiches tried to shove pieces of bread under the doors, or through cracks

in windows broken by booming eruptions. The cats mewled pite-
ously and some people were infuriated — with the owners of the
animals or the soldiers or both — and the mood on the street began to slowly turn sour.

I stood on a grassy hill to take a few notes, and a man who looked
remarkably like the actor Charles Bronson asked me if I was a journalist. I admitted that I was, and he said I should tell the world that
Ecuador's politicians didn't care about their people. They were
thieves. "If corruption was a sport," he said, "our politicians would
be world champions." There was no danger from Tungurahua, he
said. The stories in the paper, the evacuation of Baños: It was all
just a way to shift the spotlight away from incompetence and corruption.

"You don't think there is any danger?"

"None at all," the man said. In fact, he had some clothes and
food in a daypack and he was going to elude the police and the military. He'd stay in Baños.

"Are there others who are going to stay?"

"Many, I think."

"Good luck to you," I said, because I was thinking about Harry
Truman, who'd been buried in boiling mud as the north flank of
Mount St. Helens rolled over his Spirit Lake Lodge.

"Good luck to you, too," the man replied. And it occurred to me
that if he was Harry Truman, then I was Reid Blackburn.

In the distance, the procession was approaching the police line,
and it appeared that the men carrying the Virgin were not going to
stop and turn back along the agreed-upon procession route. The
police, unwilling to use riot batons on Virgin-carrying citizens, retreated back one block, then another. As the police moved their
lines, several dozen people broke out of the crowd and ran up a
wooded hillside, easily outdistancing pursuing police. I guessed
that they too were going to stay. No one I talked to seemed to think
the town was in any danger at all.

"Because," Sergeant Aedo told me later, "they don't have the information. Six weeks ago, I would have agreed with them."

The five hours allotted for the visit had elapsed. Several shafts of
slanting light fell on the square as the Virgin was brought back and
placed in a pickup truck for her own evacuation. It had turned cold
and windy. In the empty side streets, behind the military and police

lines, the wind picked up piles of black ash and sent them spinning about in shadowy whirlwinds. The ash stung my eyes, and I could taste the grit in my mouth.

The police moved slowly down the back streets behind attack dogs straining at their leashes. People were being gathered up and herded toward the buses. Small groups emerged from every alley pursued by the dogs in a kind of bitter slow motion. I felt a drop of rain, and then several. Finally, the sky opened up and the rain fell hard, rattling the leaves of the trees lining the square.

The people of Baños, some of them crying, began boarding their buses. Once again, I sat next to Daniel, the guide. His eyes, I noticed, were moist. He looked out into the rain and said, "Our city cries for us."

Postscript: On January 21, a month after I left Ecuador, Jamil Mahuad fled the national palace following a chaotic but bloodless coup. A junta — composed of a military chief, a former president of the supreme court, and an indigenous leader — declared itself in control of the government. The following day, after discussing foreign aid and investment with representatives of the United States, the junta declared itself dissolved and returned power to the constitutionally elected government. The new president, former vice president Gustavo Noboa, now faces many of the problems that defeated Mahuad: a collapsing economy, an angry indigenous population, and widespread corruption.

Previous to the coup, on January 5, four thousand angry evacuees, wielding sticks and throwing rocks, stormed police lines and reentered the city of Baños — and stayed. The Geophysical Institute in Quito says seismic activity on Tungurahua is expected to become more intense.

PHILIP CAPUTO

Among the Man-Eaters

FROM *National Geographic Adventure*

THERE ARE FEW WORDS as disturbing as *man-eater*. Instantly, it dissolves hundreds of thousands of years of human progress and carries us back to our humble beginnings, when we were puny hominids, slouching across the African savanna, huddling in fireless caves, waiting for death to rush us from out of the long grass. The thought of being devoured offends our sense of human dignity, subverts our cherished belief that we are higher beings, "the paragon of animals," to borrow a line from *Hamlet*. The man-eater's actions say to us, "I don't care if you're the president of the United States, the queen of England, the inventor of the microchip, or just an ordinary Joe or Jill; you're no paragon in *my* book, but the same as a zebra or gazelle — a source of protein. In fact, I'd rather hunt you, because you're so slow and feeble."

We didn't know if the big male lion in front of us had ever tasted human flesh. He did inhabit a region of Kenya that had given birth to the two most infamous man-eating lions in history, and that still harbors lions with a proclivity to hunt man: Only two years ago, a cattle herder had been killed and devoured by a lion not far from where this male now lay looking at us with eyes that glowed like brass in firelight. He must have gone four hundred pounds, and he was ugly in the way certain prizefighters are ugly — not a photogenic, Oscar De La Hoya sort of lion, but a Jake LaMotta lion, with only a scruff of a mane, his face and hide scarred from the thorny country he lived in, or from battles with rival lions, or from the kicks of the zebra and buffalo he killed for food. He was only twenty-five feet away, but we were safe — provided we stayed in our

Land Rover. Panting in the late afternoon heat, his gaze impassive, he rested in the shade of a tall bush beside the carcass of a young Cape buffalo killed the night before. Around him, well fed and yawning, five lionesses lazed in the short yellow grass. Two cubs licked and nibbled the buffalo's hindquarters, the ragged strips of meat in the hollowed-out cavity showing bright red under the black skin. Nothing else remained of the animal except the horned head, the front hooves, and a few scattered bones.

Photographer Rob Howard and I were taking pictures from the roof, using it to support our bulky three-hundred-millimeter lenses. Inside, my wife, Leslie, observed through binoculars, while our guides, Iain Allan and Clive Ward, kept an eye on things.

I ran out of film and dropped through the roof hatch to fetch another roll from my camera bag. Rob stood up, trying for another angle. Immediately, the drowsy, indifferent expression went out of the male's eyes; they focused on Rob with absolute concentration. Rob's camera continued to whir and click, and I wondered if he noticed that he'd disturbed the lion. Now, with its stare still fixed on him, it grunted, first out of one side of its mouth, then the other, gathered its forepaws into itself, and raised its haunches. The long, black-tufted tail switched in the grass.

"Say, Rob, might be a good idea to sit down again," Iain advised in an undertone. "Move slowly, though."

He had barely finished this instruction when the lion made a noise like a man clearing his throat, only a good deal louder, and lunged across half the distance between us and him, swatting the air with one paw before he stopped. Rob tumbled through the roof hatch, almost landing on top of me in a clatter of camera equipment, a flailing of arms and legs.

"Jesus Christ!" he said, obviously impressed. The big male had settled down again, although his tail continued to sweep back and forth.

"The short, happy life of Rob Howard," I wisecracked. "It's embarrassing to see a man lose his nerve like that." A bit of bravado.

We were going to spend only part of this safari in a vehicle. For the rest, we would try to track and photograph lions on foot. How would my own nerve hold up then? Perhaps Rob was wondering the same thing about himself. He asked Iain if the lion could have jumped on the roof.

"Could have, but he wouldn't have," Iain replied, a smile cracking across his rough, ruddy face. "That was just a demonstration, to
let you know the rules. Of course, you had no way of knowing that."

There was a lot we didn't know about these Tsavo lions — practically everything — and we had come to Kenya to begin filling in
the gaps in our knowledge. After hiring Iain, whose safari company, Tropical Ice, is one of the most experienced in the country,
we journeyed by Land Rover from Nairobi to the eastern section of
Tsavo National Park — the largest in Kenya, with an area of 8,034
square miles (the size of Massachusetts). Here, some two hundred
miles southeast of Nairobi, you can get at least a taste of the wide-
open wilds that Isak Dinesen described in *Out of Africa* and that avi-
ator-adventurer Beryl Markham explored by air. It is the Africa
that's all but vanished from the rest of Kenya's national parks and
game reserves, which have become vast outdoor zoos, except that
the animals are free while the visitors are caged in minivans.

Iain loves Tsavo — the dense palm and saltbush forests of the
river valleys, the endless red and khaki plains. "Africa without any
fat on it," he called it. "It's raw and primitive and it doesn't tolerate
fools or forgive mistakes."

But Tsavo also has a dark history that's centuries old. Its name
means "Place of Slaughter" in a local language — a reference to in-
tertribal massacres committed by Masai warriors in the distant past.
Ivory traders told spooky tales about men who vanished from their
midst when their caravans stopped at the Tsavo River for water and
rest. The traders blamed the mysterious disappearances on evil
spirits.

The region's forbidding reputation spread worldwide in 1898,
when two lions literally stopped the British Empire in its tracks by
killing and eating an estimated 140 people, most of them workers
building a railroad bridge over the Tsavo River, in what was then
called the East Africa Protectorate. The predators' reign of terror
lasted nine months, until they were hunted down and shot by the
British army engineer in charge of the project, John H. Patterson.
Working as a team, the lions sneaked into the camps at night,
snatched men from their tents, and consumed them. Patterson,
who'd had considerable experience hunting tigers in India, devised ingenious traps and ruses to bring the animals to bay. But

they outwitted him time and again, proving so crafty that the work-men — mostly contract laborers imported from India — came to believe the ancient legends about body-snatching demons, adding their own anti-imperial spin to the myth. The lions, they said, were the incarnate spirits of African chieftains angered by the building of a railroad through their ancestral lands. The workers would lie in their tents, listening to the beasts roar in the darkness. When the roars stopped, the men would call out to each other, "Beware, brothers, the devil is coming!"

In 1907, Patterson, by then a lieutenant colonel, published a book about the ordeal, *The Man-Eaters of Tsavo,* which is widely re-garded as the greatest saga in the annals of big-game hunting. Still in print, it has inspired two feature films, *Bwana Devil* in 1952 and *The Ghost and the Darkness* in 1996, with Val Kilmer portraying Patterson.

While lecturing in the United States, seventeen years after the book's publication, Patterson sold the lions' skins and skulls to the Field Museum of Natural History in Chicago. A taxidermist turned the hides into lifelike mounts and they were put on exhibit, where they have been ever since, a source of grim fascination to count-less visitors. I saw them when I was in high school, and though I can't remember any other exhibit I looked at that day, I've never forgotten those two lions, poised on a replica of sandstone, one crouched, the other standing with right paw slightly raised, both looking intently in the same direction. They had no manes, and the absence of the adornment that gives postcard lions such a ma-jestic appearance made them look sinister. It was as if nature had dispensed with distracting ornamentation to show the beasts in their essence — stripped-down assemblies of muscle and teeth and claws, whose sole purpose was to kill. But it was their eyes that im-pressed me most. They were glass facsimiles, yet they possessed a fixed, attentive, concentrated expression that must have been in the living eyes when they spotted human prey, decades before, on the plains of Africa.

Patterson's account of their raids reads like a gothic novel. Here's how he describes his discovery of the remains of his Sikh crew leader, Ungan Singh, who had been seized by one of the lions the previous night: "The ground all round was covered with blood and morsels of flesh and bones, but the head had been left intact, save for the holes made by the lion's tusks. It was the most grue-some sight I had ever seen."

Singh was one of the lions' early victims, and his ghastly death sent Patterson in avenging pursuit. He didn't know what he was in for, but he found out soon enough. The construction camps were scattered up and down the railroad right-of-way: The lions would strike at a particular camp one night and Patterson would stake it out the next, waiting with his .303 rifle — but the cats always seemed to know where he was, and would attack elsewhere.

The workmen, meanwhile, surrounded their camps with high *bomas,* or protective fences, made from thorny *Commiphora* shrubs. For a while, the attacks stopped. One night a few workers figured it was safe to sleep outside their tent but inside the *boma* — a bad de-cision. One of the lions forced its way through the fence and, ig-noring the stones and firebrands that the workers threw, grabbed a man and dragged him through the thorns. It was joined by its part-ner, and the two savored their meal within earshot of the man's friends.

Perhaps Patterson's worst memory was of the night when he was in his *boma* and both lions carried their most recent kill close to him. It was too dark to aim and fire. He sat there, listening to the crunching of bones and to what he described as a contented "purr-ing" — sounds that he could not get out of his head for days.

Patterson finally got the upper hand in December 1898. He lashed a partly eaten donkey carcass to a tree stump as bait, built a shooting platform for his protection, and waited. When the lion crept in, it ignored the bait and instead began to circle Patterson's rickety perch. Patterson blazed away into the brush; the lion's snarls grew weaker and weaker, and finally ceased. The next day, the first man-eater's body was recovered. It measured nine feet, eight inches from nose to tail tip, and was so heavy it required eight men to carry it back to camp.

To dispatch its partner, Patterson tied three live goats to a length of railroad track, then hid in a shanty nearby. The lion came just before dawn, killed one of the goats, and began to carry it away — along with the other two goats and the 250-pound rail. Patterson fired, missing the lion but killing one of the goats. The lion es-caped.

The dogged Patterson stalked it for the next two weeks, and

finally managed to wound it. He and his gun bearer followed the bloody spoor for a quarter mile until at last they spotted their quarry. Patterson took careful aim and fired. The lion charged. A second shot bowled it over, but it rose and charged again. Patterson fired a third time without effect. He then joined his terrified gun bearer in a nearby tree, from which he finally dropped the lion with a fourth slug. When he climbed down, he was stunned to see the lion jump up and charge him again. He pumped two more rounds into it — one in its chest, another in its head — and the huge cat went down for good. The reign of terror was over.

Throughout history, the beast with a taste for human flesh has been regarded as an aberration, even as an outlaw. Patterson's book often refers to the lions in terms commonly applied to criminals or psychopaths. Even the more objective scientific literature tends to explain man-eating as the exception that proves the rule: Humans are not normally on the predator's grocery list. Lions are generally believed to turn to man-eating only when injuries or old age prevent them from pursuing their usual prey.

It's true that old, sick, or wounded lions have been responsible for most attacks on people. However, a team of researchers from Chicago's Field Museum headed by Dr. Bruce Patterson (no relation to the colonel) has come up with — well, it would be an exaggeration to say "evidence" — tantalizing *hints* that there may be some lions with a more or less genetic predisposition to prey on humans, even when strong and healthy enough to bring down a zebra or a buffalo. The explanation for this behavior would then subtly but significantly shift from the pathological to the Darwinian: Conditions in a lion's environment, as much as changes in its physiology, can drive it to hunt people — and there's nothing aberrant or "criminal" about it.

Still, such a beast poses a mystery, and the key to that mystery may be found in the lions of Tsavo, which truly are a different breed of cat from the glorious, regal lions of, say, the Serengeti. Most Tsavo males are maneless, and larger than the Serengeti male, which measures 36 inches at the shoulder and weighs between 385 and 410 pounds. Tsavo lions are up to a foot taller and can tip the scales at about 460 to 520 pounds, giving you a cat the size of a small grizzly. They are also distinguished by their behavior.

On the plains, the adult male's role is to mate and protect the pride, leaving the hunting to females. In Tsavo, where scarcity of game makes prides smaller, males share in the hunting, and may even do most of it.

"There's no doubt in my mind that Tsavo lions are different," Iain told us on the drive from Nairobi. "They're total opportunists, killing machines that will attack and eat even little African hares. They're also more cunning than pride lions, often killing from ambush instead of stalk-and-spring. There's something sinister about them."

Iain is not a big-cat biologist, but twenty-eight years of leading walking and driving safaris in Kenya and Tanzania have given him the kind of direct experience that compensates for any lack of scientific training. And he's never had an experience more direct, or more terrifying, than the one he had on a Tsavo safari last July.

It was early in the afternoon, the time when he usually checks in with his Nairobi office by satellite phone. He ambled down to the wide, sandy banks of the Galana River, where reception was better than it was in his tree-shrouded tent camp. As he chatted with his secretary, he observed a bushbuck poke its way through a saltbush thicket some distance downriver, then begin to drink. Suddenly, the animal raised its head and froze; an instant later, a lioness sprang from the saltbush still farther downriver, and the bushbuck bolted in Iain's direction, the lioness in pursuit. When she was about fifty yards from Iain, without breaking stride she veered off and headed straight for him, bursts of sand flying behind her as she ran. In a microsecond that seemed like minutes, Iain realized that he needn't worry about her teeth and claws; he was going to be killed by the impact of three hundred pounds of sinew and muscle smashing into him at twenty-five miles an hour. When she was only twenty feet from where he stood, she veered again, kicked sand all over him, and vanished.

Iain suspects that the lioness charged him because she was confused, annoyed, or curious. "That," he said, "is the closest I've ever come to getting killed."

If he had been, he would have joined a long roster of Tsavo lion victims, the most recent being that cattle herder, taken in July 1998. Are the lions of Tsavo predisposed to prey on people? Do they represent a subspecies of lion? Why are they maneless? Why are they larger than average? Can they tell us anything new about the king of beasts? Those are the questions that prompted us to go to Tsavo.

On our first day, after settling into Iain's tent camp on the Voi (Goshi) River, we drove down a red laterite road to the Aruba Dam. There is a small lake behind the dam, where Samuel Andanje, a young researcher with the Kenya Wildlife Service, directed us to the scar-faced male and his harem of five females. They were part of a pride of twenty-three lions, said Andanje, who spends his nights locating the animals by their roars and his days tracking them in a Land Rover.

Shortly after the male had sent Rob tumbling back into our truck, the females, with the cubs in tow, moved off toward the lake to drink. They made a fine sight in the golden afternoon light, walking slowly through the dun-colored grass with movements that suggested water flowing. Scarface remained behind to eat his fill of the buffalo before the jackals and hyenas got to it.

As the sun lowered, we heard a series of throaty grunts from the male lion, which Clive said were a call to the females and cubs to return. Clive Ward is fifty-six years old, tall and spare, with the face of an ascetic and a clipped way of speaking that sometimes leaves the words trapped in his mouth. Like the fifty-two-year-old Iain, he has guided safaris for years, and is an alpinist by avocation. He and Iain have led countless parties of trekkers up Mount Kilimanjaro and Mount Kenya, and have scaled many of the world's major peaks together. Over the years, they have developed a relationship that seems to combine war-buddy comradeship with the easy familiarity of an old married couple; they bicker now and then, and needle each other, but beneath the bickering and needling, you sense an abiding bond knit on sheer rock faces and icy crags and long, hot tramps through the African bush.

As the lions padded silently through the grass, we left — it was growing dark — and came upon a lone lioness, lying at the junction of the road and the two-track that led to camp. She didn't move as the Land Rover passed within six feet of her. She seemed to regard the intersection as hers, and, of course, it was.

The big storks roosting in the branches of trees along the Voi riverbed looked ominous in the twilight. Up ahead and across the river, waterless now in the dry season, the glow of kerosene lamps and a campfire made a more cheerful sight.

Iain believes that you don't need to practice being miserable: His safaris hark back to the stylish roughing-it of a bygone age — commodious wall tents with cots, a large, communal mess tent, outdoor showers, portable privies in canvas enclosures, laundry service, and a six-man staff to do the cooking and camp chores. On an open fire, Kahiu, the cook, whips up meals equal to anything served in Nairobi restaurants, and you wash them down with South African and Italian wines, making you feel pretty *pukka sahib.*

After dinner, we sat around the campfire on folding chairs, and once, when the wind turned, we heard lions roaring in the distance. The sound inspired Iain to offer a sequel to the tale of his encounter with the charging lioness.

"After she disappeared, I had the feeling that she'd come into camp, so I ran back and told my clients to get in their tents and zip them up, and warned the staff that a lion was in camp. Well, they looked at me as if to say that the old boy had had too much sun, and when I didn't see the lioness for a while, I figured they were right. I was about to tell my clients that they could come on out when I turned around and saw eight Africans running like hell for our pickup, with the lioness running among them — not after them, but *right in the middle of them.* The men leaped up to the truck bed in one bound. I think that old girl was very confused: She'd started off chasing a bushbuck, ended up in a camp full of people, tents, vehicles — things she'd never seen — and must have wondered, 'How did I get into this mess?' She ran out, but stopped at the edge of camp and stayed there all day. Just sat there, like the lioness we saw a little while ago."

"What good did zipping up tent flaps do?" I asked. "She could have shredded that thin canvas if she wanted to."

"Lions don't recognize a closed tent as anything; they can't be bothered," Iain explained. "Just last August, in Zimbabwe, a young Englishman, the nephew of an earl, was on a camping safari. He went into his tent and fell asleep without closing the flaps. Sometime during the night, a lioness got close to his tent. He woke up and ran out, scared as hell, right into a mob of other lions. Lions like things that run, same as any cat. When they got through with him, I don't think there was anything left."

This was not a bedtime story to tell in lion country. When Leslie and I went to our tent, we not only secured the flaps, we zipped up the covers to the mesh ventilation windows — and could barely breathe the stifling air. I wasn't encouraged by Iain's assurance that lions couldn't be bothered with tents. Hadn't the man-eaters of Tsavo barged into the tents of the construction crews? But maybe the workmen hadn't closed the flaps, I thought. My sole armament was a K-bar, the ten-inch trench knife issued to me when I was in the Marine Corps in Vietnam. It was resting in its sheath on the night table next to my cot, but it seemed to me that the best thing I could do with it in the event of a lion attack would be to fall on it and save the lion the trouble.

"Jambo!" a staff member called from outside our tent: hello in Swahili. *"Jambo,"* we answered, and got dressed by lantern light. After breakfast, and with dawn erasing the last morning stars, we rolled out to the Aruba Dam to look for Scarface and his family.

They were not where we had left them. We drove along slowly, looking for pugmarks in the soft, rust-colored earth, until we heard a deep bass groan that ended in a chesty cough. It was so loud we thought the lion was only fifty yards away. We set off in the direction of the sound, bouncing over a prairie of short, dry grass tinted pale gold by the early morning sun, Clive, Rob, and I standing with our heads poking out of the roof hatches.

"Ah, there he is," said Iain, at the wheel.

"Him all right," Clive seconded.

I spend a lot of time in the woods, and am not bad at spotting game, but I had no idea what they were talking about.

"It's the ears, you look for the ears sticking above the grass when you're looking for a lion," Iain said, driving on. And then I saw them — two triangles that could have been mistaken for knots in a stump if they hadn't moved. We were twenty or thirty yards away when he stood up, with a movement fluid and unhurried, and I thought, Christ, if you were on foot, you would trip over him before you knew he was there, and that would be the last thing you would ever know in this world. Ugly-handsome Scarface went down a game trail at the leonine version of a stroll, then up over a rise and down toward a marsh, its green swath spread between the tawny ridges. We stayed with him all the way, keeping a respectful distance. He was one big boy, and if he was a man-eater, this is what he would do after he killed you: flay off your skin with his tongue, which is covered with small spines that give it the texture of coarse-grained sandpaper and are used to bring nutritious blood to the surface; next, he would bite into your abdomen or groin, open you up, and scoop out your entrails and internal organs and consume them, because they are rich in protein, your liver especially; then he would savor your meatiest parts, thighs and buttocks, followed by your arms, shoulders, and calves. The bones would be left for the hyenas, which have stronger jaws. Vultures and jackals would take care of your head and whatever scraps of flesh remained, so that, a few hours after your sudden death, it would be as though you had never existed. There is a terrible thoroughness to the mechanics of death in Africa, and we are not exempt.

Scarface led us right to his harem, and then, after posing on a knoll, he moved off into the marsh, the lionesses and cubs following soon after.

"That's that for now," said Iain. "Have to come back in the late afternoon. Let's look up Sam and try to find the rest of this pride."

Sam Andanje led us to a remote stretch of the Voi, and we followed his Land Rover through *Commiphora* scrub. I mentioned the *bomas* that Patterson's laborers had constructed, and how the lions had found ways through them, with the canniness of trained guerrillas infiltrating an enemy's barbed wire. Four-footed killers with above-average IQs.

"I don't doubt but that the lions had the whole thing totally wired," Iain remarked. "The difference between people and animals is that we can see the big picture, and figure out how to survive in any environment, but within their area of specialization, most animals are as smart as we are, maybe smarter." He paused, chewing over a further thought. "Take a look at this country. It's sparse and harsh — there aren't any huge herds of wildebeest, like the kind you get in the Masai Mara or the Serengeti. Tsavo lions have to take what they can get, whatever comes along. I'm convinced that they have territories they know as well as you know your backyard, with their ambush places all staked out. They're clever. They know where to be and when."

We found no lions, and by 10:30, the quest was hopeless. It was nearly one hundred degrees Fahrenheit, and the cats were laid up,

deep within the thickets. In the late afternoon, we returned to the
marsh near the Aruba Dam. There, Scarface's harem lolled with
the cubs on the slope overlooking the marsh, where a solitary bull
elephant grazed. Iain parked about thirty yards from the lions, and
we began observing and photographing.

Later, as the sun dropped below the Taita Hills and a sundowner
began to blow, the lions stirred. A small herd of Grant's gazelles
daintily walked down into the marsh to graze, and the biggest lioness, the dominant female, raised her head and fastened her gaze
on them.

"She's looking for a slight limp in one of the gazelles," Iain observed. "Any sign of weakness — but gazelle isn't a lion's favored
prey. They're so fast, and there isn't much meat on them, so it's
hardly worth the effort. Lions are lazy hunters." Gesturing to the
marsh, he returned to the theme of feline intelligence. "A lot of
thought went into choosing this position, above the swamp and
with most of its prey upwind, so they can see or scent almost anything that comes along. It's perfect buffalo country. The sun's low-
ering, they're rested, and the lions will be getting hungry soon."

On our fourth morning in Tsavo, Iain's staff struck the tents, in
preparation for moving to his "walking safari" campsite at a place
called Durusikale, on the Galana River. If you want to experience
the Africa of Isak Dinesen, then you have to do it on shank's mare.

Roused at 4:30 A.M. by another *"Jambo,"* we breakfasted under
the Southern Cross, and then drove northward, down a road paral-
leling a riverbed called the Hatulo Bisani, where we had seen a
large herd of Cape buffalo the day before. It was Iain's theory that
a lion pride might be trailing them. During the long rains of November, the Hatulo Bisani would be a torrent; now, with a mere
trickle flowing between wide swaths of bright green sedge, it resembled a river of grass.

We found fresh pugmarks in the road, followed them for a while,
then lost them when they angled off into the scrub. A short distance ahead, the buffalo, maybe six hundred of them, grazed in the
riverbed, their gray-black bodies looking like boulders.

We sat there eyeball to eyeball with one of the biggest, strongest,
fiercest animals in Africa — an animal that helps to explain why
Tsavo lions are so big, and why they're likely to turn man-eater.

Cape buffalo are among the most numerous of Tsavo's herd animals, and lions prey on them. Lions elsewhere do so only when deprived of easier game, and even then only in large bands; no average-sized lion will take down a 1,500-pound Cape buffalo alone. In other words, the lions of Tsavo are big because their favored prey is big, and because the dense, brushy country compels them to hunt in small groups. Still, no matter how hefty a lion gets, hunting buffalo is a risky business. Recently, Andanje found a lion stomped to death by a buffalo. More frequently, the cats suffer broken bones and puncture wounds; they then turn to easier prey, like livestock — and the people who tend it.

Tom Gnoske and Dr. Julian Kerbis Peterhans, members of the research team from the Field Museum, have discovered an interesting twist to such behavior: A lion that becomes a man-eater because it's injured doesn't go back to its traditional prey even after it recovers. Eating people, Gnoske says, "is an easy way to make a living."

Intriguingly, one of the Tsavo man-eaters Patterson killed had a severely broken canine tooth with an exposed root. The tooth was well worn and polished, and the entire skull had undergone "cranial remodeling" in response to the trauma, indicating that the injury was an old one. It's in the record that at least one man-eater had been prowling about Tsavo before Patterson and his bridge-building gangs arrived in March 1898. A railroad surveyor, R. O. Preston, lost several members of his crew to a man-eater near the Tsavo River early in 1897. When Preston and his men searched for remains, they found the skulls and bones of individuals who had been killed earlier still. There is no proof that an injury was the lion's "motive" for turning man-eater, but it's a plausible explanation. He might have been kicked in the jaw by a buffalo and lost a tooth; he stuck to preying on humans after the injury healed, having found out how safe and convenient it was. The arrival of the railroad workers, packed into tent camps, would have been manna from leonine heaven.

But what about his partner, who was in prime health? The Field Museum researchers speculate that an epidemic of rinderpest disease may have played a role in the lion's change of eating habits. In the early 1890s, the disease all but wiped out buffalo and domestic cattle. With its usual prey eliminated, the starving lion had to look to villages and construction camps for its meals.

Another, more disquieting, explanation lies elsewhere — with the elephants of Tsavo.

We turned off the Hatulo Bisani road and started down the Galana river road toward the campsite, some twenty-five miles downstream. Partway there, we stopped to climb one of the Sobo rocks, a series of sandstone outcrops, to scan with our binoculars for game. The Galana, fed by melting snows on Mount Kilimanjaro, showed a brassy brown as it slid slowly between galleries of saltbush and doum palm toward its distant meeting with the Indian Ocean. Beyond the river, the scorched plains rose and fell, seemingly without end. And on a far-off ridge, we saw one of Africa's primitive, elemental sights — a procession of elephants, raising dust as they migrated to the river to drink and cool themselves in the midday heat.

Forgetting our lion quest for the moment, we returned to the Land Rover and cut cross-country toward the herd, drawing close enough to count the animals — about sixty altogether, the calves trotting alongside their mothers, a huge matriarch out front, other old females guarding the flanks and rear, tusks flashing in the harsh sunlight.

Iain and Clive are elephant enthusiasts. When they saw the herd shambling toward the Galana, they drove off to a spot on the river where we had a good chance of observing the animals at close hand. We picnicked in the shade of a tamarind tree, with a broad, sandy beach in front of us. Twenty minutes later, the elephants arrived, moving within a hundred yards of where we sat. They came on down with a gliding, stiff-legged gait. The marvelous thing was how silent they were, passing through the saltbush with barely a rustle. It seemed to us that we were beholding Tsavo's wild soul made flesh.

With cat-burglar creeps, we positioned ourselves on the shore, watching and photographing for almost an hour. The animals' trunks curved into their mouths or bent back to spray their heads with water. An incredible organ, the elephant's trunk: It contains 40,000 separate muscles and tendons, and serves the elephant as a hand that feeds, a nose, a drinking straw, a built-in shower, and a weapon, all in one.

Tsavo elephants have all the reason in the world to fear and hate people. Slaughtering them for their ivory is a very old story, going back to ancient times. And the caravans that once passed through Tsavo laden with tusks may hold another explanation for the man-eating tendencies of Tsavo lions.

Dr. Chapurukha Kusimba, an anthropological archaeologist, grew up in Kenya hearing the story of the man-eaters and Patterson's epic hunt. Now an associate curator of African anthropology at the Field Museum, he began working with the Tsavo lion research team in 1994. Studying the traditional caravan routes from the interior to the coast, Kusimba learned that the caravans carried slaves as well as ivory. The Tsavo River was an important stop, where traders refreshed themselves and restocked their water supplies before moving on. However, historical texts suggest that they disposed of unnecessary cargo first: Captives too sick or weak to travel farther were abandoned there to die.

With so many corpses around, predators in the vicinity would have had an abundance of people to feed on. From there, it wouldn't have been a big step for the cats to go after living people. That may explain the myths about "evil spirits" — the men who mysteriously disappeared from the caravans' campsites had been seized not by devils but by lions. The slave and ivory caravans had passed through Tsavo for centuries — and that leads us to the truly disturbing aspect of the theory. *Panthera leo* is a social animal, capable of adopting "cultural traditions" that are passed on from generation to generation. If a lioness is hunting people, her young will grow to regard them as a normal part of their diet, and pass that knowledge on to their own young. The upshot is that Patterson's man-eaters may have done what they did not because they were handicapped by injuries, or even because their traditional prey had been wiped out, but simply because they came from a man-eating lineage so long that an appetite for human flesh was ingrained in them. Stalking and devouring the "paragon of animals" wasn't the exception, but their rule.

That's just a theory, but if you're in a tent in lion country it's the kind to make you wake up at 2:00 in the morning and hear the pad of a lion's paws in every rustle outside; to mistake your wife's breathing for a lion's; to picture him creeping up on the thin canvas that separates you from him; and to know that he isn't there out of curiosity or because he smelled the food in the cook's tent or because he winded a zebra herd beyond camp and is only passing by, but because he's scented *you* and *you* are what he's after; the kind of supposition to make you imagine the horror of what it's like to feel him bite down on your ankle or shoulder with his strong jaws and then drag you out and run off with you, wonderful, indispensable you, apple of your mother's eye, and you screaming and scratching and kicking and punching, all to no avail, until he releases his grip to free his jaws to crush your windpipe, and the last sensation you have is of his hot breath in your face.

Such were my waking nightmares that night. And yet, only that afternoon, I had been as captivated by a lion as Joy Adamson had been by Elsa. We had left camp on a game drive, and rounded a bend in the road a few miles downriver, and suddenly she was there, walking purposefully ahead of us. There was nothing beautiful about her: Old scratches and cuts marred her skin like sewn rips in a threadbare sofa, and her ribs showed, though not in a way to suggest starvation so much as a spare toughness. If the sleek pride lions of the Serengeti are the haute bourgeoisie of the leonine world, Tsavo lions are the proletariat, blue-collar cats that have to work hard for a meager living. I recalled Iain's description of Tsavo as a land intolerant of fools and unforgiving of mistakes. This lioness blended right into such a landscape; she looked neither tolerant nor forgiving, but very focused. We trailed her, but she was never alarmed. Now and then, she threw a glance at us, just to check on our distance or our behavior. If we edged too close, she simply angled away, maintaining a space of perhaps fifteen yards. A lady with a mission, she went on through the intermittent saltbush with the steady, unflagging pace of a veteran foot soldier.

After she covered some two miles, the lioness began to call with low grunts. We figured she was trying to locate her pride, but if they answered, we did not hear them. Another quarter of a mile, and she stopped and called more loudly — a sound that seemed to come from her belly instead of her throat, part moan, part cough. *Wa-uggh, wa-uggh.* In a moment, two cubs bounded from a saltbush thicket a hundred yards away. They leaped on their mother, licking face and flanks, and she licked theirs.

With her cubs following, the lioness retraced her steps, and we again followed. The wary cubs often stopped to stare or hiss at us.

Iain speculated that she had stashed the cubs in the saltbush to go scouting. Now she was leading the cubs back to the pride.

It would be good if she led us to the pride; our four-day foot safari was to begin the next morning, and knowing where the pride was would give us an objective. I love walking in the wild, but I love walking with a purpose even more. The lioness pressed on with her journey, and then she and the cubs pulled one of the vanishing acts that seem to be a Tsavo lion specialty. We looked for ten minutes; then, as suddenly as they'd disappeared, they reappeared, wading across the river. They stopped on a sandbar in midstream. There the cubs gamboled for a while, one mounting its forepaws on its mother's hindquarters and allowing her to pull it along as she looked for a spot to complete the crossing.

"All we need now is background music from *Born Free*," Iain remarked, but I thought of Santiago's dream in *The Old Man and the Sea*, his dream of lions on the beach.

The lioness plunged into the river and swam the channel, the cubs paddling after her. The three climbed the bank and were swallowed by the saltbush. We were sorry to see the lioness go; for all her scruffy appearance, we had grown fond of her and her self-possessed air. Still, she looked awfully lean, and I said that I would have felt better about her prospects if I had seen her and the cubs reunited with their pride.

"Don't worry about her," Iain commented. "She's in complete command of her situation."

I'm not sure how, in the span of a few hours, I went from feeling sorry for a real lion to being in abject terror of an imaginary one. At 2:00 in the morning, the rational brain doesn't function as well as it does at 2:00 in the afternoon, and you start thinking with the older brain, that cesspit of primeval dreads. Or maybe my heebie-jeebies were a reaction to another of Iain's bedtime stories, told over another of Kahiu's superb dinners: grilled eggplant, pumpkin soup, and bread pudding with hot cream.

A Texas couple and their two sons were on safari with Tropical Ice. One midnight, Iain was awakened by the parents' screams: "Iain! They're here! They're coming in!" He tumbled out of bed, unzipped his tent flap, and saw a lioness walk past him. Worse, he could hear other lions in the underbrush near camp — and the crunching of bones. Iain shouted to his clients to get on the floors of their tents and cover themselves with their mattresses. More lions appeared, playfully batting at the couple's tent, as if to tease the frightened occupants. Iain, who was trapped in his own tent, yelled to his two armed Masai guards, who had managed to sleep through the commotion. As they approached the thicket in which Iain had heard the hideous crunching noise, they were greeted by growls. The Masai did not live up to their reputation as fearless lion hunters; they fled in panic. It turned out that the lions were guarding their kill, which wasn't a person, but a warthog. Iain attempted to drive them off by clapping his hands — a sound that normally frightens lions, because no other animal makes it. It had no effect on these lions, who eventually just sauntered away.

The next day, as Iain brought the pickup around, he saw what he termed "a horrifying sight." A lioness was strolling alongside the woman's tent, which was open at one end. As calmly as he could, Iain told her to come out, but not to run, and get in the car. She had no sooner jumped in and shut the door than the lioness rounded the corner and walked into the tent. Had the woman still been inside, the lioness would have killed her. "Maybe not eaten her," Iain added, reassuringly, "but definitely killed her, because she would have tried to run."

Dangers imagined are always worse than dangers confronted. I was in good spirits the next morning, and actually looking forward to facing a lion on foot, if for no other reason than to conquer my fear. To protect us, Iain had contracted two Kenya Wildlife Service rangers, Adan and Hassan, who were armed with semiautomatic assault rifles. Dressed in jaunty berets, camouflage uniforms, and combat boots, they looked more like commandos than park rangers. Only safaris with special permission from the park's senior warden are allowed into the vast area north of the Galana; the guards are strongly recommended.

I hoped that Adan and Hassan would not imitate the behavior of the Masai in Iain's story. If they did, we didn't have much else in the way of self-defense: my trusty K-bar; Iain's Gurkha kris, a souvenir from a trek in the Himalaya; and Clive's Masai short sword, called a *simi*. African lore is full of stories about strong men who have killed lions with knives, but lions weren't the only dangerous game we might encounter. The saltbush forests easily conceal elephants, Cape buffalo, and hippopotamuses, which kill more people in Africa than any other mammal. Since Tropical Ice started running safaris in 1978, Iain's guards have rarely had to fire over the heads of elephants, and have never shot a lion, but they have had to kill six hippos, which are very stubborn and very aggressive.

With Hassan on point and Adan as rear guard, we waded the warm Galana to the north side, Iain instructing us to stay close together so that we would sound not like seven average-sized things but like one big thing — an elephant — to deter crocodiles. We saw one of the reptiles, a nine- or ten-footer, fifteen minutes after we'd forded. We continued upriver toward the Sobo rocks, and ran into a dozen hippos, entirely submerged except for the tops of their dark heads and their piggish, protruding eyes. They tolerated our photographing them for a while, but when we crept closer, one big bull lunged from the water with astonishing speed, his cavernous mouth open and threatening. A warning, which we heeded by moving on.

The morning was overcast and breezy, but by 10:00 the air was hot and searing — reminiscent of Arizona in July. We had the whole immense wild to ourselves, because most tourists are unwilling to walk miles in triple-digit temperatures, and too timid to confront wild creatures on foot. What a difference, to observe game animals on their own terms. To photograph them, we had to read the wind as a hunter does, practicing stealth and watching for the slightest motion. We stalked up close to a band of Cape buffalo and a small elephant herd, and the experience was far more satisfying than driving up to them. Sweating, exercising caution and bushcraft, we earned the right to bag them on film.

We were on the last mile of the trek when we found pugmarks in the sand, leading straight along the shore toward a grove of doum palms some three hundred yards away. They were deep and well defined — that is, recent. Iain and I fell into a discussion as to just how recent. Clive, looking ahead with unaided eye, said they were very recent, because two lions were laid up under the palms. Clive pointed, and Iain and I raised our binoculars.

"It's a log," I said. "A big palm log."

Iain concurred.

"I am telling you, lions," Clive insisted peevishly. "Two bloody lions. One's maned, too."

Then Adan said, "Lions, one hundred percent," but he spoke too loudly. The log lifted its head.

My binoculars framed an atypical Tsavo lion, a Metro-Goldwyn-Mayer emblem with a golden mane, lying in the shade with his companion and gazing straight back at us. With the palms overhead, the scene looked biblical.

The easterly wind favored us. We began a stalk, heading up over the embankment to approach the lions from above, Rob and I with our cameras ready, Adan with his rifle at low port, prepared to shoot if necessary. Hassan's was braced on his shoulder, the muzzle pointing backward at the rest of us. Iain pushed the rifle barrel aside. Hassan shifted the gun to the crook of his arm, holding it upside down as if he were cradling a baby, and sauntered along like a man strolling in Hyde Park, instead of in Tsavo with two big lions just ahead. A less than reassuring guard. I decided to grab his rifle if I had to.

We filed along a game trail between the saltbush and the riverbank, closing the distance. The idea was to capture an image of lions up close — while on foot. All right, what was the difference between a picture taken from a car and one taken on foot? I don't know, only that there seemed to be a difference. Listen to the ancient Roman Stoic Epictetus: "Reflect that the chief source of all evils to man, and of baseness and cowardice, is not death, but the fear of death." Still true, I'd say. The real point of life is to be brave; it is to master fear of death, which is the genesis of all fears. And one of the exercises by which you can steel yourself to that fear is to confront something that could break your neck with one swipe of its paw.

I don't wish to exaggerate the emotions of the moment. None of us was trembling. Instead, we were apprehensive, in the old sense of the word. We apprehended, in a state of heightened awareness — alert to every sound and movement. Coming abreast of the palm grove, Iain walked in a crouch, and we followed suit, trailing him and Hassan over the lip of the embankment to look down into the pool of shade beneath the trees. I raised my camera.

The lions were gone. They must have fled at the sound of our voices, though we never saw them move. Their tracks disappeared into the brush. It was as though they had dematerialized.

Two hours into the next day's trek, we found evidence of an old lion kill: the skull and horns of a big Cape buffalo, resting in the grass beside a *lugga,* or dry streambed. Iain and Clive poked around, studying the area like homicide detectives.

"Probably an old bull, alone," said Iain. "The lions were down in the *lugga,* behind that big bush, three of them. They sprang at the buffalo from the side, just as he was about to come down the bank."

But that was all the evidence we saw of lions that morning. By 11:00, with my shirt soaked through with sweat and my eyeballs feeling sunburned, we crossed back to the south side of the Galana, where we were picked up in a Land Cruiser — and were told that we need not have walked ten miles to find lions; they had found us. Soon after we left, four males had appeared on the north side of the river, almost directly across from camp. By now they had moved off.

I took a nap after lunch, took some notes, then sat shirtless and shoeless in my camp, my baked brain a perfect tabula rasa. Iain appeared, walking fast over the Bermuda grass. Gesturing, he told us in a whisper to follow him, and to be quiet. The four lions had returned.

With cameras and binoculars, we ran on tiptoe. Across the river, between two hundred and three hundred yards downstream, two of the four were crouched on the bank, drinking. Their hides so perfectly matched the sand and beige rock that they seemed made of the same stuff. I put the binoculars on them. They lacked manes, and I would have thought they were females, but their size suggested otherwise. Thirst slaked, one turned and padded up the bank, and it was clear that he was a male. He disappeared into a clump of doum palm; the second drank awhile longer, then joined his friend. A moment later, the first lion emerged to walk slowly into the saltbush behind the palms, the other following shortly afterward, and then a third.

"See how relaxed they are?" said Iain, softly. "They're not acting as if they're aware we're here. If they are, and they're this casual about it, we may have some major problems tonight."

Just as I got out of my seat to fetch my field notes from my tent, the fourth lion showed up. He caught my movement and stopped, turning his head to face in our direction. Carefully raising my binoculars, I eased back down, and had the unsettling impression that I was staring into the lion's face, and he into mine, from a distance

of, say, ten yards. Crouched low, the joints of his bent forelegs forming triangles, his shoulders a mound of muscle, sinew, and tendons,
he was so still that he could have been a carving. Like the others, he
had no mane.

No one knows the reason for this characteristic. It is thought by
some that it evolved in Tsavo males because a mane is a liability in
such thick, thornbush country. Another theory is that pride lions
on the plains sport manes as symbols of power and health to attract
females and warn off rival males. A mane would be useless for those
purposes in Tsavo, where vision is often limited to a few yards. However, bald male lions do occur throughout sub-Saharan Africa,
though they tend to be found most frequently in harsh scrub-bush
habitats similar to Tsavo's. What's really intriguing is that some experts in leonine behavior believe they have identified a historical
trend in man-eating, which can be traced geographically to such
environments. If they are correct, it could mean that maneless
lions are more likely to prey on humans.

You can ask Wayne Hosek about that. Hosek, a fifty-six-year-old
California estate planner and hunter, was born in Chicago; he had
also seen the Tsavo man-eaters in his school days, and had become
mesmerized by Patterson's saga. Many years later, in 1991, he was
on a shooting safari near Zambia's Luangwa National Parks, a region of dense bush. People in the town of Mfuwe, near where
Hosek was hunting with a professional guide and trackers, told him
that they had been terrorized by a huge lion that had killed and
eaten six of their neighbors. They thought it was a female, because
it had no mane. Local hunters had shot six lionesses, believing
each was the one responsible, but the attacks continued. The villagers pleaded with Hosek to rid them of the menace. For the next
week, he and his guide virtually relived Patterson's experiences.
Tracks told them that the lion wasn't just big, it was enormous.
But it also was canny, outsmarting them time after time. It always
seemed to know where they were and how to avoid them. As Hosek
describes it, the experience ceased to be a sport and became a kind
of war. Finally, concealed in a ground blind, Hosek killed the lion
with one shot, from a range of seventy yards. The lion indeed was
without a mane, but it was a male — and huge. Four feet at the
shoulder and ten feet, six inches from its nose to the tip of its tail, it
weighed five hundred pounds — the biggest man-eating lion on
record.

The nature of the environment, the size of the lion, the absence of a mane — Hosek's trophy fit in with the theories. I reflected on that, gazing at the big fellow across the river. He crept down to the edge of the bank, lowered his head, and drank, pausing to look at us again. He then leisurely climbed back up and lay down in the shade. If he was concerned about us, he didn't show it.

"What did you mean, if they know we're here and are casual about it that we could be in for problems tonight?" I whispered to Iain.

"They won't attack, but they could come into camp." He didn't say what led him to make such a prediction, and I didn't ask.

That night, as we sat around the campfire, the lions began to roar from across the river. It was deep and resonant, a sound like no other.

The finish line for that day's walk was the starting point for the next. Driving there, we saw two of the lion quartet on a beach, quite a ways off, but they were soon gone. From 8:00 in the morning till noon, we trudged ten miles to Sala Hill, which rises as a perfect pyramid out of the savanna, but we could not find the pride that the four males and the scruffy lioness belonged to.

We made a more concentrated effort the following day, beginning at the spot where we had seen the female and cubs cross the Galana. Distinct pugmarks were printed in the fine sand near a stand of doum palm. The strong sundowner winds in Tsavo scour animal tracks pretty quickly, so the prints must have been made last night or early in the morning. There were more on the sandbar, where the cubs had cavorted with their mother three days earlier, and on the opposite bank. One set of tracks led us into the salt-bush, and to a lion's day bed — a patch of flattened grass and dirt — but we lost them farther on, where the earth was like pavement and covered with foot-high yellow grass.

"You can see why that movie called them ghosts," Iain said, referring to *The Ghost and the Darkness*. "They're always in ambush mode. They stay hidden, come out to hunt and kill, then hide again. They *are* ghosts."

His commentary was borne out a little farther upriver, when we struck the track of the two males spotted from the truck the previous day. Again we followed it; again we lost it. The lions could have been anywhere or nowhere. As Adan pushed into the saltbush, his rifle at the ready, I mentally compared Tsavo lions not to ghosts, but to the Vietcong: masters of concealment, of hit and run, showing themselves only when they chose. I was beginning to appreciate what Patterson had endured a century ago. It was an adventure for me to track these lions, but I would not have wanted to be charged with the task of finding and killing them.

We continued upriver. Then Adan found another set of prints. "These are very new," whispered Iain, pointing at one. "This is now."

A dry wind blew through the acacias, the palm fronds rattled. I flinched when a sand grouse flushed five feet away. Great predators can make their presence known, even when they aren't seen or heard. When such monarchs are near, your senses quicken, for the simple reason that your life may depend on it. I had experienced that keenness of perception several times in Alaska, coming upon grizzly tracks, and once in Arizona, crossing the fresh prints of a cougar while I was quail hunting, but I'd never experienced it as deeply as in those haunted thickets of Tsavo. There was something else as well. To walk unarmed in the lion's kingdom demands a submission not unlike the submission required of us in the presence of the divine, and it graces those who walk there with the humility that is not humiliation. I was acutely aware of being in a place where I, as a man, did not hold dominion, but had to cede dominion to a thing grander, stronger, and more adept than I.

"I believe that if one of us, right now, tried to walk back to camp alone, we wouldn't make it," Iain said. "The lions would study you, see that you're alone and defenseless, and attack." Suddenly, he stopped, wrinkled his nose, and said, "Smell that?"

I shook my head. My sense of smell was the only one that had not been heightened; I suffer from allergies and my head was stuffed. In fact, one of the things I'm allergic to is cats.

"A kill. There's something dead, rotting in there," said Iain, gesturing at a thicket.

The wind eddied a bit, and I caught it — a little like skunk, a little like week-old garbage.

Adan and Hassan pushed into the saltbush, while we who were unarmed waited in the open. When the two rangers emerged, several minutes later, they reported they had found nothing except hyena and jackal tracks, indicating that the carcass, wherever it was, had been abandoned by the lions and was now the property of scavengers.

The trek ended at the palm grove across from camp, where the four males had laired up. A lot of pugmarks, and some stains in the sand where the lions had urinated, but nothing more.

"Make a perfect movie set, wouldn't it?" Clive whispered. It was two days later, and we had just made our way through the saltbush and entered a grove of old doum palm. The trunks of the high trees were worn smooth where elephants had rubbed up against them, and the lanes between the trees were like shadowy halls, some blocked by flood-wrack from the rainy season — barricades of logs and fronds behind which a dozen lions could have lurked unseen. We expected to hear a low, menacing growl at any moment, an expectation that was not fulfilled until, making a circle, we came out of the trees and reentered the saltbush. The sound wasn't a growl, however — more of a loud grunt or bellow.

What happened next happened all at once. A cloud of dust rose from behind a thicket, Adan whipped around, leveling his rifle, and Iain said, "Get behind me!" to Leslie and me. Just as we did, certain that we were about to be charged by a lion, an elephant appeared, not twenty yards to our right. It was a young female of some two or three tons, shaking her head angrily, her ears flared. She stomped and scuffed the earth, then started toward us. Adan fired a shot over her head to scare her off. She stood her ground and let out a trumpet, her ears flaring again, dust rising from her feet, dust spewing from her hide as she tossed her great head back and forth. Iain yelled to Adan in Swahili. Adan fired again, and for an instant I thought he'd shot her — some trick of light made a puff of dust flying from her shoulder look like the impact of a bullet. In the next instant, as the female ran off, I realized that he'd put the second round over her head.

Iain lit into Adan, all in Swahili, but it was plain that the ranger was getting a royal dressing-down. I couldn't understand why.

"Rangers are supposed to know that you don't have to shoot at an elephant to scare it off," Iain explained. "That female was old enough to have seen other elephants shot by poachers. You had to have been here in the eighties to appreciate it. Elephants are traumatized by the sound of gunfire. They're very intelligent animals, and it's not necessary to fire over their heads. A handclap will do it, or just shouting. What we try to do on a foot safari is to observe without disturbing the animals, and move on without them ever being aware that humans are around."

Before heading back to Nairobi, we made a pilgrimage to the "Man-eaters' Den." After Patterson had eliminated the two "brutes," as he called the lions, work resumed on the Tsavo River bridge. While waiting for a shipment of construction materials, he took a break to explore some rocky hills near his camp and to do some recreational hunting. He was in a dry riverbed, pursuing a rhino, when he spotted something that stopped him cold.

"I saw on the other side a fearsome-looking cave which seemed to run back for a considerable distance under the rocky bank," Patterson wrote. "Round the entrance and inside the cavern I was thunderstruck to find a number of human bones with here and there a copper bangle such as the natives wear. Beyond all doubt, the man-eaters' den!"

After taking a photograph, he left his find, and from that day in early 1899 until recently, its location was lost to history. Patterson's characterization of it as a lions' den has aroused controversy and skepticism among naturalists and zoologists for a century: Lions are generally not known to be denning animals (the tale of Daniel in the lion's den notwithstanding).

In 1996, the Field Museum team endeavored to determine who or what had been the cave's true occupants. That year and the next, Kusimba, Kerbis Peterhans, Gnoske, and Andanje made extensive searches southwest of the Tsavo River bridge — the direction Patterson said he'd followed on his excursion. Nothing was found until April 1997, when Gnoske, after rereading Patterson's descriptions and comparing them to the landscape, realized that Patterson's directions had been way off: The "rocky hills" mentioned in the book were not southwest of the bridge, but northwest.

The day after making that determination, Gnoske, Kerbis Peterhans, and Andanje found a cave in a shady riverbed only a mile from the bridge. It perfectly matched the one in Patterson's photograph. After ninety-eight years, the man-eaters' den had been rediscovered.

But was it the man-eaters' den? The next year, the team sifted through the dirt to recover human bones and examine them for teeth marks; if there were any, the researchers could determine if they had been made by lions, hyenas, or leopards. They looked for the copper bangles Patterson had seen, as well as for human teeth to distinguish between Asians and Africans; Asian teeth would be all but incontrovertible proof that the victims had been the Indian railway workers.

The result of that work was surprising, though inconclusive. Kusimba believes that the legendary cave was never a lions' den, nor any sort of den, but in all likelihood a traditional burial cave of the ancient Taita people, who once inhabited the Tsavo region. Gnoske and Kerbis Peterhans, on the other hand, favor a theory that the bones in the cave were, in fact, the remains of lion victims, though they were probably dragged there by hyenas.

Earlier in the trip, when Rob was shooting pictures at park headquarters, Kusimba took him to the cave. Now Rob would show it to us. Iain and Clive, who had never seen the cave, were as eager for a look as Leslie and I. So, with Rob in the lead, the guides became the guided. After thrashing around for a while, we came to a ravine. Rob shouted. And there it was, with a corridor between two big boulders leading beneath an overhang and into a cavern.

"Well, I don't think it looks so fearsome," said Iain, who doesn't have a high opinion of Patterson, considering him to have been an imperial martinet, a so-so hunter, and something of a grandstander.

I agreed that the cool, shady spot was almost idyllic. Then again, we were not trying to build a bridge in the African wilderness and, at the same time, hunt down two clever cats that were using our workforce as a fast-food restaurant. To Patterson, with his memories of his workers' screams, of his crew leader's gruesome remains, of the tense, interminable nights waiting with his rifle, the cave could well have appeared "fearsome." And given the ignorance about lion behavior that prevailed in his time, it was understandable why he may have mistaken a burial cave for a man-eater's den. Imperial martinet or not, he did pretty well with what he had.

That said, I did find Patterson's characterization of his adversaries as brutes and outlaws objectionable. I recalled our second-to-last morning in Tsavo, as we sat in camp and watched a zebra herd warily come down to the far bank of the Galana to drink. They had been waiting on the ledge above the river for a long time, suffering from what Iain termed "the paradox of survival." The animals were parched, but feared that a lion or crocodile was waiting for them at the river's edge — lions and crocs know that zebras must drink eventually. And so the whole herd stood still, gazing at the river with what seemed to us equal measures of longing and dread, until the desperation of their thirst overcame their fear. Even so, they did not rush down with abandon, but watered in orderly stages. A dozen or so animals would drink, while the others waited their turn and the stallions stood watch. If one group got greedy and took too long, the stallions would let out a series of loud, sharp brays. It was a strange, distressful sound, falling somewhere between a whinny and a bark.

A layman should not anthropomorphize, but to me, the stallions seemed to be saying, "You've had enough, get a move on, we don't have much time." In a way, I identified with them. They were prey; and, out there, so was I. But that recognition did not offend my sense of human dignity. The offense was to my human pride. Nothing wrong with a little pride, except when it becomes excessive. If I had been in Patterson's boots, I would have pursued the lions with as much determination as he — after all, his first responsibility was to finish the bridge and protect his workers' lives — but I don't think I would have regarded the lions as savage brutes violating some law of heaven. If anything, they were only obeying the fundamental law of all creation, which is survival.

To realize that I shared something in common with the wary, anxious zebras was merely to acknowledge my true place in nature where nature is wild, the stage on which the drama of predator and prey is played out.

ANDREW COCKBURN

Iran: Are You Ready?

FROM *Condé Nast Traveler*

THE FIRST TIME I arrived at Mehrabad Airport, gateway to Tehran, the officer in the immigration booth gave me a chilly look and followed it up with a curt declaration that my visa was invalid and I would have to leave on the next plane. Only after a long and nervous wait on an uncomfortable orange plastic bucket seat was I finally allowed through. That was in 1994, and I had arrived from the land of the Great Satan — America. Now I nervously scanned the two immigration booths ahead of me, gauging which official had the least aggressively unkempt beard. Would this time be different?

In 1998, the year following his election, President Mohammad Khatami, anxious to attract visitors and their cash, gave TV interviews urging Americans to come visit. A U.S. wrestling team was showered with gifts at the great Tehran bazaar — traditionally the lair of the most hard-line supporters of the Iranian revolution. Indeed, it appeared that the domination of Iran by vocally anti-Western hard-liners was over. But then the pendulum seemed to swing back again. In the past two years, liberal pro-Khatami newspapers have been closed by the supreme religious leadership. The extraordinarily popular Gholamhossein Karbaschi, mayor of Tehran and an important Khatami ally, was arrested in 1998 and jailed on dubious charges of corruption. In July of last year, proreform students at Tehran University were attacked by officially sanctioned right-wing hoodlums, and at least three of them were killed. I wondered now if I had missed the political "Tehran spring."

Finally, it was my turn at the immigration booth. "Welcome to

Iran," said the customs official, with a broad smile as he stamped my passport. Through the glass doors of the terminal, I could see the sun glinting off the winter snows on the rocky peaks of the Alborz Mountains, which loom like ramparts on the northern edge of the city. Taking a deep breath of mercifully unpolluted air (copious spring rains had cleared out much of the usual smog), I stepped once again into the Islamic Republic.

On the curb, a middle-aged lady was struggling to heft her suitcase onto a trolley. Like all women in Iran, she concealed her hair carefully with a headscarf. I gave a helping shove, and she thanked me in fluted English upper-class tones — a foreigner forced into cultural harmony by the regulations. Once upon a time, before the revolution, foreign visitors were clearly recognizable, and numerous. Americans in particular flocked by the tens of thousands to secure the lion's share of the shah's spending spree. Because 60 percent of the population has been born since the revolution, memory of this now lives on only in older people, who will suddenly start reminiscing about neighbors long departed home to Texas, or a military training course they attended at some air force base in Georgia. But in the past few years the famous sites of Iran, and even some very out-of-the-way spots, have again become frequented by Westerners, including Americans. "We've never had any trouble," says Tina Patterson of Distant Horizons, which has been organizing trips to Iran for the past three years. "At the beginning, the local guides were incredibly tense about being in the company of Americans, but all that has changed. They are totally relaxed now."

Amid the crooked alleyways of Abianeh, an ancient village of rose red mud houses climbing the side of a mountain valley about two hundred miles southeast of Tehran, a wizened woman remarked to me matter-of-factly, "We had a coachload of Americans last week, men and women." In fact, the Abianites are becoming rather blasé about visitors from the outside world, who are drawn by the village's relaxed air of isolated antiquity. "You must go there," a sophisticated north Tehran matron urged me. "We drive down whenever we can."

I was sitting outside the village bakery, waiting in a line of housewives for the evening's fresh bread. Inside, the bakers, their faces glistening from the heat, rolled the dough into dinner-plate-sized disks, then slapped them inside the open-mouthed oven. The scene looked as traditional as the baggy trousers and flowered shawls of the villagers, but the bakery had opened only recently, the friendly women explained as they beckoned me to jump the line — a product of prosperity brought by the flow of visitors.

Change had come even more dramatically to Tehran. Always a less than inspiring monument to the cement mixer, the city appeared to have sprouted upward. In the north Tehran foothills, the traditional lair of the affluent, elegant villas and gardens had given way to towering apartment blocks. Downtown, the giant poster of the American flag on Charimkhan Boulevard — with skulls in place of stars and the stripes depicted as falling bombs — was still there, but no one gave me, a foreigner, a second glance. Everywhere, streams of black-cloaked women flowed like flocks of birds.

"A woman modestly dressed is as a pearl in its shell," proclaimed the poster I bought at a newsstand, a call to preserve the most visible symbol of Ayatollah Khomeini's revolution: the injunction that women cover everything but their face and hands. Foreign visitors eagerly monitor the degree of feminine hair on view as a progress chart of liberalization — as if the status of a revolution that toppled a corrupt and dictatorial monarchy, wiped out a ruling class, and militantly defied the United States could be gauged by the visibility of a hairline.

"That's all the foreign press writes about," sighed my friend Mariam, as she expertly piloted us through the heart-stopping anarchy of Tehran traffic a few days after I arrived. "One paper even said that women are allowed to drive again. But we never stopped driving! What do they think this place is, Saudi Arabia?" Certainly no one looked askance at a male (me) being driven by a female. At an intersection, Ayatollah Khamenei, successor to Ayatollah Khomeini as supreme leader and guardian of the precepts of Islamic law, peered down at us from a huge billboard. On other posters, Khamenei shared equal billing with the grim visage of Khomeini himself. The genial features of President Khatami were nowhere to be seen: He has forbidden such displays of himself.

As a highly educated divorcée making her own way in Tehran, my companion is a vivid symbol of the divide between the outside world's abstract but persistent notions about Iran and the ambiguous reality. Now an executive with a large foreign firm, she had returned to the country just after the revolution, at a time when a large proportion of the middle class were fleeing into exile, where they remained through the long years of Khomeini's rule and the terrible war with Iraq. Always fiercely patriotic, Mariam was laughing now at the eagerness with which we outsiders search for evidence to show that the Iranian revolution is over. "There are lots of little changes," she admitted, "but you have to live here to notice them. For example, this year no one bothered the kids at *chahar shanbeh souri* [a pre-Islamic folk custom in which children jump over a fire to welcome the new year]. For years they stopped anyone doing it. This year all the children were jumping over fires in the streets."

We pulled into the forecourt of my hotel, and I automatically reached over to shake Mariam's hand as the doorman opened the car door. "No, no," she said, mocking my gaucherie. "Not in public."

The strict codes of public behavior instituted by Khomeini after the revolution — no intimate contact, such as handshaking, between the sexes — are still ruthlessly enforced. In private, especially if fevered rumors among the older generation are to be believed, things are very different. "When they are at home, the young people do everything," whispered Hossein, a major industrialist who divides his time between Tehran and Düsseldorf. We were tucking into a delicious dish of *shireen,* a fish from the Persian Gulf somewhat akin to swordfish, in an upscale north Tehran restaurant. His friend Jafar, an architect who had returned from years of exile in the West to seek his fortune in Khatami's Iran, confirmed this: "They have parties where everyone takes their clothes off!" I expressed skepticism. "Well," conceded Jafar, who stringently preserves an ancien régime elegance in the midst of scruffy Tehran, "bathing-costume parties. They all dance in swimsuits — boys and girls."

"For the young people," hissed Hossein, "sex is political." Only up to a point, surely, I suggested. But such doubts were brushed aside by my prosperous middle-aged friends as betraying a lack of understanding of current conditions. Perhaps they were right. For the guardians of the Islamic revolution, sex often seems to be a very political matter indeed. Just that morning a small item in the papers had reported that in Abadan, far to the south, a young woman had hanged herself with her scarf in her prison cell. The poor girl had been caught strolling in a public park with a young man not related to her, and had been hauled off to what was described as the "Headquarters for Enjoining the Good and Forbidding the Evil."

By the time coffee arrived, the talk at our table had become almost inaudible, because the conversation had turned to politics and the increasingly bitter struggle between conservative clerics, or mullahs, fighting to maintain the supremacy of Islamic rule (as exercised by them) against the coalition of liberals, leftists, and progressive businessmen, like my friends, lined up behind the avuncular Khatami. Beyond the simple headline of liberal versus conservative, the political struggle quickly descends into Byzantine complexity. It is not, for example, a straightforward fight between the clergy and the rest. Khatami himself, and many of his closest allies in the government, are also clerics. Some of them, in their younger days, were the leading lights of the 1979 seizure of the American embassy.

At the heart of the issue appears to be the recognition among the disparate coalition backing Khatami — ranging from resolute free-marketeers to unregenerate leftists (including several of the former hostage takers) — that the course set by the revolution has reached a dead end. In the beginning, Ayatollah Khomeini decreed that ultimate political power should rest with the supreme religious authority — in short, him. But the moral authority of the religious leadership disappeared a decade ago with the old revolutionary's death. His successor, Ayatollah Khamenei, opposed Khatami's election as president in 1997 only to have 70 percent of the people reject his wishes.

Even in Khomeini's time, a substantial faction among the clergy thought that mixing religion and politics could only be bad for religion, a prediction that has been amply vindicated — tellingly, I never saw people praying in the street at prayer time in Iran, as one does in countries such as Turkey, where religion is a locus of opposition. The mullahs who moved out of the mosques and seminaries to run the government have become widely reviled, thanks to an assiduously earned reputation for corruption and mismanagement. The economic situation, despite the recent rise in world oil prices, remains dire, with unemployment running perhaps as high as 30 percent and inflation hovering relentlessly between 25 and 40 percent. Concrete reminders of the economic problems came in the form of the same regular request in cafés, taxis, and even on the street: "You are from America? Europe? Can you help me get a visa?"

For anything more than superficial change, the linchpin of religious supremacy in politics has to be removed, which would be a fundamental rejection of Khomeini's legacy. "That will not happen," Iranian journalist Shahriar Radpur told me flatly. "The reason those [liberal] newspapers were closed recently was because some writer, even in the most oblique way, questioned the notion of *velayat-i faghi,* the doctrine of religious supremacy."

As it so happened, I had a connection in high clerical places. On my previous visit I had made friends with a powerful ayatollah, Mohammad Doa'ie. A mutual friend outside the country had given me his number, though without mentioning that Doa'ie controls the powerful Etela'at newspaper and publishing group and had published a book of mine (regardless of copyright) the very week I called. Doa'ie was hugely embarrassed when I arrived on his doorstep completely unaware that he was my Iranian publisher. Once he realized that I was not there to claim royalties, he gave me his name to drop. This turned out to be much more useful than whatever few devalued rials my book might have earned, because Doa'ie is an influential man. He had been very close to Ayatollah Khomeini himself, attending to him during his exile in Iraq, and had been with him on the momentous flight back to Tehran and power in 1979. "We all expected to be killed when we landed," he once told me.

I was curious to find out what my powerful friend now thought about the current political confrontation between the liberals and the conservatives. And I was relieved to find that he was foursquare behind President Khatami. "He stands for liberty of thinking, of talking, of writing," Doa'ie told me in his austerely simple corporate office. "There is a minority that refuses to cooperate, but the mentality of this country is changing." Looking hopefully at my notebook, he added, "It is the main goal of the government to make the outside world aware of this."

Thus, things are not always what they seem in Iran. During my dinner with Hossein and Jafar, for example, a group of young people strolled into the restaurant and took a table behind us. The three women in the group were wearing the ubiquitous black *hijab*. But I caught a whiff of expensive perfume as they passed, and could not help noticing that they were carrying open bottles of Coke — a common means of smuggling liquor into a restaurant. (The highly efficient bootlegging industry can sometimes create problems for the unwary. In the shady garden of a house in north Tehran, I reached to pour myself a glass of common Sava water from an unopened and sealed bottle. It was one-hundred-proof vodka.)

Driving home just after midnight, Hossein, Jafar, and I found the expressways into the heart of the city clogged to a degree unusual even for Tehran. The syrupy flutes of "Shower of Love," a current hit, poured from the windows of battered cars, all apparently bulging with at least three generations. In the parks, families strolled under the trees. Everywhere in the warm night there was the sound of running water from the streams flowing through the *jupes,* the wide gutters on the side of every downhill street in Tehran, fed by the melting snow high above us. The *basiji,* the youthful shock troops of the Islamic revolution, whose appointed tasks include the suppression of "immorality" (such as boys meeting girls), were nowhere to be seen. Their low profile is reportedly one effect of President Khatami's liberal influence, although the story of the dead girl in Abadan made it sound as if things are different outside the capital.

My first excursion into the Iranian hinterland on this trip was not a wholly happy one. I engaged the services of Mr. Hamidi, a professional guide. So anxious had Mr. Hamidi been to demonstrate his antiregime credentials, at least in the presence of a foreigner with no other English speakers in the vicinity, that at every pothole (a frequent occurrence) he would invariably exclaim, "See the state of our roads! Am I to blame? Are you? No! It is the government." The sight of a turbaned mullah in any kind of vehicle, new or old, drove him to paroxysms of anticlerical indignation. "My money paid for that car!" As an alternative, he fell into vocal reveries about his happy times in the imperial forces of his majesty the shah. As the long miles sped by, I found my clerical-revolutionary sympathies mounting.

My jaunt with Mr. Hamidi took me to Mashhad, the pilgrim city a fourteen-hour drive northeast of Tehran, to see the golden-domed shrine of Imam Reza, who had died there in the ninth century. The Shiite branch of Islam traces its origins to a dispute over the rightful succession to the Prophet Muhammad that began in A.D. 661 with the assassination of his son-in-law Ali and the subsequent betrayal and death of Ali's son Hussein in 688. They were, respectively, the first and second imams — those revered by Shiites as the legitimate successors to the Prophet — and were followed by nine others who, for the most part, also came to a sad end. Thanks presumably to these sanguinary beginnings, Shiism puts a premium on suffering and martyrdom, and therefore finds much appeal among those struggling against a ruling establishment, as the Iranians did against the Ottoman Turks in the sixteenth century, when they converted to Shiism. Ali and Hussein died in Iraq, which consequently hosts the major shrines. Iran has had to make do with less prominent figures, like Reza, the eighth imam.

Despite the widespread mutterings against the clerical hierarchy, religious devotion at the shrine in Mashhad — an enormous complex complete with a fifteenth-century mosque with a golden portal and a stunning, 150-foot-high greenish blue dome — was running at a high pitch. There was an international flavor to the crowd: a group of ladies from Zanzibar, Saudi Shiites, as well as a large Russian-speaking contingent from the Muslim republics of the former Soviet Union (the frontier of Turkmenistan is only forty miles away). At the heart of the shrine, a heaving mob jostled to reach the silver screen around the tomb. Small children on their parents' shoulders swayed forward over the heads of the throng to touch the holy relic. An old man, consumed by fervor, turned away with tears running down his grizzled cheeks. I kept accidentally stepping on the heads of ecstatic worshipers who had sunk down in prayer by my stockinged feet.

True to form, Mr. Hamidi spoiled things. "Let us go now," he remarked with a sniff. "These people leave me a little short of oxygen."

*

I decided I needed a more genial guide, and begged my friend Barham, temporarily back in Iran after a prolonged postrevolutionary foreign exile on an organic vegetable farm in Wisconsin, for his services as guide, driver, and translator. Barham agreed, and we set off in his battered but heroically rugged Volvo to see how the rest of his country was doing.

Our first stop was Qom, seventy-five miles south of Tehran, whose claim to fame rests on the shrine of Fatima, sister of Imam Reza. This was, in fact, my second visit to the holy city, famously ground zero for the Iranian brand of fundamentalism. I had made my previous trip courtesy of Ayatollah Doa'ie, who had arranged my visit as a special treat, complete with a high-powered mullah escort. As might be expected of the country's major theological training site, the streets were a sea of clerical turbans and black chadors. Anxious to be a good guest, I joined in Friday prayers at the big mosque with such enthusiasm that the attendant mullahs thought they had a possible convert on their hands. One rather sinister cleric asked me if I wanted to kill Salman Rushdie.

Eschewing a second religious experience in Qom, I was resolved to press on to the south, but we were not to leave the city before one of Barham's much patched tires gave up the ghost and subsided onto the rim. Events then followed a routine Iranian pattern: That is to say, our jack did not work; a passing motorcyclist threw himself off his bike and under the sagging car to help; a tire repair shop magically materialized around the next corner (at the intercession of Fatima, perhaps); and the tire shop attendant launched into a voluble diatribe about prices, prostitutes, and the iniquities of the regime.

His refrain was to become increasingly familiar as I traveled around the country: "Prices keep rising [gas had just gone up by a third and bread by 50 percent], wages stay where they are. There's no way to make a living. The mullahs are corrupt. I'm a religious man, but these guys are not. We elected a man from our village to the Majlis [the Parliament]. He was honest and tried to do something, but they framed him for corruption. There's no freedom here. If I go someplace with my cousin, they question her about her relationship to me." He invoked an example of decay that I was to hear repeated many times in other cities: "A lot of women are turning into whores because of the economic situation — even in Qom!"

South of Qom, we raced along the two-lane blacktop that skirts the great salt desert, Dasht-e-Kavir, shimmering away to our left. Off to our right stretched mountains of naked rock still capped with peaks of white from the heavy winter snowfall. The road stretched all the way to the lawless Pakistani border, linking the string of ancient cities along the edge of the desert — Ardestan, Nain, Yazd, Kerman. Occasionally a strip of brilliant green, startling in its contrast with the surrounding aridity, showed where water runoff from the mountains had been caught and put to use.

In the villages I could see beauty in the form of the old mud buildings — houses, granaries, sometimes big fortified structures — as well as rather less lovely new brick homes. Far to the south lay Bam, the great sand-colored mud-brick fortress town, whose walls turn rose pink at sunset. Bam is now being heavily promoted by the government as a tourist destination. Home to as many as thirteen thousand people in its heyday as a trading center four hundred years ago, the old town, surmounted by the towering citadel, is now deserted (though there is a new and unprepossessing town nearby).

Far more lively is Isfahan, a city that once upon a time was as large and affluent as London or Paris. "Isfahan is half the world," the inhabitants used to boast in its glory days of the seventeenth century, when Shah Abbas, one of those rulers who combine ruthlessness with taste and style, moved his capital here and spent the next thirty years building it into one of the jewels of the world. Despite the sprawling industrial plants on its outskirts, the city is still a gem. The long tree-lined boulevards lead to the Zaindeh River, flanked for most of its length by parks and crossed by the most beautiful bridges I have ever seen. These graceful stone constructions are parks in themselves, and every evening I would see Isfahanis strolling back and forth or simply gazing peacefully at the water rushing by.

The centerpiece of Abbas's surviving legacy is the Meidun-e Imam Square (renamed Imam Khomeini Square). It is vast, more than five hundred yards long, and enclosed by a continuous line of low buildings inset with recessed arches. Halfway down one side stands the seven-story Ali Qapu Palace, massive yet graceful. From the great balcony under a roof supported by slim wooden columns, the shah would watch the polo matches in the square, where the stone goalposts still stand nearly three hundred years after the last ball was banged home. The other three sides of the square are each bisected by a similarly striking interruption — the shah's exquisite personal mosque, the entrance to the bazaar, and the gateway to the stunning Masjed-e Imam mosque, one of the great constructions of the world.

Sitting under the intricate blue tiles of the entrance portal to the great mosque one evening, watching them change hue as the sun set, I looked across the peaceful expanse at the palace where the shahs governed their empire, received ambassadors from distant countries, or perhaps gazed across the roofscape to the mountains, a prospect that is little changed today. Thanks to an enlightened initiative in modern city planning (Karbaschi used to be the governor here), no modern high-rises obtruded on the view, and in the quiet dusk, as the moon rose, the clip-clop of hooves from the tourist carriages circling Shah Abbas's polo field obscured the hum of traffic.

Abbas used to hold memorable bashes here, ending only when all concerned sank into a stupor. The party I attended in Isfahan was quite different. The occasion was a *sur,* a traditional reception in honor of a pilgrim returning from Mecca. In this instance the honoree was the mother of Sae'id, Barham's garage mechanic in Tehran, who had come down to his native city for the event. The garden of his family home in a working-class district of Isfahan had been tented over and festooned with colored lights, and rows of little tables were arranged around the sides. One half was reserved for the men, the other for the women, although ladies showed no hesitation in coming over to chat, though not to linger, at our corner table. They had shed their daytime black chadors in favor of more festive patterned shawls. Idly, I suggested to Barham that he ask how many of these ladies would have been covered up before the revolution. "Even to ask would be insulting," he said quickly. "They have never dressed any other way." At one point in the evening all the women disappeared, bearing armfuls of flowers. They had dashed next door to greet a neighbor just back from a pilgrimage to Karbala in Iraq, the site of the martyrdom of Imam Hussein in A.D. 688. We were obviously a long way from the sophisticates of north Tehran.

I munched away amid the polite small talk. By now I had been in the country long enough to have gotten used to the customary friendliness of Iranians, the fact that I was a stranger visiting from the United States making no difference whatsoever. It was Barham who got us into trouble.

One of our fellow guests, a man in his early forties who described himself as a "retired accountant," set things off by announcing that, generally, everything was in fine shape and that any economic problems were caused by "excess" in people's appetites, not to mention the U.S. embargo. He was all for the moral code of the Islamic Republic, declaring that "there are two things I won't compromise: my religion and my wife's honor."

Barham dove into the fray, discoursing hotly on the lack of freedom of the Iranian young, widespread corruption among officials, runaway inflation, and other common complaints. The mood of the group around us started to sour. Soon a worried-looking Sae'id sidled up and suggested that perhaps it was time for us to go home. "They look on you as a foreigner," he said woundingly to Barham. "You don't talk back to the Hezbollahi [proclerical hard-liners] in that way. It is better to stay silent."

Even before the revolution, Isfahanis had a reputation for being stingy. On the basis of my personal experience, I concluded that this was an unwarranted slur. The taxi driver who brought us home from the party declined payment, a common practice in retail transactions here and elsewhere in Iran, though not in the bazaars. I have always liked the bazaars of the Middle East, bewildering medieval shopping malls. The Isfahani version, in its present quarters since the days of Shah Abbas, did not disappoint: miles of stalls selling everything from gold to soap powder, not to mention the inlaid and painted boxes for which the city is famous. The hardware shops were well stocked with *shallaghs* — practical-looking flails made of chains attached to a stout wooden handle — for the faithful to scourge themselves with. After all, it was coming up on Moharram, the high season for self-flagellation in memory of the martyred imams. Some alleyways are devoted to gold, others to silver. Sometimes the covered passages give out on to little squares open to the sky, with ornamental pools in the middle.

There is a theological school somewhere in there, though I don't think I could ever find it again. But I could always find my way to the teashops, either the two above the plaza entrance to the bazaar, opposite the great mosque, where one can peacefully contemplate Isfahan at roof level, or, even better, the one off the top right-hand side of the plaza, where you make a right, and then another right, and then go through the brassware stall and turn left at the end of the passage. I loved that last one: every inch of wall space covered with pictures, mostly of sports stars but with space for Imam Ali and Mosaddeq, the nationalist prime minister who was ejected by the CIA in 1953, and an extraordinary collection of glass lamps and ornaments. This seemed the spot to drop by for a glass of tea, a bowl of the delicious staple *abgusht,* a thick stew of fatty lamb and lentils, and a soothing water pipe, and to while away half an hour in the middle of the afternoon or chat about the terrible state of business.

Most of all the bazaar had carpets, dozens and dozens of stalls selling thousands upon thousands of carpets — more, it seemed, than there could possibly be floors in the world for them to cover. Many were destined for upscale emporia in Austria and Germany, where they sell for multiples of the prices negotiated in the recesses of the bazaar. None can go directly to the United States, said the dealers sadly, because of the embargo. On the other hand, if I really wanted one, it was clear that it could find its way to my door "for a little extra on the price."

On the way back to Tehran, we made a late-night stop in Qom for gas. Pulling out of the city with a full tank, we spotted a white VW loaded with three laughing mullahs in their robes and round hats as well as a woman in a chador. Suddenly, the mullah in the back pulled off his hat and grasped the woman beside him in a passionate embrace. Other people in the traffic saw it too, but they were not laughing.

We got lost when we finally reached the capital that night. Too many roads had been renamed for martyrs since the days of Barham's youth. For two hours we crisscrossed the silent avenues of the vast city while millions slept around us, waiting for the unknown new day that is coming.

GRETEL EHRLICH

The Endless Hunt

FROM *National Geographic Adventure*

A YOUNG INUIT FRIEND asked if I had come to Greenland from California by dogsled. He had never traveled any other way and didn't realize that the entire world wasn't covered by ice. At age seven, he had never seen a car or a highway or been in an airplane, and he assumed the world was flat. He is part of a group of Polar Eskimos in northwest Greenland who still share in an ice-age culture that began more than four thousand years ago, when nomadic boreal hunters began walking from Ellesmere Island across the ice to Greenland. Many of their ancient practices — hunting with harpoons, wearing skins, and traveling by dogsled — have survived despite modernizing influences that began at the turn of the century, when the explorer Robert Peary gave them rifles. The Arctic cold and ice have kept these hardy and efficient people isolated even today.

I began going to Greenland in 1993 to get above tree line. I was still recovering from being struck by lightning, which had affected my heart and made it impossible to go to altitude, where I feel most at home. In Greenland, I experienced tree line as a product of latitude, not just altitude. I had already read the ten volumes of expedition notes of Arctic explorer and national hero Knud Rasmussen, and when I met the Greenlandic people, my summer idyll turned into seven years of Arctic peregrinations that may never end.

This latest journey is taking place in April; I am traveling to Qaanaaq, the northernmost town in the world, where I will join two Inuit subsistence hunters — Jens Danielsen and Mikile Kristiansen, friends with whom I have been traveling since I first came to Greenland — on their spring trip up the coast to hunt seal, walrus, small birds called dovekies, and polar bear.

Despite their Danish names (Greenland, once a Danish colony, is now largely self-governing), Jens and Mikile are Eskimos, descendants of hunters who walked the Bering Land Bridge from Siberia to Alaska, across the Canadian Arctic, and, finally, to Greenland, following the tracks of polar bears, the migration of caribou and birds, the breathing holes of seals, the cracks in the ice where walrus and whales were found.

Greenland is 1,500 miles long and is crowned by a 700,000-square-mile sheet of ice whose summit is 11,000 feet high. The habitable fringe of land that peeks out from this icy mass is mostly rock, to which houses are bolted. No roads connect villages; transportation is by dogsled or boat, or the occasional helicopter taxi that can be summoned at a formidable price, weather permitting. The closest town to the south would take one and a half months to reach by dogsled from Qaanaaq.

The ice came in October and now paves the entire polar north — rivers, oceans, and fjords are all solid white. Like old skin, it is pinched, pocked, and nicked, pressed up into towering hummocks and bejeweled by stranded calf ice sticking up here and there like hunks of beveled glass.

The arrival of a helicopter is still an event in any Arctic village. Snow flies as we land, and families and friends press forward to greet their loved ones. Qaanaaq, a town of 650 people and 2,000 dogs in the northwestern corner of Greenland, is built on a hill facing a fjord. Down on the ice, there is always activity: Sleds are lined up, dogs are being fed or harnessed, hunters are coming home from a day's or month's journey or are just taking off. It's said that the Polar Eskimo begins and ends life with traveling. Even at home, they are always preparing for the next journey.

Jens Danielsen comes for me in the morning. Tall and rotund, he has a deep, gentle voice and a belly laugh that can make the ice shake. He wears sweatpants and tennis shoes despite biting cold. Almost forty, he's already beginning to gray at the temples. Jens estimates that he travels more than 3,500 miles a year by dogsled while hunting for food for his family. When not on the ice, he is a politician, heading up the Avanersuaq hunting council, a job that

requires him to go below the Arctic Circle to Nuuk, Greenland's
capital city. There, he testifies in front of Parliament in an effort
to preserve the traditional lifestyle of northern hunters. So far,
they've been able to restrict the use of snowmobiles (in Qaanaaq,
one is owned by the hospital for emergencies), limit the number of
motorized boats in the summer so as not to disrupt the hunting of
narwhals using kayaks, and dictate the means by which animals are
to be killed. Rifles are used to hunt seals and polar bears. Harpoons
are used on narwhals and walrus.

A northern hunter's year could be said to begin when the new
ice comes in late September or early October. They hunt walrus by
dogsled in the fall. After the sun goes below the horizon on October 24, the dark months last until February. By moonlight, seals are
hunted with nets set under the ice. Spring means bearded and
ringed seals, polar bears, narwhals, rabbits, and foxes, and when
the dovekie migration begins around May 10, hunters climb talus
slopes and catch the birds with nets. In summer, narwhals are har-
pooned from kayaks.

To say that Jens, Mikile, and the other villagers are subsistence
hunters is perhaps stretching the truth. A couple times a year, in
late summer when it can make it through the ice, a supply boat
comes and delivers goods from Denmark: wood, building supplies,
paint, heating oil, and other necessities. It is also possible to buy
small quantities of imported Danish foods — brought in by helicopter — at the tiny, sparsely stocked grocery store, but most villagers can't afford to live on Danish lamb and chicken, and, furthermore, prefer not to. During bouts of bad weather, no supplies
come at all. These are hunters who, at the end of the twentieth century, have chosen to stay put and live by the harpoon, gun, and
sled.

At the last minute, Jens's wife, Ilaitsuk, a strong, handsome
woman a few years older than her husband, decides to come with
us. *"Issi,"* she says, rubbing her arms. Cold. Before getting on the
sled, she and I change into *annuraat ammit*— skins. We pull on
nannuk, polar bear pants; *kapatak,* fox-skin anoraks; *kamikpak,*
polar bear boots lined with *ukaleq,* arctic hare; and *aiqqatit,* sealskin mittens. Then we prepare to head north in search of animals
whose meat we will live on and whose skins Jens, Mikile, and their
families will wear.

   Mikile has joined the hunting trip because he needs a new pair
of polar bear pants. He has already packed his sled and has begun
harnessing his dogs. In his mid-thirties, Mikile is small and wiry,
with a gentle demeanor and face. He is traveling light and carries
only one passenger, photographer Chris Anderson.

   Thule-style sleds are twelve to fourteen feet long, with upturned
front runners and a bed lashed onto the frame. Jens lays our
duffels on a tarp, and Ilaitsuk places caribou hides on top. The
load is tied down, and a rifle is shoved under the lash-rope. The
Danielsens' five-year-old grandson, Merseqaq, who is going with us,
lies on the skins with a big smile. The dogs, which are chained on
long lines when not being used, are eager to get to work. Jens
bends at the waist to untangle the trace lines — something he will
do hundreds of times during our journey. As soon as the dogs feel
the lines being hooked to the sled, they charge off out of sheer
excitement — there is no way to stop them — and the wild ride
begins.

   We careen down narrow paths through the village. Bystanders,
children, and dogs jump out of the way. Jens leaps off as we approach the rough ice at the shoreline. Walking in front of the team,
he whistles so they will follow him as Ilaitsuk steadies the sled from
behind. We tip, tilt, and bump. The dogs are not harnessed two by
two as they are in Alaska but fan out on lines of varying lengths.
This way, they can position themselves however they want, rest
when they need to, or align themselves with a friend. Ilaitsuk
and Jens run hard and jump on the sled. I've been holding the little boy. Soon, we bump down onto smooth ice. Jens snaps the
iparautaq (whip) over the dogs' heads as they trot across the frozen
sea.

   We head west, then straight north past a long line of stranded
icebergs that, in summer, when there is open water, will eventually
be taken south by the Labrador current from Baffin Bay to Davis
Strait, then into the North Atlantic. In winter, the icebergs are
frozen in place. They stand like small cities with glinting towers,
natural arches that bridge gaping portholes through which more
icebergs can be seen.

   Jens snaps the whip above the dogs' backs. "*Ai, ai, ai, ai . . .* ," he
sings out in a high falsetto, urging them to go faster. Snow-covered
ice rolls beneath us, and the coastline, a walled fortress, slides by.

On a dogsled, there is no physical control — no rudder, no brakes, no reins. Only voice commands and the sound of the whip and the promise of food if the hunt is good, which is perhaps why these half-wild, half-starved dogs obey. A dogtrot — the speed at which we move up Greenland's northwest coast — is about four miles an hour. Dog farts float by, and the sound of panting is the one rhythm that seems to keep our minds from flying away.

Half an hour north of Qaanaaq, the snow deepens, and the dogs slow down. They are already pulling seven hundred pounds. We follow the track of a sled that is carrying a coffin. Earlier this week, a young hunter died in an accident on the ice in front of Qaanaaq where schoolchildren were playing. Now his body is being taken home to Siorapaluk, a subsistence hunting village of a few dozen people up the coast from here. Some say the hunter was suicidal. "There are troubles everywhere. Even here," Jens says, clasping his tiny grandson on his lap at the front of the sled. *"Harru, harru!"* (go left), he yells to the dogs. *"Atsuk, atsuk!"* (Go right.) When his grandson mimics the commands, Jens turns and smiles.

We stop twice to make tea. The old Primus stove is lit and placed inside a wooden box to shelter the flame from the wind. Hunks of ice are chipped off an iceberg, stuffed into the pot, and melted for water. Danish cookies are passed. A whole frozen halibut, brought from home, is stuck headfirst into the snow. Mikile, Ilaitsuk, and Jens begin hacking at its side and eating chunks of "frozen sushi." The dogs roll in the snow to cool themselves, while we stand and shiver.

The closer we get to Siorapaluk, the colder it gets. Jens unties a dog, which had become lame, from the front of the sled, and throws him back into the pack. Appearances count: It wouldn't look right to arrive in a village with an injured dog. We slide around a bend, and Robertson Fjord opens up. Three glaciers lap at the frozen fjord, and the ice cap rises pale and still behind snowy mountains. Where one begins and the other ends is hard to tell. On the far, east-facing side of the fjord, the village comes into view. It has taken us eight hours to get here.

We make camp out on the ice in front of the village, pushing the two sleds together to serve as our *igliq* (sleeping platform) and raising a crude, bloodstained canvas tent over them. When I look up, something catches my eye: The funeral procession is winding up the snowy path above the houses. Six men are carrying the hunter's coffin. We hear faint singing — hymns — then the mourners gather in a knot as the wooden casket is laid down on the snow, blessed, and stored in a shed, where it will stay until the ground thaws enough for burial.

When the sun slips behind the mountains, the temperature plummets to eighteen degrees below zero. All six of us crowd into the tent. Shoulder to shoulder, leg to leg, we are bodies seeking other bodies for warmth. With our feet on the ice floor, we sip tea and eat cookies and go to bed with no dinner. When we live on the ice, we eat what we hunt — in the spring, that means ringed seals, walrus, or polar bears. But we did not hunt today.

The sound of thirty dogs crooning and howling wakes me. I look across the row of bodies stuffed into sleeping bags. Jens is holding his grandson against his barrel chest. They open their eyes: two moon faces smiling at the canine chorus. There are gunshots. Mikile sticks his head out of the tent, then falls back on the *igliq*, grunting. "They shot at something but missed," he says. "At what?" I ask. *"Nanoq, immaqa"* (a polar bear, maybe), he says, smiling mischievously.

Bright sun, frigid breeze. It must be midday. We sit in silence, watching ice melt for tea water. *"Issi,"* Ilaitsuk says again. Cold. My companions speak very little English, and my Greenlandic is, well, rudimentary. Some days we talk hardly at all. Other times we pool our dictionaries and enjoy a feast of words. I try to memorize such useful phrases as *"nauk tupilaghuunnguaju,"* which means "you fool"; and *"taquliktooq,"* "dark-colored dog with a white blaze over its eye." But often, I fail, which just makes for more merriment.

Today, we break camp quietly. The pace of the preparations is deceptive: It looks laid-back because Inuit hunters don't waste energy with theatrics or melodrama. Instead, they work quietly, steadily, and quickly. Before I know it, Jens is hooking the trace lines to the sled. I grab the little boy and make a flying leap as Ilaitsuk and Jens jump aboard the already fast-moving sled. Jens laughs at his grandson for not being ready, and the boy cries, which makes Jens laugh harder. This is the Eskimo way of teaching children to have a sense of humor and to pay attention and act with precision — lessons that will later preserve their lives.

Snow begins pelting us. "The weather and the hunter are not such good friends," Jens says. "If a hunter waits for good weather, well, he may starve. He may starve anyway. But if he goes out when conditions are bad, he may fall through the ice and never be seen again. That's how it is here."

Snow deepens, and the dogtrot slows to a walk. On our right, brown cliffs rise in sheer folds striped with avalanche chutes criss-crossed by the tracks of arctic hares. *"Ukaleq, ukaleq,"* Ilaitsuk cries out. Jens whistles the dogs to a stop. Ilaitsuk points excitedly. The rabbits' hides provide liners for *kamiks* (boots), and their flesh is eaten. We look: They are white against a white slope and bounce behind outcrops of boulders. No luck. On the ice, there are no seals. What will the six of us plus thirty dogs eat tonight?

As we round a bend and a rocky knob, a large bay opens up. We travel slowly across its wide mouth. Looking inward, I see a field of talcum powder, then a cliff of ice: the snout of an enormous glacier made of turquoise, light, and rock, carrying streambed debris like rooftop ornaments. My eyes move from the ice cap above to the frozen fjord below. Bands of color reveal the rhythm of ablation and accumulation for what it is: the noise and silence of time — Arctic time — which is all light or all dark and has no hours or days. When you're on a dogsled, the twenty-four-hour day turns into something elastic, and our human habits move all the way around the clock; we find ourselves eating dinner at breakfast time, sleeping in the all-day light, and traveling in the all-light night. What we care about is not a schedule but warmth and food and good weather as we push far north of the last village and see ahead only cold and snow and a growing hunger that makes us ache.

We change course. The going has been torturously slow. Instead of following the coastline straight north, we now veer out onto the frozen ocean; we follow a lead in the ice, looking for seals. The snow comes on harder. The cowl of a storm approaches, crossing Ellesmere Island, pulling over the hundred-mile-wide face of Humboldt glacier. Wind whips the storm's dark edge; it fibrillates like a raven's wing feathers, and as it pulls over, the great dome light of inland ice goes dark.

There are breathing holes all along the crack, but no *uuttuq* — seals that have hauled themselves out on ice — which are usually common in the spring. We keep going in a westward direction, away from the historic camping sites of Neqi, where we will sleep tonight, and Etah.

All afternoon and evening, we travel in a storm. I remember a hunter once telling me about getting vertigo. "Sometimes when we are on our dogsleds and there is bad fog or snow, we feel lost. We can't tell where the sky is, where the ice. It feels like we are moving upside down." But today we aren't lost. "We can tell by wind direction," the same hunter told me, "and if we keep traveling at the same angle to the drifting snow, we're okay."

All is white. We stop for tea, pulling the two sleds close together and lashing a tarp between for a windbreak. We scrounge through our duffels for food. Chris finds a jar of peanut butter. I'm dismayed to see the words REDUCED FAT on the label. Never mind. We spread it on crackers, then drink tea and share a bittersweet chocolate bar. Bittersweet is what I am feeling right now: happy to be in Greenland among old friends but getting hungrier with each bite I take.

It's easy to see how episodes of famine have frequently swept through the Arctic, how quickly hunting can go bad, how hunger dominates. Before stores and helicopters, pan-Arctic cannibalism was common. After people ate their dogs and boiled sealskins, they ate human flesh — almost always the bodies of those who had already died. It was the key to survival, repellent as it was. Peter Freuchen, a Danish explorer who traveled with Knud Rasmussen for fourteen years, wrote of the practice: "At Pingerqaling I met a remarkable woman, Atakutaluk. I had heard of her before as being the foremost lady of Fury and Hecla Strait — she was important because she had once eaten her husband and three of her children."

Freuchen went on to describe the ordeal. Atakutaluk's tribe had been traveling across Baffin Island when a warm spell hit and it became impossible to use a sled. There were no animals in the area. When they ran out of food, they ate their dogs, then the weaker people in their hunting party. When Freuchen met Atakutaluk, she said, "Look here, Pita. Don't let your face be narrow for this. I got a new husband, and I got with him three new children. They are all named for the dead ones that only served to keep me alive so they could be reborn."

We head north again, crossing back over a large piece of frozen ocean. Rabbit tracks crisscross in front of us, but we see no animals. The edge of the storm frays, letting light flood through. Snow, ice, and air glisten. Ilaitsuk and I tip our faces up to the sun. Its warmth is a blessing, and for a few moments, we close our eyes and doze.

There's a yell. Ilaitsuk scrambles to her knees and looks around. It is Mikile far ahead of us. He's up on his knees on his fast-moving sled: *"Nanoq! Nanoq!"* he yells, pointing, and then we see: A polar bear is trotting across the head of a wide fjord.

Jens's dogs take off in that direction. Mikile has already cut two of his dogs loose, and they chase the bear. He releases two more. *"Pequoq, pequoq,"* Jens yells, urging his dogs to go faster. It is then that we see that there is a cub, struggling in deep snow to keep up. The mother stops, wheels around, and runs back. Mikile's loose dogs catch up and hold the bear at bay. Because she has a young one, she will not be killed; an abandoned cub would never survive.

Now we are between the cub and the she-bear. Repeatedly, she stops, stands, and whirls around to go back to her cub. The dogs close in: She paws, snarls, and runs again. Then something goes terribly wrong: One of the dogs spies the cub. Before we can get there, the dog is on the cub and goes for his jugular. We rush to the young bear's rescue, but the distances are so great and the going is so slow that by the time we make it, the dog is shaking the cub by his neck and has been joined by other dogs. Mikile and Jens leap off their sleds and beat the dogs away with their whip handles, but it is too late. The cub is badly hurt.

We stay with the cub while Mikile catches up with the mother. The cub is alive but weak. A large flap of skin and flesh hangs down. Even though he's dazed and unsteady, he's still feisty. He snarls and paws at us as we approach. Jens throws a soft loop around his leg and pulls him behind the sled to keep him out of the fray; then we let him rest. Maybe he will recover enough for us to send him back to his mother.

Far ahead, the mother bear starts to get away, but the loose dogs catch up and slow her progress. Near the far side of the fjord, the bear darts west, taking refuge behind a broken, stranded iceberg. Mikile cuts more dogs loose when the first ones begin to tire. The bear stands in her icy enclosure, coming out to charge the dogs as they approach. She doesn't look for her cub; she is fighting for her own life.

The sun is out, and the bear is hot. She scoops up a pawful of snow and eats it. The slab of ice against which she rests is blue and shaped in a wide V, like an open book whose sides are melting in the spring sun. The dogs surround her in a semicircle, jumping forward to snap at her, testing their own courage, but leaping back when she charges them.

Five hundred yards behind Mikile, we watch over the cub. If we get too close, he snaps. Sometimes he stands, but he's weak. He begins panting. His eyes roll back; he staggers and is dead.

Jens ties a loop around his neck, and we pull the cub like a toy behind the sled. Mikile turns as we approach. "Is the cub dead?" he asks. Jens says that he is. The decision is made: Mikile will shoot the mother. I ask if killing her is necessary — after all, she is a young bear that can have more cubs — but my Greenlandic is unintelligible. I plead for her life using English verbs and Greenlandic nouns. Jens says, "It is up to Mikile."

Mikile, whose polar bear pants are worn almost all the way through, listens, then quietly loads his rifle. We are standing close to the bear, close enough for her to attack us, but she has eyes only for the dogs. Standing on her toes, she lays her elbow on top of the berg and looks out.

Silently, I root for her: Go, go. These are the last moments of her life, and I'm watching them tick by. Does she know she is doomed? Once again I plead for her life, but I get only questioning looks from the hunters. I feel sick. Peeking over the top of the ice, the bear slumps back halfheartedly. She is tired, her cub is gone, and there is no escape.

Ilaitsuk covers Merseqaq's ears as Mikile raises his rifle. The boy is frightened. He has seen the cub die, and he doesn't want to see any more.

The bear's nose, eyes, and claws are black dots in a world of white, a world that, for her, holds no clues about human ambivalence. She gives me the same hard stare she would give a seal — after all, I'm just part of the food chain. It is the same stare Mikile gives her now, not hard from lack of feeling but from the necessity to survive. I understand how important it is for a hunter to get a polar bear. She will be the source of food, and her skin will be used for much-needed winter clothing. It is solely because of the polar bear pants and boots that we don't freeze to death. Nevertheless, I feel that I am a witness to an execution.

The bear's fur is pale yellow, and the ice wall is blue. The sun is hot. Time melts. What I know about life and death, cold and hunger, seems irrelevant. There are three gunshots. A paw goes up in agony and scratches the ice wall. She rolls on her back and is dead.

I kneel down by her. The fur is thick between her claws. There is the sound of gurgling. It's too early in the year for running water. Then I see that it is her blood pouring from the gunshot wound that killed her.

Mikile ties his dogs back in with the others. Knives are sharpened. Tea water is put on to boil. We roll up our sleeves in the late afternoon sun. Ilaitsuk glasses the ice for other animals; Merseqaq is on the snow beside the bear and puts his tiny hand on her large paw.

The bear is laid out on her back. Jens puts the tip of his knife on her umbilicus and makes an upward cut to her neck. The fine tip travels up under her chin and through her black lip as if to keep her from talking.

Soon enough she is disrobed. The skin is laid out on the snow, and, after the blood is wiped off, it is folded in quarters and laid carefully in a gunnysack on the sled. Then her body is dismembered, and the pieces are also stowed under the tarp, so when we put away our teacups and start northwest toward Neqi, she is beneath us in pieces and we are riding her, this bear that, according to Inuit legends, can hear and understand everything human beings say. We travel the rest of the day in silence.

We cross the wide mouth of the fjord and continue on to Neqi, a camp used by Inuit hunters and European explorers for hundreds of years. There is no village, only a cabin, low and wide, set at the tip of a long thumb of land sticking out from between two glaciers. The cabin looks down on the frozen Smith Sound. The word *neqi* means "meat," and this was a place where meat caches were laid in for hunters and explorers on their way to the far north of Greenland or to the North Pole. We push our sleds up through the hummocks to the cabin. The meat racks are crowded with walrus flippers, dead dogs, and bits of hacked-up seals. Half sanctuary, half charnel ground.

We stand on the ice terrace in front of the cabin. Looking out at the wide expanse of frozen ocean, we salute the rarely seen sun. Its warmth drives into us, and for the first time, we relax. A hidden beer emerges from Jens's duffel bag and is passed around.

The strangled cry of a fox floats out over the frozen bay where we shot the bear. Now a band of fog rises from that place, a blindfold covering the labanotations — the script of the bear's death dance: where she stopped, wheeled around, attacked, and kept running; the hieroglyphics of blood and tracks; and the hollows in the snow where the dogs rested after the chase. I'm glad I can't see.

A Primus is lit, and water is put on to boil. Then the backstrap of the polar bear — the most tender part — is thrown in the pot. It's so warm, we take off our anoraks and hats. Jens passes paper plates. *"Nanoq. Nanoq,"* he says in a low voice. "The polar bear is king. We have to eat her in a special way. We boil her like the seal, but we pay special respects to her so her soul shall not have too much difficulty getting home."

After twenty minutes, chunks of meat are doled out. They steam on our plates. *"Qujanaq,"* I say, thanking Mikile, Jens, and, most of all, the bear. The meat is tender and good, almost like buffalo.

Later, we get into our sleeping bags and lie on the *igliq*. It is still warm, and no one can sleep. Jens and Ilaitsuk hold their grandson between them as Jens begins a story: "A long time ago, when shamans still flew underwater and animals could talk, there was a woman named Anoritoq who lived on that point of land north of Etah. The name Anoritoq means 'windswept one.' This woman had no husband, and her only son was killed by a hunter out of jealousy, because the young boy had no father but was becoming a great hunter anyway. After her son died, a hunter brought the woman a polar bear cub, which she raised just like a son. The bear learned the language of the Eskimo and played with the other children. When he grew up, he hunted seals and was very successful. But she worried about him. She was afraid a hunter might kill him, because he was, after all, a bear, and his skin was needed for clothing. She tried covering him with soot to make him dark, but one day, when some of his white fur was showing, a hunter killed him. She was so sad, she stopped eating and went outside and stayed there all the time and looked at the sea. Then, she changed into a stone. Now when we go bear hunting in that area, we put a piece of seal fat on the rock and pray for a good hunt."

*

Morning. We follow the coast north to Pitoravik. It's not a long trip. From there, we will determine our route to Etah — either up and over part of the inland ice or following the coast if there is no open water or pressure ice. A wind begins to blow as Jens and Mikile take off to investigate the trail over the glacier. They are gone several hours, and when they come back, they shake their heads. "The drifts are too deep and the crevasses too wide, and the snow hides them," Jens says. "Down below, the ice is badly broken with open water. Too dangerous. We'll wait until morning. If the weather is good, we'll try to go over the top. If not, then we'll go to the ice edge out there, toward Canada, and hunt walrus and narwhal."

In the morning, the weather is no better. A continuous, mesmerizing snow falls. "I think the hunting will be better out there," Jens says, using our vantage point to look out over Smith Sound. Beyond, Ellesmere Island is a blue line of mountains with a ruffle of white clouds. We descend and go in a southwesterly direction toward the island of Kiatak.

For three or four days, we travel in weather that keeps closing down on us. When we stop to rest the dogs, Ilaitsuk, Merseqaq, and I play tag on the ice to keep warm. The child never complains. When his feet get cold, he merely points to his toes, and Ilaitsuk puts on the overboots she sewed together when we were in the cabin at Neqi. Then he sits at the front of the sled, wind-blasted and happy, echoing his grandfather's commands, snapping the long whip, already becoming a man.

Patience and strength of mind are the hunter's virtues. Also, flexibility and humor. Jens shoots at a seal and misses. Another one catches his scent and dives down into its hole. He returns to the sled, laughing at his failures, explaining to Mikile exactly what he did wrong. Later, he reverts to winter-style seal hunting called *agluhiutuq,* hunting at the *agluq* (breathing hole). But even this fails.

We continue on. *"Hikup hinaa,"* Jens says. The ice edge. That's what we are now looking for. There we will find plentiful seal, walrus, and narwhal. My stomach growls, and I think of the legend of the Great Famine, when winters followed one after the other, with no spring, summer, or fall in between. Jens says that this last winter and spring have been the coldest in his memory. Ironically, colder weather in the Arctic may be a side effect of global warming. As pieces of the ice cap melt and calve into the ocean, the water temperature in parts of the far north cools, as, in turn, does the air. Maybe global warming will cancel itself out, I say. Jens doesn't understand my "Greenenglish." *"Issi,"* he says, rubbing his arms. Cold. "Maybe we will have to eat each other like they did in the old days," he says, smiling sweetly.

For the Eskimo, solitude is a sign of sheer unhappiness. It is thought to be a perversion and absolutely undesirable. Packed tightly together on the sled, we are fur-wrapped, rendered motionless by cold. It's good to be pressed between human bodies. We scan the ice for animals. Shadows made by standing bits of ice look like seals.

Then we do see one, a black comma lying on the alabaster extravagance.

Jens and Mikile stop their dogs. Jens mounts his rifle on a movable blind — a small stand with a white sailcloth to hide his face. The snow is shin-deep, but the wind is right. He creeps forward, then lies down on his belly, sighting in his rifle. All thirty dogs sit at attention, with ears pricked. When they stop panting, the world goes silent. As soon as they hear the muffled crack of the gun, off they go, running toward Jens as they have been trained to do.

We stand in a semicircle around a pool of blood, backs to the wind. Quickly and quietly, Jens flenses the seal. He cuts out the liver, warm and steaming, holds it on the end of his knife, and offers it to us. This is an Inuit delicacy. Eating the steaming liver has helped to save starving hunters. In gratitude, we all have a bite. Our mouths and chins drip with blood. There is a slightly salty taste to the lukewarm meat.

Ilaitsuk folds the sealskin and lays it under the tarp alongside the polar bear skin. Jens cuts a notch through the back flipper for a handhold and drags the pink body, looking ever more diminutive, over the front of the sled. Lash lines are pulled tight, and we take off as snow swirls.

We are still traveling at 10:30 in the evening when the storm breaks. We watch the dark edge pull past, moving faster than the sled. Under clear skies, the temperature plummets to somewhere near twenty degrees below zero.

One seal for thirty dogs and six humans isn't very much meat.

We stop at an iceberg and hack out slabs of ice, then make camp. As Ilaitsuk and I unload the sleds, Jens and Mikile cut up seal meat. The dogs line up in rows, avidly waiting for food. It has been two days since they've eaten fresh meat. A chunk is flung through the air, then another and another. Jens's and Mikile's aims are so perfect, every dog gets its share, and the faster they eat, the more they get.

Jens cuts up the remaining seal for our dinner. Inside the tent, we watch as lumps of meat churn in brown water. As the hut warms up, we strip down. Merseqaq's tiny red T-shirt reads: I LOVE ELE-PHANTS, though he has never seen one and probably never will.

We eat in silence, using our pocketknives and fingers. A loaf of bread is passed. We each have a slice, then drink tea and share a handful of cookies. After, Ilaitsuk sets a piece of plywood in a plastic bucket and stretches the sealskin over the top edge. With her *ulu* — a curved knife with a wooden handle — she scrapes the blubber from the skin in strong, downward thrusts. When the hide is clean, she turns to her *kiliutaq* — a small, square knife used to scrape the brownish pink oil out of a fur.

Ilaitsuk lets me have a try at scraping. I'm so afraid I'll cut through and ruin the skin, I barely scratch the surface.

Later, lying in my sleeping bag, I listen to wind. Jens tells stories about the woman who adopted a bear, the hunter who married a fox, and the origin of fog. His voice goes soft, and the words drone, putting us into a sweet trance of sleep so pleasurable that I don't know if I'll ever be able to sleep again without those stories.

In the next days, we search for the ice edge, camping on the ice wherever we find ourselves at the end of the night. We travel straight west from the tip of Kiatak Island out onto the frozen ocean between Greenland and Ellesmere Island. On the way, Jens teaches his grandson voice commands and how to use the whip without touching the backs of the animals. "Will Merseqaq be a hunter, too?" I ask. Jens says, "I am teaching him what he needs to know. Then the decision will be up to him. He has to love this more than anything."

When we reach a line of icebergs, Jens and Mikile clamber to the top and glass the entire expanse of ice to the west. It feels as if we're already halfway across Smith Sound. Jens comes back shaking his head. "There is no open water," he says incredulously. "It is ice all the way to Canada." This has never happened before in any spring in memory. It is May 8.

We turn south to an area where sea currents churn at the ice. Maybe there will be an ice edge there. Down the coast at Kap Parry, we meet two hunters who are coming from the other direction. As usual, there is a long silence, then a casual question about open water. They shake their heads. No ice edge this way, either.

That night, I lie in my sleeping bag, squeezed tightly between Mikile and Ilaitsuk. "I feel as if we are stuck in winter," Mikile said earlier, looking frustrated. He has a big family to feed. Along with Jens, he is considered one of the best hunters in Qaanaaq, but even he can't kill enough game if spring never comes. We lie awake listening to wind.

At midday, we climb an iceberg that is shaped like the Sydney Opera House, to see if the ice edge has appeared. Jens shakes his head no. As we climb down, Mikile yells and points: *"Nanoq."* Far out, a polar bear dances across the silvered horizon, blessedly too distant for us to hunt. A mirage takes him instead of a bullet, a band of mirrored light floating up from the ice floor. It takes his dancing legs and turns them into waves of spring heat still trying to make its way past the frigid tail end of winter.

Finally we head for home, traveling along the east side of Kiatak. Walls of red rock rise in amphitheaters; arctic hares race across snow-dappled turf and grass. A raven swoops by, and a fox floats its gray tail along the steep sidehill. Near the bottom of the cliff, icicles hang at odd angles from beds of rock. We pass over a floor of broken platelets that look as if they'd been held up like mirrors, then tossed down and broken, making the sled tip this way and that. Some pieces of ice are so exquisite that I ask Jens to stop so I can stare at them: a finely etched surface overlaid with another layer of ice punctured by what look like stars.

The dogs bring me back. They fight and fart and snarl and pant. One of them, Pappi, is in heat, and the other dogs can think of nothing except getting to her. Pappi slinks behind the others, clamping her tail down and refusing to pull. Then the males fall back, too, fighting one another, and the sled eventually comes to a stop. Jens unties Pappi and fastens her behind the sled, but this doesn't work, either. She falls and is dragged and can't get up.

Finally Jens cuts Pappi loose. There's a moment of relief, as if she had been freed from a tight world of ice and cold and discipline. Ilaitsuk looks at me and smiles. Her face is strong in the late evening sun. The boy is ensconced in his grandfather's lap, wearing dark glasses. We have failed to bring home much meat, but Jens shrugs it off, reminding me that worrying has no place in the Arctic. He and all those before him have survived day by day for four thousand years, and one bad hunting trip won't set him back. There is always tomorrow.

Now Pappi is running free and happy. Jens urges her to go on ahead. The snow is hard and icy, and the sled careens as the dogs give chase. Sometimes when we are airborne, flying over moguls, little Merseqaq gets on his hands and knees and squeals with delight. The cold and hunger and terrible hunting conditions are behind us now, and as we near Qaanaaq, the dogs, ever optimistic, run very fast.

MICHAEL FINKEL

Desperate Passage

FROM *The New York Times Magazine*

DOWN IN THE HOLD, beneath the deck boards, where we were
denied most of the sun's light but none of its fire, it sometimes
seemed as if there were nothing but eyes. The boat was twenty-
three feet long, powered solely by two small sails. There were forty-
one people below and five above. All but myself and a photographer were Haitian citizens fleeing their country, hoping to start a
new life in the United States. The hold was lined with scrap wood
and framed with hand-hewn joists, as in an old mine tunnel, and
when I looked into the darkness it was impossible to tell where one
person ended and another began. We were compressed together,
limbs entangled, heads upon laps, a mass so dense there was
scarcely room for motion. Conversation had all but ceased. If not
for the shifting and blinking of eyes there'd be little sign that anyone was alive.

Twenty hours before, the faces of the people around me seemed
bright with the prospect of reaching a new country. Now, as the ar-
duousness of the crossing became clear, their stares conveyed the
flat helplessness of fear. David, whose journey I had followed from
his hometown of Port-au-Prince, buried his head in his hands. He
hadn't moved for hours. "I'm thinking of someplace else," is all he
would reveal. Stephen, who had helped round up the passengers,
looked anxiously out the hold's square opening, four feet over our
heads, where he could see a corner of the sail and a strip of cloud-
less sky. "I can't swim," he admitted softly. Kenton, a thirteen-year-
old boy, sat in a puddle of vomit and trembled as though crying,
only there were no tears. I was concerned about the severity of

Kenton's dehydration and could not shake the thought that he wasn't going to make it. "Some people get to America, and some people die," David had said. "Me, I'll take either one. I'm just not taking Haiti anymore."

It had been six weeks since David had made that pronouncement. This was in mid-March of 2000, in Port-au-Prince, soon after Haiti's national elections had been postponed for the fifth time and the country was entering its second year without a parliament or regional officials. David sold mahogany carvings on a street corner not far from the United States embassy. He spoke beautiful English, spiced with pitch-perfect sarcasm. His name wasn't really David, he said, but it's what people called him. He offered no surname. He said he'd once lived in America but had been deported. He informed me, matter-of-factly, that he was selling souvenirs in order to raise funds to pay a boat owner to take him back.

David was not alone in his desire to leave Haiti. In the previous six months, Haitians had been fleeing their country in numbers unseen since 1994, when a military coup tried to oust Jean-Bertrand Aristide, who was president at the time. Haiti's poverty level, always alarming, in recent years has escalated to even higher levels. Today, nearly 80 percent of Haitians live in abject conditions. Fewer than one in fifty has a steady wage-earning job; per capita income hovers around $250, less than one-tenth the Latin American average. Haitians once believed that Aristide might change things, but he was no longer in power, and the endless delays in elections, the recent spate of political killings, and the general sense of spiraling violence and corruption has led to a palpable feeling of despair. In February, the U.S. State Department released the results of a survey conducted in nine Haitian cities. Based on the study, two-thirds of Haitians — approximately 4,690,000 people — "would leave Haiti if given the means and opportunity." If they were going to leave, though, most would have to do so illegally; each year, the United States issues about ten thousand immigration visas to Haitian citizens, satisfying about one-fifth of 1 percent of the estimated demand.

To illegally enter America, Haitians typically embark on a two-step journey, taking a boat first to the Bahamas and then later to Florida. In the first five months of 2000, the United States and

Bahamian Coast Guards picked up more than a thousand Haitians, most on marginally seaworthy vessels. This was twice the number caught in all of 1999. Late April was an especially busy time. On April 22, the U.S. Coast Guard rescued 200 Haitians after their boat ran aground near Harbor Island, in the Bahamas. Three days later, 123 Haitian migrants were plucked from a sinking ship off the coast of Great Inagua Island. Three days after that, 278 Haitians were spotted by Bahamian authorities on a beach on Flamingo Cay, stranded after their boat had drifted for nearly a week. By the time rescuers arrived, 14 people had died from dehydration; as many as 18 others had perished during the journey. These were merely the larger incidents. Most boats leaving Haiti carry fewer than 50 passengers.

Such stories did not deter David. He said he was committed to making the trip, no matter the risks. His frankness was unusual. Around foreigners, most Haitians are reserved and secretive. David was boastful and loud. It's been said that Creole, the lingua franca of Haiti, is 10 percent grammar and 90 percent attitude, and David exercised this ratio to utmost effectiveness. It also helped that he was big, well over six feet and bricked with muscle. His head was shaved bald; a sliver of mustache shaded his upper lip. He was twenty-five years old. He used his size and his personality as a form of self-defense: the slums of Port-au-Prince are as dangerous as any in the world, and David, who had once been homeless for more than a year, had acquired the sort of street credentials that lent his words more weight than those of a policeman or soldier. He now lived in a broken-down neighborhood called Projet Droullard, where he shared a one-room hovel with thirteen others — the one mattress was suspended on cinder blocks so that people could sleep not only on but also beneath it. David was a natural leader, fluent in English, French, and Creole. His walk was the chest-forward type of a boxer entering the ring. Despite his apparent candor, it was difficult to know what was really on his mind. Even his smile was ambiguous — the broader he grinned, the less happy he appeared.

The high season for illegal immigration is April through September. The seas this time of year tend to be calm, except for the occasional hurricane. Last May I mentioned to David that I, along with a photographer named Chris Anderson, wanted to document a voyage from Haiti to America. I told David that if he was ready to make the trip, I'd pay him $30 a day to aid as guide and translator. He was skeptical at first, suspicious that we were working under-cover for the CIA to apprehend smugglers. But after repeated as-surances, and after showing him the supplies we'd brought for the voyage — self-inflating life vests (including one for David), vinyl rain jackets, waterproof flashlights, Power Bars, and a first-aid kit — his wariness diminished. I offered him an advance payment of one day's salary.

"Okay," he said. "It's a deal." He promised he'd be ready to leave early the next morning.

David was at our hotel at 5:30 A.M., wearing blue jeans, sandals, and a T-shirt and carrying a black plastic bag. Inside the bag was a second T-shirt, a pair of socks, a tin bowl, a metal spoon, and a Bi-ble. In his pocket was a small bundle of money. This was all he took with him. Later, he bought a toothbrush.

David opened his Bible and read Psalm 23 aloud: *Yea, though I walk through the valley of the shadow of death.* Then we walked to the bus station, sidestepping the stray dogs and open sewers. We boarded an old school bus, thirty-six seats, seventy-two passengers, and headed north, along the coast, to Île de la Tortue — Turtle Is-land — one of the three major boatbuilding centers in Haiti. David knew the island well. A year earlier, he'd spent a month there try-ing to gain a berth on a boat. Like many Haitians who can't afford such a trip, he volunteered to work. Seven days a week, he hiked deep into the island's interior, where a few swatches of forest still remained, and hacked down pine trees with a machete, hauling them back to be cut and hammered into a ship. For his efforts, Da-vid was served one meal a day, a bowlful of rice and beans. After thirty days of labor there was still no sign he'd be allowed onto a boat, so he returned to his mahogany stand in Port-au-Prince.

The bus rattled over the washboard roads and the sun bore down hard, even at 7:00 in the morning, and the men in the sugarcane fields were shirtless and glistening. A roadside billboard, faded and peeling, advertised Carnival Cruise Lines. LES BELLES CROI-SIÈRES, read the slogan — the Beautiful Cruises. At noon, we transferred to the bed of a pickup truck, the passing land gradually surrendering fertility until everything was brown. Five hours later the road ended at the rough-edged shipping town of Port-de-Paix, where we boarded a dilapidated ferry and set off on the hourlong crossing to Île Tortue, a fin-shaped wisp of land twenty miles long and four miles wide. Here, said David, is where he'd begin his trip to America.

There are at least seven villages on Île Tortue — its population is about 30,000 — but no roads, no telephones, no running water, no electricity, and no police. Transportation is strictly by foot, via a web of thin trails lined with cactus bushes. David walked the trails, up and down the steep seafront bluffs, until he stopped at La Vallée, a collection of huts scattered randomly along the shore. On the beach I counted seventeen boats under construction. They looked like the skeletons of beached whales. Most were less than thirty feet long, but two were of the same cargo-ship girth as the boat that had tried a rare Haiti-to-Florida nonstop last January but was intercepted by the Coast Guard off Key Biscayne. Three hundred ninety-five Haitians, fourteen Dominicans, and two Chinese passengers were shoehorned aboard, all of whom were returned to Haiti. According to survivors' reports, ten people had suffocated during the crossing, the bodies tossed overboard.

The boats at La Vallée were being assembled entirely with scrap wood and rusty nails; the only tools I saw were hammers and machetes. David said a boat left Île Tortue about once every two or three days during the high season. He thought the same was true at the other two boatbuilding spots — Cap-Haïtien, in the north, and Gonaïves, in the west. This worked out to about a boat a day, forty or more Haitians leaving every twenty-four hours.

The first step in getting onto a boat at Île Tortue, David said, is to gain the endorsement of one of the local officials, who are often referred to as elders. Such approval, he explained, is required whether you are a foreigner or not — and foreigners occasionally come to Haiti to arrange their passage to America. A meeting with the elder in La Vallée was scheduled. David bought a bottle of five-star rum as an offering, and we walked to his home.

The meeting was tense. David, Chris, and I crouched on miniature wooden stools on the porch of the elder's house, waiting for him to arrive. About a dozen other people were present, all men. They looked us over sharply and did not speak or smile. When the official appeared, he introduced himself as Mr. Evon. He did not seem especially old for an elder, though perhaps I shouldn't have been surprised; the average life expectancy for men in Haiti is less than fifty years. When Haitian men discuss serious matters, they tend to sit very close and frequently touch each other's arms. David placed both his hands upon Mr. Evon and attested, in Creole, to the availability of funds for the trip and to our honesty.

"What are your plans?" asked Mr. Evon.

"To go to America," David said. "To start my life."

"And if God does not wish it?"

"Then I will go to the bottom of the sea."

That evening, several of the men who had been present during our interview with Mr. Evon came to visit, one at a time. They were performing what David called a *vit ron* — a quick roundup, trying to gather potential passengers for the boat they were each affiliated with. David chose an amiable man named Stephen Bellot, who claimed to be filling a ship that was likely to leave in a matter of days. Stephen was also a member of one of the more prominent families on Île Tortue. He was twenty-eight years old, lanky and loose-limbed, with rheumy eyes and a wiggly way of walking that made me think, at times, that he'd make an excellent template for a cartoon character. In many ways, he seemed David's opposite. Where David practically perspired bravado, Stephen was tentative and polite. His words were often lost in the wind, and he had a nervous habit of rubbing his thumbs across his forefingers, as if they were little violins. He had been raised on Île Tortue and, though he'd moved to Port-au-Prince to study English, he seemed to lack David's city savvy. In Port-au-Prince, Stephen had worked for several years as a high school teacher — chemistry and English were his specialties. He was paid $35 a month. He'd returned to Île Tortue six months before in order to catch a boat to America. The prospect of leaving, he admitted, both inspired and intimidated him. "I've never been anywhere," he told me. "Not even across the border to the Dominican Republic." He said he'd set up a meeting with a boat owner the next day.

The boat owner lived on the mainland, in Port-de-Paix. Stephen's mother and brother and grandmother and several of his cousins lived in a small house nearby, and Stephen took us there while he went off to find the captain. An open sewer ran on either side of the two-room cinder-block home; insects formed a thrumming cloud about everyone's head. There was a TV but no electricity. The lines had been down for some time, and nobody knew when they'd be repaired. Sleep was accomplished in shifts — at all times, it seemed, four or five people were in the home's one bed. The sole decoration was a poster advertising Miami Beach. We waited there for eleven hours. The grandmother, bone thin, sat against a wall and did not move. Another woman scrubbed clothing with a washboard and stone. "Everyone in Haiti has been to prison," David once said, "because Haiti is a prison."

The captain arrived at sunset. His name was Gilbert Marko; he was thirty-one years old. He was wearing the nicest clothing I'd seen in Haiti — genuine Wrangler blue jeans, a gingham button-down shirt, and shiny wingtips. He had opaque eyes and an uncommonly round head, and tiny, high-set ears. There was an air about him of scarcely suppressed intensity, like a person who has recently eaten a jalapeño pepper. The meeting went well. David explained that his decision to leave had not been a hasty one — he mentioned his previous trip to Île Tortue and his time in America. Stephen said we all understood the risks. Both David and Stephen declared their support for us. This seemed good enough for Gilbert. He said he'd been to the Bahamas many times. He had seven children by five women and was gradually trying to get everyone to America. He spoke excellent English, jingly with Bahamian rhythms.

His boat, he said, was new — this would only be its second crossing. There would be plenty of water and food, he insisted, and no more than twenty-five passengers. He was taking family members and wanted a safe, hassle-free trip. His boat was heading to Nassau, the Bahamian capital. The crossing could take four days if the wind was good, and as many as eight days if it was not. We'd have no engine.

Most people who make it to America, Gilbert explained, do so only after working in the Bahamas for several months, usually picking crops or cleaning hotel rooms. According to Gilbert, the final segment of the trip, typically a ninety-minute shot by powerboat from the Bimini Islands, Bahamas, to Broward Beach, Florida, costs about $3,000 a person. Often, he said, an American boat owner pilots this leg — ten people in his craft, a nice profit for a half-day's work.

Eventually, talk came around to money for Gilbert's segment of the trip. Nothing in Haiti has a set price, and the fee for a crossing is especially variable, often depending on the quality of the boat. Virtually every Haitian is handing over his life savings. The price most frequently quoted for an illegal trip to the Bahamas was 10,000 gourdes — about $530. Fees ten times as high had also been mentioned. Rumor on Île Tortue was that the two Chinese passengers on the Key Biscayne boat had paid $20,000 apiece. Gilbert said that a significant percentage of his income goes directly to the local elders, who in turn make sure that no other Haitian authorities become overly concerned with the business on Île Tortue.

After several hours of negotiations, Gilbert agreed to transport Chris and me for $1,200 each, and David and Stephen, who were each given credit for rounding us up, for $300 each.

Gilbert had named his boat *Believe in God*. It was anchored (next to the *Thank You Jesus*) off the shore of La Vallée, where it had been built. If you were to ask a second-grader to draw a boat, the result would probably look a lot like the *Believe in God*. It was painted a sort of brackish white, with red and black detailing. The mast was a thin pine, no doubt dragged out of the hills of Île Tortue. There was no safety gear, no maps, no life rafts, no tool kit, and no nautical instruments of any type save for an ancient compass. The deck boards were misaligned. With the exception of the hold, there was no shelter from the elements. Not a single thought had been given to comfort. It had taken three weeks to build, said Gilbert, and had cost $4,000. It was his first boat.

Gilbert explained that he needed to return to Port-de-Paix to purchase supplies, but that it'd be best if we remained on the boat. The rest of his passengers, he said, were waiting in safe houses. "We'll be set to go in three or four hours," he said as he and his crew boarded a return ferry.

Time in Haiti is an extraordinarily flexible concept, so when eight hours passed and there was no sign of our crew, we were not concerned. Night came, and still no word. Soon, twenty-four hours had passed since Gilbert's departure. Then thirty. David became convinced that we had been set up. We'd handed over all our money and everyone had disappeared. Boat-smuggling cons were nothing new. The most common one, David said, involved sailing around Haiti and the Dominican Republic two or three times and then dropping everyone off on a deserted Haitian island and telling them they're in the Bahamas. A more insidious scam, he mentioned, involved taking passengers a mile out to sea and then tossing them overboard. It happens, he insisted. But this, said David, was a new one. He was furious, but for a funny reason. "They stole all that money," he said, "and I'm not even getting any."

David was wrong. After dark, Gilbert and his crew docked a ferry alongside the *Believe in God*. They had picked up about thirty other Haitians — mostly young, mostly male — from the safe houses, and the passengers huddled together as if in a herd, each clutching a small bag of personal belongings. Their faces registered a mix of worry and confusion and excitement — the mind-jumble of a life-altering moment. Things had been terribly delayed, Gilbert said, though he offered no further details. I saw our supplies for the trip: a hundred-pound bag of flour, two fifty-five-gallon water drums, four bunches of plantains, a sack of charcoal, and a rooster in a cardboard box. This did not seem nearly enough for what could be a weeklong trip, but at least it was something. I'd been told that many boats leave without any food at all.

The passengers transferred from the ferry to the *Believe in God,* and Gilbert sent everyone but his crew down to the hold. We pushed against one another, trying to establish small plots of territory. David's size in such a situation was suddenly a disadvantage — he had difficulty contorting himself to fit the parameters of the hold and had to squat with his knees tucked up against his chest, a little-boy position. For the first time since I'd met him he appeared weak, and more than a bit tense. Throughout our long wait, David had been a study in nonchalance. "I'm not nervous; I'm not excited; I'm just ready to leave," he'd said the previous day. Perhaps now, as the gravity of the situation dawned on him, he realized what he was about to undergo.

"Wasn't it like this last time you crossed?" I asked. David flashed me an unfamiliar look and touched my arm and said, "I need to tell you something," and finally, in the strange confessional that is the hold of a boat, he told me a little of his past. The first time he'd gone to America, he said, he'd flown on an airplane. He was nine years old. His mother had been granted an immigration visa, and she took David and his two brothers and a sister to Naples, Florida. Soon after, his mother died of AIDS. He had never known his father. He fell into bad company, and at age seventeen spent nine months in jail for stealing a car. At nineteen, he served a year and five days in jail for selling marijuana and then was deported. That was seven years ago. In Naples, he said, his friends had called him Six-Four, a moniker bestowed because of his penchant for stealing 1964 Chevy Impalas. He admitted to me that if he returned to Naples, where his sister lived, he was concerned he'd have to become Six-Four again in order to afford to live there. In America, he mentioned, there is shame in poverty — a shame you don't feel in Haiti. "People are always looking at the poor Haitians who just stepped off their banana boat," he said. This was something, he suggested, that Stephen might find a painful lesson.

The view from the hold, through the scuttle, was like watching a play from the orchestra pit. Gilbert handed each crew member an envelope stuffed with money, as if at a wedding. Nobody was satisfied, of course, and an argument ensued that lasted into the dawn. Down in the hold, where everyone was crushed together, frustration mounted. Occasionally curses were yelled up. When it was clear there was no more money to distribute, the crew demanded spots on the boat for family members. Gilbert acquiesced, and the crew left the ship to inform their relatives. Soon there were thirty-five people on board, then forty. Hours passed. There was no room in the hold to do anything but sit, and so that is what we did. People calmed down. Waiting consumes a significant portion of life in Haiti, and this was merely another delay. The sun rode its arc; heat escaping through the scuttle blurred the sky. A container of water was passed about, but only a few mouthfuls were available for each person. Forty-two people were aboard. Then forty-six. It was difficult to breathe, as though the air had turned to gauze. David and Stephen could not have been pressed closer to each other if they'd been wrestling. There had been murders on these journeys, and suicides and suffocations. Now I could see why. "We came to this country on slave boats," David said, "and we're going to leave on slave boats."

There was a sudden pounding of feet on the deck and a man — an old man, with veiny legs and missing teeth — dropped headfirst into the hold. Gilbert jumped after him, seized the old man by his hair, and flung him out. I heard the hollow sounds of blows being landed, and then a splash, and the attempted stowaway was gone.

Everything was quiet for a moment, a settling, and then there was again commotion on deck, but it was choreographed commotion, and the sails were raised, a mainsail and a bed-sheet-sized jib, two wedges of white against the cobalt sky. We'd already been in the hold ten hours, but still the boat did not leave. There was a clipped squawk from above, and the rooster was slaughtered. Then Gilbert came down to our quarters — he'd tied a fuchsia bandanna about his head — and crawled to the very front, where there was a tiny door with a padlock. He stuck his head inside the cubby and hung a few flags, sprayed perfumed water, and chanted. "Voodoo prayers," said David. When he emerged he crawled through the hold and methodically sprinkled the top of everyone's head with the perfume. Then he climbed onto the deck and barked a command, and the *Believe in God* set sail.

The poorest country and the richest country in the Western Hemisphere are separated by six hundred miles of open ocean. It's a treacherous expanse of water. The positioning of the Caribbean Islands relative to the Gulf Stream creates what is known as a Venturi effect — a funneling action that can result in a rapid buildup of wind and waves. Meteorologists often call the region "hurricane alley." For a boat without nautical charts, the area is a minefield of shallows and sandbars and reefs. It is not uncommon for inexperienced sailors to become sucked into the Gulf Stream and fail to reach their destination. "If you miss South Florida," said Commander Christopher Carter of the Coast Guard, who has sixteen years' experience patrolling the Caribbean, "your next stop is North Carolina. Then Nova Scotia. We've never found any migrants alive in Nova Scotia, but we've had ships wash ashore there."

Initially, the waves out past the tip of Île Tortue were modest, four or five feet at most, the whitecaps no more than a froth of curlicues. Still, the sensation in the hold was of tumbling unsteadiness. The hold was below the waterline, and the sloshing of the surf was both amplified and distorted — the sounds of digestion, it occurred to me, and I thought more than once of Jonah, trapped in the belly of a whale. When the boat was sideswiped by an especially aggressive wave, the stress against the hull invariably produced a noise like someone stepping on a plastic cup. Water came in through the cracks. Every time this happened, David and Stephen glanced at each other and arched their eyebrows, as if to ask, Is this the one that's going to put us under? When building a boat, David had said, it was common to steal nails from other ships, ham-

mer them straight and reuse them. I wondered how many nails had
been pulled from our boat. As the waves broke upon us, the hull
boards bellied and bowed, straining against the pressure. There
was a pump aboard, a primitive one, consisting of a rubber-
wrapped broom handle and a plastic pipe that ran down to the bottom of the hold. Someone on deck continuously had to work the
broom handle up and down, and still we were sitting in water. The
energy of the ocean against the precariousness of our boat seemed
a cruel mismatch.

Nearly everyone in the hold kept their bags with them at all
times; clearly, a few of the possessions were meant to foster good
luck. One man repeatedly furled and unfurled a little blue flag
upon which was drawn a *vévé* — a symbolic design intended to in-
voke a voodoo spirit. Stephen fingered a necklace, carved from a
bit of coconut, that a relative had brought him from the Bahamas.
Another man read from a scrap of a paperback book, Chapters 29
through 33 of a work called *Garden of Lies*. David often held his
Bible to his chest. I had my own charm. It was a device called
an Emergency Position-Indicating Radio Beacon, or EPIRB. When
triggered, an EPIRB transmits a distress signal to the Coast Guard
via satellite, indicating its exact position in the water. I was assured
by the company that manufactured the beacon that if I activated it
anywhere in the Caribbean, help would be no more than six hours
away. The EPIRB was a foot tall, vaguely cylindrical, and neon yellow. I kept it stashed in my backpack, which I clasped always in my
lap. Nobody except Chris, the photographer, knew it was there.

The heat in the hold seemed to transcend temperature. It had
become an object, a weight — something solid and heavy, settling
upon us like a dentist's X-ray vest. There was no way to shove it
aside. Air did not circulate, wind was shut out. Thirst was a constant
dilemma. At times, the desire to drink crowded out all other notions. Even as Gilbert was sending around a water container, my
first thought was when we'd have another. We had 110 gallons of
water on board, and forty-six people. In desert conditions, it's recommended that a person drink about one gallon per day. It was as
hot as any desert down there. Hotter. That meant we had a two-day
supply. But we were merely sitting, so perhaps half a gallon would
be enough. That's four days. The trip, though, could take eight
days. If it did we'd be in serious trouble.

Finding a comfortable position in the hold was hopeless. The hull was V-shaped, and large waves sent everyone sliding into the center, tossing us about like laundry. I exchanged hellos with the people around me — Wesley and Tijuan and Wedell and Andien — but there seemed nothing further to say. Every hour, an electronic watch chirped from somewhere in the dark. From here and there came the murmurs of sleep. The occasional, taut conversations between Stephen and David consisted primarily of reveries about reaching America. David said that he wanted to work in the fields, picking tomatoes or watermelon. His dream was to marry an American woman. Stephen's fantasy was to own a pickup truck, a red one.

The rules of the boat had been established by Gilbert. Eight people were allowed on deck at once; the rest had to remain in the hold. Six spots were reserved by Gilbert and the crew. The other two were filled on a rotating basis — a pair from the deck switched with a pair from the hold every twenty minutes or so. This meant each person would be allowed out about once every six hours. A crowded deck, Gilbert explained, would interfere with the crew and rouse the suspicions of passing boats. More important, people were needed in the hold to provide ballast — too much weight up top and the boat would tip.

Of the forty-six people on the boat, five were women. They were crammed together into the nether reaches of the hold, visible only as silhouettes. The farther back one crawled into the hold, the hotter it got. Where the women were it must have been crippling. Occasionally they braided one another's hair, but they appeared never to speak. They were the last to be offered time on deck, and their shifts seemed significantly shorter than those of the men.

The oldest person on the boat was a forty-year-old passenger named Desimeme; the youngest was thirteen-year-old Kenton. The average age was about twenty-five. Unlike the migrants of the early nineties, who tended more heavily to be families and rural peasants, most Haitian escapees are now young, urban males. The reason for this shift is probably an economic one. In recent years, according to people on Île Tortue, the price for a crossing has become vastly inflated, and women and farmers are two of Haiti's lowest-paid groups.

Two hours after leaving, the seasickness began. There was a commotion in the rear of the hold, and people started shouting, and a yellow bucket — at one time it was a margarine container — was tossed below. It was passed back. The man who was sick filled it up, and the bucket was sent forward, handed up, dumped overboard and passed back down. A dozen pairs of hands reached for it. The yellow bucket went back and forth. It also served as our bathroom, an unavoidable humiliation we each had to endure. Not everyone could wait for the bucket to arrive, and in transferring the container in pitching seas it was sometimes upended. The contents mingled with the water that sloshed ankle-deep about the bottom of the hold. The stench was overpowering.

One of the sickest people on board was Kenton, the thirteen-year-old boy. He lay jackknifed next to me in the hold, clutching his stomach, too ill to grab for the bucket. I slipped him a seasickness pill, but he was unable to keep it down. Kenton was a cousin of one of the crew members. He had been one of the last people to board the boat. In the scramble to fill the final spots, there was no room for both him and his parents, so he was sent on alone. His parents, I'd overheard, had promised that they'd be on the very next boat, and when Kenton boarded he was bubbly and smiling, as if this were going to be a grand adventure. Now he was obviously petrified, but also infused with an especially salient dose of Haitian mettle — as he grew weaker he kept about him an iron face. Never once did he cry out. He had clearly selected a favorite shirt for the voyage: a New York Knicks basketball jersey.

This did not seem like the appropriate time to eat, but dinner was ready. The boat's stove, on deck, was an old automobile tire rim filled with charcoal. There was also a large aluminum pot and a ladle. The meal consisted of dumplings and broth — actually, boiled flour balls and hot water. Most people had brought a bowl and spoon with them, and the servings were passed about in the same manner as the bucket. When the dumplings were finished, Hanson, one of the crew members, came down into the hold. He was grasping a plastic bag that was one of his personal possessions. Inside the bag was an Île Tortue specialty — ground peanuts and sugar. He produced a spoon from his pocket, dipped it into the bag, and fed a spoonful to the man nearest him, carefully cupping his chin as if administering medicine. Then he wormed his way through the hold, inserting a heaping spoon into everyone's mouth. His generosity was appreciated, but the meal did little to help settle people's stomachs. The yellow bucket was again in great demand.

Hours trickled by. There was nothing to do, no form of diversion. The boat swayed, the sun shone, the heat intensified. People were sick; people were quiet. Eyes gradually dimmed. Everyone seemed to have withdrawn into themselves, as in the first stages of shock. Heads bobbed and hung, fists clenched and opened. Thirst was like a tight collar about our throats. It was the noiselessness of the suffering that made it truly frightening — the silent panic of deep fear.

Shortly before sunset, when we'd been at sea nearly twelve hours, I was allowed to take my second stint on deck. By now there was nothing around us but water. The western sky was going red and our shadows were at full stretch. The sail snapped and strained against its rigging; the waves, at last, sounded like waves. Gilbert was standing at the prow, gazing at the horizon, a hand cupped above his eyes, and as I watched him a look of concern came across his face. He snapped around, distressed, and shouted one word: "Hamilton!" Everyone on deck froze. He shouted it again. Then he pointed to where he'd been staring, and there, in the distance, was a ship of military styling, marring the smooth seam between sea and sky. Immediately, I was herded back into the hold.

A Hamilton, Stephen whispered, is Haitian slang for a Coast Guard ship — it's also, not coincidentally, the name of an actual ship. The news flashed through the hold, and in reflexive response everyone crushed deeper into the rear, away from the opening, as though this would help avoid detection. Gilbert paced the deck, manic. He sent two of the crew members down with us, and then he, too, descended. He burrowed toward his cubby, shoving people aside, unlocked the door, and wedged himself in. And then he began to chant, in a steady tone both dirgelike and defiant. The song paid homage to Agwe, the voodoo spirit of the sea, and when Gilbert emerged, still chanting, several people in the hold took up the tune, and then he climbed up and the crew began chanting, too. It was an ethereal tune, sung wholly without joy, a signal of desperate unity that seemed to imply we'd sooner drift to Nova Scotia than abandon our mission. Some of these people, it seemed, really were willing to sacrifice their lives to try and get to America. Our captain was one of them.

Over the singing came another sound, an odd buzz. Then there were unfamiliar voices — non-Haitian voices, speaking French. In the hold, people snapped out of their stupor. Stephen grabbed his necklace. David chewed on the meat of his hand. I stood up and peeked out. The buzz was coming from a motorized raft that had pulled beside us. Six people were aboard, wearing orange life vests imprinted with the words U.S. COAST GUARD. Gilbert was sitting atop one of our water drums, arms folded, flashing our interlopers a withering look. Words were shouted back and forth — questions from the Coast Guard, blunt rejoinders from Gilbert.

"Where are you headed?"

"Miami."

"Do you have docking papers?"

"No."

"What are you transporting?"

"Rice."

"Can we have permission to board?"

"No."

There was nothing further. In the hold everyone was motionless. People tried not to breathe. Some had their palms pushed together in prayer. One man pressed his fingertips to his forehead. Soon I heard the buzz again, this time receding, and the Coast Guard was gone. Gilbert crouched beside the scuttle and spoke. This had happened on his last crossing, he said. The Coast Guard just comes and sniffs around. They were looking for drugs, but now they've gone. Then he mentioned one additional item. As a precaution, he said, nobody would be allowed onto the deck, indefinitely.

The reaction to this news was subtle but profound. There was a general exhalation, as if we'd each been kicked in the stomach, and then a brief burst of conversation — more talking than at any time since we'd set sail. The thought of those precious minutes on deck had been the chief incentive for enduring the long hours below. With Gilbert's announcement, something inside of me — some scaffolding of fortitude — broke. We'd been at sea maybe fourteen hours; we had a hundred to go, minimum. Ideas swirled about my head, expanding and consuming like wildfire. I thought of drowning, I thought of starving, I thought of withering from thirst.

Then, as if he'd read my mind, David took my right hand and

held it. He held it a long time, and I felt calmer. He looked at my
eyes; I looked at his. This much was clear: David wasn't willing to
heed his own words. He wasn't prepared to die. He was terrified,
too. This wasn't something we discussed until much later, though
he eventually admitted it.

When David let go of my hand, the swirling thoughts returned. I
wrestled with the idea of triggering the EPIRB. People were weak
— I was weak — and it occurred to me that I had the means to save
lives. But though pressing the button might lead to our rescue, it
would certainly dash everyone's dreams. There was also the concern that I'd be caught setting it off, the repercussions of which I
did not want to ponder. I made a decision.

"Chris," I said. I was whispering.

"Yes."

"I'm going to use the thing."

"Don't."

"Don't?"

"No, don't. Wait."

"How long?"

"Just wait."

"I don't think I can."

"Just wait a little."

"Okay. I'll wait a little."

I waited a little, a minute at a time. Four more hours passed. Then,
abruptly, the buzz returned. Two buzzes. This time there was no
conversation, only the clatter of Coast Guard boots landing on our
deck. At first, it seemed as though there might be violence. The
mood in the hold was one of reckless, nothing-to-lose defiance. I
could see it in the set of people's jaws, and in the vigor that suddenly leaped back into their eyes. This was our boat; strangers were
not invited — they were to be pummeled and tossed overboard,
like the old man who had tried to stow away. Then lights were
shined into the hold, strong ones. We were blinded. There was no
place for us to move. The idea of revolt died as quickly as it had ig-
nited. Eighteen hours after we'd set sail, the trip was over.

Six at a time, we were loaded into rubber boats and transported
to the Coast Guard cutter *Forward,* a ship 270 feet long and nine
stories high. It was 4:00 in the morning. Nobody struggled, no

weapons were drawn. We were frisked and placed in quarantine on the flight deck, in a helicopter hangar. Three Haitians were so weak from dehydration that they needed assistance walking. The Coast Guard officers were surprised to see journalists on board, but we were processed with the Haitians. We were each supplied with a blanket, a pair of flip-flops, and a toothbrush. We were given as much water as we could drink. We were examined by a doctor. The *Forward*'s crew members wore two layers of latex gloves whenever they were around us.

The *Forward*'s commanding officer, a nineteen-year Coast Guard veteran named Dan MacLeod, came onto the flight deck. He pulled me aside. The Coast Guard, he said, had not lost sight of our boat since we'd first been spotted. He'd spent the previous four hours contacting Haitian authorities, working to secure an S.N.O. — a Statement of No Objection — that would permit the Coast Guard to stop a Haitian boat in international waters. When David and Stephen learned of this, they were furious. There is the feeling among many Haitians of abandonment by the United States — or worse, of manipulation. American troops helped restore Aristide to power, then they vanished. Now, because there is democracy in Haiti, the United States has a simple excuse for rejecting Haitian citizenship claims: Haitians are economic, not political migrants. For those Haitians who do enter America illegally — the United States Border Patrol estimates that between 6,000 and 12,000 do so each year — it is far better to try to seep into the fabric of the Haitian-American community than to apply for asylum. In 1999, 92 percent of Haitian asylum claims were rejected.

As soon as the Haitian government granted permission, the Coast Guard had boarded our boat. Though illegal migrants were suspected to be on board — two large water barrels seemed a bit much for just a crew — the official reason the boat had been inter- cepted, Officer MacLeod told me, was because we were heading straight for a reef. "You were off course from Haiti about two de- grees," he said. "That's not bad for seat-of-the-pants sailing, but you were heading directly for the Great Inagua reef. You hadn't altered your course in three hours, and it was dark out. When we boarded your vessel you were 2,200 yards from the reef. You'd have hit it in less than forty minutes."

Our boat running against a reef could have been lethal. The hull, probably, would have split. The current over the reef, Officer

MacLeod informed me, is unswimmably strong. The reef is as sharp as a cheese grater. The Epirb would not have helped.

Even if we'd managed to avoid the reef — if, by some good fortune, we'd changed course at the last minute — we were still in danger. Officer MacLeod asked me if I'd felt the boat become steadier as the night progressed. I said I had. "That's the first sure sign you're sinking," he said. There was more. "You were in three-to-four-foot seas. At six-foot seas, you'd have been in a serious situation, and six-foot seas are not uncommon here. Six-foot seas would've taken that boat down." When I mentioned that we'd expected the trip to take four or five days, Officer MacLeod laughed. "They were selling you a story," he said. In the eighteen hours since leaving Haiti, we had covered thirty miles. We'd had excellent conditions. The distance from Haiti to Nassau was 450 miles. Even with miraculous wind, it could have taken us ten days. The doctor on board said we'd most likely have been dealing with fatalities within forty-eight hours.

The next day, it turned out, was almost windless. It was hotter than ever. And the seas were choppy — seven feet at times, one officer reported. Another high-ranking officer added one more bit of information: a Coast Guard ship hadn't been in these waters at any time in the past two weeks. The *Forward* happened to be heading in for refueling when we were spotted.

Our trip, it appeared, had all the makings of a suicide mission. If there had been no Epirb and no Coast Guard, it's very likely that the *Believe in God* would have vanished without a trace. And our craft, said Officer MacLeod, was one of the sturdier sailboats he has seen — probably in the top 20 percent. Most boats that make it, he mentioned, have a small motor. I wondered how many Haitians have perished attempting such a crossing. "That's got to be a very scary statistic," said Ron Labrec, a Coast Guard public affairs officer, though he wouldn't hazard a guess. He said it's impossible to accurately determine how many migrants are leaving Haiti and what percentage of them make it to shore.

But given the extraordinary number of people fleeing on marginal sailboats, it seems very likely that there are several hundred unrecorded deaths each year. Illegal migration has been going on for decades. It is not difficult to imagine that there are thousands of Haitian bodies on the bottom of the Caribbean.

We spent two days on the *Forward,* circling slowly in the sea, while it was determined where we would be dropped off. On May 16, everyone was deposited on Great Inagua Island and turned over to Bahamian authorities. Chris and I were released and the Haitians were placed in a detention center. The next day they were flown to Nassau and held in another detention center, where they were interviewed by representatives of the United Nations High Commission for Refugees. None were found to qualify for refugee status.

As for the *Believe in God*, the boat came to a swift end. The night we were captured, we stood along the rail of the flight deck as the *Forward*'s spotlight was trained on our boat. It looked tiny in the ink-dark sea. The sail was still up, though the boat was listing heavily. Officer MacLeod had just started telling me about its unseaworthiness. "Watch," he said. With nobody pumping water from it, the hold had been filling up fast. As I looked, the mast leaned farther and farther down, as if bowing to the sea, until it touched the water. Then the boat slowly began to sink.

After two weeks in the Nassau detention center, all forty-four Haitians were flown to Port-au-Prince. They received no punishment from Haitian authorities. The next morning, Gilbert returned to Île Tortue, already formulating plans for purchasing a second boat and trying to cross once more. Stephen also went home to Île Tortue, but was undecided as to whether he'd try the journey again. David went back to Port-au-Prince, back to his small mahogany stand, back to his crumbling shack, where his personal space consisted of a single nail from which he hung the same black plastic bag he'd had on the boat. He said he felt lucky to be alive. He said he would not try again by boat, not ever. Instead, he explained, he was planning on sneaking overland into the Dominican Republic. There were plenty of tourists there and he'd be able to sell more mahogany. He told me he was already studying a new language, learning from a Spanish translation of *The Cat in the Hat* that he'd found in the street.

IAN FRAZIER

Desert Hideaway

FROM *The Atlantic Monthly*

LOS ANGELES is a desert (or almost), but sometimes you want
even more desert. What you do then is get in the car and take the
10 to the 405 to the 5 to the 14, or the 55 to the 91 to the 15, or
some other combination of highways heading roughly northeast
from the city, and after an hour and a half or two hours the expanses of pavement have narrowed, the sky is a bright blue tinged
with smog, and empty, unmistakable desert is all around. Brown
hills dotted with small bushes as regularly spaced as beard stubble
rise on the horizon; low brush beside the road holds shreds of fluttering trash. A canyon is filled with boulders heaped up like paper-
work you'll never get to. Then comes a broad flat plain of nothing
but gray sand and rocks, with a single anomalous object — an orange traffic cone, the hood from a barbecue grill — resting in the
middle distance, as if to aid perspective.

If you stay on the 15 toward Las Vegas and night falls, the four
lanes of headlights and taillights become a string dwindling far
across the darkness. Suddenly, at the Nevada border, the lit-up casino town of Primm appears, as gaudy as a funhouse entrance. I
don't go that way, though; for some reason, Las Vegas does not interest me. Instead I take the 14 north through the high-desert town
of Mojave. Just past there a field of wind turbines hums in the wind,
the long, propellerlike blades on towers eighty feet high throwing
giant shadows as they turn, some clockwise, some counterclock-
wise. Across the highway from them, to the west, an airfield full of
used passenger jets bleaches in the sun. The map shows the Los Angeles Aqueduct as a blue line running nearby. In fact the aqueduct

here is an imposing white pipe eight feet across that wanders the
contours of the dirt-bike-furrowed hills like a garden hose. From
14 I cut across on a two-lane road to the old mining town of
Randsburg, and from there continue to Trona, a lakeside town
whose lake dried up 20,000 years ago, leaving a bone white salt flat
that is said to contain half the natural elements known to man.
IMC Chemicals, a sprawling enterprise, now mines the flat; Trona
smells like sulfur and is windy, gritty, and hot. Past Trona, over
some hills and across another vast and shimmering desert flat, is
the western boundary of Death Valley National Park.

Death Valley is the largest national park in the lower forty-eight
states, and it includes more than three million acres of wilderness.
At its center is the long, low desert valley from which the park takes
its name. Toward the east side of the valley is a fancy inn, the Furnace Creek Inn, and an eighteen-hole golf course. The first time I
went to Death Valley was to play golf. I had wondered what a golf
course in the desert, 214 feet below sea level, would be like. When I
got to the pro shop, a high wind was whipping the tamarisk trees
that enclose the course, and dark storm clouds were pouring over
the barren Panamint Range to the west like spilled paint. The guy
in the pro shop said the storm was supposed to hit in an hour, but if
I wanted to play, it was my money. The bad weather had emptied
the course, a situation I like; I am such an indifferent golfer that I
prefer there be no witnesses. Also, I am afraid of injuring somebody. I teed off, occasionally running down to a green to reset a
flag knocked over by the wind. By the time I reached the fifth hole,
the storm had turned to the north, the wind had dropped, and the
sun emerging on the horizon lit the course like a klieg light.
Mourning doves were eating the recently sown grass seed on the
tees, and a pair of coyotes had emerged to stalk the ducks and Canada geese gabbling in the hazards. A coyote with eyes only for the
waterfowl was sitting on his haunches on the fringe of the seventh
green.

    The village of Furnace Creek sits in a natural oasis and makes a
green rectangle on the desert floor. Along with the inn and the golf
course there are campgrounds, a motel, and the headquarters of
the Park Service. Tour buses and little rental cars come and go, and
tourists — many of them Germans, who seem to have a thing for

deserts — line up at the cash registers in the gift shop. Just a step on the other side of the tamarisk-tree border extreme desert begins. One afternoon I ducked through the trees at a corner of the golf course and walked across desert like gray pie crust to the village of the Timbisha Shoshone Indians, a half mile or so away. I had heard that the Timbisha had been highhandedly evicted from the oasis years ago. Among the irregularly spaced mobile homes of the Timbisha village I found the one belonging to the tribal chairman, Pauline Esteves, a dour, heavyset woman in her seventies. After many questions about who I was and what I wanted to know, she reluctantly agreed to talk to me. Sitting with her head in her hands at her dining-room table, she said that people who write about her almost always get everything wrong. To my questions about Timbisha history she responded first by staring back at me, irritatedly and long.

She said that the Timbisha people had lived here for thousands of years; that they had been the first to use the natural springs at Furnace Creek to cultivate the land; that a mining company had dispossessed them and bulldozed their houses in the 1920s; that the golf course was near where her house used to be; that despite such incursions the Timbisha had never left and didn't intend to leave. She added that they found the name Death Valley insulting. I asked about a local landmark, and what the Timbisha name for it had been. She buried her face in her hands for a while in silence. Then she looked at me and said, "Impossible to translate." She said that the tribe had been working for decades to get their land back but that she doubted they ever would. (A few weeks after I talked to her, I saw in the paper that the federal government had agreed to return 300 acres of land at Furnace Creek oasis to the Timbisha, along with about 7,200 acres outside the park. Congress has yet to approve the plan: I have a feeling that Pauline Esteves will believe it when she sees it.)

In the evenings I sat in my motel room and listened to the whirring of the lawn sprinklers on the golf course and read a book called *Desert Shadows: A True Story of the Charles Manson Family in Death Valley*, by Bob Murphy, which I had bought in a little museum in a nearby town. The woman minding the museum had said it was an interesting book, and it is. When I got to the end of it, I went back to the beginning and read parts over again. Somehow I was in a mood to think about Charles Manson. Manson was arrested — in Death Valley, as it happened — thirty years ago last October. He and his followers roamed all over this desert back then, on foot and in chopped Volkswagen dune buggies, and they used it for a hideout. At the time of his arrest Manson was wanted only for auto theft and for torching an earthmover belonging to the Park Service; his involvement in the famous murders in L.A. came out afterward.

Desert Shadows says that Manson was captured at a cabin on the Barker ranch, his remote hideaway in an isolated part of Death Valley, up a canyon called Goler Wash. The book describes how difficult it is to drive or even hike up the canyon, and refers to it as "treacherous" Goler Wash. I considered: Would I like to see a place like that — the desert hideout of a deranged killer? I decided that, all in all, I would not. Then I thought about it some more and decided that I actually would.

I spent a day driving and asking around to locate Goler Wash, which is in the Panamint Range in the park's southwestern corner. Early one morning I drove to the ghost town of Ballarat, and then continued south about sixteen miles on a road of gravel and sand to the foot of Goler Wash. I left my car, took a daypack with sandwiches and sunblock and water, and started up the canyon.

You might miss the entrance if you didn't know it was there: From a distance the canyon looks like just another seam in the mountain front. But within fifty yards high walls rise up to enclose a passage about the width of two cars, and the way winds between the walls like a narrow street in lower Manhattan. Grayish dawn light showed the canyon as I ascended; though the time was past sunrise, the sun would not get there for a while. This was the sort of place that needs the accompaniment of foreboding minor chords on a bass viol. But when I stopped and listened, I heard not a sound. As I went on, the stones clicking under my feet at a steep part seemed indiscreetly loud.

After about a mile the canyon opened out, and I could see farther. The sun lit the top of one ridge, and then slid to the next. I passed greenery — mesquite trees, scrubby willows — and thumb-shaped cacti poking from the canyon walls. In the crook of a switchback was a spring, upwelling and dark-tinted among creepers and weeds. After another few miles the day became hot. The sun, now

overhead, filled the widened canyon with a fierce brightness un-
marred by any shade. The silence remained vast. A raven glided
over a ridge, and I thought of the Manson family members, some of
them young women with babies, hiking up this track barefoot back
in 1969. Then I began to think about 1969 in general, and what an
unhinged year it was, and how the insane expression in Charles
Manson's eyes in that photograph of him on the cover of *Life* magazine seemed an apt image for that time. I had begun to give myself the creeps when I was distracted by the sound of an engine,
and then by the sight of a bright red ATV coming up the road. It
stopped beside me, and its window rolled down. In it were Scott
and Marv, businessmen from suburban Chicago, who were tooling
around the desert in Marv's high-tech, diesel-powered, tanklike,
very expensive Hummer while their wives played blackjack in Vegas. They were looking for Manson's hideout too. They had read
about it in a guidebook. They offered me a ride, and I hopped in.

Marv was dark and stocky, Scott blond and thinner. Scott was
driving. Each was smoking a big cigar. Scott said he especially
wanted to find Manson's bus, which their guidebook also mentioned. In 1968 Manson drove the family's green and white school
bus up to the Barker ranch, in what was perhaps the only noncrimi-
nal real achievement of his life. According to the guidebook, the
bus was still there. As Scott negotiated the road's dicey parts, occasionally adjusting a control on the dash in order to add extra air to
the Hummer's tires and raise the vehicle's underside an inch or
two over the high spots, he kept saying, "I can't *believe* he got a
school bus up here!" At a vista point with desert waste stretching
beyond, Scott said, "Marv, when I look at scenery like this, I feel
small." Marv puffed his cigar and said, "Drive, Scott. Just drive."

Marv told me about his glass-and-mirror company and how it
had installed the mirrors in the Chicago-area mansion of the basketball star Michael Jordan. As the throbbing Hummer motored
upward, Scott kept saying, "The Hummer loves this, Marv. He loves
this place."

The Barker ranch is on a tributary canyon that joins Goler Wash
from the south. We took a couple of wrong canyons before we
found it. Then we passed another spring, hung a right, squeezed
through a narrow defile and under a low-hanging cottonwood, and
there was the Barker cabin. The cabin where Charles Manson and

his followers were captured is a trim one-story structure of local stone set against a low hillside and surrounded by willows, cottonwoods, and a pomegranate tree that was blooming crimson. An ingenious network of plastic pipes connected to a spring irrigates the grounds. It's the sort of place one comes across unexpectedly now and again in America — a homemade utopia, or (in this case) dystopia.

No one lives there. The cabin now belongs to the Park Service, which maintains it as a backcountry stopover for hikers and other off-road travelers. A notice on the door lists the rules for visitors, and another warns that the house and its contents are protected under the Archaeological Resources Protection Act of 1979 and the American Antiquities Act of 1906. Scott and Marv and I poked around — no sign of the historic school bus, disappointingly — and then we shook hands and they continued on their way, following a route that would take them over the mountains and into the valley from the western side. Three minutes after they left, the silence had returned. The sun now stood directly above; I had never before been anyplace so still at midday.

Gingerly, I went through the cabin a second time. Its dimensions — of windows and ceiling and doorways — seemed slightly miniaturized. The man who built it (I later learned), in the forties, was a former L.A. police detective with a small wife, and she liked the reduced scale of Pullman sleeping cars. Perhaps this smaller scale also appealed to the five-foot-two-inch Manson. The highway patrolman who arrested Manson found him hiding in a little cupboard in the bathroom, under the sink. The cupboard is now gone, and most of the fixtures are too. Past visitors to the cabin have left behind playing cards, books, a bird's nest with feathers stuck in it on the mantelpiece, *Far Side* cartoons, animal vertebrae, candles, .45- and .22-caliber shell casings, a bottle of dishwashing soap, a pitching wedge, nonperishable foods, and an oil painting of the view from the front porch. In an outbuilding I found only a set of bedsprings and, on the wall, a map of the Orion Nebula.

The Park Service or someone has provided the cabin with a guest book. It was nearly full, with entries dating from several years to just a few days before. Being in the cabin made me jumpy, so I took the book outside and read it sitting on the edge of the porch, in the shade. Entries from polite Europeans with good handwriting complimenting us Americans on our magnificent scenery alternated with all-capital-letter scrawls from apparent fans of Manson: "HELTER SKELTER DUDE! WELL HERE'S TO ANOTHER YEAR OF KILLIN!" There were ballpoint sketches of Manson, and mystifying symbols, and obscure references to the date of his arrest; a ranger at Park Service headquarters had told me that members of the Manson family come back to the cabin sometimes. As I was reading a comment signed by someone named Feral Jenny, suddenly I heard what sounded like a scream from the hillside above. I don't know what it could have been — a coyote or a wild burro, maybe. Unobtrusively I stood up to see where the sound had come from. I looked all around, but I saw nothing besides a dilapidated fence at the edge of the property, some weeds along it, some tire tracks in the dirt dwindling away, the bare and hot hillsides, and over all a bright blue western sky of endless, careless possibility.

PETER HESSLER

View from the Bridge

FROM *The New Yorker*

ON MY THIRD DAY in Dandong, I woke up at 2:00 in the morning with a thief in my hotel room. It was a midrange Chinese hotel, $10 a night, and Dandong was a midrange Chinese city, the sort of place you wouldn't pay much attention to if it weren't across the Yalu River from North Korea. But having North Korea five hundred meters away changed everything. Dandong promoted itself as "China's Biggest Border City," and the riverfront was lined with telescopes that could be rented by tourists, most of whom were Chinese hoping to catch their first glimpse of a foreign nation. The telescopes had signs that advertised: LEAVE THE COUNTRY FOR JUST ONE YUAN! For nine more, you could catch a ride on a speedboat and get a closer look at the North Koreans, who, during the heat of the day, swam in the shallows off their riverbank. On days deemed auspicious for getting married, it was a Dandong tradition for Chinese newlyweds to rent a boat, put life preservers over their wedding clothes, and buzz the North Korean shore.

There was a lot to think about in Dandong, and that was probably why I had forgotten to close my window that night. Because my room was on the second floor, I'd thought I was safe from intruders, but I hadn't noticed the foot-wide ledge that ran just below the window. Nor had I bothered to put my money belt and passport under my pillow; instead, I'd left them on a dresser, along with my camera, my wallet, my reporter's notebook, and a pair of shorts. The thief was scooping everything up when I awoke. For an instant, neither of us moved.

I sat up in bed and shouted, and he turned and ran for the door. I chased him down the hallway, wearing nothing but a pair of boxers. We rounded a corner, skidding on the tile floor. I caught him at the end of the hallway, by a stairwell.

I hit him as hard as I could. His hands were full of my belongings, and every time I punched him he dropped something. I slugged him and my camera popped out; I hit him again and there was my money belt; another punch and my shorts flew up in the air. After he had dropped everything, he ran down the hall, trying to find a door that would open, while I continued to shout and throw punches. At last, he found an unlocked door that led to an empty room and an open window. He jumped. I ran to the window and leaned out. The thief had been lucky — there was an overhang just below the sill. I heard his footsteps as he rounded the corner of the building. He was still running hard.

During the struggle, I had wrenched the middle finger of my left hand, so the hotel's night manager accompanied me to the Dandong hospital. It took us awhile to wake up the doctor who was on duty. He yawned, popped the finger back in place, and took an X-ray of it. The finger looked crooked, so the doctor yanked it out of its socket again, and then put it back in place. This time, the X-ray machine failed to work, and the doctor said that I'd have to return later in the morning, when a technician would be on duty. I went to the police station, where I reported the crime, answered some questions, and filled out some forms. Finally, at 5:00 A.M., I went back to bed. I didn't sleep well.

A couple of hours later, the hotel owner showed up to escort me back to the hospital. He was a handsome man, who gelled his hair so that it swept, blue-black, across his forehead. He wore a new white button-down shirt and well-pressed slacks. He apologized profusely about the robbery, and introduced himself.

"My name is Li Peng," he said.

"The same name as the former premier?" I asked.

"Yes," he said. He smiled in a tired way, and I could see that I wasn't the first person to have made this observation. Li Peng strongly advocated the use of force against Beijing students and workers in the protests of 1989, and he is the least popular leader in China. After the Tiananmen Square massacre, a Hong Kong newspaper reported that angry citizens were harassing twenty Beijing residents who happened to be named Li Peng. At least one of them had applied formally for a change of name.

"Do you like Li Peng?" I asked the hotel owner.

"No," he said, using English for emphasis. It was clear that he wanted to talk about something else. He asked me about the robbery.

I had already told the police everything I could recall about the thief: he had black hair, and he was somewhere between the ages of twenty and forty. He was smaller than me. I told the police that I wouldn't recognize him if I saw him again.

This vagueness had bothered them: How could you break your finger on another human being and remember nothing about him? It bothered me as well. I could remember details of the chase with incredible vividness — mostly, I remembered the overwhelming anger I'd felt, a rage that now scared me. The man himself was a blur in my mind. I could see that it also perplexed Li Peng, who wrinkled his brow.

"Was it a child?" he asked.

"No," I said. "It wasn't a child."

"But how did you catch him so easily?"

"I don't know."

"Do you have thieves in your America?"

I told Li Peng that there were thieves in America, but that they carried guns and you didn't run after them.

"Most thieves here in China have knives," he said. "What kind of thief doesn't carry a knife? That's why I think he was a child."

"He wasn't a child. I know that for certain."

"But why didn't he fight back? Why did you catch him so easily?" He sounded almost disappointed.

"I don't know," I said.

The police had followed the same line of questioning, and it was beginning to annoy me. The implication was clear: Only a thief of unusual ineptitude would be caught and beaten by a foreigner at 2:00 in the morning, and so there must have been something seriously wrong with him. The police offered various excuses. He must have been a drunk. Or a cripple. Or an idiot who was desperately poor. Dandong, the police emphasized, was a modern, orderly city, with a growing tourist industry. It wasn't the sort of place where a foreigner woke up in the middle of the night with a common thief in his room.

Nobody suggested what I suspected — that the man was a North

Korean refugee. The police had assured me that there were few refugees along this part of the border, because Sinuiju, the North Korean city across the river, was relatively well-off. People in Sinuiju ate twice a day, according to Dandong residents who had relatives there. But I knew that farther east, where a famine had been particularly severe, an estimated 70,000 North Koreans were fleeing to China every year. It seemed likely that at least a handful of them had made their way to Dandong. This possibility distressed me. If the locals wanted the thief to have been disabled, I wanted him to be perfectly normal and fit. It disturbed me to think that I'd viciously punched a man who was starving.

Both Li Peng and I were silent for a while, and then he thought of another possibility.

"Probably he was a heroin addict. That would explain why he was so weak."

"Are there a lot of heroin addicts around here?" I asked.

"Oh, no," Li Peng said quickly. "I don't think there are any in Dandong."

Apart from the North Korean swimmers, the main tourist attraction in town was the Yalu River Broken Bridge, which had once connected Dandong and Sinuiju. In November 1950, during the first year of the Korean War, American bombers destroyed most of the bridge when General MacArthur's troops made their push toward China's border. In Chinese, the war is known as "the war of resistance against America and in support of Korea." It is estimated that a million Chinese died in the fighting.

Today, the Chinese half of the Yalu River bridge is still standing. Tourists can walk to the end of it, look at the bombed-out wreckage, and pay one yuan to stare through a telescope at the North Koreans. One morning after the aborted theft, I paid a yuan and looked through the telescope. As usual, the North Koreans were swimming. The worker at the telescope asked me what country I was from. I told him.

"If America and China had a war today, who do you think would win?" he asked.

"I don't think America and China will have a war today."

"But if they did," he said, "who do you think would win?"

"I really don't know," I said. It seemed like a good time to ask him how business was going. He said it was fine, and he added that he had a photography stand where tourists could dress up and have their picture taken with the wreckage of the bridge in the background. They could wear either traditional Korean costume or a full Chinese military uniform, with a helmet and a plastic rifle.

Another vendor on the bridge ran a café where tourists could buy *Titanic* ice cream bars, with pictures of Leonardo DiCaprio and Kate Winslet on the wrappers. The café manager explained that although the bridge was state-owned, private entrepreneurs were allowed to rent space for their telescopes and soft drink stands. It was an example of "socialism with Chinese characteristics." The ice cream man paid five hundred yuan a month for his café. On summer nights, he slept on the bridge, where the river breeze was cool.

The bridge was at one end of the Dandong Border Cooperative Economic Zone, which the locals referred to as the Open District. They were very proud of the Open District, because it showed how far Dandong had come during the past ten years, after China's capitalist-style reforms finally started to take hold in this part of the country. People told me that a decade ago the Open District had been nothing but peasant shacks and makeshift docks. Now there were restaurants, coffee shops, ice cream parlors, and karaoke halls. At the western end of the Open District, a luxury apartment complex, with Western-style villas, was under construction. It was called the European Flower Garden. The eastern end of the Open District featured the bombed-out bridge and the Gateway to the Country Hunting Park. Between the bridge and the luxury apartments there was a twenty-four-hour venereal-disease clinic and the Finland Bathing and Pleasure Center, a massage parlor whose marquee featured a photograph of a topless foreign woman taking a shower.

The Gateway to the Country Hunting Park was one of the recreational options available to Dandong's tourists, a place where they could hunt "wild" quail, pigeons, pheasants, and rabbits. The birds were tethered to the ground, and, for one yuan, tourists could shoot at them with either a .22-caliber rifle or a bow and arrow. For three yuan, they could take a potshot at a rabbit that was also tied to the ground. They were allowed to eat anything they killed. I never saw anybody shoot at the rabbit. It was too expensive.

One day, I watched two tourists from Guangdong hunt the quail. The young couple were in their early twenties, nicely dressed, and the man was very drunk. He missed so badly that the quail didn't even strain at their tethers. They just sat there in the sunshine. They were the most bored-looking quail I've ever seen.

"I'm too drunk," the man from Guangdong said to his girlfriend. "I want you to shoot instead."

"I don't want to shoot the gun," she said. "It's too loud."

"Here," he said. "You shoot it. I'm too drunk. I can't shoot straight."

"I don't want to."

"Go ahead. It's easy."

The man showed her how she could rest the gun on the fence so that it would be simpler to aim. Usually, customers weren't allowed to do that, but the park keepers were willing to make an exception because the couple had traveled all the way from Guangdong. I was sitting nearby, listening to the conversation and trying to remember which Hemingway story it recalled. In the best stories there were always guns, animals, women, and drunk people bickering. The only difference was that in Hemingway stories the animals were never tied to the ground.

Finally, the man persuaded his girlfriend to pick up the .22 and the keeper helped her prop the gun up on the fence. She shot three bullets, and every time she squealed and covered her ears. She missed badly. The quail appeared to have fallen asleep. It was late afternoon. Later, after it got dark, the Open District was a riot of lights, neon and fluorescence blazing from the restaurants and karaoke bars and the Finland Bathing and Pleasure Center. Meanwhile, across the Yalu, there was complete darkness on the North Korean shore. There was no electricity over there. The North Koreans didn't go swimming at night.

I got to know a couple of the local boat pilots, and several times a day they'd drive me along the banks of North Korea. We'd cruise by run-down tourist boats that were empty except for the portraits of Kim Il Sung and Kim Jong Il on the walls, and we'd pass factories that looked abandoned. On the sandy stretches, hundreds of North Koreans were swimming. The children smiled and waved when we went by. Farther upstream, where the river narrowed, it wasn't unusual for adventurous young Chinese to swim across the Yalu, touch the far side, and swim back again. There weren't any North Koreans swimming to China. On the Sinuiju bank, armed soldiers stood stiffly at their posts, watching over the swimmers. They were like lifeguards with guns.

One day, we cruised past a barge where soldiers were unloading bags of grain marked "USA," which had been donated through the United Nations World Food Program. I asked the pilot to draw closer. When we got to within thirty feet of the barge, one of the soldiers glared at me and made an obscene Korean gesture: a fist with his thumb poking out between the fingers. We sped off.

"All that food will go to the soldiers and the cadres," the pilot said. "None of the common people will get it."

He spoke matter-of-factly — the way those in Dandong did when I asked about their neighbors. They were quick to say that the North Koreans were poor and that they had bad leadership, but then they'd shrug and say, *"Meiyou yisi"* — "It's not interesting." They weren't concerned by the North Koreans' poverty or by their isolation; everybody who had lived in China through the sixties and seventies had seen enough of that.

Ordinary Chinese tourists buzzed the Korean shore simply because it was the closest they'd ever get to a foreign country; wealthy tourists, however, could enter North Korea on organized tours. Passports weren't required; the regulations were lax because the Chinese government was pretty sure that no one would want to stay on the other side of the river.

Every morning, tour groups of upper-class Chinese met in front of my hotel before leaving for North Korea, and one day I watched a guide give a briefing. The guide explained that the tourists should be careful to show respect when they visited memorials to the North Korean leaders, and he said that they should avoid taking photographs of people laboring, because the North Koreans might accuse them of focusing on poverty. The North Koreans are proud people, and the Chinese need to be conscious of this, he said. Also, when visiting the thirty-eighth parallel, it was important that the Chinese not shout "Hello!" at any American soldiers on the other side.

"You'll notice that it's not as developed as China," the guide said. "You shouldn't tell the North Koreans that they need to reform and open up, or that they should study the example of our China. And remember that many of their tour guides speak very good Chinese, so be careful what you say."

One day, I met a Chinese veteran of the Korean War. He had

been in the navy and hadn't seen much action during the war, but in 1964 he'd been wounded in a battle off the coast of Taiwan. He was sixty-four years old and had been a member of the Communist Party for four decades. He walked with a limp. The enemy who wounded him had been Taiwanese, but his weapon was American-made. The veteran pointed this out very carefully. As far as he was concerned, everything had gone downhill after Mao died. "Nowadays too many things aren't certain," he said. "Some of the retired people don't get their pensions. And some people are too rich while others are too poor." He disagreed with the views of the younger generation, including those of his twenty-six-year-old son, who had turned down a perfectly good government job to join a private firm. The firm paid more, but there wasn't as much stability. Was this, he asked, how Americans lived? And had his son learned to think this way from the foreign teachers at his college?

I asked the veteran about the situation across the border, and he said that North Korea had a leadership problem. "When Kim Il Sung was alive, he was like Chairman Mao — everybody worshiped him. But Kim Il Sung's son isn't as great as his father. He's too young and he hasn't been hardened by war. If you look at Kim Il Sung's life, he experienced war as a small boy. That's why he became a great man."

My hotel room picked up North Korean television, which was one reason that I continued to stay there even after the attempted robbery. The other reason was that Li Peng gave me free food and drinks at the beer garden out in front. I had become a local celebrity — the Foreigner Who Broke His Finger Fighting the Thief.

When it rained, I sat in my hotel room eating cookies and watching North Korean television. North Korean television had everything that fascinated me about Chinese television, but more of it. There were more military variety shows, more patriotic bands, more heroic leaders. The songs were more cloying. The smiles were bigger. The uniforms were more uniform. There were more programs of singing and dancing children wearing heavy makeup.

I got to the point where I could watch North Korean television for nearly an uninterrupted hour. There was the news, which consisted of showing the front page of a newspaper while a commentator read it. There was the great leader, Kim Jong Il, wearing dark glasses and pointing at maps. An army choir, some violinists, and

some singers — all dripping with medals. Kim Jong Il visiting a factory. Children in makeup bouncing across a stage. Kim Jong Il in
the T'aebaek Mountains. Pyongyang at night. Miners working happily. Children singing. Kim Jong Il.

At night, I dreamed of being robbed. I'd wake up, my heart rac-
ing, and I'd lie there trying to recall what the thief had looked like.
But mostly I remembered what he had felt like. I remembered his
body recoiling from one of the blows, and I remembered hitting
him again. I found myself thinking about my anger and his fear —
the two emotions shifted uneasily in my mind. What had made me
keep punching him, even after he'd dropped my valuables? And
why had he not fought back?

On my last afternoon in Dandong, the river was full of Chinese
wedding boats. At any given moment, there were half a dozen on
the water, the couples posing in the prows as they glided past the
North Korean shore. The wealthy couples hired big two-tier cruis-
ers; the others rented little motor launches. All of them followed
the same route — a scoot out to the ruined bridge; a pause for
photographs; a slow cruise along the banks of North Korea. The
Chinese brides wore bright dresses of all colors — white and pink
and orange and purple — and they stood in the prows of the boats
like flowering figureheads. It was a hot afternoon and the North
Koreans were swimming again.

I went out with a pilot named Ni Shichao, and we zipped in and
out of the flotilla of wedding boats. Ni Shichao explained that it
was a very auspicious day on the lunar calendar — the sixth day of
the sixth month — which was why there were so many weddings.
But on the whole, he said, there were fewer weddings than usual
this year.

"People think that years ending in nine are bad luck," he explained. "I don't believe it myself, but many people do. In eighty-
nine there was the disturbance" — a euphemism for what happened around Tiananmen Square — "and in seventy-nine there
was the trial of the Gang of Four. Sixty-nine was the Cultural Revolution. Fifty-nine was when your America bombed the bridge."

He paused and thought for a moment. "No, that was in nineteen-
fifty," he said, shaking his head. "Anyway, something bad happened
in fifty-nine."

That had been the climax of the Great Leap Forward, when Mao's mad push for greater industrial production resulted in a famine that killed an estimated 30 million people. But Chinese history books brushed over this disaster. As with many Chinese, Ni Shichao had a shaky grasp of recent history; he had also made a mistake about the Gang of Four trial, which took place in 1980 and 1981.

"What about nineteen-forty-nine?" I asked.

"That was when the new China was founded," he said. He paused again. We were in the shadow of the ruined bridge; the slow-moving Yalu flowed blue beneath us. "That year wasn't the same as the others," he went on. "That was a good year, of course."

A week after leaving Dandong, I went east to Tumen, a Chinese city on North Korea's northern border. Tumen was poor; it had none of Dandong's energy and development, but it still drew hordes of refugees from North Korea. The Tumen River was narrow here, and this stretch of the North Korean countryside was reported to have suffered some of the worst effects of the famine that had been devastating the country since 1995. Almost nobody went swimming in the murky Tumen River. The border was heavily guarded on both sides. The Chinese promenade had a few souvenir stands and telescopes, but there weren't many tourists. You couldn't see much across the river.

I walked along the promenade and passed a child sitting in the shade. I approached him from the back, thinking that it was a local boy about seven years old, but then I saw his face, and I stopped. I had never seen so many different ages in a single person. He had the body of a young child, but from his face I could see that he was older, probably fourteen or fifteen. The corners were wrinkled, the skin shriveled like an old man's, and there was a gray dullness in his gaze that startled me.

I stared at the boy and realized that he was a North Korean who had come here to beg. In that moment, everything I'd glimpsed about this closed-off country — the swimmers and the soldiers and the television programs — slipped away. The boy gazed back. Finally, I fumbled for my wallet and pulled out some money. He accepted it without changing his expression. Neither of us said anything. I felt his eyes on my back as I walked away.

PICO IYER

Why We Travel

FROM *Salon Travel*

WE TRAVEL, initially, to lose ourselves; and we travel, next, to find ourselves. We travel to open our hearts and eyes and learn more about the world than our newspapers will accommodate. We travel to bring what little we can, in our ignorance and knowledge, to those parts of the globe whose riches are differently dispersed. And we travel, in essence, to become young fools again — to slow time down and get taken in, and fall in love once more. The beauty of this whole process was best described, perhaps, before people even took to frequent flying, by George Santayana in his lapidary essay "The Philosophy of Travel." We "need sometimes," the Harvard philosopher wrote, "to escape into open solitudes, into aimlessness, into the moral holiday of running some pure hazard, in order to sharpen the edge of life, to taste hardship, and to be compelled to work desperately for a moment at no matter what."

I like that stress on work, since never more than on the road are we shown how proportional our blessings are to the difficulty that precedes them; and I like the stress on a holiday that's "moral" since we fall into our ethical habits as easily as into our beds at night. Few of us ever forget the connection between "travel" and "travail," and I know that I travel in large part in search of hardship — both my own, which I want to feel, and others', which I need to see. Travel in that sense guides us toward a better balance of wisdom and compassion — of seeing the world clearly, and yet feeling it truly. For seeing without feeling can obviously be uncaring; while feeling without seeing can be blind.

Yet for me the first great joy of traveling is simply the luxury of leaving all my beliefs and certainties at home, and seeing everything I thought I knew in a different light, and from a crooked angle. In that regard, even a Kentucky Fried Chicken outlet (in Beijing) or a scratchy revival showing of *Wild Orchids* (on the Champs-Elysées) can be both novelty and revelation: In China, after all, people will pay a whole week's wages to eat with Colonel Sanders, and in Paris, Mickey Rourke is regarded as the greatest actor since Jerry Lewis.

If a Mongolian restaurant seems exotic to us in Evanston, Illinois, it only follows that a McDonald's would seem equally exotic in Ulan Bator — or, at least, equally far from everything expected. Though it's fashionable nowadays to draw a distinction between the "tourist" and the "traveler," perhaps the real distinction lies between those who leave their assumptions at home and those who don't: Among those who don't, a tourist is just someone who complains, "Nothing here is the way it is at home," while a traveler is one who grumbles, "Everything here is the same as it is in Cairo — or Cuzco or Kathmandu." It's all very much the same.

But for the rest of us, the sovereign freedom of traveling comes from the fact that it whirls you around and turns you upside down, and stands everything you took for granted on its head. If a diploma can famously be a passport (to a journey through hard realism), a passport can be a diploma (for a crash course in cultural relativism). And the first lesson we learn on the road, whether we like it or not, is how provisional and provincial are the things we imagine to be universal. When you go to North Korea, for example, you really do feel as if you've landed on a different planet — and the North Koreans doubtless feel that they're being visited by an extraterrestrial too (or else they simply assume that you, as they do, receive orders every morning from the Central Committee on what clothes to wear and what route to use when walking to work, and you, as they do, have loudspeakers in your bedroom broadcasting propaganda every morning at dawn, and you, as they do, have your radios fixed so as to receive only a single channel).

We travel, then, in part just to shake up our complacencies by seeing all the moral and political urgencies, the life-and-death dilemmas, that we seldom have to face at home. And we travel to fill in the gaps left by tomorrow's headlines: When you drive down the streets of Port-au-Prince, for example, where there is almost no paving and women relieve themselves next to mountains of trash, your notions of the Internet and a "one world order" grow usefully revised. Travel is the best way we have of rescuing the humanity of places, and saving them from abstraction and ideology.

And in the process, we also get saved from abstraction ourselves, and come to see how much we can bring to the places we visit, and how much we can become a kind of carrier pigeon — an anti–Federal Express, if you like — in transporting back and forth what every culture needs. I find that I always take Michael Jordan posters to Kyoto and bring woven ikebana baskets back to California; I invariably travel to Cuba with a suitcase piled high with bottles of Tylenol and bars of soap and come back with one piled high with salsa tapes, and hopes, and letters to long-lost brothers.

But more significantly, we carry values and beliefs and news to the places we go, and in many parts of the world, we become walking video screens and living newspapers, the only channels that can take people out of the censored limits of their homelands. In closed or impoverished places, like Pagan or Lhasa or Havana, we are the eyes and ears of the people we meet, their only contact with the world outside and, very often, the closest, quite literally, they will ever come to Michael Jackson or Bill Clinton. Not the least of the challenges of travel, therefore, is learning how to import — and export — dreams with tenderness.

By now all of us have heard (too often) the old Proust line about how the real voyage of discovery consists not in seeing new places but in seeing with new eyes. Yet one of the subtler beauties of travel is that it enables you to bring new eyes to the people you encounter. Thus even as holidays help you appreciate your own home more — not least by seeing it through a distant admirer's eyes — they help you bring newly appreciative — distant — eyes to the places you visit. You can teach them what they have to celebrate as much as you celebrate what they have to teach. This, I think, is how tourism, which so obviously destroys cultures, can also resuscitate or revive them, how it has created new "traditional" dances in Bali, and caused craftsmen in India to pay new attention to their works. If the first thing we can bring the Cubans is a real and balanced sense of what contemporary America is like, the second — and perhaps more important — thing we can bring them is a fresh and renewed sense of how special are the warmth and beauty of their country, for those who can compare it with other places around the globe.

Thus travel spins us round in two ways at once: It shows us the sights and values and issues that we might ordinarily ignore; but it also, and more deeply, shows us all the parts of ourselves that might otherwise grow rusty. For in traveling to a truly foreign place, we inevitably travel to moods and states of mind and hidden inward passages that we'd otherwise seldom have cause to visit.

On the most basic level, when I'm in Thailand, though a teetotaler who usually goes to bed at 9:00 P.M., I stay up till dawn in the local bars; and in Tibet, though not a real Buddhist, I spend days on end in temples, listening to the chants of sutras. I go to Iceland to visit the lunar spaces within me, and, in the uncanny quietude and emptiness of that vast and treeless world, to tap parts of myself generally obscured by chatter and routine.

We travel, then, in search of both self and anonymity — and, of course, in finding the one we apprehend the other. Abroad, we are wonderfully free of caste and job and standing; we are, as Hazlitt puts it, just the "gentlemen in the parlour," and people cannot put a name or tag to us. And precisely because we are clarified in this way, and freed of inessential labels, we have the opportunity to come into contact with more essential parts of ourselves (which may begin to explain why we may feel most alive when far from home).

Abroad is the place where we stay up late, follow impulse, and find ourselves as wide open as when we are in love. We live without a past or future, for a moment at least, and are ourselves up for grabs and open to interpretation. We even may become mysterious — to others, at first, and sometimes to ourselves — and, as no less a dignitary than Oliver Cromwell once noted, "A man never goes so far as when he doesn't know where he is going."

There are, of course, great dangers to this, as to every kind of freedom, but the great promise of it is that, traveling, we are born again, and able to return at moments to a younger and a more open kind of self. Traveling is a way to reverse time, to a small extent, and make a day last a year — or at least forty-five hours — and traveling is an easy way of surrounding ourselves, as in childhood, with what we cannot understand. Language facilitates this cracking open, for when we go to France, we often migrate to French and the more childlike self, simple and polite, that speaking a foreign language educes. Even when I'm not speaking pidgin English in Hanoi, I'm simplified in a positive way, and concerned not with expressing myself but simply with making sense.

So travel, for many of us, is a quest for not just the unknown but the unknowing; I, at least, travel in search of an innocent eye that can return me to a more innocent self. I tend to believe more abroad than I do at home (which, though treacherous again, can at least help me to extend my vision), and I tend to be more easily excited abroad, and even kinder. And since no one I meet can "place" me — no one can fix me in my résumé — I can remake myself for better, as well as, of course, for worse (if travel is notoriously a cradle for false identities, it can also, at its best, be a crucible for truer ones). In this way, travel can be a kind of monasticism on the move: On the road, we often live more simply (even when staying in a luxury hotel), with no more possessions than we can carry, and surrendering ourselves to chance.

And that is why many of us travel in search not of answers but of better questions. I, like many people, tend to ask questions of the places I visit, and relish most the ones that ask the most searching questions back of me. In Paraguay, for example, where one car in every two is stolen, and two-thirds of the goods on sale are smuggled, I have to rethink my every Californian assumption. And in Thailand, where many young women give up their bodies in order to protect their families — to become better Buddhists — I have to question my own too-ready judgments.

"The ideal travel book," Christopher Isherwood once said, "should be perhaps a little like a crime story in which you're in search of something." And it's the best kind of something, I would add, if it's one that you can never quite find.

I remember, in fact, after my first trips to Southeast Asia, more than a decade ago, how I would come back to my apartment in New York and lie in my bed, kept up by something more than jet lag, playing back in my memory, over and over, all that I had experienced, and paging wistfully through my photographs and reading and rereading my diaries, as if to extract some mystery from them. Anyone witnessing this strange scene would have drawn the right conclusion: I was in love.

For if every true love affair can feel like a journey to a foreign country, where you can't quite speak the language and you don't know where you're going and you're pulled ever deeper into the inviting darkness, every trip to a foreign country can be a love affair, where you're left puzzling over who you are and whom you've fallen in love with. All the great travel books are love stories, by some reckoning — from the *Odyssey* and the *Aeneid* to the *Divine Comedy* and the New Testament — and all good trips are, like love, about being carried out of yourself and deposited in the midst of terror and wonder.

And what this metaphor also brings home to us is that all travel is a two-way transaction, as we too easily forget, and if warfare is one model of the meeting of nations, romance is another. For what we all too often ignore when we go abroad is that we are objects of scrutiny as much as the people we scrutinize, and we are being consumed by the cultures we consume, as much on the road as when we are at home. At the very least, we are objects of speculation (and even desire) who can seem as exotic to the people around us as they do to us.

We are the comic props in Japanese home movies, the oddities in Malian anecdotes, and the fall guys in Chinese jokes; we are the moving postcards or bizarre *objets trouvés* that villagers in Peru will later tell their friends about. If travel is about the meeting of realities, it is no less about the mating of illusions: You give me my dreamed-of vision of Tibet, and I'll give you your wished-for California. And in truth, many of us, even (or especially) the ones who are fleeing America abroad, will get taken, willy-nilly, as symbols of the American Dream.

That, in fact, is perhaps the most central and most wrenching of the questions travel proposes to us: how to respond to the dream that people tender to you? Do you encourage their notions of a Land of Milk and Honey across the horizon, even if it is the same land you've abandoned? Or do you try to dampen their enthusiasm for a place that exists only in the mind? To quicken their dreams may, after all, be to matchmake them with an illusion; yet to dash them may be to strip them of the one possession that sustains them in adversity.

That whole complex interaction — not unlike the dilemmas we face with those we love (how do we balance truthfulness and tact?) — is partly the reason why so many of the great travel writers, by

nature, are enthusiasts: not just Pierre Loti, who famously, in-
famously, fell in love wherever he alighted (an archetypal sailor
leaving offspring in the form of *Madame Butterfly* myths), but also
Henry Miller, D. H. Lawrence, and Graham Greene, all of whom
bore out the hidden truth that we are optimists abroad as readily as
pessimists at home. None of them was by any means blind to the
deficiencies of the places around them, but all, having chosen to
go there, chose to find something to admire.

All, in that sense, believed in "being moved" as one of the points
of taking trips, and "being transported" by private as well as public
means; all saw that "ecstasy" ("ex-stasis") tells us that our highest
moments come when we're not stationary, and that epiphany can
follow movement as much as it precipitates it. I remember once
asking the great travel writer Norman Lewis if he'd ever be interested in writing on apartheid South Africa. He looked at me, astonished. "To write well about a thing," he said, "I've got to like it!"

At the same time, as all this is intrinsic to travel, from Ovid to
O'Rourke, travel itself is changing as the world does, and with it,
the mandate of the travel writer. It's not enough to go to the ends
of the earth these days (not least because the ends of the earth are
often coming to you); and where a writer like Jan Morris could, a
few years ago, achieve something miraculous simply by voyaging to
all the great cities of the globe, now anyone with a Visa card can do
that. So where Morris, in effect, was chronicling the last days of the
empire, a younger travel writer is in a better position to chart the
first days of a new empire, postnational, global, mobile, and yet as
diligent as the Raj in transporting its props and its values around
the world.

In the mid-nineteenth century, the British famously sent the Bible and Shakespeare and cricket round the world; now a more international kind of empire is sending Madonna and the Simpsons
and Brad Pitt. And the way in which each culture takes in this common pool of references tells you as much about them as their indigenous products might. Madonna in an Islamic country, after all,
sounds radically different from Madonna in a Confucian one, and
neither begins to mean the same as Madonna on East 14th Street.
When you go to a McDonald's outlet in Kyoto, you will find Teri-
yaki McBurgers and Bacon Potato Pies. The place mats offer maps
of the great temples of the city, and the posters all around broadcast the wonders of San Francisco. And — most crucial of all — the

young people eating their Big Macs, with baseball caps worn backward and tight 501 jeans, are still utterly and inalienably Japanese in the way they move, they nod, they sip their oolong teas — and never to be mistaken for the patrons of a McDonald's outlet in Rio, Morocco, or Managua. These days a whole new realm of exotica arises out of the way one culture colors and appropriates the products of another.

The other factor complicating and exciting all of this is people, who are, more and more, themselves as many-tongued and mongrel as cities like Sydney or Toronto or Hong Kong. I am in many ways an increasingly typical specimen, if only because I was born, as the son of Indian parents, in England, moved to America at seven, and cannot really call myself an Indian, an American, or an Englishman. I was, in short, a traveler at birth, for whom even a visit to the candy store was a trip through a foreign world where no one I saw quite matched my parents' inheritance, or my own. And though some of this is involuntary and tragic — the number of refugees in the world, which came to just 2.5 million in 1970, is now at least 27.4 million — it does involve, for some of us, the chance to be transnational in a happier sense, able to adapt anywhere, used to being outsiders everywhere, and forced to fashion our own rigorous sense of home. (And if nowhere is quite home, we can be optimists everywhere.)

Besides, even those who don't move around the world find the world moving more and more around them. Walk just six blocks in Queens or Berkeley, and you're traveling through several cultures in as many minutes; get into a cab outside the White House, and you're often in a piece of Addis Ababa. And technology too compounds this (sometimes deceptive) sense of availability, so that many people feel they can travel around the world without leaving the room — through cyberspace or CD-ROMs, videos and virtual travel. There are many challenges in this, of course, in what it says about essential notions of family and community and loyalty, and in the worry that air-conditioned, purely synthetic versions of places may replace the real thing — not to mention the fact that the world seems increasingly in flux, a moving target quicker than our notions of it. But there is, for the traveler at least, the sense that learning about home and learning about a foreign world can be one and the same thing.

All of us feel this from the cradle, and know, in some sense, that all the significant movement we ever take is internal. We travel when we see a movie, strike up a new friendship, get held up. Novels are often journeys as much as travel books are fictions; and though this has been true since at least as long ago as Sir John Mandeville's colorful fourteenth-century accounts of a Far East he'd never visited, it's an even more shadowy distinction now, as genre distinctions join other borders in collapsing.

In Mary Morris's *House Arrest*, a thinly disguised account of Castro's Cuba, the novelist reiterates, on the copyright page, "All dialogue is invented. Isabella, her family, the inhabitants, and even *la isla* itself are creations of the author's imagination." On page 172, however, we read, "*La isla*, of course, does exist. Don't let anyone fool you about that. It just feels as if it doesn't. But it does." No wonder the travel-writer narrator — a fictional construct (or not)? — confesses to devoting her travel magazine column to places that never existed. "Erewhon," after all, the undiscovered land in Samuel Butler's great travel novel, is just "nowhere" rearranged.

Travel, then, is a voyage into that famously subjective zone, the imagination, and what the traveler brings back is — and has to be — an ineffable compound of himself and the place, what's really there and what's only in him. Thus Bruce Chatwin's books seem to dance around the distinction between fact and fancy. V. S. Naipaul's recent book *A Way in the World* was published as a nonfictional "series" in England and a "novel" in the United States. And when some of the stories in Paul Theroux's half-invented memoir, *My Other Life,* were published in *The New Yorker,* they were slyly categorized as "Fact and Fiction."

And since travel is, in a sense, about the conspiracy of perception and imagination, the two great travel writers, for me, to whom I constantly return are Emerson and Thoreau (the one who famously advised that "traveling is a fool's paradise," and the other who "traveled a good deal in Concord"). Both of them insist on the fact that reality is our creation, and that we invent the places we see as much as we do the books that we read. What we find outside ourselves has to be inside ourselves for us to find it. Or, as Sir Thomas Browne sagely put it, "We carry within us the wonders we seek without us. There is Africa and her prodigies in us."

So, if more and more of us have to carry our sense of home inside us, we also — Emerson and Thoreau remind us — have to carry with us our sense of destination. The most valuable Pacifics we explore will always be the vast expanses within us, and the most important Northwest Crossings the thresholds we cross in the heart. The virtue of finding a gilded pavilion in Kyoto is that it allows you to take back a more lasting, private Golden Temple to your office in Rockefeller Center.

And even as the world seems to grow more exhausted, our travels do not, and some of the finest travel books in recent years have been those that undertake a parallel journey, matching the physical steps of a pilgrimage with the metaphysical steps of a questioning (as in Peter Matthiessen's great *The Snow Leopard*), or chronicling a trip to the farthest reaches of human strangeness (as in Oliver Sacks's *Island of the Colorblind*, which features a journey not just to a remote atoll in the Pacific but to a realm where people actually see light differently). The most distant shores, we are constantly reminded, lie within the person asleep at our side.

So travel, at heart, is just a quick way of keeping our minds mobile and awake. As Santayana, the heir to Emerson and Thoreau with whom I began, wrote, "There is wisdom in turning as often as possible from the familiar to the unfamiliar; it keeps the mind nimble; it kills prejudice, and it fosters humor." Romantic poets inaugurated an era of travel because they were the great apostles of open eyes. Buddhist monks are often vagabonds, in part because they believe in wakefulness. And if travel is like love, it is, in the end, mostly because it's a heightened state of awareness, in which we are mindful, receptive, undimmed by familiarity and ready to be transformed. That is why the best trips, like the best love affairs, never really end.

KATHLEEN LEE

Into the Heart of the Middle Kingdom

FROM *Condé Nast Traveler*

LIAO INHALED on his cigarette like he was blowtorching his lungs, tapped a hard fingernail against one of my tiles, and said in Chinese, "You should have played that one." I was playing mahjongg — badly. The other players — two men who played fiercely and rapidly and a woman wearing the latest Chinese fashion, a tight chiffon dress slit to her hips and a pair of heels with ankle-length nylon socks — smoked while I contemplated my tiles. The woman played coolly, as if she didn't care who won. They were all patient, which is typical of the Chinese, who seem to have levels of sheer tolerance that would elevate most people to nirvana.

I couldn't concentrate: Too much was happening on this weekday afternoon at the Jin River Park. Liao's constant conversation, for instance. "In the summer, tea is my savior," he said, twisting off the lid of his tea jar and drinking. He had lustrous thick hair and bad teeth. We spoke a mix of Chinese and English, Liao interjecting "Do you understand?" with manic regularity. I had talked to him every day since I'd arrived in Chengdu, the capital of Sichuan Province, but he had an endearing amnesia. Today he'd said, "You live in Brazil, right?" No. His conversation required no prompting. "Chinese people are more concerned with social rules. Westerners are more honest." Was he talking about the way I played mahjongg?

A few feet from our concrete table under a shady elm, a troop of soldiers marched into the park, dropped to their bellies, and began desultory target practice with unloaded weapons. They appeared to be aiming at pedestrians strolling along the opposite bank. Mysterious. How could they lie with their noses so close to the stinking waters of the Jin River, peppered with garbage and bubbling with methane? From a nearby primary school came the sweet innocence of children singing "Twinkle, Twinkle, Little Star" in Chinese. Itinerant barbers snipped people's hair. Beneath the sounds of bicycle bells and honking horns from the street were the clicks of mah-jongg tiles, the snap of cards, and the sharp clap of wooden chess pieces. Nobody appeared distracted, except me. Perhaps the ability to focus in the midst of bustle is what living in China, among an intimate mass of a billion people, teaches you.

When I first came to the country — and to Sichuan Province — in 1987, I was really just in transit. China hardly figured in my imagination: I was going to India. But you can't just pass through this land; it takes you by the throat.

At first I thought everyone was angry, an exoticized anger in a language that sounded like music sans melody. Then I realized that the Chinese were like my Italian relatives: loud. I began to like the country and its people; the chaos and noise of human exchange was oddly familiar, while nearly everything else, from the language (which I didn't yet speak) to the bedding (towels for pillowcases), was delightfully strange. From that first trip, Sichuan Province stood out as extraordinary. Chengdu was livelier, Sichuanese people warmer, the markets more colorful, the countryside more vivid than other places in China. Sichuan satisfied every expectation I unconsciously held about the country: peasants in emerald rice fields, mountains laced with mist, temples with tiled, upcurved roofs. In Sichuan, you can experience the China of the late twentieth century and the old China of willow-patterned plates and the wild China that we rarely imagine. This was the China that I knew I had to return to.

Sichuan, meaning "Four Rivers," is roughly the size of France, and landlocked near the center of the country. In the eastern part, where most of the province's 110 million residents live, lies the fertile Red Basin, with a subtropical climate and rich soil. Three harvests a year are produced here in a rigorous cycle from muddy fields to luscious greenery. Sichuan is China's Iowa, California, and Kansas: a combination heartland, breadbasket, and gateway to the west — minus John Deere. Instead of tractors and combines, you

see men with wooden plows slung over their shoulders leading water buffalo into muddy fields, and women bent between rows of
plump cabbages. China relies on Sichuanese agriculture, profits
from which power the economic success of the province.

There's a saying: "When the rest of the country is at peace,
Sichuan is the last brought to heel." In China, Sichuan is famous
for its spicy food and its residents' independent-mindedness, a
stubborn quality connected to the province's main physical feature: mountains. Sichuan is ringed and sliced by forbidding alpine
ranges. The west, in particular, with more herd animals than humans, is pleated with wild, high peaks. These have served to both
isolate and insulate Sichuan from mainstream China. Little surprise then, that it was Sichuan native Deng Xiaoping — tenacious,
peppery, inventive — who orchestrated China's economic metamorphosis from communism to the present idiosyncratic blend of
capitalism and socialism.

As you move from the farmland of eastern Sichuan into the
mountains and high plains of the west, civilizing influences thin,
cowed by the untamed sweeps of exhilaratingly empty land beneath plattered skies. This is China's Wild West. The pressures of
materialism dwindle as the pressures of survival intensify. Produce
grows in patches hewn from the raw, luminous terrain, and un-
fenced grasslands surge, oceanlike, to the horizon. The fiercely autonomous people who inhabit these immense distances are Tibetan, Hui Muslim, and Qiang, three of China's ethnic minority
groups. From western Sichuan, the central government feels remote, and residents do what they like. In response to the atmosphere of lawlessness that prevails in the region, Chengdu is thick
with soldiers poised for trouble, either in Sichuan or to its west in
Tibet.

Visiting a Chinese city is like deboning a fish: If you do it right,
it's terrific; if not, you eat bones. Within fifteen minutes of my arrival in Chengdu, I began to think that all of China was under
construction. Buildings were rising and falling — it was often hard
to tell which. Chengdu's old half-timbered structures — resembling sixteenth-century English cottages — were disintegrating or
were being sledgehammered away without nostalgia. Blocky new
white-tiled buildings fingered the skyline, and I was convinced that
their blue windows were meant to give the illusion of blue skies, be-

çause in Chengdu, they say dogs bark when the sun — an intruding stranger — emerges. Chengdu's skies weren't blue, but the sun lit the gray into an opalescent brilliance gone powdery with pollution.

The way to experience a Chinese city is to wander its streets, and the way to wander its streets is on a bicycle. So, on my first morning, I rented a Flying Pigeon and wobbled into the mass of bicyclists maneuvering among food carts, pedestrians, cars, buses, pedicabs, motorbikes, fruit sellers with baskets of peaches swinging from either side of shoulder poles, all coming from different directions. Fortunately, people in Chengdu ride at a conversational pace; unfortunately, they appear to daydream. Traffic lights are loosely adhered to, and lane dividers are merely decorative; it was a hip-to-bumper, face-to-windshield scrum.

After running into only two cyclists, when I swerved to avoid someone spitting (the signature habit in China), I arrived at the massive concrete statue of Mao planted at the top of Renmin (People's) Street. The chairman's statue resembles the smaller plastic one of Colonel Sanders outside a KFC several hundred yards away: two big-chested men, one with an arm outstretched in blessing, the other with an arm outstretched in welcome, both apparently benevolent. They meet across a huge square where nobody is allowed on the grass. Of the two, Mao is the controversial figure.

"Mao was a great man who made mistakes," said a woman with a sparse puff of white hair. "He improved life for the peasants. Everyone was equal — no rich or poor. Yes, there were terrible things." She shrugged and chased after her grandson, who was heading for the forbidden grass. Clearly, the present was more absorbing than the past.

A few minutes later, I met Liao for the first time. He refused to absolve Mao. "He was selfish, an egomaniac. I can never forgive him," he said. "During the Cultural Revolution I learned nothing, the schools were closed, and other, worse things happened." For a minute he looked as if he might cry or punch somebody. Abruptly he switched from Mao to mah-jongg and asked if I could play; he too had little desire to review the past.

Back on my bike, I headed south down Renmin Street, stopping to watch department store employees performing exercises to a routine blasting from a PA system. Lined up in their uniforms outside the store, sullen young women twisted and flapped beneath the stern gaze of a manageress. They were not happy Socialist workers forging a healthy Socialist future. These group calisthenics used to be carried out with a willed desire to believe in socialism. Now what was there to believe in? China had changed quickly and deeply, and with the changes came cynicism, born of the gap between Socialist rhetoric and capitalist reality. These women understood the vacuousness of a Socialist activity attached to a capitalist enterprise.

Next came the street markets between Renmin and Hongxing streets, selling lychees, freshly folded dumplings, blue-skinned chickens, pet crickets woven into basket cages, frothy pink hair ribbons. A woman talked on her cellular phone while the duck she had purchased was dipped in a vat of boiling water and then plucked. New technology was in everyone's pockets, but the Chinese people were not about to buy their meat wrapped in plastic on a foam tray in a fifteen-aisle supermarket.

I bought a triangle-shaped bread from a woman selling them warm from a basket on the back of her bike. She had a broad, placid face and wore her hair tucked into a white cotton cap. Soft and flat, the bread had scallions and a sprinkling of crushed cardamom and anise; two pie-shaped slices cost less than 10 cents. When I opened my wallet, the vendor spotted a picture I carried of myself at the age of five. "That's you," she shouted. A delighted crowd gathered to examine and comment on my younger self; they love children, they loved my former innocence.

At Wangjianglou Park I stopped for a rest: instant relief. The noise of traffic was held at bay, replaced by the susurrus of breezes through bamboo. I dutifully viewed the sluggish Jin River from the pagoda-style Ming dynasty River Viewing Pavilion, which had thick pads of moss growing on its roof tiles. (Dates and dynasties: I attach people to time periods. Tang is Charlemagne, Ming is Shakespeare, Qing is Napoleon.) Then I strolled curved paths beside lotus-flowered lakes and watched a ballroom dance class. Nobody appeared self-conscious; the Chinese can dance badly in front of anyone. Beside the dancers, a shirtless man practiced tai chi, arms sweeping the air, legs lifting and landing as if he might fall through the earth if he weren't careful.

At a teahouse pavilion of dark, polished wood overlooking a quiet lake, I settled into a reclining bamboo chair and, for 50 cents, drank an endless cup of fragrant tea refilled by a roving band of pourers. It was served in a handleless porcelain cup fitted into a tight saucer. You sweep the curved lid over the surface of the water, brushing back floating tea leaves. Sip, sweep, sip. I was surrounded by the warm din of conversation, the scraping of chairs being arranged, the cracking of sunflower seeds, and the rustling of newspapers. A middle-aged woman offered me a loquat, somebody else wanted to know who I thought would win the World Cup. While I eavesdropped on conversations about prices, illness, and love, several people hovered nearby to see the novelty of English being written, and two ear pickers persistently offered to pick my ears.

Beneath China's convulsing urban landscape lay the unperturbed, ancient heart of Chengdu. Back on my bike, I turned down a narrow alley and found people playing games and gossiping. It's easy to imagine these scenes a hundred years ago and a hundred years from now. Something remains untouchable in Chinese culture; it is the oldest continuous civilization, and it has the distinction of converting conquerors — the Mongols (thirteenth century) and the Manchus (seventeenth) — to its own beliefs, rather than the other way around.

At one table, Zhao, a chemist with orange, tobacco-stained fingernails, played Chinese bridge and talked, cigarette trembling between his lips. His troubles began in the 1950s, when Mao encouraged intellectuals to speak freely during the Hundred Flowers Campaign. "I said some things and was sent to Gansu Province for two years of reeducation."

I wanted to know what he'd said, but he concentrated on the elegantly narrow cards in his hand. "It was a hard life, but simple — only survival mattered." Things worsened: First, his wife died, and then, in 1958, a three-year famine began in the countryside, killing 30 million people — a famine brought about by corrupt and irresponsible government policies. "I was lucky," Zhao said. "I lived near a lake and we ate fish but nothing else."

Eventually Zhao's name was cleared and he was invited back to the science institute where he worked. But an intellectual life was too complicated, so he returned to Chengdu and became a furniture maker. He lived a calm life until 1967, when the Cultural Revolution propelled the country into chaos. "But I didn't worry,"

Zhao said, squinting through his own cigarette smoke. "If I was a ti-ger, I was already a dead tiger." He inhaled and held the smoke carefully, luxuriously. "We got our food with coupons and did noth-ing. Many people suffered, especially in Sichuan. For me, I was al-ready dead." He threw a card with a sharp crack. "After Mao died, I got a job as a chemistry teacher in a middle school."

I looked at the other players in that shadowed alley, each with his own story of suffering. How was it that Zhao, and others, weren't bitter and angry? "Chinese people don't complain, they accept things as they are," Zhao explained. "That's why we aren't angry."

I rode into the sunless streets where the action never ceased: a Chinese-medicine doctor applying glass cups to a man's back, blind fortunetellers awaiting customers, a masseuse performing a head massage. People sat on bits of newspaper; families strolled and talked. Some women wore slippers and pajamas, as if they were in their own backyard. This was nothing like life in America, with its locked doors and fenced yards.

Swift bats swooped over the darkening river water. At the park beside the Jin River, Liao was still playing mah-jongg. "We meet again," he shouted. "It's destiny." His eyes blinked rapidly behind his tilted glasses, and he smiled crookedly with the air of a slightly crazed comedian.

Long-distance bus travel in China is like a Zen meditation: an exer-cise in uncomfortable concentration. At the end of a ten-hour ride to Songpan in the Min Mountains north of Chengdu, I was actually reluctant to leave my fellow passengers. We were dirty and tired of being close, yet a strange bond had developed between us. I said goodbye to the mother with whom I'd shared snacks, and whose baby had wet my lap, and my seat partner who'd slept with his head bumping my shoulder. I thanked the bus driver, a heroically calm man. While competing for his piece of the busy road, he had argued with passengers over fares, scrambled for change from a metal box, and fought back mounds of luggage that threatened to collapse onto him.

I came here to do a horse trek into Sichuan's legendary moun-tains. Songpan, a scrappy town that was once a Qing dynasty garri-son, is demarcated by meat. One half of the main street is Muslim, where mutton and yak are sold; the other is Chinese, where pork is sold. Besides the majority, who are Han Chinese, Tibetan, Hui Muslim, and Qiang people live in the area, and they do so harmoniously, though this hasn't always been true.

I wandered along the main street, past a Hui man wearing a white Muslim skullcap and enthusiastically hawking yak and mutton kabobs. He threw his head back and flashed a mouth full of gold teeth; the mutton was surprisingly tender, but I chewed on the yak until my jaw ached. Two Tibetan men with horses in tow sauntered by, wearing long black coats, one shoulder free of a coat sleeve, as if for easy access to the knives tucked into their red sashes. I took their disheveled hair as evidence of a wild ride into town. In an open-fronted shop, I tried on a heavy Tibetan necklace of turquoise and coral chunks strung between carved silver beads, and made the solemn-faced shopkeeper laugh when I bent under its weight. Back on the street, a yak carcass — dinosaur-sized bones and gaping, airy nave of a rib cage — marked a corner. Was it that I had never seen such enormous bones or was it that I rarely saw an entire carcass?

Cowboys and China do not mix easily in the imagination. I had no notion what to expect the next morning when I met my Songpan cowboys: Li, the head wrangler, had dreamy eyes and an Elvis lock of hair on his forehead; Ermao blushed easily and tried to disguise his boyish charm behind cigarettes. They slouched sloppily in saddles that were really just big pads, their feet, in thin tennis shoes, dangling free of the carved metal stirrups. They did not wear hats. I was dismayed to notice that the horses were already tired and caked with mud, and I didn't like the jitteriness of my assigned mount — a belligerent black gelding. I swung into the saddle, and the horse rolled his eyes and promptly dumped me in the middle of the street. Li and Ermao dismounted, mortified at the sight of me lying on my back; I lay for a minute, watching the tails of two yaks as they insolently swished past.

After Ermao and I switched horses — he didn't want to ride the black horse either — we climbed steeply away from Songpan, past Tibetan villages with prayer flags beating rhythmically in the sharp wind. The sun was dim in a flat, pale sky. I tried conversing with Tibetan women wearing their braids wrapped around their heads with scarves and coral beads, but they didn't speak Mandarin and I don't speak Tibetan. A group of high-spirited Tibetans trotted past in a burst of laughter behind a train of lumber-loaded yaks, heavy heads swinging with a gloomy, romantic air.

At the top of a pass, Li pointed out the ruin of a stone corral. "We used to work in a commune," he said. "All the horses were kept here. Nobody owned animals." He looked disapproving, and I had to admit that communal cowboys didn't sound like a happy combination. He continued, "Now that we have an economy, I want to buy a car." The difficulties of the past only moved Li to pursue his goals with greater energy.

We dropped into a valley where the Tibetan town of Munigou rested between folds of forested hills and a wrinkled river. Munigou was as pristine and tidy as anything made in Switzerland: neat fields fenced with delicately woven slender branches. Woodpiles, whose size attested to the wealth of the owner, looked as if they had been stacked by mathematicians. The white disks of satellite dishes, sprinkled among the houses, advertised the village's prosperity, the source of which was farming and animal husbandry. Still, there was no farm machinery, just the bent backs of women in the fields. The traditional two-story houses had a first floor for animals, made of stone, and a second floor for people, made of wood, with carved verandas and wood shutters; all boards planed by hand, all joints wood.

We rode out of Munigou, passing a red-robed monk on a bicycle, wearing a white mesh fedora with the letters CORLDW DUP on the band. Secret code for "World Cup"? Ermao, too young to care about life before private ownership, talked blithely about the two cows, three horses, and forty goats his family owned and the girlfriend he had just broken up with: "If you sleep with a girl, you have to marry her." Meanwhile, I wondered where we were going to sleep. My saddle was a canvas bag packed with a Tibetan tent (no floor) and a quilt. No sleeping bags, no pads, no cookstove. I didn't know where we were or what would happen next, yet I relished the anticipation of the unexpected. I like travel that resembles a chaotic Christmas, with mysterious gifts awaiting unveiling. Impending surprise turned my surroundings exotic: the blazing clarity of pines against an aqua sky, the slanting lemon afternoon light.

We didn't camp out, we slept on plank beds in a plywood hut at the top of a valley north of Munigou, where three of Li's friends had a small shop and a restaurant. Ermao led the horses into a high pasture, while Li and his friends waded into the stream to catch lizards, like boys. I wondered if they were groping around slick stones in search of dinner: stir-fried lizard? The thin-lipped man in charge threaded a line through the chin of each of the five captured creatures, then strung them between two saplings to dry, where they wriggled and flipped their tails. As it turned out, they were not slated for our dinner but were to be sold in town for use as medicine.

Mr. Thinlips deftly chopped vegetables on a log, then kneaded dough. He built a fire in a wood-burning stove and began preparing Tibetan noodle soup while Li spread a quilt over a board in a corner of the hut, then threw a Tibetan coat, lined with a mangy sheepskin, on top of it: my bed and bedding. I lay down for a rest and sighed. It was just as it looked — hard and cold.

After dinner, we sat beside a sparking campfire; the rustling of water, the snapping of pitch, a few stars between clouds softening the edges of the night, the sound of horse's teeth crashing through fava beans. It was beautiful; it was China. A generator started up in the building across the stream, and karaoke drowned the night sounds, disco lights colored the trees overhead. The Chinese are masters of one-stop entertainment. If a place has one feature — beautiful scenery, say — it can only be enhanced by the addition of other attractions: karaoke, children's rides, balloons that can be shot for prizes. This means that temples, parks, or scenic areas might have the atmosphere of an amusement park. China's recent history, notably devoid of entertainment, seems a reasonable enough excuse for the excess.

In the lobby of my hotel back in Chengdu, an old-time China traveler told me, "Get on a bus to Xiaojin. Go over the snowy mountain, and get off in Siguniangshan. There's a guesthouse and three valleys. Spectacular."

"Over the snowy mountain" sounded like directions to a fairyland. Then, when I discovered that Siguniangshan, in the Qionglai Mountains, wasn't on my map, and that there was no road drawn to Xiaojin, I had to go. Maps are my downfall: I'm enticed by small print or an isolated name far from roads. I can't resist going "nowhere." Still, the bus to Xiaojin was crowded — so crowded that I had to sit on the board over the engine, beside the driver, which gave me an arresting view of our approaching fate.

Five hours outside Chengdu, the pavement ended and we started to climb a half-built road. For three hours, including stops to cool the boiling engine, we pitched up a rock and mud strip about as wide as dental floss cut into the mountainside, scraping past trucks going in the other direction and swerving to avoid frightened yaks. Except there was no room to swerve. I couldn't see the bottom of the valley, just thousands of feet of sharp air. The driver snacked nervously, fiddling with drinks and bags of salted plums; I watched the road and strategized a disaster plan. If we rolled, I would curl up and cover my head with my hands. I held my pack in my lap, hoping to avoid being impaled on the gearshift. Work crews stood beside their tents, perched on the road's sheer lip. I was awed by these unheralded men and women, hacking China's infrastructure out of this severe landscape.

We drove into the blindness of clouds, and I put my head in my hands; I was in an old bus that sounded like a beast in pain on an abysmal road with zero visibility. When we emerged abruptly into clarity, only the driver and I were awake to witness frothing clouds ascending the mountains in fat, languorous swells. The surrounding peaks cut into the sky in splintered piles with needle-sharp silhouettes. At the crest, I imagined the prayer flags were flapping for us as we began to hurtle down the other side at a speed that shook the entire bus almost to pieces. I got off in the dusty one-street town of Siguniangshan, stunned to have arrived. That ten-hour bus ride was all-consuming: I had forgotten that I had a destination.

Siguniangshan (Four Girls Mountain) is the name of both the town and the pyramid-shaped peak above it. Legend has it that four sisters turned themselves into a mountain in order to protect the local villagers. As I trudged up the street, tucking my chin to keep swirling dust out of my eyes, Tibetan women peered from shops selling tools, yarn, rope, cigarettes; men lifted their heads from inside truck engines; all squinted at me with surprise and suspicion. "One person?" they asked. Obviously, few came here alone. I now understood the romance and power of Sichuan's mountains — this had not been an easy place to get to.

In the morning, I teamed with a sister, brother, and wife trio from Shanghai in a jeep going to Changping Valley. They put a live chicken they'd bought for lunch into a box and then into the jeep, where it sat meekly at my feet. Our Tibetan guide wiped his forehead with his sleeve; he looked hung-over.

We entered Double Bridge Valley through a rock-walled slit that widened into pink-carpeted meadows cut by a clear, hard-running stream. Herders — the women spinning and knitting as they walked — followed sheep and pigs up the mangled dirt road. A boy in overlarge pants sang a mournful song syncopated by sheep bells. Higher up, the waterfalls began: fat, white spouts; thin slides of sweat on the mountain's brow.

We stopped for the driver to tighten bolts in the engine, shaken loose by the rough road. Yu, the sister, told me, "My teacher used to say, 'If you travel, it must be to seek difference.'" She brushed mud off her white tennis shoes and straightened her crisp blue slacks. We discussed culinary differences and changes within China. Born in 1968, she vividly remembered a time when all she ate was cabbage and rice. But, like everyone I met in Sichuan, she focused on the present. "Now there is so much meat and so many choices, though I'm afraid I've only eaten Chinese food."

At lunchtime we entered a stone hut. Three pots hung over a central fire, the walls were furry with soot, a lump of yak cheese sat in a damp corner. The guide wrung and slit the chicken's neck, the Tibetan owner of the hut went to pick mushrooms, I hiked up past horses and yaks poking their heads through bushes to gaze at me.

The sheer, high grandeur could have been Yosemite, except that no tourist in Yosemite would bring a live chicken for lunch. At the top of the valley there were vertical rock faces, a cream and cappuccino glacier, and spiky peaks piercing a cobalt sky. I stopped in a spear of silvery light, delighted to have found this empty, magical place where the sounds of wind and water fluttered at the edges of a delicious solitude.

JANET MALCOLM

Travels with Chekhov

FROM *The New Yorker*

AFTER THEY HAVE SLEPT TOGETHER for the first time, Dmitri Dmitrich Gurov and Anna Sergeyevna Von Diderits, the hero and heroine of Anton Chekhov's story "The Lady with the Dog" (1899), drive out at dawn to a village near Yalta called Oreanda, where they sit on a bench near a church and look down on the sea. "Yalta was hardly visible through the morning mist; white clouds stood motionless on the mountain-tops," Chekhov writes at the start of the famous passage that continues:

> The leaves did not stir on the trees, grasshoppers chirruped, and the monotonous hollow sound of the sea rising up from below, spoke of the peace, of the eternal sleep awaiting us. So it must have sounded when there was no Yalta, no Oreanda here; so it sounds now, and it will sound as indifferently and monotonously when we are all no more. And in this constancy, in this complete indifference to the life and death of each of us, there lies hid, perhaps, a pledge of our eternal salvation, of the unceasing movement of life upon earth, of unceasing progress towards perfection. Sitting beside a young woman who in the dawn seemed so lovely, soothed and spellbound in these magical surroundings — the sea, mountains, clouds, the open sky — Gurov thought how in reality everything is beautiful in this world when one reflects: everything except what we think or do ourselves when we forget our human dignity and the higher aims of our existence.

Today, I am sitting on that same bench near the church looking at the same view. Beside me is my English-speaking guide, Nina (I know no Russian), and a quarter of a mile away a driver named Yevgeny waits in his car at the entrance to the footpath leading to the lookout point where Gurov and Anna sat, not yet aware of the great love that lay before them. I am a character in a new drama: the absurdist farce of the literary pilgrim who leaves the magical pages of a work of genius and travels to an "original scene," which can only fall short of his expectations. However, because Nina and Yevgeny have gone to some trouble to find the spot, I pretend to be thrilled by it. Nina — a large woman in her late sixties, with short, straight blond hair, forget-me-not-blue eyes, and an open, passionate nature — is gratified. She breaks into song. "It's a big, wide, wonderful world that we live in," she sings, and then asks, "Do you know this song?" When I say I do, she tells me that Deanna Durbin sang it in the 1948 film *For the Love of Mary.*

"Do you like Deanna Durbin?" she asks. I say yes.

"I adore Deanna Durbin," Nina says. "I have adored her since I was a girl."

She tells me of a chance encounter in a church in Yalta, two years earlier, with an Englishwoman named Muriel, who turned out to be another adorer of Deanna Durbin, and who subsequently invited her to the annual conference of an organization called the Deanna Durbin Society, which was held that year in Scarborough, England. Nina owns videos of all Deanna Durbin's movies and knows all the songs Deanna Durbin sang. She offers to give me the address of the Deanna Durbin Society.

Nina was born and educated in St. Petersburg and, after studying languages at the university there, became an Intourist guide, presently moving to Yalta. She has retired, and, like most retirees in the former Soviet Union, she cannot live on her pension. She now hires out as an independent guide and waits for assignments from the Hotel Yalta, currently the only habitable hotel in the town. My trip to Yalta is a stroke of good fortune for her; she had not worked for a long time when the call from the hotel came.

It is the second day of my acquaintance with Nina, the third day of my stay at the Hotel Yalta, and the ninth day of my trip to the former Soviet Union. I have worked my way south from St. Petersburg and Moscow. My arrival in Yalta was marked by an incident that rather dramatically brought into view something that had lain just below my consciousness as I pursued my itinerary of visits to houses where Chekhov lived and places he had written about. I had flown from Moscow to Simferopol, the nearest town to Yalta with an airport, an hour-and-a-half drive away. Chekhov lived in Yalta during much of the last five years of his life. (He died in July 1904.) At that time, exile to places with mild climates, like the Crimea and the Riviera, was the favored therapy for tuberculosis, into whose last stages Chekhov was entering in the late 1890s. He built a handsome villa a few miles outside the city center, in a suburb called Autka, and also bought a small cottage on the water in a seaside Tatar village called Gurzuf. He wrote *The Three Sisters* and *The Cherry Orchard*, as well as "The Lady with the Dog" and "The Bishop," in these houses.

At the Simferopol airport, as I stood in line at the immigration counter waiting to have my passport and visa stamped, I saw, as if in a dream's slow motion, a man in the baggage area on the other side of a glass panel walk out of the building with my suitcase in his hand. The hallucination proved to be real. In a daze, I filled out a lost-luggage form and followed an English-speaking woman who worked for the Hotel Yalta to a car in the parking lot. She said she would trace my luggage and disappeared. The driver — the same Yevgeny who now sits in the car in Oreanda — drove me to the hotel in silence, his English and my Russian in exact equilibrium.

As we neared the Black Sea coast, the Ukrainian farm country gave way to a terrain resembling — and, in the variety and beauty of its vegetation, surpassing — that of the Riviera corniches. The winding road offered views of mountains and glimpses of the sea below. But when the Hotel Yalta came into view I caught my breath at its spectacular ugliness. It is a monstrous building — erected in 1975, with a capacity of 2,500 people — that is like a brute's blow in the face of the countryside. Its scale would be problematic anywhere, and on the hillside above Yalta it is catastrophic. Hundreds of — possibly a thousand — identical balconies jut out from a glass-and-concrete façade. The approach is an American supermarket-style parking lot. The vast low-ceilinged lobby, with black marble floors and metallic walls, looks as if a failing bank had been crossed with a seedy nightclub. In one corner there is a bar, and along one wall stands a row of slot machines. A great expanse of empty black marble floor lies between the slot machines and the hotel's front desk. When I entered the lobby, it was almost completely empty: two or three men were playing the slot machines and a couple sat at the bar. At the reception desk, I was given a key to a

room on the fourth floor, and, after walking down an almost satiri-
cally long empty corridor, I opened the door to a cubicle about
eight by twelve feet, pleasingly furnished in the blond-wood Scandi-
navian Modern style of the fifties and sixties, and affording just
enough room for a double bed, a small round table with two chairs,
an armchair, and a minuscule refrigerator. My little balcony — like
its myriad replicas — offered a glimpse of the sea and a view of
large swimming pools, tennis courts, various outbuildings, and an
auditorium. No one was in the pools or on the courts, but American popular music blared out of a loudspeaker. I shut the glass
door to muffle the sound and hopefully opened the refrigerator. It
was empty. In the bathroom, I found serviceable fixtures and a
soap dish of plastic made to resemble brown marble.

On my arrival, an unsmiling young man named Igor, who spoke
fluent English, had approached me in the lobby and led me to his
office, where he enumerated the activities that had been arranged
for the next two days with Nina and Yevgeny. These had been pre-
paid, and he wanted me to understand that anything more would
cost extra. (The trip to Oreanda would be one such addition.)
When I mentioned my lost luggage and asked if there was somewhere I could buy a nightgown and a change of clothes, he looked
at his watch and said that if I walked down to the town — a twenty-
or thirty-minute walk — I might still find some clothing stores
open.

As I walked to the town in the late-afternoon sunlight, down a road
fragrant with smells of the trees and shrubs and wildflowers that
lined it, and left the horrible hotel behind, I felt a stir of happiness.
Though it was May, St. Petersburg had been icily wintry and Moscow only a few degrees warmer. But here it was true spring; the air
was fresh and soft. In a few months — I knew from "The Lady with
the Dog" — Yalta would be hot and dusty. On the day Gurov and
Anna became lovers, "it was sultry indoors, while in the street the
wind whirled the dust round and round and blew people's hats off.
It was a thirsty day, and Gurov often went into the pavilion, and
pressed Anna Sergeyevna to have syrup and water or an ice. One
did not know what to do with oneself." In the evening, after min-
gling with a crowd at the harbor that has gathered to meet a ship
coming in, Gurov kisses Anna, and they go to her hotel. After they

have made love, Anna sits dejected, "like 'the woman who was a sin-
ner' in an old fashioned picture," and Gurov callously cuts himself
a slice of watermelon and eats it "without haste." Gurov's unforget-
table gesture — the mark of the cold roué that he is — only deepens the mystery and heightens the poignancy of his later transformation into a man capable of serious love.

As I walked on, small village houses of a familiar old sort began
to appear. Yalta seemed untouched by the hands that had heaved
my monstrous hotel into the hillside above it. Along the seafront,
some changes had of course taken place since Gurov and Anna
strolled there. In the square opposite the harbor stood a huge
statue of Lenin, gesturing toward the sea; and the harbor itself had
become the site of a kiddie park, outfitted with garishly colored
cartoon figures. The shops along the tree-lined promenade — selling film and suntan lotion and mermaid dolls and souvenir china
— had a neglected, unvisited air; perhaps business would pick up
in the hot, dusty season. Many were closed for the day, among them
the clothing stores. When Chekhov visited Yalta for the first time,
in July 1888, he disparaged it thus to his sister Maria:

> Yalta is a mixture of something European that reminds one of the views
> of Nice, with something cheap and shoddy. The box-like hotels in which
> unhappy consumptives are pining, the impudent Tatar faces, the ladies'
> bustles with their very undisguised expression of something very abomi-
> nable, the faces of the idle rich, longing for cheap adventures, the smell
> of perfumery instead of the scent of the cedars and the sea, the misera-
> ble dirty pier, the melancholy lights far out at sea, the prattle of young la-
> dies and gentlemen who have crowded here in order to admire nature
> of which they have no idea — all this taken together produces such a de-
> pressing effect and is so overwhelming that one begins to blame oneself
> for being biased and unfair.

I began my ascent back up the hill. The sun was nearing the horizon, and there was a chill in the air. The weight of being thousands
of miles from home with nothing to wear but the clothes on my
back fell on me. I tried to pull myself together, to rise above my
petty obsession with the loss of a few garments, and to that end invoked Chekhov and the heightened sense of what is important in
life that gleams out of his work. The shadow of mortality hovers
over his texts; his characters repeatedly remind one another that

"we all have to die" and that "life is not given twice." Chekhov himself needed no such reminders: the last decade of his life was a daily struggle with increasingly virulent pulmonary and intestinal tuberculosis. And yet when he was dying, in the spa of Badenweiler, where he had stupidly been sent by a specialist, he wrote letters to Maria in which he repeatedly complained not about his fate but about how badly German women dressed. "Nowhere do women dress so abominably. . . . I have not seen one beautiful woman, nor one who was not trimmed with some kind of absurd braid," he wrote on June 8, 1904, and then, on June 28 — in his last letter to anyone and his last comment on anything — "There is not a single decently dressed German woman. The lack of taste makes one depressed."

I continued climbing the hill, in the inflexible grip of unhappiness over my lost clothes. And then the realization came: the recognition that when my suitcase was taken something else had been restored to me — feeling itself. Until the mishap at the airport, I had not felt anything very much. Without knowing exactly why, I have always found travel writing a little boring, and now the reason seemed clear: travel itself is a low-key emotional experience, a pallid affair in comparison with ordinary life. When Gurov picks up Anna at an outdoor restaurant (approaching her through her dog), they converse thus:

"Have you been long in Yalta?" [he says].
"Five days."
"And I have already dragged out a fortnight here." There was a brief silence.
"Time goes fast, and yet it is so dull here!" she said, not looking at him.
"That's only the fashion to say it is dull here. A provincial will live in Belyov or Zhidra and not be dull, and when he comes here it's 'Oh the dullness! Oh, the dust!' One would think he came from Granada."

Although the passage functions (as Vladimir Nabokov pointed out) as an illustration of Gurov's attractive wit, it also expresses the truth that had just been revealed to me, and that Chekhov's Yalta exile revealed to him — that our homes are Granada. They are where the action is; they are where the riches of experience are distributed. On our travels, we stand before paintings and look at scenery, and sometimes we are moved, but rarely are we as engaged with life as we are in the course of any ordinary day in our usual surroundings. Only when faced with one of the inevitable minor hardships of travel do we break out of the trance of tourism and once again feel the sharp savor of the real. ("I have never met anyone who was less a tourist," Maxim Kovalevsky, a professor of sociology whom Chekhov met in Nice in 1897, wrote of his compatriot, and went on to say that "visiting museums, art galleries, and ruins exhausted rather than delighted him. . . . In Rome I found myself obliged to assume the role of guide, showing him the Forum, the ruins of the palace of the Caesars, the Capitol. To all of this he remained more or less indifferent.") Chekhov was deeply bored in Yalta before he built his house and put in his garden, and even afterward he felt as if he had been banished, and that life was elsewhere. When he wrote of the three sisters'. yearning for Moscow, he was expressing his own sense of exile. "One does not know what to do with oneself."

Chekhov's villa in Autka — Nina took me there on our first day together — is a two-story stucco house of distinguished, unornamented, faintly Moorish architecture, with an extensive, well-ordered garden and spacious rooms that look out over Yalta to the sea. Maria Chekhova, who lived until 1957, preserved the house and garden, fending off Nazi occupiers during the war and enduring the insults of the Stalin and Khrushchev periods. It remains furnished as in Chekhov's time: handsomely, simply, elegantly. As Chekhov cared about women's dress (it does not go unnoted in his work, and is always significant), he cared about the furnishings of his houses. Perhaps his love of order and elegance was innate, but more likely it was a reaction against the disorder and harshness of his early family life. His father, Pavel Yegorovich, was the son of a serf who had managed to buy his freedom and that of his wife and children. Pavel rose in the world and became the owner of a grocery store in Taganrog, a town with a large foreign (mostly Greek) population, on the sea of Azov, in southern Russia. The store, as Chekhov's best biographer, Ernest J. Simmons, characterizes it, resembled a New England general store — selling things like kerosene, tobacco, yarn, nails, and home remedies — though, unlike a New England store, it also sold vodka, which was consumed on the premises in a separate room. In Simmons's description, the place had "filthy debris on the floor, torn soiled oilcloth on the counters, and in summer, swarms of flies settled everywhere. An unpleasant mélange of odors emanated from the exposed goods: the sugar smelled of kerosene, the coffee of herring. Brazen rats prowled about the stock."

Chekhov's oldest brother, Alexander, in a memoir of Anton, wrote of a freezing winter night on which "the future writer," then a nine-year-old schoolboy, was dragged by his father from the warm room where he was doing his homework and made to mind the unheated store. The account lays stress on the cruelty of the father and the misery of the boy, and is crudely written, in a sort of penny-dreadful style. The reticent Anton himself left no memoir of his childhood sorrows, though there are passages in his stories that are assumed to refer to them. In his long story "Three Years" (1895), for example, the hero, Laptev, says to his wife, "I can remember my father correcting me — or, to speak plainly, beating me — before I was five years old. He used to thrash me with a birch, pull my ears, hit me on the head, and every morning when I woke up my first thought was whether he would beat me that day." In a letter of 1894, to his publisher and close friend Alexei Suvorin, Chekhov permitted himself the bitter reflection that "I acquired my belief in progress when still a child; I could not help believing in it, because the difference between the period when they flogged me and the period when they stopped flogging me was enormous." Chekhov had what he described to another correspondent, in 1899, as "autobiographophobia." The correspondent was Grigory Rossolimo, who had been a classmate in medical school, and had written to Chekhov to ask him for an autobiography for an album he was assembling for a class reunion — which Chekhov supplied, but not before expressing his reluctance to write about himself. Seven years earlier, when V. A. Tikhonov, the editor of a journal called *Sever,* asked him for biographical information to accompany a photograph, Chekhov made this reply:

> Do you need my biography? Here it is. In 1860 I was born in Taganrog. In 1879 I finished my studies in the Taganrog school. In 1884 I finished my studies in the medical school of Moscow University. In 1888 I received the Pushkin Prize. In 1890 I made a trip to Sakhalin across Siberia and back by sea. In 1891 I toured Europe, where I drank splendid wine and ate oysters. In 1892 I strolled with V. A. Tikhonov at [the writer Shcheglov's] name day party. I began to write in 1879 in *Strekosa.* My col-

lections of stories are Motley Stories, Twilight, Stories, Gloomy People, and the novella The Duel. I have also sinned in the realm of drama, although moderately. I have been translated into all languages with the exception of the foreign ones. However, I was translated into German quite a while ago. The Czechs and Serbs also approve of me. And the French also relate to me. I grasped the secrets of love at the age of thirteen. I remain on excellent terms with friends, both physicians and writers. I am a bachelor. I would like a pension. I busy myself with medicine to such an extent that this summer I am going to perform some autopsies, something I have not done for two or three years. Among writers I prefer Tolstoy, among physicians, Zakharin. However, this is all rubbish. Write what you want. If there are no facts, substitute something lyrical.

Maxim Gorky wrote of Chekhov that "in the presence of Anton Pavlovich, everyone felt an unconscious desire to be simpler, more truthful, more himself." Chekhov's mock biography produces a similar chastening effect. After reading it, one can only regard any attempt at self-description that is longer and less playful as pretentious and rather ridiculous.

"This morning, I felt giddy," Nina tells me at the lookout in Oreanda. "I was afraid I would not be able to come today. Fortunately, I am better." I question her about her symptoms and urge her to see a doctor. She explains that she hasn't the money for a doctor — doctors can no longer get by on their salaries from the state and now charge for their services. I ask if there are clinics, and she says yes, but they are overcrowded — one has to wait interminably. She finally agrees to go to a clinic the next day to have her blood pressure checked. Nina and I took to each other immediately. She is extremely likable. Because she is large and I am small, she has taken to giving me impulsive bear hugs and calling me her little one — for lack of a better equivalent for the Russian diminutive. Over the two days we have been together, I have received an increasing sense of the pathos of her life. She is poor. Her apartment is too small, she says, to keep a cat in. The dress she is wearing was given to her by an Englishwoman whose guide she was a few years ago. She is grateful when clients give her leftover shampoo and hand cream; nothing is too small. Earlier in the day, during a visit to the Livadia Palace, where the Yalta agreement was signed, she told me that as a young child she lived through the nine-hundred-day siege of Leningrad. Her grandparents died during the siege, and her parents' lives, she said, had been shortened because of the sacrifices they made for their children. Now, as she talks about the leftover shampoo, I think about the large tip I will give her at the end of the day, anticipating her surprise and pleasure. Then a suspicion enters my mind: Has she been putting on an act and playing on my sympathy precisely so that I will give her money? A week earlier, in St. Petersburg, someone else had used the term "putting on an act." I had been walking along the Nevsky Prospect with my guide, Nelly, when I was stopped in my tracks by the horrifying sight of an old woman lying face down on the pavement, convulsively shaking, a cane on the ground just out of reach of the trembling hand from which it had fallen. As I started to go to her aid, Nelly put her hand on my arm and said, "She lies here like this every day. She is a beggar." She added, "I don't know if she's putting on an act or not." I looked at her in disbelief. "Even if she's acting, she must be in great need," Nelly allowed. I then noticed a paper box with a few coins in it sitting on the ground near the cane. As the occasional passerby added a coin to the box, the woman took no notice; she simply continued to shake.

If Nina is acting, I think, she too must be impelled by desperation, but I decide that she is on the level. There is an atmosphere of truth about her. She is like one of Chekhov's guileless innocents; she is Anna Sergeyevna in late middle age. We rise from the seat and walk over to a semicircular stone pavilion at the edge of the cliff. Names and initials have been penciled on or scratched into the stone. In Chekhov's story "Lights," the hero, an engineer named Ananyev, speaks of a decisive youthful encounter in a stone summerhouse above the sea, and offers this theory of graffiti:

> When a man in a melancholy mood is left *tête-à-tête* with the sea, or any landscape which seems to him grandiose, there is always, for some reason, mixed with melancholy, a conviction that he will live and die in obscurity, and he reflectively snatches up a pencil and hastens to write his name on the first thing that comes handy. And that, I suppose, is why all convenient solitary nooks like my summer-house are always scrawled over in pencil or carved with pen-knives.

Ananyev is another of Chekhov's redeemed womanizers, though he undergoes his transformation of soul after hideously betraying

the story's gentle, trusting heroine, Kisotchka. The story was written eleven years before "The Lady with the Dog," and it was not
well received. "I was not entirely satisfied with your latest story," the
novelist and playwright Ivan Shcheglov wrote to Chekhov on May
29, 1888, and went on:

> Of course I swallowed it in one gulp, there is no question about that, be-
> cause everything you write is so appetizing and real that it can be easily
> and pleasantly swallowed. But that finale — "You can't figure out any-
> thing in this world . . ." — is abrupt; it is certainly the writer's job to fig-
> ure out what goes on in the heart of his hero; otherwise his psychology
> will remain unclear.

Chekhov replied, on June 9:

> I take the liberty of disagreeing with you. A psychologist should not pre-
> tend to understand what he does not understand. Moreover, a psycholo-
> gist should not convey the impression that he understands what no one
> understands. We shall not play the charlatan, and we will declare frankly
> that nothing is clear in this world. Only fools and charlatans know and
> understand everything.

To Suvorin, who had also criticized the story's apparent incon-
clusiveness (his letter has not survived), Chekhov wrote:

> The artist is not meant to be a judge of his characters and what they say;
> his only job is to be an impartial witness. I heard two Russians in a mud-
> dled conversation about pessimism, a conversation that solved nothing;
> all I am bound to do is reproduce that conversation exactly as I heard it.
> Drawing conclusions is up to the jury, that is, the readers. My only job is
> to be talented, that is, to know how to distinguish important testimony
> from unimportant, to place my characters in the proper light and speak
> their language.

These disclaimers — which have been much quoted and are of a
piece with what we know of Chekhov's attractive unpretentiousness
— cannot be taken at face value, of course. Chekhov understood
his characters very well (he invented them, after all), and his stories are hardly deadpan journalistic narratives. But his pose of journalistic uninquisitiveness is no mere writer's waffle produced to
ward off unwelcome discussion. It refers to something that is actually present in the work, to a kind of bark of the prosaic in which
Chekhov consistently encases a story's vital poetic core, as if such

protection were necessary for its survival. The stories have a straightforward, natural, rational, modern surface; they have been described as modest, delicate, gray. In fact, they are wild and strange, archaic and brilliantly colored. But the wildness and strangeness and archaism and brilliant colors are concealed, as are the complexity and difficulty. "Everything you write is so appetizing and real that it can be easily and pleasantly swallowed." We swallow a Chekhov story as if it were an ice, and we cannot account for our sense of repletion.

To be sure, all works of literary realism practice a kind of benevolent deception, lulling us into the state we enter at night when we mistake the fantastic productions of our imaginations for actual events. But Chekhov succeeds so well in rendering his illusion of realism and in hiding the traces of his surrealism that he remains the most misunderstood — as well as the most beloved — of the nineteenth-century Russian geniuses. In Russia, no less than in our country, possibly even more than in our country, Chekhov attracts a kind of sickening piety. You utter the word *Chekhov* and people arrange their features as if a baby deer had come into the room. "Ah, Chekhov!" my guide in Moscow — a plump, blond, heavily made-up woman named Sonia — had exclaimed. "He is not a Russian writer. He is a writer for all humanity!" Chekhov would have relished Sonia. He might have — in fact he had — used her as a character. She was a dead ringer for Natasha, the crass sister-in-law in *The Three Sisters,* who pushes her way into control of the Prozorov household and pushes out the three delicate, refined sisters. Sonia saw her job as guide as an exercise in control, and over the two days I spent with her I grew to detest her — though never in the serious way one comes to detest Natasha. My struggle with Sonia was almost always over small-stake points of touristic arrangement; and her power to get to me was, of course, further blunted by my journalist's wicked awareness of the incalculable journalistic value of poor character. After delivering herself of her estimate of Chekhov, Sonia went on to speak of her unpleasant experience with certain previous American clients who had put her down. "They considered themselves superior to me," she said, but when I asked her how they had shown this she couldn't say. "I just felt it." Then she added (as I somehow knew she would) that it was never the rich Americans who made her feel inferior, always the other kind.

One of my major battles with Sonia was over the issue of a two-hour visit to the Armory in the Kremlin, scheduled for the next day and, in Sonia's view, the high point of my — of every — trip to Russia. I asked her what was in the Armory, and, when she told me that it was a "magnificent" collection of armor and ancient gold and gems and Fabergé eggs, I said that that kind of thing didn't interest me, and that I would just as soon skip it. Sonia looked at me as if I had gone mad. Then she abruptly said that skipping the Armory was impossible: the tour was scheduled, and it was too late to change the schedule. I repeated that I would prefer not to go to the Armory, and Sonia lapsed into silence. We were in a car, on our way to Melikhovo, Chekhov's country house, forty miles south of Moscow. Sonia began to converse in Russian with Vladimir, the driver, and continued to do so for many miles. In St. Petersburg, when Nelly spoke to our driver Sergei — usually to give him some direction — she did so tersely and apologetically. Sonia used her talk with the driver as a form of punishment. Finally, she turned to me, and said, "It is essential that you see the Armory — even for only forty-five minutes." "All right," I said. But Sonia was not satisfied. My attitude was so clearly wrong. "Tell me something," Sonia said. "When you were in St. Petersburg, did you go to the Hermitage?" "Yes," I said. "Well," Sonia said in a tone of triumph, "the Armory is much more important than the Hermitage."

When we arrived at Melikhovo, I recognized the house from pictures I had seen, but was surprised by the grounds, which were a disorderly spread of wild vegetation, haphazardly placed trees, and untended flower beds. There seemed to be no plan; the grounds made no sense as the setting for a house. Chekhov bought Melikhovo in the winter of 1892 and moved there with his parents, his sister, and his younger brothers in the spring. It was a small, run-down estate, which Chekhov rapidly transformed: the uncomfortable house was made snug and agreeable, kitchen and flower gardens were put in, an orchard was planted, a pond dug, the surrounding fields planted with rye and clover and oats. It was characteristic of Chekhov to make things work; thirteen years earlier, he had arrived in Moscow, to start medical school, and pulled his family out of poverty by what seems like sheer force of character. The father's store had failed, and he had fled to Moscow to escape debtor's prison. Alexander and Nikolai were already in Moscow studying at the university, and the mother and sister and younger brothers followed; but sixteen-year-old Anton was left behind in Taganrog to finish high school. Little is known about the three years Chekhov spent alone in Taganrog. He boarded with the man who had, like Lopakhin in *The Cherry Orchard,* bailed out the family at a crucial moment for the price of their home. He was not a brilliant student, but he graduated and received a scholarship from the town for his further studies. He was a tall, robust boy, with a large head, a genial nature, and a gift for comedy. (He had entertained his family and now entertained his classmates with imitations and skits.)

When Chekhov rejoined his family in Moscow, in 1880, the possessor of what the critic James Wood has called a "strange, sourceless maturity," he quickly became its head. The authoritarian father, now a pitiable failure, had allowed the family to sink into disorderly destitution. The elder brothers made contributions — Alexander through writing sketches for humor magazines, and Nikolai through magazine illustrations — but they lived dissolute lives, and only when Anton, too, began writing humorous sketches did the family's fortunes change. He wrote strictly for money; if some other way of making money had come to hand, he would have taken it. The humor writing was wretchedly paid, but Chekhov wrote so quickly and easily and unceasingly that he was able to bring in considerable income. In the early writings, no hint of the author of "The Duel" and "The Lady with the Dog" is to be found. Most of the sketches were broadly humorous, like pieces in college humor magazines, and if some of them are less juvenile than others, and a few make one smile, none of them are distinguished. Chekhov began to show signs of becoming Chekhov only when he turned his hand to writing short fiction that wasn't funny. By 1886, his writing was attracting serious critical attention as well as bringing in real money. Because of Chekhov's earnings from his writings (he never made any money as a physician; he mostly treated peasants, free), the family was able to move to progressively better quarters in Moscow. The purchase of Melikhovo was a culminating product of Chekhov's literary success — and of the illusion (one that Russian writers, Chekhov included, are particularly good at mocking) that life in the country is a solution to the problem of living.

With his characteristic energy and dispatch, Chekhov organized his family so that there was a productive division of labor — the mother cooked, the sister took care of the kitchen garden, the youngest brother, Ivan, did the agriculture, and Anton took charge of horticulture, for which he proved to have great talent. (The father, who had been and remained a religious fanatic, would retreat to his room for his observances and the mixing of herbal remedies.) Chekhov came remarkably close to living out his pastoral ideal, and even passed the test that city people who moved to the country in nineteenth-century Russia invariably, ingloriously flunked — of being helpful to the peasants. Chekhov built three schools, donated his services as a doctor, and worked in famine and cholera relief — all the while writing some of his best stories and almost never being without a houseful of visitors. (His frequent, abrupt removals to Moscow or St. Petersburg suggest that the problem of living remained.)

I recognized the house. Actually, however, I was seeing not the one in the photographs — which had been torn down in the 1920s — but a replica, built in the late 1940s. (Resurrecting destroyed buildings seems to be a national tic. In Moscow, I saw a huge church with gold domes which was a recently completed replica of one of the churches Stalin had wantonly torn down.) The interiors had been carefully restored, re-created from photographs supplied by Maria Chekhova, then in her eighties. The rooms were small and appealingly furnished; they gave a sense of a pleasant, very well run home. The walls were covered with Morris-print-like wallpapers, and over them paintings and family photographs hung in dense arrangements. Everything was simple, handsome, unaffected. But I think that Chekhov would have found it absurd. The idea of rebuilding his house from scratch would have offended his sense of the fitness of things. I can imagine the look of irony on his face as he walked through the rooms — and listened to the prepared speech of our tour guide, Ludmilla. Ludmilla was a youngish woman with glasses, dressed in trousers and a shabby maroon snow jacket, who was full of knowledge of Chekhov's life but had read little of his work. She spoke of Chekhov with a radiant expression on her face. She told me (through Sonia) that a good deal of the furniture and many objects in the house were original; when the house was being torn down, the local peasants had sacked it but during the restoration returned much of what they had taken. I asked if they had been forced to do so by the Soviet authorities, and she said, "Oh, no. They did so gladly. Everyone loved Anton Pavlovich." When I questioned her about how she came to be working at the museum, she gave a long reply: She had never been able to read Chekhov; his writing left her cold. But one day she visited Melikhovo (she lived in a nearby town) and while in the house had some sort of incredible spiritual experience, which she cannot explain. She kept returning to Melikhovo — it drew her like a magnet — and finally the director of the museum had given her a job.

After finishing the tour of the ersatz house and the disorderly garden, Ludmilla walked out to the exit with Sonia and me, and from her answer to one of my questions it appeared that she wasn't paid for her work. "So you work here as a volunteer," I said. "No," she said. She just wasn't paid, the way many people in Russia were not being paid now. Wages were frequently "delayed" for months, even years. I asked Ludmilla how she lived if she wasn't paid. Did she have another job that did pay? Sonia — not relaying my question — looked at me angrily and said, "We will not talk about this. This is not your subject. We will talk about Chekhov."

I debated with myself whether to challenge Sonia, and decided I would. I said, "Look, if we're going to talk about Chekhov, we need to say that Anton Pavlovich cared about truth above all else. He did not look away from reality. People not being paid for work is something he would have talked about — not brushed away with 'Let's talk about Chekhov.'" I sounded a little ridiculous to myself — like someone doing an imitation of a character in a socialist-realist novel — but I enjoyed Sonia's discomposure, and when she started to answer I cut her off with "Tell Ludmilla what I just said." Sonia obeyed, and Ludmilla, smiling her sweet smile, said, "This is why I find it hard to read Chekhov. There is too much sadness in it. It is his spirituality that attracts me — the spirituality I receive from learning about his life."

On the drive back to Moscow, Sonia praised the "good taste" of Melikhovo, before relapsing into conversation with Vladimir. He was a large, swarthy man of about fifty, wearing a black leather coat and exuding a New York taxi driver's gruff *savoir-faire*. The contrast between him and Sergei, my St. Petersburg driver, a slender young

man who dressed in jeans and carried a book, was like the contrast
between St. Petersburg and Moscow themselves. St. Petersburg was
small and faded and elegant and a little unreal; Moscow was big
and unlovely and the real thing in a city. St. Petersburg came at you
sideways; Moscow immediately delivered the message of its scale
and power. Chekhov loved Moscow and had reserved feelings
about St. Petersburg, even though his literary career only got properly under way when, in 1882, the St. Petersburg editor and publisher A. N. Leiken invited him to write for his humorous weekly
Fragments and then moved into full gear when he began writing for
Suvorin's St. Petersburg newspaper *New Times*. He would visit St.
Petersburg, first to see Leiken and then Suvorin, but he never really warmed to the city. In his fiction, people from St. Petersburg
tend to be suspect (in "An Anonymous Story," an unsympathetic
character named Orlov is described as a St. Petersburg dandy) or
apologetic ("I was born in cold, idle Petersburg," the sympathetic
Tuzenbach says in *The Three Sisters*). In St. Petersburg, Chekhov suffered the worst literary failure of his life, with *The Seagull* — compa-
rable to Henry James's failure with *Guy Domville*. At its première, at
the Alexandrinsky Theatre in 1896, it was booed and jeered, and
the reviews were savage. The failure is generally attributed to a special circumstance of the première: it was a benefit for a beloved
comic actress named E. I. Levkeeva, and so the audience was
largely made up of Levkeeva fans, who expected hilarity and, to
their disbelief and growing outrage, got Symbolism. At its next performance, which was attended by a normal Petersburg audience,
The Seagull was calmly and appreciatively received and positive criticism began to appear in the newspapers. But by that time Chekhov
had crawled away to Melikhovo, and believed that he was finished
as a playwright. "Never again will I write plays or have them staged,"
he wrote to Suvorin.

Because of Chekhov's slender and ambivalent ties to St. Petersburg, the city has no Chekhov museum, but a few of his letters and
manuscripts have strayed into its Pushkin Museum, and on the
morning of my first day in Nelly's charge she took me to inspect
them. We sat at a table covered with dark green cloth, opposite a
young, round-faced archivist named Tatyana, who displayed each
document like a jeweler displaying a costly necklace or brooch.
(Once, when Nelly reached out her hand toward a document,
Tatyana playfully slapped it.) Chekhov's small, spidery handwrit-

ing, very delicate and light, brought to mind Tolstoy's description of him as reported by Maxim Gorky: "What a dear, beautiful man; he is modest and quiet like a girl. And he walks like a girl." One of Tatyana's exhibits was a letter of 1887 to the writer Dmitri Grigorovich, commenting on a story of Grigorovich's called "Karelin's Dream." Today, Grigorovich's work is no longer read; his name figures in literary history largely because of a fan letter he wrote to Chekhov in March 1886. At the time, Grigorovich was sixty-four and one of the major literary celebrities of the day. He wrote to tell the twenty-six-year-old Chekhov, "You have *real* talent — a talent which places you in the front rank among writers in the new generation." Grigorovich went on to counsel Chekhov to slow down, to stop writing so much, to save himself for large, serious literary effort. "Cease to write hurriedly. I do not know what your financial situation is. If it is poor, it would be better for you to go hungry, as we did in our day, and save your impressions for a mature, finished work, written not in one sitting but during the happy hours of inspiration."

Chekhov wrote back:

Your letter, my kind, warmly beloved herald of glad tidings, struck me like a thunderbolt. I nearly wept, I was profoundly moved, and even now I feel that it has left a deep imprint on my soul. . . . I, indeed, can find neither words nor actions to show my gratitude. You know with what eyes ordinary people look upon such outstanding people like yourself, hence you may realize what your letter means for my self-esteem. . . . I am as in a daze. I lack the ability to judge whether or not I merit this great reward.

Chekhov went on to acknowledge the haste and carelessness with which he wrote:

I don't recall a single tale of mine over which I have worked more than a day, and "The Hunter," which pleased you, I wrote in the bathhouse! I have written my stories the way reporters write up their notes about fires — mechanically, half-consciously, caring nothing about either the reader or myself.

And:

What first drove me to take a critical view of my writing was . . . a letter from Suvorin. I began to think of writing some purposeful piece, but nevertheless I did not have faith in my own literary direction.

And now, all of a sudden, your letter arrived. You must forgive the comparison, but it had the same effect on me as a government order "to get out of the city in twenty-four hours." That is, I suddenly felt the need for haste, to get out of this rut, where I am stuck, as quickly as possible.

In his letter about "Karelin's Dream," Chekhov gives a remarkable account of the way being cold at night gets into one's dreams:

When at night the quilt falls off I begin to dream of huge slippery stones, of cold autumnal water, naked banks — and all this dim, misty, without a patch of blue sky; sad and dejected like one who has lost his way, I look at the stones and feel that for some reason I cannot avoid crossing a deep river; I see then small tugs that drag huge barges, floating beams. . . . All this is infinitely gray, damp, and dismal. When I run from the river I come across the fallen cemetery gates, funerals, my school teachers. . . . And all the time I am cold through and through with that oppressive nightmare-like cold which is impossible in waking life, and which is only felt by those who are asleep. . . . When I feel cold I always dream of my teacher of scripture, a learned priest of imposing appearance, who insulted my mother when I was a little boy; I dream of vindictive, implacable, intriguing people, smiling with spiteful glee — such as one can never see in waking life. The laughter at the carriage window is a characteristic symptom of Karelin's nightmare. When in dreams one feels the presence of some evil will, the inevitable ruin brought about by some outside force, one always hears something like such laughter.

These dreams, in their atmosphere of dread and uncanniness, put one in mind of the novels of Dostoyevsky and the paintings of Edvard Munch, and hint at anxieties of which Chekhov preferred never to speak. Chekhov's biographers regularly note his elusive reserve, even as they attempt to break it down. With the opening of the Soviet archives, hitherto unknown details of Chekhov's love life and sex life have emerged. But the value of this new information — much of it derived from passages or phrases cut out of Chekhov's published letters by the puritanical Soviet censorship, and absurdly said to make him "more human" — is questionable. That Chekhov was not uninterested in or prudish about sex is hardly revealed by his use of a coarse word in a letter; it is implicit in the stories and plays. Chekhov would be unperturbed, and probably even amused, by the stir the restored cuts have created — as if the documentary proof of sexual escapades or of incidents of impotence disclosed anything essential about him, anything that crosses the boundary between his inner and outer life. Chekhov's privacy is safe from the biographer's attempts upon it — as, indeed, are all privacies, even those of the most apparently open and even exhibitionistic natures. The letters and journals we leave behind and the impressions we have made on our contemporaries are the mere husk of the kernel of our essential life. When we die, the kernel is buried with us. This is the horror and pity of death and the reason for the inescapable triviality of biography.

The attentive reader of Chekhov will notice a piece of plagiarism I have just committed. The image of the kernel and the husk comes from another famous passage in "The Lady with the Dog," one that appears in its last section. Gurov, as you will recall, after parting with Anna at the end of the summer and returning to his loveless marriage in Moscow, found that he couldn't get her out of his mind, traveled to the provincial town where she lived with the husband *she* didn't love, and is now clandestinely meeting with her in a hotel in Moscow, to which she comes every month or so, telling her husband she is seeing a specialist. One snowy morning, on his way to the hotel, Gurov reflects on his situation (all the while conversing with his daughter, whom he will drop off at school before proceeding to his tryst):

> He had two lives: one, open, seen and known by all who cared to know, full of relative truth and of relative falsehood, exactly like the lives of his friends and acquaintances; and another life running its course in secret. And through some strange, perhaps accidental, conjunction of circumstances, everything that was essential, of interest and of value to him, everything in which he was sincere and did not deceive himself, everything that made the kernel of his life, was hidden from other people; and all that was false in him, the sheath in which he hid himself to conceal the truth — such, for instance, as his work in the bank, his discussions at the club . . . his presence with his wife at anniversary festivities — all that was open. And he judged of others by himself, not believing in what he saw, and always believing that every man had his real, most interesting life under the cover of secrecy and under the cover of night. All personal life rested on secrecy, and possibly it was partly on that account that civilized man was so nervously anxious that personal privacy should be respected.

"The Lady with the Dog" is said to be Chekhov's riposte to *Anna Karenina,* his defense of illicit love against Tolstoy's harsh (if ambivalent) condemnation of it. But Chekhov's Anna (if this is what it is) bears no real resemblance to Tolstoy's; comparing the two only draws attention to the differences between Chekhov's realism and Tolstoy's. Gurov is no Vronsky, and Anna Von Diderits is no Anna Karenina. Neither of the Chekhov characters has the particularity, the vivid lifelikeness of the Tolstoy lovers. They are rather indistinct, more like figures in an allegory than like characters in a novel. Nor is Chekhov concerned, as Tolstoy is, with adultery as a social phenomenon. In *Anna Karenina,* the lovers occupy only a section of a crowded canvas; in "The Lady with the Dog," the lovers fill the canvas. Other people appear in the story — the crowd at the Yalta harbor, a Moscow official with whom Gurov plays cards, the daughter he walks to school, a couple of servants — but they are shadowy figures, without names. (Even the dog is unnamed — when Gurov arrives at Anna's house, and sees a servant walking it, Chekhov makes a point of noting that "in his excitement he could not remember the dog's name.") The story has a close, hermetic atmosphere. No one knows of the affair, or suspects its existence. It is as if it were taking place in a sealed box made of dark glass from which the lovers can see out but no one can see in. The story enacts what the passage about Gurov's double life states. It can be read as an allegory of interiority. The beauty of Gurov and Anna's secret love — and of interior life — is precisely its hiddenness. Chekhov often said that he hated lies more than anything. "The Lady with the Dog" plays with the paradox that a lie — a husband deceiving a wife or a wife deceiving a husband — can be the fulcrum of truth of feeling, a vehicle of authenticity. (Tolstoy would argue that this is the kind of self-deception adulterers classically indulge in, and that a lie is a lie.) But the story's most interesting and complicated paradox lies in the inversion of the inner/outer formula by which imaginative literature is perforce propelled. Even as Gurov hugs his secret to himself, we know all about it. If privacy is life's most precious possession, it is fiction's least considered one. A fictional character is a being who has no privacy, and who stands before the reader with his "real, most interesting life" nakedly exposed. We never see people in life as clearly as we see the people in novels, stories, and plays; there is a veil between ourselves and even our closest intimates, blurring us to each other. By intimacy we mean something much more modest than the glaring exposure to which the souls of fictional characters are regularly held up. We know things about Gurov and Anna — especially about Gurov, since the story is told from his point of view — that they don't know about each other, and feel no discomfort in our voyeurism. We consider it our due as readers. It does not occur to us that the privacy rights we are so nervously anxious to safeguard for ourselves should be extended to fictional characters. But, interestingly, it does seem to occur to Chekhov. If he cannot draw the mantle of reticence over his characters that he draws over himself — and still call himself a fiction writer — he can stop short of fully exercising his fiction writer's privilege of omniscience. He can hold back, he can leave his characters a little obscured, their motives a little mysterious. It is this reticence that Shcheglov and Suvorin were responding to in their criticism of "Lights." Chekhov's replies, with their appealing expressions of epistemological humility and journalistic detachment, skirt the issue, putting his interlocutors off the scent of his characters' secrets.

In a story called "Difficult People," written in 1886, we can see the shoot from which Gurov's meditation on double life will grow. A dreadful row has taken place at a provincial family dinner table between an authoritarian father and a rebellious son. The son storms out of the house and, full of bitterness and hatred, sets off for Moscow on foot. Then:

"Look out!" He heard behind him a loud voice.
An old lady of his acquaintance, a landowner of the neighborhood, drove past him in a light, elegant landau. He bowed to her, and smiled all over his face. And at once he caught himself in that smile, which was so out of keeping with his gloomy mood. Where did it come from if his whole heart was full of vexation and misery. And he thought nature itself had given man this capacity for lying, that even in difficult moments of spiritual strain he might be able to hide the secrets of his nest as the fox and the wild duck do. Every family has its joys and its horrors, but however great they may be, it's hard for an outsider's eye to see them; they are a secret.

Chekhov hid the secrets of his literary nest as well as those of his personal one; he was closemouthed about his compositional methods and destroyed most of his drafts. But he didn't merely withhold information about his literary practice; the practice itself was a kind of exercise in withholding. In his letter of 1886 to Grigoro-vich, Chekhov noted his curious habit of doing everything he could not to "waste" on any story "the images and scenes dear to me which — God knows why — I have treasured and kept carefully hidden," and, writing to Suvorin in October 1888, he again cited "the images which seem best to me, which I love and jealously guard, lest I spend and spoil them," adding, "All that I now write displeases and bores me, but what sits in my head interests, excites and moves me."

In the much anthologized story "The Kiss" (1887), Chekhov gave brilliant form to his sense of the danger of dislodging what sits in one's head from its place of safety. A brigade on the march spends the night in a provincial town, and its nineteen officers are invited for evening tea at the house of the local squire, a retired lieutenant general named Von Rabbek. The central consciousness of the story is Ryabovitch, "a little officer in spectacles, with sloping shoulders, and whiskers like a lynx's," who thinks of himself as "the shyest, most modest, and most undistinguished officer in the whole bri-gade." At Von Rabbek's house, Ryabovitch is struck by the social adroitness of the host and hostess and their grown son and daugh-ter, who have invited the officers strictly out of duty, and at a time when it is inconvenient to do so — they are having a house party — but who put on a dazzling performance of hospitality. "Von Rabbek and this family skillfully drew the officers into the discussion, and meanwhile kept a sharp lookout over their glasses and mouths, to see whether all of them were drinking, whether all had enough sugar, why some one was not eating cakes or not drinking brandy. And the longer Ryabovitch watched and listened, the more he was attracted by this insincere but splendidly disciplined family." Dur-ing a period of dancing, in which Ryabovitch does not participate ("He had never once danced in his whole life, and he had never once in his life put his arm round the waist of a respectable woman"), he follows the Von Rabbek son and some officers to a bil-liard room in another part of the house, and then, feeling himself in the way (he does not play billiards, either), decides to return to the drawing room. But in retracing his steps Ryabovitch makes a wrong turn and finds himself in a small dark room. Suddenly, a young woman rushes toward him, murmurs "At last!" and kisses him. Realizing her mistake — she had come to the room for a lovers' tryst, clearly — she shrieks and runs off. The encounter has a momentous effect on Ryabovitch. It is almost like a conversion experience:

> Something strange was happening to him. . . . His neck, round which soft, fragrant arms had so lately been clasped, seemed to him to be anointed with oil; on his left cheek near his moustache where the unknown had kissed him there was a faint chilly tingling sensation, as from peppermint drops. . . . He was full of a strange new feeling which grew stronger and stronger. . . . He quite forgot that he was round-shouldered and uninteresting, that he had lynx-like whiskers and an "undistinguished appearance." (That was how his appearance had been described by some ladies whose conversation he had accidentally overheard.)

The next morning, the brigade leaves the town, and throughout the day's march Ryabovitch remains under the spell of the kiss, which has acted on his imagination like a powerful drug, releasing delicious fantasies of romantic love. At the end of the day, in the tent after supper, he feels the need to tell his comrades about his adventure:

> He began describing very minutely the incident of the kiss, and a moment later relapsed into silence. . . . In the course of that moment he had told everything, and it surprised him dreadfully to find how short a time it took him to tell it. He had imagined that he could have been telling the story of the kiss till next morning.

One of the officers, a sleazy womanizer named Lobytko, is moved to respond with a crude story about a sexual encounter in a train. Ryabovitch vows "never to confide again." Twelve years later, Chekhov will write another version of this scene, in "The Lady with the Dog." After Gurov returns home from Yalta, he is "tormented by an intense desire to confide his memories to some one," and one evening, as he is leaving a Moscow club, he impulsively says to an official with whom he has been playing cards:

> "If only you knew what a fascinating woman I made the acquaintance of in Yalta!"

The official got into his sledge and was driving away, but turned sud-
denly and shouted:
"Dmitri Dmitrich!"
"What?"
"You were right this evening: the sturgeon was a bit too strong!"

In both cases, something lovely and precious has been defiled by
the vulgar gaze of the outer world. Both men immediately regret
their impulse to confide. But the telling scene in "The Kiss" has an
additional moral — a literary one. Ryabovitch makes the painful
discovery that every novice writer makes about the gap that lies between thinking and writing. ("It surprised him dreadfully to find
how short a time it took him to tell it.") The gossamer images that
sit in one's head have to be transformed into some more durable
material — that of artful narration — if they are not to dissolve
into nothing when they hit the chilly outer air. Chekhov lodges the
cautionary incident of Ryabovitch's artless blurting out within his
own artful narration. What poor Ryabovitch fails to communicate
to his comrades in his amateur's innocence Chekhov succeeds in
communicating to us with his professional's guile. He is like the
practiced Von Rabbeks, who perform their function of giving pleasure because they must and because they know how. "You can do
nothing by wisdom and holiness if God has not given you the gift,"
a monk in "On Easter Eve" (1886) says in a discussion of the
poetics of certain hymns of praise in the Russian Orthodox liturgy
called *akathistoi*. "Everything must be harmonious, brief, and complete. . . . Every line must be beautified in every way; there must be
flowers and lightning and wind and sun and all the objects of the
visible world." Chekhov's own literary enterprise could hardly be
better described. His stories and plays — even the darkest among
them — are hymns of praise. Flowers and lightning and wind and
sun and all the objects of the visible world appear in them as they
appear in the work of no other writer. In almost every Chekhov
work there is a moment when we suddenly feel as Ryabovitch felt
when the young woman entered the room and kissed him.

LAWRENCE MILLMAN

Daughter of the Wind

FROM *Islands*

AT TIMES during my visit to the Mediterranean island of Pantelleria the wind sounded like a pneumatic drill gone awry, at other times like the high-pitched howling of Eskimo sled dogs, and at still other times like a melancholy riff from a bluesman's sax. Once it managed a pretty good imitation of Frank Sinatra crooning "I've Got You under My Skin," albeit with an uncharacteristic vibrato. Another time it whisked off my cap and deposited it unceremoniously on a nearby Bronze Age tomb, laughing shrilly as I went to retrieve it.

Alternately bullying, keening, buffeting, and whistling, the wind on Pantelleria blows twelve knots or more virtually every day of the year, including the day I arrived. On that day a sirocco was scattering bits of the Sahara around the island.

The legendary ill wind, sometimes referred to as "the African pest," reputedly causes indolence, insomnia, and even depression. I asked the waiter at my hotel whether he was feeling any of its effects. Perhaps he regarded diners through a fog of ennui?

He shook his head rather more vigorously than one is supposed to shake a head when a sirocco is blowing.

"Pantescans feel out of sorts only when there is no wind," he said.

A mistral blew in that evening. A cleansing wind, it swept away all evidence of the Sahara. When I went out for a postprandial stroll, instead of being blown north by the sirocco, I found myself blown in a southerly direction, which became southwesterly with the arrival of a levanter. I braced myself against being picked up and flung to Tunisia, whose flickering fairyland of lights forty-four miles away looked almost close enough to touch.

I know what you're thinking: that not even the wind god Aeolus, try as he might, could have flung me all the way to Tunisian shores. But on an island where 2,500-year-old cisterns are still in use, where donkeys move with nineteen different gaits and the fabled voyager Ulysses is spoken of like a contemporary, anything seems possible, even a levitation across forty-four miles of sea.

So it was not altogether surprising that when I woke up the next morning, I heard the wind imitating the Three Tenors in a knock-down, drag-out fight. (Pavarotti, being the heaviest, won.)

At first I felt a bit disoriented, although not so much by the island's bravura winds as by its apparent borrowings from other places. The volcanic landscape reminded me of Iceland, the architecture suggested Bible lands, the baking sun evoked Africa, and the stone wall traceries put me in mind of Ireland's Aran Islands. Jets of steam issuing from the ground made me think of Yellowstone, while the place names — Bukkuram, for instance, or Farkikala — seemed to have been stolen from *The Arabian Nights.*

This curious hodgepodge isle is, in fact, part of Italy. Most of my traveled friends had never heard of it; one, a waggish Irishman, said, "Pantelleria? Sounds like a good place for stealing knickers off clotheslines." (The name actually is a corruption of the Arabic phrase *bint-al rion,* which means "daughter of the wind.") Another friend *had* heard of it: His first wife had run off with an Italian nobleman, and the place they chose to hide from the world was Pantelleria.

Once upon a time, however, everyone had heard of the island. Bronze Age people from North Africa, Phoenicians, Romans, Carthaginians, Vandals, Byzantines, Arabs, Normans, Turkish sea raiders, Spanish, and Bourbons — all passed through its continually revolving door, marauding, setting up a government, working the island's obsidian deposits, or just pausing from their travels for a while. Such is the virtue, or the burden, of being located at the intersection of time-honored Mediterranean shipping lanes.

In 1860 Italy annexed the thirty-two-square-mile island and began sending political undesirables there. Mussolini, in the 1930s, referred to it as "The Black Pearl of the Mediterranean" and, in an unusual use for a pearl, made the island a military base, with the result that the Allies carpet-bombed it during World War II. The port town of Pantelleria was flattened; after the war it was rebuilt in ugly low-rise concrete. To bomb it again, an unkind person might say, would be a mercy.

After so many assaults and flattenings, you might think this would be a paranoid island, given to the constant nagging question: What unwanted visitor will batter at our door next? But Pantelleria is more or less free from neurosis. "I embrace everything," it seems to say, and then proceeds to assimilate whatever fetches up on its shores, be it an architectural style, a foreign physiognomy, or a method of cooking fish. In doing so, it has managed not only to keep its sanity but also, paradoxically, to remain unlike anything else.

Consider the island's traditional *dammuso* houses. With their barrel vaults, white stucco domes, three-foot-thick walls, and cubic shapes, they suggest the work of invaders — certainly the Arabs, possibly the Phoenicians, and maybe even Bronze Age Sesioti, who constructed similarly domelike mausoleums. At the same time, *dammusi* are so peculiar to Pantelleria, so spare and basaltic, that they suggest not human influence so much as a geology that's taken a skilled architectural turn.

If life's a beach, then life has bypassed Pantelleria; the island has no beaches. Instead, its shoreline consists of basalt so fierce that a person who elects to lie on it runs the risk of impalement. So the wise visitor does as Pantescans themselves do; he looks inland, away from the invader-dark sea.

Thus it was that one day I went for a backcountry trek with a local naturalist named Giuseppe. Giuseppe's English was nearly as bad as my Italian, a fact that became apparent when a brass-colored mutt tried to mate with my leg. "This god wants sex," Giuseppe observed. No matter. My guide possessed the innate Italian talent for making gestures speak as eloquently as words.

From the village of Sibà, we walked north into the teeth of a wind that sounded like an amalgam of Philip Glass's music and flapping laundry. Within half an hour it had shifted to the mellow throatiness of early Billie Holiday.

But the musicality was no boon to agriculture. The olive trees here looked like bonsai versions of the proverbially hardy Mediterranean evergreen; they'd been trained to grow outward rather than upward, in order to avoid being snipped off by the wind. Nearby grapevines were surrounded by windbreaks of cactus; where the cactus had blown over, the poor vines looked like victims of an anti-botanical blitzkrieg.

In one vineyard Giuseppe bent down and picked up a white terra-cotta shard. "Punic," he said. A moment later he picked up a reddish piece of ceramic. "Roman," he declared. Then he pointed to a few blue and white tiles and told me they were Arab, probably from around the year 1000. All of the island's influences seemed to be at our feet.

"Is this an archaeological site?" I asked.

"No," he said, "just an ordinary Pantescan vineyard."

We passed several *dammusi* so Middle Eastern in appearance that I half expected to see Arab script on their walls. Their domed roofs, designed to collect rainwater and channel it to underground cisterns, gleamed in the midday sun like giant white bubbles. In front of one, a large-paunched man with burst shirt buttons was splayed over a bench and drinking heartily from a flagon of wine — an image straight out of Brueghel.

The scrub brush of Mediterranean *macchia* soon replaced the terraced vineyards. The resinous scent, comprising bush oak, maritime pine, rock rose, honeysuckle, and myrtle, nearly lifted me off my feet. I also saw enough wild herbs — thyme, fennel, rosemary, sage, oregano, and borage to name a few — to stock a kitchen cabinet. Giuseppe pointed to some pale pink mallow flowers: Did I know they made a superior herbal tea? Then he pointed to some rue *(Ruta chaliepensis)* and said Pantescans use it to make an unguent for hemorrhoids.

Later I read that the island hosts more than 570 varieties of plants. All thanks to the incessant winds that blow such an abundance of seeds here from Europe and North Africa (and bring relief to local hemorrhoid sufferers).

We now began climbing a partially collapsed volcanic cone called Gelfiser. There was black scoriaceous rock everywhere, including the inside of my hiking boot. Where there wasn't rock, there were fissures in the rock — Gelfiser is derived from Arabic words meaning "fissure mountain." I stepped into one of these fissures and ended up with a colorful souvenir of the island on the lower part of my leg.

At one point I looked around, and there seemed to be nothing but unspoiled, untrammeled nature in every direction. "Marlboro Country," Giuseppe announced with a sweeping gesture of his hand. Yet we were no more than a few miles "as the cow flies" (in Giuseppe's phase) from the modest bustle of Pantelleria Town, and even closer to an American hilltop radar facility.

At last we arrived at our destination, a large cave extending deep into Gelfiser. Recently, a friend of Giuseppe's had descended into the bowels of this cave and discovered a rusty Norman sword sticking upright in the rock. Shades of Excalibur! Now Giuseppe wanted to search for other relics, possibly bits of ceramic, possibly bones, that might help explain what the mysterious sword was doing there.

We began rappelling into the cave's gloom. The passage was tight, and it soon got tighter. All at once I felt violently claustrophobic. It was too dark for me to read my Italian dictionary, so I just yelled out "claustrophobia" in English. As it happened, the word was almost exactly the same in Italian.

"No more *caverna* for you, my friend," Giuseppe said after we were outside again. Well, that wasn't entirely true. We investigated another, less deep cave and found a scattering of Arab tiles just inside the entrance. I got the impression that you could bend down almost anywhere on Pantelleria, even seemingly inaccessible places, and pick up some sort of artifact.

As we hiked back, the Mediterranean suddenly came into view. Peacock blue around the island, it clung to the horizon like a filament of liquid silver.

"*Bello,* eh?" I said.

"*Puah!*" Giuseppe exclaimed, half in jest but half-seriously, too. He said he'd grown up with such a strong dislike of the sea that he never learned to swim and, to this day, refused to eat seafood, even the Pantescan specialty *couscous di pesce.* A member of his family had been kidnapped by Turkish sea raiders, he said by way of explanation. He gestured northwest to indicate where they'd come from.

I asked him when this unfortunate incident had occurred.

"Not long ago," he said, adding, "in the seventeenth century."

Wherever I went on Pantelleria, I felt vigilant eyes gazing in my direction.

The chinks in the Bronze Age tombs at Mursia seemed to be

squinting at me as if they were trying to figure out whether I was friend or foe, harmless visitor or rapacious sea raider. *Dammuso* windows seemed to look at me hopefully, as if I might turn out to be another Giorgio Armani. In Gadir the underwear-to-evening-wear designer had bought and renovated a set of *dammusi,* thus providing them with a role considerably more elegant than the one to which history had accustomed them.

Pantescans themselves often gazed at me as if I were from another planet. Once, when I was clambering down from the hill of San Marco, site of first a Punic acropolis, then a Roman one, an old woman interrupted her journey to the well, set down her buckets, and gave me a stare that must have lasted a full minute.

At the time I assumed the woman was only registering her curiosity about outsiders. And with my "Shiitake Happens" T-shirt, my Ouje-Bougoumou Cree cap, and my diligent scribbling, I was a slightly more flagrant outsider than most. But when I discovered a dead fritillary butterfly floating in my cappuccino the next morning, I became concerned. Then in short order I wrenched my knee doing the gentlest of sidestrokes in Specchio di Venere lake and nearly got blown off the vertiginous cliffs at Salto la Vecchia by a sudden gust of wind.

Aha, I told myself, you've been given *malocciu,* otherwise known as the evil eye.

People who believe in this affliction say it can reduce whole cities to ruin. I didn't feel like waiting around to see whether I myself would be reduced to ruin, so I paid a visit to a squat, ancient woman named Angela. Angela was one of the island's evil-eye doctors.

First thing Angela asked me was more or less the same question I'd been asked on small islands in the Pacific, in the Caribbean, and indeed all over the world: Did I know her cousin in Brooklyn? She seemed astonished when I told her I hardly knew a soul in Brooklyn.

Then she got down to business. She brought out a pasta bowl and filled it with water, added a dash of salt, and then held it next to my chest and began uttering a succession of barely audible paternosters and Ave Marias. After making the sign of the cross over the bowl, she put three drops of olive oil in the water. If the drops dispersed over the surface, I'd been *pigghiatu ad occiu* (literally, "taken by the eye"), she said; if not, I was just having a run of bad luck.

The drops formed solid globules on the water.

I was relieved. More than relieved, exultant. Seldom have I been so pleased with my own bad luck. I offered Angela several thousand lire, but she said she never accepted money for her services. So, in return for those services, I promised to phone her cousin in Brooklyn when I got home. (I did make the call, only to learn that the cousin had died some years ago. News travels slowly to outposts like Pantelleria.)

As for the woman who'd given me such a lingering stare, I later found out that she was half-blind and probably thought I was one of her pigs, escaped from its pen.

"We are not Sicilian," Pantescans declare, adding that their immediate neighbors to the north are either arrogant or mafiosi, or sometimes both. Certain Pantescans will even deny being Italian; their ancestry is Arab, they'll tell you, or if not exclusively Arab, at least an Arab-Italian mix, with perhaps a dollop of Spaniard thrown in for good measure.

In regard to their hospitality, Pantescans did in fact strike me as being more Arab than European. I could imagine them wining and dining Mother Teresa and Attila the Hun with equal devotion to their respective needs. Certainly, they looked after *my* needs in much the same way a desert Bedouin might look after a famished guest.

For instance, when I inquired about the taste of moray eels, a local delicacy, a toothsome fillet of moray appeared on my plate the next day. Or I would wander into a bar, only to have a glass of vintage *passito* wine pressed on me with the bartender's compliments. Or I'd have peanut butter graciously put before me at mealtime, on the assumption that it was my national food.

At one point I mentioned my interest in mushrooms to one of my guides, and an hour later he showed up with a bucketful of mud. Apparently, my pronunciation of *funghi,* the word for mushrooms, sounded not unlike *fanghi,* the word for muds, and rather than question my sanity (the guest is always right), he'd gone out and gathered the choicest muds he could find.

But it was the offerings of wine that I'll most remember. Along with the capers, wine is Pantelleria's most important export, and I often felt I was being considered for the role of the island's North American jobber. I'd be marveling at some local sight, a two-thousand-year-old Punic cistern, say, or the artful stonework surrounding a so-called Arab garden, and there'd be a polite tap on my shoulder. The next thing I knew, I'd be seated on the shaded veranda of a farmer's *dammuso* with a beaker-sized glass of wine in front of me.

Pantescan wines tend to be heady. *Very* heady. For the *passito* version of a muscatel, the aromatic *zibibbo* grapes unique to the island are spread out to dry for three weeks. (*Passito* comes from the word meaning "sun-dried.")

As the grapes lose their water, their flavor intensifies and their sugar content increases. The result is a high-octane wine whose alcohol content is typically 16 percent or more.

The island's *passito* reputedly put the notorious rake Casanova in a libidinous mood. It did not have that effect on me. After two or three glasses I wouldn't have recognized my libido if it had announced itself with a flourish of trumpets. Nor could I tell whether I was being buffeted by blasts of wind or swaying back and forth of my own accord. Doubtless some of what I took to be Pantelleria's bluster was really the consequence of my visits to *dammuso* verandas.

Moreover I felt obliged to drink less prudently than I would have drunk at home. As one of my guides informed me, "It's bad manners to stop with just one glass. The farmer will think you don't like his wine."

Eventually I began taking to the high country so as not to seem unmannerly. Even there I was not immune from local hospitality. Late one afternoon I encountered a farmer tending his vineyard on the upper slope of Monte Gibele. Just coincidentally, he happened to have a bottle of homemade *passito* in his donkey's saddle pack.

I can't remember drinking the bottle with him, but I'm sure I did, because when I looked out to sea a short while later, I saw a Roman trireme approaching the island.

I blinked. The trireme turned into the passenger-and-car ferry that links Pantelleria with Trapani in Sicily. I blinked again to make sure. The ship remained indisputably modern.

Still, this is an island with at least one foot in the past, although perhaps not the past of Roman triremes. It seemed to me to occupy a space in time somewhere in the 1930s, or so I felt after seeing faded photographs of Mussolini in several of the island's bars. One of the Pantescans who regaled me with wine — a sweet-spirited, leprechaunish man in his early eighties — told me he ranked Mussolini with Garibaldi and Count Cavour as the three greatest Italian heroes.

I confess that I wasn't troubled by this enthusiasm for a man whose rating elsewhere isn't very high. The picture of Mussolini I got from Pantescans was not of history's strutting despot but of a public-minded padrone who improved local schools and helped fund the island's first real roads.

"Il Duce looked after us, *signore*," my leprechaunish friend told me. He said he had presented Mussolini with a bottle of *passito* on the occasion of the dictator's visit to Pantelleria. On hearing this, I had a sudden vision of Il Duce staggering back and forth in a merry dance that belied the true grimness of fascism.

Partially because of its leisurely, old-fashioned pace, but also because my wrenched knee continued to bother me, I became a lumbering creature on Pantelleria. One of my guides told me the best way to unwrench my knee was to go swimming in the same place where I had wrenched it, the Specchio di Venere — the mirror of Venus — so named because the goddess used the lake's unrippled surface to gaze on her own lovely visage.

I returned to Specchio di Venere one bright, levanter-blown day. The lake was so churned up that Venus would have seen only a murky image of herself. Undaunted, I waded through mineral-packed ooze and began paddling around in the highly alkaline water.

The sulfurous smell reminded me of similar lakes, old volcanic craters, in Iceland. This lake also had the roundish shape of a volcanic crater. Where would I come down, I wondered, if an eruption occurred? Tunisia? Palermo? On top of Signor Armani's *dammuso*?

But no eruption occurred, and after an hour or so of sulfur and alkalinity, my knee felt better. Much better.

I shouldn't have been surprised by the knee's improvement. After all, Pantelleria's geology has long been known for its healing powers. Near the main town, there's a saunalike cave whose steam has eased bodily aches and pains since Roman times. In Benikulà, there's another cave whose hot vapors are a balm for rheumatism sufferers. All over the island, in fact, there are caves, hot springs, miniature geysers called *favare*, and thermomineral waters where you can sweat, burn, or rinse away your ills.

And on the island's west coast, there's the Grotta di Sataria (Cave of Good Health), popularly known as Calypso's Cave. Here, according to legend, the Homeric wanderer Ulysses spent seven years cavorting with the sea nymph Calypso, a prisoner of her seductive powers. Nowadays the inhabitants of the nearby village of Scauri use the cave for their own romantic trysts.

Toward the end of my trip I found myself reclining in a pool of hot water at Calypso's Cave. Time seemed to dissolve, past and present merged, and a few feet away I noticed Ulysses and Calypso — or was it a couple from Scauri — locked in an amorous embrace. Roman centurions dropped by for a soak and gossiped about their emperor's various excesses. Arabs knelt toward Mecca. A certain leprechaunish old man proffered a beaker-sized glass of wine.

Earlier in the day the wind had been in a tumultuous mood, but now it was singing something blithe and airy by Mozart. Resting in the pool, I felt blithe and airy myself — and also more than a little envious: What a lucky fellow Ulysses was to be stuck for seven years on this most salubrious of islands.

SUSAN MINOT

This We Came to Know Afterward

FROM *McSweeney's*

A LITTLE OVER TWO YEARS ago I went to Africa to write a story about the children of northern Uganda who are abducted by roaming rebel groups and enslaved as soldiers. It's a horrendous story. Their towns are raided, their parents murdered, and they, children between the ages of eight and eighteen, are held captive in the bush, made to fight and steal, and kill. The girls are often raped or forced to be "wives" to their captors. However, the raiding groups, though brutal, are not well organized, and because children can be as wily as they are adaptable, many manage to escape. Some four thousand of them had so far — during skirmishes with government troops, or if camp was hastily abandoned. They may wander for days until they find help, and often return to their villages to discover that their parents are dead or have moved away.

Two weeks after I returned to New York to write the piece, a very similar story was published in a national magazine, and so the magazine which had originally shown interest in my story now felt the story was not new enough.

It was not a new story then. And it's definitely not a new story now.

Angelina Auytum in TriBeCa, at the Filmmaker's Dinner

I first heard about the abducted children in the fall of 1997 in New York, at a dinner in TriBeCa at a filmmaker's loft. It was a Sunday night and one of the dozen or so people at the table was a Ugandan woman in her mid-forties, slim, wearing a long green and yellow and brown flowered dress. Her name was Angelina Auytum. She'd been flown from Uganda by Human Rights Watch, to be honored at a fundraising banquet the next night, at which she could make a plea for her cause.

Angelina had helped start a group in northern Uganda called the Concerned Parents Association. Her daughter, Charlotte, was one of the 10,000 kidnapped children. Over a year before, Charlotte, aged fifteen, was attending a girls' boarding school run by Italian nuns, about a half-hour drive away from where Angelina lives with the rest of her family. One night, the gates were stormed by a group of rebels who broke into one of the dormitories, tied 139 girls together with a rope, and led them into the bush. A nun, Sister Rachele, followed. By morning she had caught up with the rebels and, rosary in hand, begged the commander to let her girls go. For some reason he agreed to release some of them — 109 were freed — but he kept 30 with him.

The rebels call themselves the Lord's Resistance Army, and are led by a man named Joseph Kony. Though he purports to want to overthrow the government, his troops spend most of their time looting from and killing people of his own tribe, the Acholi, native to northern Uganda. They have been active for over twelve years, during which the Ugandan government has done little to stop them.

The relationship between the current Ugandan government and the Acholi, Angelina explained, is very complicated. The Lord's Resistance Army is allied with the Sudanese government, because the Sudanese, unfriendly with their neighbors to the south, are interested in any group undermining Ugandan stability. In southern Sudan, Kony maintains camps with hundreds if not thousands of abducted children — perhaps 80 percent of the army is made up of abducted children — and there he enjoys Sudan's hospitality: complimentary guns, vehicles, and food.

Charlotte had been gone over a year; she was now nearly seventeen. Angelina had heard that Charlotte was made to be "wife" to one of the commanders. She said that if Charlotte returned pregnant with a rebel's child she'd want to kill that child. It was, she said, the way many of the parents felt. She knew this was wrong. Perhaps, she suggested, she needed counseling on this point.

"What can be done?" asked a man at the table, frowning, holding the stem of his wineglass between thumb and forefinger.

Put pressure on governments, Angelina said. Let people know.

The man nodded. We all nodded. No one knew what that meant.

The next night Angelina spoke at the Human Rights banquet. I heard from friends who attended the dinner that she was more reserved in her formal speech, and seemed tired. She thanked Human Rights Watch and UNICEF and Amnesty International and everyone who was helping her. She said she'd met a lot of nice people and there had been a lot of nice dinners and the food was very good. But, she said, she couldn't eat another bite. She didn't know when her daughter had last eaten — she didn't even know where her daughter was. So she pushed her plate from her, leaving the rest of the attendees stuck — could *they*, in good conscience, eat? It was an unfair position to put her dinner guests in, but she didn't seem to care.

Uganda in the Winter of 1998

I drove to Uganda from Kenya with three friends: Simon, who'd grown up in Kenya and traveled around much of Africa, provided us with his car, a Toyota jeep, and ended up doing nearly all the driving; Dudu, born in Nairobi, wanted to videotape the trip, with the possibility of making a documentary; and Hugie, a photographer from Memphis, on his second trip to Africa. Simon and Dudu — whose name, in Swahili, means "bug" — were both in their twenties, and spoke Kiswahili.

We planned to visit Angelina Auytum at her home in Lira, to go to St. Mary's, the Catholic boarding school from which Charlotte had been abducted, and to see the rehabilitation centers nearby, where escaped children are sent before returning to their families.

We drove northeast through Kenya, and passed through the town of Karuma, where that week, according to the newspapers, houses had been torched and people murdered with machetes. The attacks were aimed at the Kikuyu, one of Kenya's largest tribes, apparently in retaliation for their not having voted for President Moi, who had just been reelected. When we stopped for gas, though, we saw no signs of unrest. The town was quiet, the afternoon still; Karuma was just a big town with warehouses and giant grocery stores, and old men sitting under gnarled trees. Covering the paved lot of the gas station were hundreds of flattened green dragonflies, as shiny as strips of green satin, like confetti from a Mardi Gras party.

North of Karuma, the road took us higher, past tea fields bright acid green under black rain clouds. On the roadside, children in blue and white uniforms were walking home from school. Many of them waved and shouted as we drove past. Nearing Uganda, the land changed and the vegetation grew more lush, with notched banana leaves blowing on the roadside, and hills, slate blue in the distance, in the form of odd, hat-shaped lumps.

Shea Oil Shields and Rock Grenades

The Acholi's military history, one they would perhaps like to forget, has in part led to the current situation.

Milton Obote led the Ugandans when, in 1962, they fought for and won independence from Great Britain. While serving under Milton Obote, the Acholi were notorious for committing horrible human rights violations. But when the tides of power shifted in 1972 and Idi Amin took over, the Acholi and Langi, also a tribe of the north, were victims of the inevitable backlash of an enemy rising to power. Nearly all of the people slaughtered by Amin were Acholi or Langi. When Obote regained power in 1979, the Acholi were back behind the guns. It was that army, under Obote II, that committed the worst atrocities. There was a famous bloodbath at Luwero, not far from Kampala, where pregnant women were disemboweled and thousands slaughtered. The Acholi were perceived as the majority of this army, and it was the Acholi who were blamed.

At that time Yoweri Museveni was the leader of a rebel group made up mostly of southerners and westerners. In 1986, Museveni ousted Obote, becoming Uganda's new president. The Acholi soldiers returned to their homes in the north, but found their cattle raided and their farmland usurped. Museveni's government, unsympathetic to the Acholi, looked the other way. To protect themselves, the Acholi's ex-soldiers formed a resistance army, the UPDA (Uganda People's Democratic Army).

A year after its inception, the UPDA was invigorated by Alice Lakwena, a healer who called her fellow Acholi to arms. Adding a strong dash of spiritual muscle, she rechristened the rebel forces the Holy Spirit Mobile Force. Lakwena, whose name means "messenger," believed that a *tipu*, or spirit, came to her in the unlikely form of a ninety-five-year-old Italian veteran of the First World War who'd drowned at a famous Ugandan tourist site, Murchison Fall.

This spirit, she asserted, guided her to help the Acholi "cleanse" themselves of the sins they'd committed as soldiers for the Ugandan army.

In 1991, President Museveni instituted Operation North, sealing off the region, restricting travel, barring the press, blocking communication. In the name of security, the Acholi were herded into camps. Rapes were committed by Ugandan soldiers while the girls' families looked helplessly on. At a place called Bucoro, the government's army buried people alive. In the climate of this sort of persecution, the Acholi found in Alice Lakwena a figure of hope and redemption. And believing in her required great leaps of faith: she instructed her followers to soak rocks in water to turn them into grenades; she told them that if they smeared themselves with shea oil it would protect them from bullets. They followed her orders, attempting to use rocks as grenades, and, after dousing themselves in oil, they ran naked into battle. Amazingly, Lakwena's troops made progress in their attempt to overthrow the government, and in 1987, they reached the outskirts of the capital before they were stopped by Museveni's army. Defeated, Lakwena disappeared into Kenya.

Kampala and the Hive of NGOs

We drove into Kampala on red dirt roads, past shops called Heart's Desire Grocery and Ice Me. It was hot, and dust swirled up from construction sites. In the city, the roads were being blocked off for leaders attending an East African economic conference. The southern half of Uganda was enjoying a period of prosperity, and Kampala had the feeling of a boomtown. Foundations were being dug for new bank branches, and businesses were opening with colorful plastic flags draped across doorways. President Museveni, one-time rebel leader, was now a champion of economic opportunity and educational reform. Many saw Uganda as the hope of Africa.

Up a hill, along leafy potholed roads, we drove past embassies barricaded behind electric gates, past converted colonial houses with signs at the end of short driveways, through a thick hive of relief organizations from all over the world: Save the Children, Oxfam, GOAL, CONCERN, World Vision. Nongovernment organizations, or NGOs, were addressing various problems in the region; in this part of the world the aid business is often the biggest business around.

Inside the open doorway of the World Vision Headquarters set out on low tables were pamphlets and fact sheets about sexually transmitted diseases, press releases on the battle against AIDS — in parts of Uganda the spread of AIDS has been reduced — and booklets on education and agricultural studies. Among the literature of alarm was a new report on the abducted children, "Breaking God's Commandments: The Destruction of Childhood by the Lord's Resistance Army," which had just been released by Amnesty International. Human Rights Watch had their version, called "The Scars of Death," focusing on the children's stories.

UNICEF's "Shattered Innocence" recorded testimonies of some of the children who'd escaped. A typical story was told by Pete O., aged fourteen:

It was around 1 A.M. and I was sleeping with my brother in a hut. Rebels arrived, kicked the door and commanded us to come out. There were about seven men and women in military uniforms carrying submachine guns, mortars and rocket propelled grenades, and pangas. When they kicked the door I was so very frightened. I could hear other doors in the compound being kicked too. They looted our house.

I was tied on the waist with ropes to a line of five other children. We were told "If you attempt to escape I will kill you." There were about 30 children tied together and we were led away into the bush toward Ato hills. At 1 P.M. we stopped in the bush to cook. We moved in the Kitgum district through the bush till we entered Sudan. We were about 500 people moving in parallel lines. The rebel leaders communicated with a radio to Sudan government soldiers whom we found waiting for us at the border.

Vehicles ferried us to a place near Juba where we stayed for a week of rest before we were taught how to shoot with guns, lay ambushes and attack. A few of us were trained to lay landmines.

While in Sudan we were treated like slaves. We would wake early to dig in the garden then dig latrines, build officers' houses with no rest and not enough to eat. We would eat leaves, grass — anything that would not kill you, you would eat. Many people were suffering from diarrhea and dysentery. There was no treatment. When you are almost dying is when you would be taken to Juba hospital.

We grew opium, which we exchanged for military uniforms. Later I was selected to come to Uganda with 200 other children. We came back through Padwat village and spent three days addressing rallies in Palabek. Then, after the fourth day, we began to abduct children. For the next two months we continued capturing and abducting children.

[During a skirmish with Ugandan government troops] I took cover and escaped. I hid in the tall bush. Other children fleeing walked over me probably thinking I was dead or in their panic did not notice me. I hid in the bush for the night, fearing the civilians who might think I was part of the rebels. In the morning, government soldiers came into the village and I reported myself to them. One almost shot me mistaking me for an active rebel. But others persuaded him to leave me alone.

I would like to go back to school. I was in Primary Three when I was abducted.

The children told of watching other children being flogged and being forced to participate in killings. One boy remembered another boy beaten "on the bare back so badly that his whole skin peeled off and only the bloody flesh could be seen" and how the pleading of that boy "keeps coming back fresh in my mind." The children said there were times they felt as if they were dreaming when they were awake, of being so dizzy they were unable to think.

The Rise of Joseph Kony

With Alice Lakwena gone, Joseph Kony appeared. He was supposedly a relative of hers, a distant cousin. He appointed himself her successor and renamed the rebel army the Lord's Resistance Army.

Kony doesn't meet with reporters, but we watched some rare footage of him in a documentary made by Danish journalists. In one part, a government official is visiting a rebel camp. The speed is slowed down and the washed-out color makes everything look surreal. People are walking by, some with army shirts on, some bare-chested, many of their faces stricken with strange hypnotic expressions, their arms jerking in sideswipes as if in a ritual gesture, dashing water from cups to the ground.

Then Joseph Kony appears. He wears a white cowboy hat, cola-colored aviator sunglasses, and a pristine white shirt. His hair is braided into thin beaded plaits that swing slowly along his face when he turns his head. He sits at a table, inwardly focused, while one of his commanders shouts through a loudspeaker to a scruffy group gathered in the woods. When Kony finally speaks, in English, he says sonorous but meaningless things like "I know I will die.

If I don't die I'm not the son of God. God created me just as he created death." At one point he refers to the abductees: "Those who
escape are like women with two vaginas — one in front and one at
the back. From the back, the wife of one man, from the front the
wife of another."

Kony was in his early twenties when he stepped into the place va-
cated by Alice Lakwena. After ten years of looting the villages of his
own tribe, killing adults, and kidnapping the children — his justi-
fication being that this was "cleansing," for their own good — Kony
no longer has the support of his fellow Acholi. However, because
their children are part of his army — they *are* his army — the
Acholi are uneasy in supporting the Ugandan government's occasional attacks on the rebels, for in a skirmish, it's the children who
are likely to be killed — Kony sends them to the front lines of any
conflict.

The Center at Kiryandongo

The curving Nile divides the south from the north. We leave Kampala in the morning and by the time we've found gas and fixed
some of the car's minor troubles, it's midday. In the afternoon we
reach the Nile. We get out of the car and stand at the broken railing of the bridge at Karuma Falls, looking down at the rapids. This
is reportedly where Idi Amin used to put on public shows of throwing people into the river, crocodiles waiting in the shallows. As
we watch the water foam, three young soldiers, guns across their
chests, approach us and tell Hugie to put away his camera. Then
they tell us to move on. We get back in the car and cross the river
into the north.

The trauma centers were created for the children who "return" —
those who manage to escape from the Lord's Resistance Army.
There are a number of centers we planned to visit in the north.
A genial man named Robby Muhumuza, at World Vision in Kampala, had explained the process of rehabilitation. First, there
is medical treatment — the children are nearly always malnour-
ished, usually with parasites and often with battle wounds. Second,
there is psychological treatment. And third, there is vocational
training — he mentioned carpentry, agriculture, bicycle repair —
to prepare them for reentry into some kind of normal life. "You ask

them what their hopes are for the future," Robby said, "they have none."

The center at Kiryandongo is at the end of a deeply rutted road. We drive through cornfields and grass towering high above the car. A group of thirty thatched huts surround a dusty playing field, with lopsided soccer goals made from stripped branches.

We are met by one of the counselors, Charles Obwonamogi. His smile is so wide it shows all his bottom teeth. Assembled counselors sit on the benches opposite us. They smile at Dudu's name, knowing some Swahili. A young woman with a threadbare T-shirt passes through the room, head down, and disappears behind a partition. "That is a client," Charles says, using the term preferred at the center. There are 185 children here, and a staff of 13 — counselors, cooks, and teachers. Betty, a nurse in her fifties, is the only one who stays overnight. I ask her how she is able to look after them all, so many of them teenagers, all having lived in such extreme circumstances.

She smiles. "They are good children."

Hugie has wandered off to take pictures. The children gather around him, laughing. Charles and I walk past a hut, dark inside. "Oh," he says. "The girls' dorm. You want to see?"

Through the narrow door is a small room so crowded with iron bunk beds there's no place to stand. Dangling from the low roof onto the top bunks are empty cardboard boxes of Close-Up toothpaste or Fortified Protein, hanging as decorations. A few girls inside are sitting heavily on the beds, skirts pulled over their knees. This is the first sight I have of their faces. They're teenagers. Their hair is cut close to their head, in the style of all the girls. Some glance over at the shadows in the doorway, some look down. There is no greeting in their expression. Their eyes seem swollen. Their mouths are closed, their lips set in a way that was not so much pinched or obstinate, but simply unyielding.

Under a spreading tree in the dappled shade, about seventy children and young adults are gathered, building chairs or sewing or just standing around. The high sound of plucked strings from homemade instruments of wire and wood drifts chimelike through the air. The boys wear T-shirts, from crisply new to threadbare, many bearing slogans: BAD TO THE BONE, CHICAGO UNI-

VERSITY, KELLY 1O, LICENSED TO KILL, DIVE IN, MEN IN
BLACK, HARD ROCK CAFE, THE YEARS OF DECAY. Some boys
are huddled around a game of stones.

Here and there in the huts or leaning on beds children have
their heads pressed low to pieces of paper, scribbling away. This is
part of their therapy — to draw their experiences in the camps.
Figures in army boots with Elvis hairdos are shooting guns with
rocket-shaped ammunition. A delicate little girl in a blue sleeveless
dress with a belted full skirt — she looks like a miniature Audrey
Hepburn in *Roman Holiday* — shows me her drawing. The red-and-
white-checked hut — that's her house — and there's her and her
sister coming out and those are the rebels who came and took
them away when they raided her village. Another drawing shows
Kony himself, with earphones on, talking on a radio. Many pictures
feature machine guns set on tripods, cars on fire. In one picture
drawn by a little boy wearing broken glasses, an ax lies on the
ground beside a dismembered leg.

When it's time to go I find Simon in the dust under the car investigating a snapped cable.

At Lira

Lira is Angelina Auytum's town. Word has been sent that we're coming. Along the red dirt pathways lining the road are streams of people. They walk, pulling goats on leashes, carrying branches on their
backs, tin basins on their heads, babies in slings. Some ride bicycles —
only men it seems — sometimes with passengers sitting sidesaddle
behind. They carry rolled beds, bound poles of green sugarcane.
We pass lopsided buses crammed with passengers. People hang on
swinging doors, or balance on the roof gripping railings.

A screen of haze has moved in, infusing everything with a silvery
light. We're hushed in the car, no music playing. A woman in a pink
dress turns slowly in the tall grass and watches us pass.

At the Lira Hotel there's a message that Angelina Auytum is waiting
in town. It's the end of the day and the streets, lined with tall ragged trees, are busy with people. The Concerned Parents Association meet on a side street next to a shop selling soda and chips. The
light is falling as we pull up. Dark figures on a cement veranda. We
get out of the car and Angelina greets me with the smile I had for-

gotten, creasing her cheekbones. There are nine other parents there, mostly women, a few men. Since receiving Leila Pakkala's message, they've been waiting all day.

We all shake hands. For each of them there is a daughter gone. As far as they know — from reports that come back with the escapees — their girls are still alive. Lilian's daughter is Rebecca. Rosemary, with the red pinafore, is the mother of a girl named Brenda. Isabelle's daughter is Louiza, whose birthday is today. We sit in chairs and talk about the origin of the Concerned Parents Association. They started off with little money, they say, just what was in their pockets. They wrote letters and contacted officials. None of their letters were answered. Angelina's trip to New York had been a big opportunity.

"We are calling up everyone in the world," they say. They're not concerned with political affiliations, and they don't want war with Sudan — that would be, as one mother says, "laying my child on the devil's altar." They want Sudan instead to realize "they are our neighbors and will always be our neighbors" and to force Kony to release their children.

Birds are swooping in the falling dusk. I notice Simon watching them, dazed from driving. Soon we are sitting in darkness, listening to silhouettes.

Initially the parents' concern was only for each of their own daughters, the girls of St. Mary's. But now they were working for all the Ugandan children abducted. "What is the point in getting my daughter when we are a team? Now we know these other children by name and we know the parents, and all the children seem to be in my daughter and all the parents seem to be in one another. We are one."

Angelina says an astonishing thing: "If it was only about pursuing my child, I know — *I know* — that by now I would have gotten her back."

St. Mary's College of Aboke

The next day we visit Charlotte's boarding school in Aboke, twenty minutes from Lira. Angelina drives with us; normally she would travel in the overpacked vans that serve as buses. She fills us in on last night's rebel activity: the rebels have attacked a trading center in Adwari, thirty kilometers away. They took six people.

We turn off the main road and pass swamps and a field of sun-flowers. We turn down a narrow road where in a field a church stands, painted incongruously in the Italian mannerist style — chalky pink, yellow, and green. We arrive at red iron gates in a high stucco wall and are let in by an elderly *mzee*. The interior of St. Mary's College is a sort of Eden of leafy trees and purple bougain-villea. Flowers spill around tree trunks; pots of fuchsia dot a ve-randa painted turquoise with crimson trim. We are met by four nuns wearing nurselike dresses with white wimples over their hair. They greet us in English, Swahili, and their native Italian. As they usher us inside a young Ugandan soldier walks by on the gravel path with a gun strapped across his back.

We are given lunch in the sisters' dining area, with the door open to an inner court, a few habits on hangers drying in the back gar-den. The serving table is covered with pasta, meat, beans, stewed tomatoes, rice, chicken, potatoes, corn. All the vegetables and fruit are grown in their gardens. As lamb chops are being cut, the rebels are discussed in patient, deliberate voices. Angelina has known the sisters for a long time — she was a student at St. Mary's herself.

"They are not too far from us today," one of the sisters says. "They are still looking for food and people."

Sister Alba, the headmistress, a jovial woman in her seventies, first came to Uganda fifty years ago and has been here ever since. She mentions a missing child.

"That boy, he was seven when the rebels took him. He is fifteen now."

The nuns nod. "Sister, it is possible."

They serve us espresso in little cups — they have even grown the coffee beans. Sister Rachele, who brought the 109 girls back the night the rebels took them, is so slight it's hard to picture her wad-ing through thick bush, much less negotiating with a rebel com-mander.

"At first we wouldn't talk," she says. "We worried it would hurt the girls." She spoons her custard. "Then we decided to speak. Now we will not stop."

"I admire your strength," says Hugie.

Angelina's face is unusually hard. "Is it strength?"

One of the sisters nods. "Before our girls we didn't do anything."

*

Sister Rachele has an open face with eyes set wide apart behind large pale glasses, a white wimple tucked halfway over her ears, and the top of a well-worn white T-shirt showing beneath the collar of her dress. She speaks in a hushed, deliberate voice, as if telling a wondrous secret. Now and then her wiry arms jut upward in amazement. She has told the story of the abduction before and, leaning forward on the veranda, she tells it well.

That week, there were rumors of the rebels being close. The school had been attacked twice before, in 1989 and again in 1991, when the rebels took food and supplies. Government troops had been stationed at the school on and off, but that morning they had been moved. October 9, 1996, was a holiday, Ugandan Independence Day, so the troops were being given a break. Still, the sisters were assured that the troops would be returning. When they hadn't arrived by that afternoon, Sister Rachele bicycled to a nearby town where she was again told the troops would come. At 8:00, Sister Alba, the headmistress, had food ready for the army soldiers, but they had not returned. The sisters discussed whether to take the girls to the village, as they sometimes did, to put them in nearby homes for the night, where they would be hidden. They decided not to, and gave the girls their supper and put them to bed early.

In the middle of the night the watchman woke up Sister Rachele.

"Sister," he said, "they are here."

"The gate," she says, "was illuminated like daylight. The dormitory was already surrounded, a light on each window. We had to make the hardest decision of our lives. We said, 'What do we do?'"

The dormitory doors were steel, and bolted from the inside — the girls locked themselves in each night. The sisters assured themselves that the girls would not open the doors.

"We said, 'Let us hide.' We threw off our habits and lay in the grass behind the banana garden." Across the courtyard they could hear the rebels banging on the doors. "We were praying, 'Let those doors hold.' Until the last we were sure the girls were inside. We never heard one voice of the girls. We saw the smoke and fire from the vehicles burned in the parish next door. Finally it was quiet. We came out and met some of the girls. 'Children, you are here,' we said. Big tears in their eyes. A little one said, 'Sister, they took all of us.' 'They took you?' 'They took all of us.'"

"Oh, the scene we saw. It was a devastation. Glass broken, sleepers, clothes . . . What shocked us was a big hole in the wall. They'd removed a whole window and used the bars as a ladder. The girls will tell you how they tried to hide, under the beds, under the mattresses. One of the little ones was raped near the church. This we came to know afterward.

"I changed my clothes. I went to the office and took some money and put it in a bag. I said, 'I must go.' John Bosco, one of our teachers, was with me. He said, 'Sister, let us go die for our girls.'

"We started walking. Bosco did not know the way. There were pieces of paper thrown — for the holiday we'd given sweets to the girls — and wrappers and Pepsi cans. He walked in front, I behind. It was seven; they were two hours ahead of us. We asked villagers, Have they passed here? We reached a swamp. The water reached me here." She indicated her breastbone. "I kept thinking of the little ones who were not so tall. We entered the water. Because of the land mines, Bosco said, 'Sister, put your feet where I put mine.' The Lord helped us.

"One of the girls, Irene, had gotten away. When I saw her she had her skirt as a blouse. We came to a hilly place. I found an identity card of one of the girls. As I bent down to pick it up, Bosco, looking ahead, said, 'Sister, they are there.'

"I am not good at telling distance. They were maybe three, four hundred meters ahead on a hill, climbing. It was one thing to follow, another thing to face them. I said, 'Bosco, what are we going to do?' He said, 'Sister, what are we going to do?' We went down into a valley and I couldn't see them, then we crossed a field and I could see they were in two lines. As we came toward them they made us raise both our hands. The guns were pointed at us and I saw their faces. They said something I couldn't understand, in Acholi. The commander came forward and asked where I had been — he meant at the school. The Lord gave me the right words. I said I hadn't been there, that I had taken Alba to Lira because she was sick. I said a small lie."

I Will Keep Thirty

"I said I had money if he would give me back the girls. 'We don't want money,' he said, but took the bag anyway. Then: 'Follow me, I will give you the girls.'

"I was full of hope — I did not expect such a welcome. We went ahead a bit and what I saw . . . three or four of our girls with three or four rebels. I tried to greet the girls but they kept their eyes down. The commander took me to another group of rebels.

"'Please be so kind as to give me the girls,' I said. I had a rosary. He said, 'What are you doing?' I said, 'I am praying.' He took out his rosary.

"[Other] children were guarding us. They had guns and necklaces of bullets. The youngest, about ten years old, were the hardest.

"He said, 'I need to send a message.' Soldiers put out a solar panel to charge batteries to send a radio signal and they waited for the sun to charge it." Just then helicopters carrying government troops, on routine surveillance, surprised them, unaware the girls were there. Sister Rachele and the girls were told to hide themselves. "The bullets were flying. The girls started to cover me to protect me. We were hiding, walking, collecting branches of cassava to make us look like walking trees." Soon the helicopters flew off.

"We had met the rebels at ten-forty. Now it was four o'clock. We sat for a while, drank water. There were a few houses nearby, a few women there. The commander sat on a stool and a lady got a plastic bag for me to sit on.

"I said, 'Please give me the girls.'

"He said, 'Don't worry. I am Mariano Lagira.'

"He told me I should wash. When I came back from washing, he told me, 'There are one hundred and thirty-nine. I will give you' — he wrote the numbers in the dirt like this — one–zero–nine. 'I will keep thirty.'

"I knelt in front of him. 'Let my girls go. Keep me here.' He said only if Kony says yes. 'Then take me to Kony,' I said."

Guess What I Had to Do

"I wrote it out — 'Dear Mr. Kony Please be so kind as to allow Mariano to release the girls.' He took the letter I wrote. But I don't know if Kony ever got that note.

"It is difficult for me to say all these things because I cannot put into words what I felt at the moment. From where I was sitting I saw a large group of my girls. And next to them, a small group.

"He said, 'You go and write the names of those girls who are remaining.' I stood up and went over there with a pen and piece of paper. I said, 'Girls, be good . . .' but I didn't finish the sentence. They started crying. They understood everything. In a second I heard an order and a quick movement and suddenly the soldiers began grabbing branches and beating the girls. One soldier jumped onto the girls. He jumped on the back of Grace. Carolyn they slapped so hard . . . the girls stopped crying.

"I was there seeing these things.

"The girls started looking at me. Then they started one by one, all of them, no not all — some of them were just looking at me — to speak. Jessica said, 'My two sisters died in a car accident and my mother is sick.' Another: 'Sister, I have asthma. Sister, I am in my period.'

"'Mariano,' I said, 'please.'

"He said, 'If you do like this I give you none of them.' I apologized.

"I couldn't write. Then Angela — she is still with them, still in Sudan — she started writing the names. I gave my rosary to Judith, the head girl, and said, 'You look after them.' I got them a sweater.

"I said, 'When we go, you must not look at us.'

"'No, Sister, we won't.'

"I had tea and biscuits with the commander. We ate. We greeted each other as great friends. He told me I should go say goodbye.

"I started calling their names. One of the girls said, 'Sister, Janet is not here. She went there.' Janet had sneaked away, trying to escape.

"Guess what I had to do? I told Angela, 'Get her. If they realize one is missing. . . .' So I had to do this. Can you imagine? She was brought back. I told Janet she was endangering her friends.

"She said, 'No, Sister, I will not try to run away again.'

"She is still in Sudan."

Sister Rachele remembers Charlotte's last words to her: "Sister, are you coming back for us?"

"You go and see the children," Sister Rachele says, knowing we are going to visit the rehabilitation centers farther north, in Gulu. "You go look and see in their eyes what they have been through. When I think that I footed for only a few hours . . . that they had to do this for months, for years . . . for kilometers and kilometers. When they return, their hands and soles of their feet are as hard as this table. Is a miracle some are surviving. In crossfire Jacqueline got a bullet in the neck, Pamela in the nose. They are just children. Can you imagine? There must be someone somewhere who can do something. Some parents are giving up. Jacqueline's mother has died of sorrow and Jacqueline does not even know . . .

"I am saying words like this, but the pain. . . ." Her eyes are red. She stares at the beaten Kleenex in her hand.

How Some Escaped

In the peaceful middle of the campus we talk to three of the St. Mary's girls who were among those thirty kept, but who have since escaped. Down at the end of the lawn we can see colored dresses passing behind the fig trees, girls walking back from class. The girls we've met are all well mannered, sliding forward on a bent knee in a curtsy when they're introduced to us, turning their faces away and softly shaking our hands. The students all perform chores — in the kitchens, in the gardens. Some girls are bent over on a platform, sifting maize. Above them is a grotto of stone and plaster with a painted statue of the Virgin Mary and just to the left, the dormitory the rebels raided. Inside are rows of beds and windows cut high in the concrete walls, with bars over them. That night in October a path was beaten diagonally across the garden from the front gates. The rebels knew exactly where they were going.

Agnes, Carolyn, and Grace each escaped at different times. The girls tell us their stories, at first choosing their words carefully, with Dudu's video camera propped in front of them. But soon they grow more relaxed, until they're interrupting each other, adding to each other's story.

Carolyn Akello has a long face and her eyes look pulled down. She gazes downward as she tells her story. After her kidnapping, her left hand became paralyzed. "Even if I could lift it, then it would fall like that." She flops her arm on her lap.

She escaped after a looting.

"It was a Sunday. They told us to go to the well to collect water. I told the other girls, 'If you do find me here tomorrow then I have not made the best use of this chance I've got in my life.' While they were boiling the water I just walked for a short distance as if I'd

gone [to the bathroom] and when I reached to there I started running.

"I met a bushy place where the grasses were long. I could not
walk through. I said, 'Let me go back.'" But she continued. As she
walked through the night she passed thatched houses Kony's
forces had raided. She was afraid of being mistaken for a rebel —
the villagers might take revenge upon her — so she kept going.
The path passed cassava gardens and came to a forest.

"I said, 'Let me rest.' While I was resting some bird came to me. I
thought the rebels were coming. I got up and looked in every direction. By then I was feeling very cold because of the dew. Even if
my body could touch a grass like this it could start shaking. At exactly six — I had a watch — I heard some clapping. I stood up. I
had just rotated around — the rebels were right there. I came to a
swamp and measured the water with a stick" — she gestures to her
chest — "and I said, 'This is nothing,' and in a minute I was across."

She ran as the sun was rising. She came to a banana plantation,
then a road, and recognized it as a road she'd reached with the rebels. She made the sign of the cross and ran toward the town of
Gulu. When she became tired she went into the bush. "Let me
climb these trees," she said to herself, to see if anyone was coming. From a small tree she could see the main road. She saw three
people.

"There was an old lady, a pregnant lady, and a young girl. They
were collecting food and taking it to town. I narrated to them my
story, and they told me, 'Don't you worry.' They told me to remove
my watch. They said, 'If the Lord is with you, you will go safely.'
They were carrying peas and sorghum and cassava. I helped them
carry with my good arm, and eighteen miles away at eleven A.M. we
reached Gulu."

She was taken to a nearby soldiers' barracks, where the escaped
children were usually brought. Eventually she was returned to her
town, where she waited at the trading center while a soldier went to
find her family.

"At four P.M. they called me to come and see my father. When I
saw him I was happy. I greeted him and I just started crying. And he
said, 'Are you really the one?' I thought I would never see you
again."

*

Agnes Ochity is an inviting fifteen-year-old, small and buxom. As she talks, she sits back in her wooden chair, an arm draped languidly over her shaved head. When she speaks of the rebels she is scornful, but smiles frequently.

She escaped with a girl named Esther. On the morning of the group's departure for Sudan, where chances for escape are greatly diminished, Esther was having second thoughts about fleeing. "I told her, 'Esther, get up.' Esther did not move. I said, 'Do you want to die, Esther? Do you want to see your parents?' Then Esther accepted my opinion."

When the rebels moved out of the camp, the girls ran. When they met with government troops, Esther wanted to go to them, but Agnes said no. "If they get you in the bush, whether you are a rebel or not, they will disturb you." Eventually a man on a bicycle found them. He gave them bananas and led them to a center.

Grace is bigger than the two other girls, but speaks in a much softer voice. After escaping, she was in the bush for three days without food. She ate sand to keep up her strength. "I said, 'I am going to die in this bush. Who will know I am dead?'" At one point she ran into two boys and two girls who also had escaped. But they didn't trust her. They had a gun and told her they were going to kill her. They brought her with them, and together they crossed a river and came across a group of huts, close to the Sudan where the Dinkas, a Sudanese tribe, live. The Dinkas caught them and also thought they were rebels.

"They were going to shoot us. I said, 'We are not bad people.' A certain old man came up, very old, and he knew English and he knew I was praying in English and he jumped in front of us and did like this" — Grace stretched out her arms — "and said, 'Leave these girls, it seems they are not bad.'"

Just a Young Person

Once, in the Sudan, a man asked Grace if she knew Joseph Kony. She did not. The man said, "People are saying Kony is ugly, but Kony is very handsome." The man was talking very seriously. "Kony," he said, "is very handsome and is going to overcome the government." Then he walked away.

Afterward she learned that the man who spoke to her was Kony himself.

Later, Kony spoke to the girls of St. Mary's. "These girls," he said, "they should know that from this day on they are soldiers." They were told they had been selected like the apostles were selected.

Grace, arms draped over her legs, says, "He's just a young person, thirty years old, brown. Hair very short. The body is small." He is said to have six children and eighteen wives.

The rebels believe it's not Kony who talks, but Lakwena talking through him, as an angel. The girls say Kony used to faint — in a trance — and when he came to he'd say he'd been in an airplane.

The girls laugh at this.

The rebels say that Kony once changed into a rotted corpse. This makes the girls laugh harder.

Talking about their time with the rebels, the girls are now giggling, slapping one another on the arm.

"When the rebels say a girl has died it means she has escaped."

"They eat rats, they eat anything they can get."

"The rebels don't like bicycles. A bicycle can report to army barracks. If they find someone on a bicycle they cut off his legs and despoil his bicycle."

"And they cut your mouth so you won't tell. They cut off your lips."

"If you are fifteen years old they say you are very old."

They were always walking. Their legs were swollen. For lunch they were given banana leaves and potato leaves. They were told Sister Rachele had left and gone to Kenya. They used to pray that Sister Rachele would not come: Kony had said he'd take her as a wife and be the first man to marry a nun.

The girls were told their families were killed.

The rebels used to pray early in the morning, but never got through the rosary. It was important to put your rosary on your chest, but when you were walking it had to be around your wrist, not your neck. Before praying under the trees you had to be barefoot and had to remove the magazine from your gun.

Each of the girls was given to a commander. Agnes was thirteen when she became a wife to a man named Labon. He used to call her Mummy; his mother's name was also Agnes.

Grace says she would like her revenge upon Mariano Lagira, the one who captured them. "He is very cruel. Maybe fifty-five. In battles he used to push us in front. He is the ugliest man I've ever seen. His mouth is like this." She pulls her mouth to the side. The girls laugh.

A pale light slants through the mango trees. It is a sweet evening.

Agnes says, "Oh, one more thing."

It happened just after they were first taken. They were called over to a group surrounding a girl lying on the ground. She was a girl from Gulu — not one of the girls from St. Mary's, but a girl they knew. "They were beating that girl with firewoods," Agnes says, "and they call all the Aboke girls that we should take this as an example and that we should all touch that girl before she dies. They called us to come kill that girl."

"In turn we got sticks and firewoods," Carolyn says.

"At first we try beating only the leg," Agnes says, her enthusiasm for telling this story beginning to fade. "We fear to beat the head," she says softly. "The [rebels] tell us, 'We are going to kill you instead.' So we beat that girl and then she died."

Agnes stares ahead at the ground. She says that girl comes to her in her dreams and says she will not forgive her.

Charlotte We Don't Hear Much About

Angelina, sitting with us, says, "They were the last to come home." In all, nine of the thirty girls have managed to escape. One, they have learned, was killed. Grace said that Charlotte tried to escape, but returned when she thought she was endangering the others. She was taken to the Sudan.

Angelina and Sister Rachele visit the rehabilitation centers regularly to see if the returnees have any news of the girls of St. Mary's. They'd gone to the centers in Gulu a month before. "We showed them a photograph of our girls," says Angelina. Some of the girls were recognized. "But Charlotte and Namahele and Miriam were never identified."

In a studio snapshot that Angelina has, Charlotte is posed in front of a painting of islands and palm fronds, standing sideways with her face full to the camera. Her head is tipped down, more inviting than shy, and her shiny hair is rolled above her temples.

She's wearing a white shirt and a purple sash at the top of a long purple skirt, posed like a bathing beauty, arm resting on curved hip.

The first Angelina heard of the kidnapping was on October 10, at 6:00 in the morning.

"Someone came banging on my door. 'Angelina, wake up. The rebels have taken them, all the girls of St. Mary's.' My God, I lost my head. I screamed and I felt helpless. My husband was confused, he didn't even know what to do. Then another neighbor heard me screaming. She came with her husband and said, 'What is the problem?' My husband had the courage to tell them. They comforted us. It was not easy. So they prayed with us a little bit, and I thought, Why sit here? Let me get going to Aboke. My husband was still looking for a means of traveling to the school, but I got out of the house. I was even shabbily dressed and I took off for the bus park and got a pickup which was going that way. I was dropped at the juncture and there caught a ride on a bicycle. The road by then was muddy. Part of the way we walked. I was at the school at seven.

"Sister Alba was there and some teachers and a few people from around. By eight the school was filled with parents. It was like a funeral, it was like a graveyard. Parents wept and at ten o'clock I got that friend of mine [Angelina's best friend, Speciosa, whose daughter was also one of the thirty and who has since died], and I said, 'What do you think?' Would we walk and follow the Sister? We mobilized a few parents and Sisters and said, 'Let us wait till Sister Rachele returns.' That night some stayed, some went home. I went back because I had a son alone at home, but there was no sleep.

"I left there at six, and at seven the next day we heard Sister Rachele was coming with some of the children. We decided to follow in that direction. We drove there with a man from Gulu, a manager of the electricity board. We met them five miles up the road. The first lot of [released] students were on a tractor. I looked through quickly and of course did not see my daughter. And I screamed. The children looking at me just told me, Mama Charlotte, you have nothing to hope for. I mean their faces told me, they didn't tell me. Their faces were telling me, We have nothing to give you now. There were about forty girls on the tractor. Some others were on foot, some were brought one by one on motorcycle. But I wanted to see the last. We waited for the last lot of girls. Sister

Rachele was there. She could not speak to me. I knew she had no good news for me at that time. I saw what she was feeling and she knew what I was feeling so we just kept quiet."

Above the Lira Line

The area north of Lira was considered dangerous. There were two main roads — the road to Kitgum was off-limits and the road to Gulu, which my three companions and I took when we left Lira, was better. We had been told — many times — that as long as we saw people along the road we didn't need to worry about rebel activity.

We were also told to ask for any news at the villages, the cross-roads of concrete buildings where women in cotton kangas sat behind pyramids of onions or papayas, their gaze sliding over the white people in the white car as we passed by.

The Hospital at Lacor

Dr. Pietro Corti has no idea who we are. The little piece of paper we hand to him has come from a doctor we met one night at a pizza place in Kampala, introducing us as journalists. Dr. Corti says he has two extra bedrooms in his house and soberly takes us in. Later he soberly says he only did so because he welcomed the opportunity to entertain ladies.

He is Italian, in his sixties, very handsome. He started Lacor Hospital with his surgeon wife and built it into one of the largest and most well respected hospitals in Uganda. It also serves as a refugee camp. Behind the gates in a spreading series of courtyards, families have set up little camps in the shade of the trees. Men with bandaged stumps sit in chairs while their families stir pots at smoldering fires; pregnant women waft by in filmy white robes; mothers splash babies beside dribbling faucets; children dance with gyrating hips and dusty feet.

Dr. Corti came to Gulu in the fifties and has lived through many chapters of Uganda's troubled history. His wife has recently died. Beloved and missed, she contracted AIDS while performing operations. Shrapnel is particularly sharp, he told us, and very dangerous to remove.

*

At dawn there is no sun yet or wind and the air is suffused with the slightest mist and slightest rosy tint. Every now and then a rooster crows — otherwise there is no sound, save the muffled sound of feet scuffing dirt.

Dudu and I have woken early and are standing at the gates of the hospital, where people stream out as if from a subway entrance. Most of the quiet throng are women and children. Having spent the night within the safety of the courtyards, with bedrolls in hand they are heading back to their villages, which at night are targets for the rebels. There are about two thousand of them heading home.

David Okello's Funeral

When we visit GUSCO — Gulu Save the Children Organization — a couple of miles from the hospital, there is a hushed funeral service in progress. A boy of fourteen has died of pneumonia and complications from wounds he received as a hostage in the bush. It is the first death at GUSCO, the best rehabilitation center in the north. David Okello's narrow plywood coffin is covered with a white sheet decorated with a cross of pink and yellow frangipani blossoms. The children who sit on the ground in the enclosure are all returnees. Many have parents waiting for them at home, though some parents are missing or dead. They will stay longer and eventually be sent on to another center, one for orphans.

They fill up the entrance courtyard, sitting on the curb of the office building, hands shadowing their eyes from the sun, arms resting across their knees. There are 270 in the center, 39 of them girls. Though the rebels abduct as many girls as boys, the boys have more opportunities to escape.

A priest holds up a candle, speaks in Lor, the local dialect. "The boy will rise together with Jesus," he says. A sea of faces looks forward. Everyone is very still. The coffin is lifted and everyone stands and moves slowly as the boy's body is carried out of the gate. A few brush tears from their eyes, but no one speaks and no face breaks its composure. David Okello's village is seven miles off the road to the south; his family will carry him and bury him there.

An administrator apologizes for having to welcome us on such a day. "But we will hide our sadness," he says. In light of the death there will be no classes today. Nor will there be any disco dancing, one of the children's favorite pastimes.

The girls' rooms have names like Star Room and Nimaro (Friendship) Room. In one room yellow foam mattresses cover half the floor, topped with black and gray wool blankets. More mattresses are stacked in a corner. A girl lies on her side, facing a peeling wall. "They are often tired," says our guide, a man named Odong.

For dinner the children are given hot food: cabbage, cowpeas, dried fish, meal, horsemeat. For lunch and breakfast: food bars — a sort of shredded cookie packed tight, made of vegetable fat, sugar, protein, wheat, and milk. Nearby families used to bring in home-cooked dishes, but with the increase in cholera it's no longer allowed.

About seventy boys sleep in four rooms of another house. The doors creak open when we enter. In an empty office at the end of the hall on metal desks are sliding piles of relief manuals. I pick up *Helping Children in Distress Development Manual 2.* Suggestions include drawing therapy and getting the children to talk.

In the yard on straw mats in the palmy shade nearly all of some fifty boys have pieces of paper and pencils. Some have set their paper on the back of their flip-flops. A boy named Simon, small for fourteen, describes the training he received from the rebels, including learning to dodge army helicopters by standing straight under branches, or lying flat. Shyly Simon shows me his warped leg and the shiny scar on his shin, still pink, where the bullet hit. I ask an older boy standing nearby what he's drawing. He looks at me for a few long moments, then walks away.

The girls sit a little apart on a mat under a tree, crocheting, legs demurely tucked to the side. Their voices are soft, barely audible. One of the youngest girls, eleven, whispers about the three weeks of target practice she had in the Sudan. Her small shoulders curve forward as she inspects a stitch in her round doily. The girl beside her busily working her needles interrupts to correct her about a gun. She means an SP9. Another girl in dotted swiss shakes her head. She thinks it was a B10.

Linda Akello was in the bush for a year and a half and is now six months pregnant with a rebel's child. She's a tall, beautiful sixteen-year-old with a narrow chin and high cheekbones, wearing a pink chiffonlike dress with wide white lapels slipping off her long shoulders. Crocheting a yellow doily, she speaks in sweet, dull tones. She will stay at GUSCO until her delivery. If it's a boy she plans to name the baby Komakech, meaning "I am unfortunate." If it's a girl, Alimochan: "I have suffered on this earth."

Through the chainlink fence, in another yard, children of the village are playing. A small boy with a hunched back swings on a crutch, a shriveled leg dangling. He smiles brightly.

Children walk along with us toward the exit. Someone hands me a drawing one of the boys has done of me — a long skirt, a bag over my shoulder with a water bottle in it. One boy notices a large scar on Hugie's forearm and asks him what happened. "Actually," says Hugie, who ran into some trouble in Memphis, "I was shot." The kids double over in bursts of laughter. The kids have never heard anything so hilarious.

Beatrice Arach is one of the administrators at GUSCO. She has tiny braids swept up in a bun, and wears a loose tie-dye dress. She sits in her office and describes the sight of the children arriving from the bush: starving, legs covered with sores, some with gunshot wounds. "If you are too sympathetic you cannot work. If you are looking at the children as human beings, every day you will be breaking." She says the children need to be dewormed and treated for dehydration. Many haven't bathed for weeks. She remembers one boy sort of crawling on the ground soiling himself. She starts to talk about David Okello, the boy who died. He liked bakery class, she says. Then she weeps.

After a day of hearing these stories I collapse on my bed in the doctor's guest room. In the quiet, I can hear the shuffling sound of two thousand people entering the hospital gates for the night.

Christine, Abducted Three Times

On the way back to Kampala we stop again at the Kiryandongo Center to talk to the children. Christine, who speaks in a sweet voice, is twenty, and has been abducted three times. We sit on mats on the ground and lean in the shade against a mud hut. Christine's year-old daughter, not from a rebel, sits quietly beside us, chewing on my sunglasses.

The first time she was abducted, Christine was with the rebels for eight months. The second time, for a year and seven months, she was given to a commander as a wife. "He was rude," she says. After her second escape she returned to her village and got married. The third time both she and her husband were abducted. Christine was raped, then let go after three days, when the rebels found out she was pregnant — they have no need for pregnant girls. When her husband returned, he abandoned her. He was now living near Kitgum. "I think he has another woman," she says.

Christine's head is solid like a Brancusi block. She has a small nose and wide lowered eyes that shift slowly from side to side when she speaks. She begins speaking English, then lapses into Lor. Betty, the head nurse, translates, tapping a small twig thoughtfully at her chin. As she tells her story, Christine implies a difference between rape and being given as a wife. I ask her how they're different.

Christine doesn't seem to understand the question. Betty, looking down, tries to explain, "Sometimes the girls are given a husband and they are forced to be a wife. They have no choice. And other times they are raped."

"Isn't it force in both cases?" I ask.

They both look at me, not understanding. "One time the girl is a wife. The other time there is violence."

"Remember us to your family," says Charles Obwonamogi. "I pray you get a blessing for your journey," says Christine. "Go in peace," says Nurse Betty.

On the road out of Kiryandongo the car got stuck — as it must on every trip. We had twenty people, many from the center, covered in mud trying to dig us out, using stones and sticks. After two hours, just as the sun was going down, we revved out of the ditch.

Dudu and I sat on the hood of the car when we sped away. A weak sunset was falling in the haze, the wind was cool. We stopped and picked up warm beer and bananas. We left behind all those children lost in the bush.

I had asked one group of girls in the rehabilitation center if there was anything they'd like me to say on their behalf. One girl shifted on her mattress and spoke forcefully. She was protesting one of the rules requiring the returnees to stay in the rehabilitation center for six weeks before they could leave. It was a new kind of imprisonment, she said. The counselor didn't translate right away. Then he cleared his throat. "She says she wants to go home."

The Clintons in Africa

That spring, 1998, President Clinton visited Uganda on a tour of Africa, the first tour of Africa by a U.S. president since Kennedy. I watched Clinton on TV shaking hands with Museveni, dancing with children in pink shirts, and making a speech under an awning protecting him from the white sun. He said he'd come so America would look upon Africa with new eyes. He talked about the light he sees in the eyes of the children.

Nowhere in the press coverage of Clinton's rounds in Africa did I see anything more about the children of the north. Later I found out that during that trip Hillary Rodham Clinton, who'd met Angelina in Washington through Human Rights Watch, gave a speech at Makere University in Kampala and mentioned Angelina, Charlotte, and the LRA abductions. The First Lady had pledged $500,000 to the Concerned Parents Association and GUSCO, and $2 million over the next three years toward a Northern Ugandan Initiative.

It was a positive gesture of support, but somehow I couldn't help thinking of the Italian doctor I'd met in Kampala, the one who had given us the piece of paper recommending us to Dr. Corti. He'd been practicing medicine in Africa for ten years, most recently at Lacor Hospital. But now he was leaving; he was fed up and discouraged. He believed the unrest in the north could be stopped if the government wanted to stop it, but they were allowing it to go on for one reason: money. Money was pouring in to solve the problems. The doctor was headed back to Europe, to start over.

But first he was going paragliding in Eritrea.

Angelina in Washington

In December of 1998 I heard from Human Rights Watch that Angelina was in Washington, D.C. I also heard that she'd learned Charlotte was pregnant. I happened to be in D.C. and I tracked Angelina down. I rode in an overheated cab listening to the radio broadcast the House Judiciary hearings — "Ms. Lewinsky's statement with regard to sexual . . . ."

I found Angelina in a paneled room speaking to a group sponsored by Senator Paul Wellstone of Minnesota, who'd taken up the cause. Most of the people in the room, which had more chairs than people, were women, and most seemed familiar with the situation. As people expressed sympathy, then held forth to demonstrate how much they knew about the complexity of the relations between President Museveni and the Sudan, I noticed Angelina was watching them with weary eyes. When someone asked her what could be done, this time she had an answer, in the form of an anecdote. One time, she said, at the zoo in Kampala, a woman tourist was standing at the monkey cage. Through the bars a monkey snatched her purse. The zookeepers entered the cage and tried chasing after the monkey, but the monkey was much faster and could scamper up the trees. One trainer took out a banana and caught the monkey's eyes. Slowly the monkey came down. In order to take the banana the monkey had to drop the purse.

Angelina suggested that President Museveni offer Joseph Kony immunity. At this point she was willing, it seemed, to accept anything to get her daughter back. Give him immunity, Angelina said, and let him give us back our children.

After her talk, Angelina was taking business cards, and slowly writing her address for those who wanted it. She greeted me warmly, but seemed exhausted. Yes, it was true, she said, Charlotte was pregnant. She was said to be looking poorly.

Two Years Later

In the last two years I've done a lot of other things that had nothing whatsoever to do with Angelina or the LRA. I even returned to Africa and sat on the roof of a Land Rover. I watched wildebeest migrating and elephants crossing rivers and lions yawning in the tall grasses of a golden dusk.

A couple of months ago at a dinner after a friend's art opening, a woman sitting across the table told me she was at a ladies lunch on the Upper East Side where a woman spoke about the kidnapped girls in Uganda. Was her name Angelina? Yes, the woman said, That's right. And what about her daughter, Charlotte? The woman shook her head. No, she was not back.

Charlotte would have had her child by now, if she's still alive.

SUSAN ORLEAN

The Place to Disappear

FROM *The New Yorker*

ALL LANGUAGES are welcome on Bangkok's Khao San Road, including Drunkard. "Hold my hand," a man fluent in Singapore slings commanded a Scottish hairdresser one night at Lucky Beer and Guest House — only in his dialect it came out soggy and rounded, more like *Hole mah han.*

"Not right now," the Scottish hairdresser said. She was a slender girl with the pinkish pallor of a milkmaid, blond hair, gray eyes, and a nose ring. She was on a six-week trip through Asia with two cute friends from Glasgow. They'd just arrived on a super-discount flight from Scotland and had checked into a $7-a-night room at one of the several hundred or so cheap guesthouses around Khao San Road — Happy Home Guest House or Nirvana Café and Guest House or Sweety's or Lek Mam's or something; they actually couldn't remember what it was called, but they knew how to find their way back. They also knew how to get from their guesthouse to the new branch of Boots, the English drugstore, which opened recently amid the T-shirt shops and travel agencies that line Khao San. Within their first few hours in Bangkok, the girls went to Boots and blew their travel budget on English soap and shampoo — same soap and shampoo they could get at home but somehow more exotic-seeming when bought in Thailand — and on snack packages of Oreos, which they worship and which are not easy to find in the United Kingdom. They thought Khao San was horrible because it was so crowded and loud and the room in the guesthouse was so dingy, but it was brilliant too, because it was so inexpensive, and there were free movies playing at all the bars, and because they'd already run into two friends from home. On top of that, finding a branch of Boots right here was almost too good to be true. What's more, Boots was super-air-conditioned, and that distinguished it from many of the other Khao San Road shops, which were open to the hot and heavy Bangkok air. Now it was close to midnight, and the girls were sitting at a rattletrap table outside Lucky Beer, eating noodles and drinking Foster's Lager and trying to figure out how to get to Laos.

"Hole mah han," the drunk repeated, and thrust his arm across the table. The three girls studied his arm, then shifted away from him. "Wow," one of the hairdresser's friends said. "He looks kind of . . . *old.*"

"Shut up," the man snapped. He yanked his arm back, wobbled to his feet, and then fell across the table, sending a saltshaker and a napkin dispenser to heaven. All the while, the girls kept talking about their schedule. It was as if the strangeness of where they were and what they were doing were absolutely ordinary: as if there were no large, smelly drunk sprawled in front of them, as if it were quite unexceptional to be three Scottish girls drinking Australian beer in Thailand on their way to Laos, and as if the world were the size of a peanut — something as compact as that, something that easy to pick up, shell, consume, as long as you were young and sturdy and brave. If you spend any time on Khao San Road, you will come to believe that this is true. Finally, the hairdresser glanced at the man, who had not moved. "Hello, sir?" she said, leaning toward his ear. "Hello? Can you hear me? Can I ask you something important? Do you remember where you're from?"

I went back to Lucky Beer the next night, but the Scottish girls were gone — off to Laos, most likely. At their table was a South African woman who taught English in Taiwan and was on her way back from massage school in Chiang Mai, in northern Thailand. The next night, she was gone too, replaced by an American couple in their twenties who'd just finished a Peace Corps assignment in Lithuania and were taking the long way home; the night after that, it was five Israelis who had just finished their military service and were stalling in Southeast Asia before starting college in Tel Aviv.

Khao San Road, one long packed block in Bangkok's Banglamphu neighborhood, was the jumping-off point for all of them, a sort of nonplace they went to in order to leave from, so they could get to the place they really wanted to go. People appear on Khao San just long enough to disappear. It is, to quote the Khao San Road Business Association's motto, "Gateway to Southeast Asia," provided that you are traveling on the cheap and have a backpack fused to your shoulders. From here you can embark on Welcome Travel's escorted tour of Chiang Mai, which guarantees contact with four different hill tribes, or the Cheap and Smile Tour to Koh Samui, or a minibus trip to Phuket or Penang or Kota Baharu, or an overland journey by open-bed pickup truck to Phnom Penh or Saigon, or a trip via some rough conveyance to India or Indonesia or Nepal or Tibet or Myanmar or anywhere you can think of — or couldn't think of, probably, until you saw it named on a travel-agency kiosk on Khao San Road and decided *that* was the place you needed to see. Everything you need to stay afloat for months of traveling — tickets, visas, laundry, guidebooks, American movies, Internet access, phone service, luggage storage — is available on Khao San Road.

Thailand, the most pliant of places, has always accommodated even the rudest of visitors. For hundreds of years, it was the junction between Chinese, Burmese, Indian, Khmer, and Vietnamese traders. Many Americans first came to know Bangkok as the comfort lounge for troops in Vietnam, and, later, as the capital of sex tourism. Starting in the early eighties, when foreigners started trekking to such places as Myanmar and Tibet and Vietnam, Thailand took on another hostessing job, because Bangkok was the safest, easiest, most Westernized place from which to launch a trip through Asia. Until then, Khao San was an unremarkable working-class neighborhood. It had a large temple called Wat Chanasongkhran, a small Muslim enclave, bakeries, motorcycle shops, grocery stores, and a surprising number of residents who were employed as traditional Thai dancers. There were some hotels in the neighborhood, frequented by Thai businesspeople. In 1985, Bonny and Anek Rakisaraseree noticed how many budget travelers — mostly young French and Australian men — were drifting around Bangkok, so they opened Bonny Guest House, the first on Khao San catering to foreign wanderers. Locals were not even permitted to rent rooms. Dozens of other guesthouses opened soon afterward, most with forbidding signs in the lobby saying N O T

ALLOW ANY THAIS TO GO UPSTAIRS. Drugs were fantastically cheap and available and quietly tolerated, despite wishful signs saying WE DO NOT WELCOME USE OR POSSESSION OF HEROIN IN GUESTHOUSE.

More than a third of Thailand's 7 million annual visitors are young, and undoubtedly many of them pass some time on Khao San. Some are Americans, but even more of them are from other countries: Australians having what they call their "o-s experience," their overseas experience, which begins in Sydney and ends six or eight months later with requisite Rough Guide– and Lonely Planet–advised stops in Goa for Christmas and in Nepal for a winter trek and in Angkor Wat for sunrise; hordes of Israelis, fresh out of the army — so many, in fact, that the best kosher food and the only Hebrew bookstore in Thailand are on Khao San Road. There are such large crowds of Japanese kids that a few guesthouses are de facto Japanese only, and you can buy a logo T-shirt of any Japanese baseball team from the vendors on the road. There are French and German and British and Canadians. Altogether, they have turned Khao San into a new sort of place — not really Thai anymore, barely Asian, overwhelmingly young, palpably transient, and anchored in the world by the Internet, where there is no actual time and no actual location. Khao San has the best foreign bookstores in Thailand, thanks to the books that backpackers sell before heading home, and it probably has the fewest prostitutes in Bangkok, partly because the guesthouses frown on overnight Thai guests, and partly because, one backpacker explained to me, most of the travelers would rather have sex with each other than with someone for hire. Khao San is now the travel hub for half the world, a place that prospers on the desire to be someplace else. The cheapest tickets on the most hair-raising of airlines can be bought in the scores of bucket shops that have collected in the neighborhood. Airlines you've never heard of, flying routes you never imagined, for prices you only dream of are the staple of Khao San travel agencies. The first time I ever heard of Khao San Road was from an American backpacker whom I met on a Bhutanese airline flight from Calcutta to Bangkok. He'd bought his ticket on Khao San Road. "I told the travel agent I didn't care how or when I got there," he said. "As long as it was cheap, I was ready to go."

I have a persistent fantasy that involves Khao San. In it, a middle-aged middlebrow middle manager from Phoenix is deposited at the western end of the road, near the Chanasongkhran police booth. He is a shocking sight, dressed in a blue business suit and a red tie and a white oxford shirt, carrying a Hartmann briefcase, and wearing a Timex. He wanders through the snarl of peddlers' carts and trinket booths. First he discards his suit for batik drawstring trousers and a hemp vest and a Che Guevara T-shirt, or knockoff Timberland cargo shorts and a Japanimation tank top, and he sells his Timex to a guy with a sign that says, WE BUY SOMETHING/CAMERA/TENT/SLEEPING BAG/WALKMAN/BACKPACK/SWISS KNIFE. He then gets a leather thong bracelet for one wrist and a silver cuff for the other, stops at Golden Lotus Tattoo for a few Chinese characters on his shoulder, gets his eyebrow pierced at Herbal House Healthy Center, has blond extensions braided into his hair, trades his briefcase for a Stüssy backpack and a Hmong fabric waistpack, watches twenty minutes of *The Phantom Menace* or *The Blair Witch Project* at Buddy Beer, goes into Hello Internet Café and registers as "zenmasterbob" on hotmail.com, falls in love with a Norwegian aromatherapist he meets in the communal shower at Joe Guest House, takes off with her on a trek through East Timor, and is never seen again.

The sidewalk vendors changed a little every day I was on Khao San. The road has a jumble of small businesses — travel agencies, Internet cafés, souvenir stores, bars — and the sidewalk and the edge of the roadbed are lined with stalls offering bootleg tapes, bogus Teva sandals, Hindu-print camisoles, and flyweight silver jewelry, along with the hair-braiders and the banana-pancake makers. A few spots had more transient occupants, and, except for the daily twitches in the exchange rate at Khao San's foreign-currency shops, they were one of the only things that distinguished one day from the next. The morning I arrived on Khao San, a nerdy Thai teenager had got a foothold halfway down one block, between Shaman Bookstore and Nadav Bead Shop, and was peddling electronic pagers. The next day he was gone, and a chatty young woman was there selling homemade burlap handbags. I began to think of the days that way — as "burlap-bag day" or "pager day" — to help tell them apart. One morning — it was miniature-mirrored-disco-ball day — I stopped to check my e-mail at Khao-San Cyber Home, a computer center set a few paces back from the sidewalk beside a stand of banana trees and a fishpond full of carp. On the street, the open-air Siam Oriental Inn was blasting a Swedish-dubbed version of *The Phantom Menace* on wide-screen TV, while across the way Buddy Beer, also open-air and also maximum volume, was showing *Wild Wild West,* and at the big bootleg-cassette booth next door an early Santana album screeched out of tinny speakers. The sounds collided like a car wreck, and even early in the day the wet, warm air smelled like Michelob and pad thai.

Inside the Khao-San Cyber Home, though, it was mercifully cool and quiet. In the front room were eight computer terminals with Pentium II microprocessors, a large and solemn photograph of King Bhumibol Adulyadej on one wall, and a Buddhist altar in the corner across from the front door. I left my shoes by the landing and padded across the floor to an open computer. On my left, a thin kid with a blond braid was instant-messaging someone in Australia. On my right, two girls were squeezed together at one terminal, tapping out a message in romanized Japanese. The more slowly and more uncomfortably and more dangerously you travel around Asia, the more rank you pull in backpacker culture — in other words, it's much cooler to go somewhere by cargo boat or pickup truck or milk train than to fly — but when it comes to computers Khao San is all speed. The first Macintosh computers in all of Thailand appeared here, and one Internet-service owner complained sourly to me that backpackers refused to use anything with Pentium I microprocessors anymore, so he had to upgrade all his machines to Pentium IIIs.

There are so many Internet outlets on Khao San Road now that the price to use a computer is probably the best in the world, and certainly the best in Asia — around 3 cents a minute, compared with, say, $5 a minute, which is what I paid to check my e-mail in Cambodia. In the past, a six-month odyssey through the Far East might have meant a few letters home and the rare long-distance phone call; now it's possible for a few cents to e-mail friends and family every day, order clothes from the Gap, and even read your local newspaper on-line. Some computer centers on Khao San stay open twenty-four hours a day. Hello Internet Café was the first in the neighborhood. Khao-San Cyber Home is one of the most recent. Until eight months ago, it wasn't a cyber home at all: it was an actual home of an actual Thai family, the Boonpojanasoontorns, who had been living on Khao San for many years. Until Chanin Boonpojanasoontorn learned about the Internet when he was at college and pushed the family to capitalize on their location, Khao-San Cyber Home computer center had been the family's living room.

Urasa Boonpojanasoontorn, the second youngest daughter, was behind the desk that day, and from time to time her father toddled by on some household task and then disappeared behind a door again. Urasa is twenty-five and has a round face and a square body and a quick, crumpled-up smile. She was wearing a white polo shirt and pleated khakis — nearly a nun's outfit on Khao San Road, where the skimpiest camisoles and the filmiest skirts are the usual backpacker gear. Urasa and her brother and sisters grew up playing soccer in the middle of the street with the other neighborhood kids, buying candy at the stores that back then stocked everyday groceries and household goods. "When I was in seventh grade," Urasa said to me, "I went outside and everything was different. The foreigners had arrived. It happened so fast! It was such a quiet place before. There were no foreigners. It changed, like, over-night, and I never went outside again." Her parents were afraid of the backpackers. Once the neighborhood changed, they insisted that the kids come home directly from school and stay away from the street. I asked her what they were afraid of. "They thought the backpackers had a different lifestyle than us," she said carefully. "Their language and their behavior were different. There were boys and girls traveling together, and the problem of drugs. And when I first saw the way the backpackers dressed . . ." She hesitated. The door behind her desk opened, and I could see her father in an easy chair, watching TV. "The way the backpackers dressed was shocking. My father and mom thought it wasn't good. I can't say what happens in other countries, but if I saw a Thai girl dressed like that I would think it wasn't good." She brightened and added, "Sometimes it was fun to hear the music from the bars. It wasn't sad when it changed. There was no more playing in the street, but then I grew up and I had other things to do. I studied hard. It's different from your culture. I had a tutor for two hours every day after school and on Saturday too."

The front door opened and three Israeli girls in pastel tank tops came in to use Khao-San Cyber Home's international long-distance service. They took their shoes off and left them by the door, a Thai tradition that most shops on Khao San forgo. Urasa decided to uphold it because she wanted her customers to see a little bit of her culture, her lifestyle, even though it meant that some backpackers in twenty-four-eyelet hiking boots chose to check their e-mail somewhere more lenient. A similar impulse accounts for the Buddhist altar and the king's portrait, though not for the enormous framed Michael Jordan poster beside her desk. "He's mine," Urasa said, tapping the glass above Jordan's eye. "I never heard about him until my sister went to college in Illinois, and she said to me, 'Urasa, you have to see this man. He is a *god*.'"

Something about Khao San Road makes you feel as though it could eat you alive. The junkies and the glue-sniffers lurking in the alleys are part of it, and so are the clean-cut kids with stiff, Ecstasy-fueled grins dancing at the cafés; the aimlessness that pervades the place is both pleasantly spacey and a little scary when you glimpse an especially blank face. Travelers do vanish in all sorts of ways. The first cybercafé I stopped in had a $10,000-reward sign on the wall which said, HAVE YOU SEEN MY SON? HE WAS BACKPACKING AROUND INDIA AND WAS LAST HEARD FROM IN MAY 1997 FROM NORTHERN INDIA. Urasa said she sees a lot of lost souls. One day, an American girl came into Khao-San Cyber Home to call her mother and could hardly talk because she was crying so hard. "She had lost her boyfriend," Urasa told me. "He disappeared from her in Nepal." Sometimes, visitors planning another kind of trip are busted and subsequently relocated to Bangkok's Ban Kwan Prison. Guesthouses often post lists of foreigners who are locked up on drug charges, and encourage you to visit Lyle Doniger, of Australia, or Alan Jon Davies, of Britain, or any number of Americans and Danes and Italians at Ban Kwan if you find yourself with nothing to do one afternoon.

The day begins at night on Khao San Road. Usually a soccer game is being broadcast from one bar and five or six movies are being broadcast from the others, and the cassette dealers are demonstrating the quality of their bootleg tapes by playing Global Trance Mission or Techno Trance Mania or Earth, Wind and Fire at top volume. Kids clutching copies of *Bangkok Groovy Map & Guide* and

Teach Yourself Indonesian and *Teach Yourself Card Games for 1* and the *Swahili Phrasebook* amble up and down the street. They emerge from the guesthouses — and their bottom-dollar rooms, with wafer-thin walls and battered mattresses — to collect in the cafés for 10-cent plates of curry chicken and "Stogarnov Steak" and beer and to shop. The first Thai head of state to travel outside the region was King Rama V, who visited Europe in 1897. He brought back Waterford crystal from Ireland, Sèvres porcelain and Baccarat goblets from France, Murano glass from Italy, Royal Crown Derby plates from England. When you visit Khao San Road, you can bring back Indian undershirts decorated with Hindu imagery, Australian Billabong sweats, Nike jackets made in Indonesia, rubber-platform faux-fur thongs from another planet, Game Boys from Japan, and a used copy of *Memoirs of a Geisha* that was published in England and sold to a secondhand bookstore in Bangkok by a New Zealander on his way to Vietnam.

At around midnight I ran into the South African English teacher from Taiwan who had been on her way back from massage school in northern Thailand the other time I'd met her. Seeing her again was both a shock and not a shock, because Khao San is so transitory a place that you imagine each encounter there to be singular, but then you realize that the world is small and this particular world of young adventurers is smaller yet, and that there is nothing extraordinary about seeing the same people, because their great adventures tend to take them to the same few places over and over again. Her name was Elizabeth, and she and I stopped at a street vendor and bought corn on the cob and sat on a curb near My House Guest House to eat. This time she'd just come back from a full-moon party on the southern Thai island of Koh Phangan, a party of two thousand travelers, most of them high on Ecstasy or pot or psychedelics, painting a herd of oxen with Day-Glo colors and dancing for hours on the edge of the sea. She now had a terrible headache, but she didn't think it was from the drugs or the late hours. She blamed a Sikh psychic she'd met that morning on Khao San who had tricked her into paying him $100 so he wouldn't curse her karma. I felt sorry for her, so I treated her to a bowl of noodle soup from a stand at the western end of the street. We were, at that moment, on the very edge of the rest of the city. Thirty paces away, on Chakrabongse Road, were a dozen bridal shops where

Thai girls bought their big white gowns; a few paces beyond that was the temple, Wat Chanasongkhran, where monks in yellow were chanting their daily sutras. All of it seemed surreal and sort of irrelevant and much farther away from Khao San Road than almost anywhere else in the universe, including outer space. Elizabeth had a travel tip for me. *The Phantom Menace* was starting at 1:00 A.M. at Buddy Beer, and if she finished her soup, and we hurried, we could make it back for the opening scene.

DAVID QUAMMEN

The Post-Communist Wolf

FROM *Outside*

IT'S TWO HOURS after sunset on this snow-clogged Romanian mountain, and in the headlight of a stalled snowmobile stand five worried people and two amused dogs. One of the dogs is a husky. Her name, Yukai, translates from a distant Indian language to mean "northern lights." Her pale gray eyes glow coldly, like tiny winter moons. One of the worried people is me. My name translates from Norwegian to mean "cow man" or, less literally, "a cattle jockey who should have stayed in his paddock" — neither of which lends me any aura of masterly attunement to present circumstances. The temperature is falling.

Unlike placid Yukai, we five humans are poorly prepared for a night's bivouac in the snow, having long since abandoned most of our gear in an ill-advised gambit to lighten our load and move faster. Three of us — myself, the American photographer Gordon Wiltsie, and a German visitor, Uli Geertz, from the conservation group Vier Pfoten ("Four Paws") — are on backcountry skis with skins, schlepping along steadily behind a biologist named Christoph Promberger and his biologist wife, Barbara Promberger-Fuerpass, who are driving the two snowmobiles.

Christoph is a lanky, thirty-four-year-old German whose raucous black hair and almond-thin, lidded eyes make him appear faintly Mongolian — that is, like a young Mongolian basketball player with a wry smile. Though officially employed by the Munich Wildlife Society, he has worked here in the Carpathian Mountains since 1993, collaborating with a Romanian counterpart named Ovidiu Ionescu, of the Forestry Research and Management Institute, to create a new conservation program called the Carpathian Large Carnivore Project. Barbara, a fair-haired Austrian, joined the project more recently and is now beginning a study of lynx. Both of them are hardy souls with considerable field experience in remote parts of the Yukon (where Christoph did his master's work on the relationship between wolves and ravens, and where later they honeymooned), so they know a thing or three about winter survival, backcountry travel, problem avoidance, snowmobile repair. But tonight's conditions, reflecting an unusually severe series of January storms and an absence of other human traffic along this road, have caught them by surprise.

Gordon and I are surprised too: that Murphy's Law, though clearly in force, seems unheard-of in Romania.

At the outset Christoph was towing a cargo sled, but that had to be cast loose and left behind. Even without it, the Skidoos have been foundering in soft six-foot drifts, and much of our energy for the past few hours has gone into pushing these infernal machines, pulling them, kicking them, cursing them, nudging them ever higher toward a peak called Fata lui Ilie, ever deeper into trouble. The sensible decision, after we'd bogged at the first steep pitch and then bogged again and again, would have been to turn back at nightfall and retreat to the valley.

Instead we went on, convincing ourselves recklessly that the going would get easier farther up. Ha. Somewhere ahead, maybe three miles, maybe five, is a cabin. We have one balky headlamp, a bit of food, matches, two pairs of snowshoes as well as the skis, but no tent and, since ditching even our packs back at the last steep switchback, no sleeping bags. The good news is that the forest is full of wolves.

"I believe the term is *goat-fucked,*" Gordon says suddenly. "A situation that's so absurdly bad, it becomes sublime." Gordon's own situation is more sublime than the rest of ours, since he's suffering from a gut-curdling intestinal flu as well as the generally shared ailments — cold hands, exhaustion, frustration, hunger, and embarrassment. "We could easily spend the night out here, without sleeping bags," he adds.

On that point I'm inclined to disagree: We could do it, yes, but it wouldn't be easy.

*

Christoph's mission with the Carpathian Large Carnivore Project is to investigate the biology and population status of Romania's three major species of predator — the wolf, the brown bear, the European lynx — and to explore measures that might help conserve those populations into the future. His immediate purpose, with this snow trek toward Fata lui Ilie, is to use the cabin as a base for three or four days of wolf trapping. The trapped wolves, if any, will be fitted with radio collars for subsequent tracking.

Since 1994, Christoph and his coworkers have collared thirteen wolves, at least three of which have been illegally shot. Two have dispersed beyond the study zone, and four others have fallen cryptically silent, probably because their transmitters failed. One of the missing animals is a female named Timis, the first Carpathian wolf Christoph ever touched. Timis, the alpha bitch in her pack, was a savvy survivor, and she opened his eyes to the range of lupine resourcefulness in Romania. Originally trapped and collared in a remote valley near the city of Brasov, Timis and her pack soon relocated themselves closer and began making nocturnal forays into town. On Brasov's south fringe was a large meadow where they could hunt rabbits, and by skulking along a sewage channel, then crossing a street or two, they could find their way to a garbage dump, rich with such toothsome possibilities as slaughterhouse scraps, feral cats, and rats. In 1996, Timis denned near the area and produced ten pups. With the aid of a remote camera set fifty meters from the den, Christoph spent many hours watching her perform the intimate chores of motherhood. But times change and idylls fade. Timis disappeared, the fate of her pups is unknown, and in the enterprising ferment of post-Communist Romania, the rabbit-filled meadow is now occupied by a Shell station and a McDonald's.

At the time of our visit, only two wolves are still transmitting, one of which is a male known as Tsiganu, recently collared in another valley not far from Brasov. The wolf population of the Carpathians is sizable, but the animals are difficult to trap — far more difficult than wolves of the Yukon or Minnesota, Christoph figures — probably because their long history of close but troubled relations with humans has left them more wary than North American wolves. Romania is an old country, rich with natural blessings but much wrinkled by conflict and paradox, and history here is a first explanation for everything, including the ecology and behavior of *Canis lupus*. Go back two thousand years, before the imperial Romans put their stamp on the place, and you find the Dacia, a fearsome indigenous people who referred to their warriors as Daois, meaning "the young wolves."

Just after World War II, wolves roamed the forests throughout Romania, even the lowland forests, with a total population of perhaps five thousand. They preyed on roe deer, red deer, and wild boar, but were also much loathed and dreaded for their depredations against livestock, especially sheep. In the 1950s the early Communist government, under a leader named Gheorghe Gheorghiu-Dej, sponsored a campaign of hunting, trapping, poisoning, and killing of pups at their dens to reduce the wolf population and make the countryside safe for Marxist-Leninist lambs. That antiwolf pogrom worked well in the lowlands, which were more thoroughly devoted to agriculture and heavy industry. On the high slopes of the Carpathians, though, where lovely beech and oak forests were protected by a tradition of conscientious forestry and where dreams and memories of freedom survived among at least a few of the hardy rural people, wolves survived too.

The Carpathians also served as a refuge for brown bear and lynx. The bear population stands currently at about 5,400, a startling multitude of *Ursus arctos* considering that in all the western United States (excluding Alaska), where we call them grizzlies, there are only about a thousand. The wolf population, at somewhere between two thousand and three thousand, represents a large fraction of all *Canis lupus* surviving between the Atlantic Ocean and Russia. Why has Romania, of all places, remained such a haven for large carnivores? The reasons involve accidents of geology, geography, ecology, politics, and the ironic circumstance that a certain Communist potentate, successor to Gheorghiu-Dej, came to fancy himself a great hunter. This of course was the pip-squeak dictator Nicolae Ceausescu, who for decades ruled Romania as though he owned it.

Born in the village of Scornicesti and apprenticed to a Bucharest shoemaker at age eleven, Nicolae Ceausescu made his way upward as a gofer to early Communist activists during their years of persecution by a fascist regime. He served time in prison, a good place for making criminal and political contacts. He was cunning, he was ambitious and efficacious though never brilliant, he bided his time, sliding into this opening and then that one, eventually gaining ultimate control as general secretary of the Communist Party in 1965. He styled himself the Conducator, a lofty title that paired him with an earlier supreme leader, Marshal Ion Antonescu, the right-wing dictator who had ruled Romania during World War II. Ceausescu distanced himself from certain Soviet policies such as the invasion of Czechoslovakia in 1968, and thereby made himself America's favorite Communist autocrat, at least during the administrations of Nixon, Ford, and Carter. His manner of domestic governance remained merely Stalinism in a Romanian hat, but for a long time the United States didn't notice.

Ceausescu's dark little shadow cast itself across Romania for twenty-five years, with the help of his Securitate apparatus of secret police and informers, which included as many as 3 million people in a nation of just 23 million. Such institutional menace wasn't uncommon in the Communist bloc, of course, but it may have weighed more heavily here, due to a certain wary, fatalistic strain in the national spirit. Romania under Ceausescu had a few brave dissenters, but not the same sort of robust underground network of dissidents that existed in the Soviet Union or, say, Czechoslovakia. There's a nervous old Romanian proverb, counseling caution: *Vorbesti de lup si lupul e la usa.* Speak of the wolf and he's at your door.

Ceausescu's industrial, economic, and social policies were as wrongheaded as they were eccentric. Though he was Stalinist in style, he had that self-important yearning for independence from Moscow, and so he pushed Romania to develop its own capacities in oil refining, mineral smelting, and heavy manufacturing. During the 1970s his industrialization initiative sucked off a huge fraction of the country's GNP and generated a big burden in foreign loans; then in the 1980s he became obsessed with paying off those loans and made the Romanian populace endure ferocious austerity in order to do it. He exported petroleum products and food while his own people suffered in underheated apartments without enough to eat. He instituted a systematization campaign, as he called it, which essentially meant bulldozing old neighborhoods and villages in order to force their inhabitants into high-rise urban housing projects, where he could better control the flow of vital resources.

His systematization created a larger proletariat living amid ugly urban blight, and his industrialization resulted in some horrendous point-source pollution problems, such as the smelter at Zlatna and the gold-reprocessing plant at Baia Mare, which just recently let slip a vast wet fart of toxic sludge from one of its containment ponds into the Danube drainage, poisoning fish downstream for miles. But for some reason Ceausescu did not become obsessed with exporting timber, and so the Carpathian highlands remained wild and sylvan while other parts of the country grew grim.

The Conducator himself lived a life of splendorous self-indulgence and paranoia, like a neurasthenic king. He had food-tasters to protect him from poisoning. He had germ obsessions like Howard Hughes. He trusted only his wife, Elena, who was his full partner in megalomania and his chief adviser on how to govern badly. With her, he sealed himself away in palatial residences, letting the people see him mainly through stagy televised ceremonials. For bolstering his ego and political luster he depended also on occasional mass rallies, for which tens of thousands of citizens were mandatorily mustered to express — or anyway, feign — adulation. The last of those, on December 21, 1989, went badly askew and led to his fall. All the other Communist leaders who got dumped during that dizzy time, from Gorbachev down, were content to go peacefully, but Nicolae Ceausescu required execution.

Ceausescu's shadow still lingers in some places, including the snowed-over road that may or may not eventually carry us to Fata lui Ilie. The forest is thick. The spruce trees are large and heavily flocked with snow. While the Skidoos are mired still again, on another steep switchback below a ridgeline, I wonder aloud whether this route was originally cut for hauling timber.

"No, this was a hunting road for Ceausescu," Christoph tells me. "He'd fly in by helicopter. And his people would come in by four-wheel-drive to organize the hunt." Among other fatuities, Ceausescu prided himself as a great killer of trophy-sized bears. Although his name went into record books and his trophies can still be seen at a museum in the town of Posada, Ceausescu's actual accomplishments were contemptible: squeezing off kill shots at animals that had been located, fattened, and baited for his convenience. The sad irony is that, so long as he arrogated the country's bear-hunting rights largely to himself, the bear population flourished. Records show that it peaked, at about eight thousand animals, in 1989. The end of that year was when the ground shifted for everyone — carnivores, citizens, and the Conductor himself. The people finally revolted, and Ceausescu, losing his nerve, tried to flee but was captured. On Christmas Day, before a firing squad, the great hunter got his.

Farther along, when we pass a spur road to Ceausescu's helicopter pad, I feel tempted to ski up and inspect it. But by now Christoph and Barbara are far ahead on the snowmobiles, Gordon is with them, and I'm skiing through darkness with only Uli's dim headlamp as a point of guidance. Ceausescu is dead, the bears are asleep, the new government is led by a center-right coalition of parliamentarians, the Carpathian forests are being privatized to their great peril, the currency is weak, the mafia is getting strong, and all idle contemplation of the pungent contingencies of recent Romanian history is best left, I realize, for a time when I'm not threatened by hypothermia.

The wolf known as Tsiganu was trapped on December 19, 1999, near a valley called Tsiganesti. The handling, collaring, and release were done by a Romanian wildlife technician named Marius Scurtu, a sturdy young man with an unassuming grin and a missing front tooth. Marius had blossomed into an important member of the Carnivore Project, absorbing well Christoph's field training in wolf capture and showing great appetite for the hard backcountry legwork. In recognition of his role, he was allowed to christen the new animal. Besides relating the wolf to that particular valley, the name he picked — Tsiganu — means "Gypsy."

At the time of trapping, Tsiganu weighed ninety-five pounds. He was notable for the lankiness of his legs and the length of his canine teeth. Since collaring, he has rejoined a small pack of four or five animals, though whether he himself is the alpha male remains uncertain. He now broadcasts his locator beeps on a frequency of 148.6 megahertz, and several times each week either Marius or another project technician goes out with a map, a radio receiver, and a directional antenna to check on him. Tsiganu seldom lets himself be seen, but from his prints and other evidence in the snow, a good tracker can learn what he has been doing. In the past month he has killed at least three roe deer, two dogs, and two sheep.

On a warmish day not long before our misadventure on the trail toward Fata lui Ilie, Gordon and I skied along with a tracker named Peter Surth. We followed him up a tight little canyon into the foothills above a village. It was slow travel, through wet heavy snow along the bank of a small stream, but within less than a mile we came to a kill. The rib cage and hide of a roe deer, partly covered by overnight snowfall, confirmed that Tsiganu and his pack hadn't gone hungry. Continuing upward, we passed an old log barn from which we could hear the companionable gurgles and neck bells of sheep, safely shut away behind a door. Moments later we met a man in country clothes, presumably the sheep owner, trudging down a steep slope. Peter spoke a few words with him, then told us the gist of the exchange. Wolves, you want wolves? the man had said. Wolves we've got, around here. Lots of them.

We angled up a slope, rising away from the creek bottom. A half-hour of climbing brought us, sweating, onto a ridge. Peter took another listen with the receiver, catching a strong signal that seemed to place Tsiganu within three hundred yards. Which direction? Well, probably there, to the northwest. But the tempo of beeps also indicated that the animal was active, not resting, and therefore his position could change fast. We hustled northwest along the ridgeline. When Peter listened again he got a much different bearing, this one suggesting that Tsiganu and his pack were below us, possibly far below, on the opposite slope of the creek valley we'd just left. Or maybe the earlier signal had been deceptive because of echo effects from the terrain. Or maybe this one was the echo.

Such are the ambiguities in tracking an animal that doesn't want to be found.

Not far from where we stood, pondering the whereabouts of Tsiganu, lay a snowbound hamlet of thatch-roofed cottages, conical haystacks, and a few shapely farmhouses with gabled and turreted tin roofs, all hung like a saddle blanket across the steep sides of the ridge. It was called Magura. It seemed a mirage of bucolic tranquillity from the late Middle Ages, but it was real.

Gordon and I had been there a few days earlier with another project worker, Andrei Blumer. In bright sunshine and stabbing cold, we had skied up from another valley on the far side, stopping to visit an elderly couple named Gheorghe and Aurica Surdu. The Surdus live in a trim little cottage they built fifty years ago to replace a five-hundred-year-old cottage on the same spot, in which Aurica had been born. Aurica is a pretty woman of seventy-some years, with a deeply lined face and a wide, jokey smile. We were greeted effusively by her, Gheorghe, and their middle-aged son, another Gheorghe but nicknamed Mosorel, who himself had boot-kicked up through the snow for a Saturday visit. Passing from deep snowbanks and icy air into a small narrow room with a low ceiling, a bare bulb, and a woodstove upon which simmered a pot of rose-hip tea, we commenced to be steam-cooked with hospitality. Aurica, wearing a headscarf and thick-waled corduroy vest, spoke as little English as Gordon and I did Romanian, but she made herself understood, and her motherly eyes missed nothing. She stood by the stove and fussed cheerily while Andrei traded news with Mosorel, Gordon thawed his lenses, and I waited for my glasses to clear. *Have some rose tea, you boys, get warm. Here, have some bread, have some cheese, don't be so skinny.* The tea was deep-simmered and laced with honey. *Have some smoked pork. And the sausage too, it's good, here, I'll cut you a bigger piece, don't you like it? You do? Then don't be shy, eat.* We had set off without lunch, so we were pushovers. *Mosorel, give them some* tsuica, *what are you waiting for?* Mosorel, grinning broadly, poured us heated shots of his mother's homemade apple-pear brandy, lightly enhanced with sugar and pepper. *Tsuica* is more than just the national moonshine; it's a form of communion, and we communed.

Mosorel's right hand was swaddled in a large white bandage. It testified to a saw accident several months earlier, Andrei explained, in which Mosorel had sliced off his pinky and broken his fourth finger while cutting up an old chest for usable lumber. Mosorel is a carpenter, sometimes. Sometimes too he's a tailor; his nickname means, roughly, "Mr. Thread." Until the saw accident he had also been pulling shifts at a factory down in the nearby town. Like his parents, who still raise pigs, cows, sheep, onions, corn, beets, potatoes, and more than enough apples and pears for *tsuica*, Mosorel is a versatile man of diverse outputs. The hand injury didn't seem to dampen his spirit, possibly because some joyous aptitude for survival runs like a dominant gene through the family, homozygous on both sides of his parentage. As the sweet liquor spread its heat in our bellies, the talk turned in that direction — to survival, and how its terms of demand had changed.

During the Communist era, Gheorghe and Aurica Surdu had been required to supply eight hundred liters of milk each year to the state. Andrei translated this fact, Aurica nodding forcefully: Yes, eight hundred. There were also quotas to be met in lambs, calves, and wool. Since the revolution, things had changed; no longer were Gheorghe and Aurica obliged to deliver up a large share of their farm produce, but market prices were so low that, rather than selling it, they fed their milk to the pigs. So, I asked simplemindedly, is life better or worse since the fall of Ceausescu? The talk rattled forward in Romanian for a few moments until Andrei paused, turned aside, and told me that Mosorel had just said something important.

"At least we're not scared now," he had said.

Just below the high village of Magura, at the mouth of the small river valley draining from Fata lui Ilie and other peaks, sits a peculiar little town called Zarnesti. Narrow streets, paved with packed snow at this time of year, run between old-style Transylvanian row houses tucked behind tall courtyard walls closed with big wooden gates. Horse-drawn sleighs jingle by, carrying passengers on the occasional Sunday outing. Heavy horse carts with rubber tires haul sacks of corn, piles of fodder, and other freight. Young mothers pull toddlers and grocery bags on metal-frame sleds. There are also a few automobiles — mostly beat-up Romanian Dacias — creeping between the snowbanks, and along the south edge of town rises, with sudden ugliness, a cluster of five-story concrete apartment blocks from the Communist era, like a histogram charting the grim triumph of central planning. Beside the train tracks sits a large pulp mill that eats trees from the surrounding forests, digests them, and extrudes the result as paper and industrial cellulose.

You can walk all afternoon along the winding lanes of Zarnesti, down to the main street, past the Orthodox church, past the pulp mill, looping back through the post office square, and not see a single neon sign. There are no restaurants and no hotels, none that I've managed to spot, anyway. Yet the population is 27,000. People live and work here, but few visit. For years Zarnesti was off-limits to travelers because of another industrial plant in town, the one commonly known as the "bicycle factory." The bicycle factory was really a munitions factory, built in 1938, when Romania was menaced by bellicose neighbors during the buildup toward World War II. Later, in the Communist era, it thrived and diversified. It produced artillery, mortars, rockets, treads for heavy equipment, boxcars, and — yes, as window dressing — a few Victoria bicycles. For decades it was Zarnesti's leading industry. But the market for Romanian-made rockets and mortars has been wan since the disintegration of the Warsaw Pact, and the bicycle factory, which once employed 13,000 people, has laid off about 5,000 since 1989. At the pulp mill, likewise, the workforce has shrunk to a fraction of its former size. The town's economy now resembles a comatose patient on a gurney, ready to be wheeled who knows where. Still, Zarnesti is filled with stalwart people, and a few of those people are energized with new ideas and new hopes.

One new idea is large-carnivore ecotourism. It began in 1995, when Christoph Promberger was contacted by a British conservation group, working through a travel agency, that had heard about the Carpathian Large Carnivore Project and wanted to bring paying visitors to this remote corner of Europe for a chance to see wolves and bears. They came — not actually to Zarnesti, but to another small community nearby — and the money spent on lodging and food, though modest, was significant to the local economy. Two years later Christoph and his colleagues repeated the experiment as an independent venture. They welcomed eight different tour groups totaling some seventy people, who were accommodated in small *pensiunes,* vacation boardinghouses run by local families. By now the wolf fieldwork had come to focus on the wooded foothills and flats of the Barsa Valley, which stretches thirty miles into the mountains above Zarnesti. Although the likelihood of actually glimpsing a wolf or a brown bear in the wild is always low, even for experienced trackers like Marius and Peter, some nature-loving travelers were quite satisfied to hike or ride horses through Carpathian forests in which a sighting, or a set of tracks, was always possible. Large carnivores, it turned out, were attracting people who wouldn't come just for the edelweiss and primrose.

One of the *pensiunes* where the travelers stay is owned by Gigi Popa, a forty-six-year-old businessman whose trim mustache, balding crown, and gently solicitous manner conceal the soul of a risk taker and a performer. Give him three shots of *tsuica,* a guitar, and an audience — he'll smile shyly, then hold the floor for an eve-

ning. Give him a window of economic opportunity — he'll climb
through it. In the 1980s, Gigi worked as a cash register repairman
for a large, inefficient government enterprise charged with servic-
ing machines all over Romania. The machines in question were
mediocre at best and destined to be obsoletized by modern electronic versions. Gigi couldn't divine all the coming upheavals, but
he could see clearly enough that mechanical Romanian cash registers were not a wave to ride into the future.

"After the revolution, I change quickly my job and my direction,"
Gigi says. He got out of cash register repair and opened a small grocery and dry goods store in the back of the house.

He was ready for the next step, not knowing what the next step
might be, when Christoph told him about English, Swiss, and German travelers who would be coming to Zarnesti, drawn by the
wolves in the mountains but needing lodging in town. Gigi
promptly remodeled his home and his identity again. He became a
pensiune-keeper, with four guest rooms ready the first summer and
another four the following year. He now plays an important part-
nership role to the Carpathian Large Carnivore Project's program
of tourism. Gigi's *pensiune* is where Gordon and I have been sleeping, for instance, when we're not sublimely *geschtuck* in the mountains.

One morning I ask Gigi the same question I asked Mosorel: Has
the new order made life better or worse? "The good thing of the
revolution is everybody can do what he have dreams," Gigi says.
"Because everybody have dreams. And in Ceausescu time you can
do no thing for your own. Must be on the same" — he makes a
glass-ceiling gesture — "level. Everybody." Whereas now, he says, a
person with initiative, wit, a few good ideas and a willingness to
gamble on them can raise himself and his family above the dreary
old limit. The bad thing, he says, is that free-market entrepreneur-
ship involves far more personal stress than a government job in
cash register maintenance.

One day in the summer of 1999, Christoph and Barbara noticed a
sizable construction job under way in the Barsa Valley, some miles
upstream from Zarnesti. The foundation was being laid for a hun-
dred-room hotel.

This was not long after Christoph had begun discussions with the town mayor about a vision of sustainable ecotourism for Zarnesti. The crucial premise of that vision was to let the Barsa Valley remain undeveloped while the infrastructure to support visitors would be built as small-scale operations down in the town. If the valley itself were consumed by suburban sprawl and recreational development, Christoph had explained, then the carnivore habitat would be badly fragmented if not destroyed, and the Large Carnivore Project would be forced to move, taking its ecotourism business with it. But if the Barsa habitat were protected, then the project could remain, channeling visitors to whatever small *pensiunes* might be available in Zarnesti. Everyone had seemed to agree that this was the sensible approach. Yet now the hotel construction revealed that someone else — an investor from the city of Brasov, fifty miles away — intended to exploit the area on an ambitious scale. And belatedly it was revealed that the town council had approved open-development zoning for the entire valley.

"So this was disaster," Christoph remembers thinking. "Absolute disaster."

Christoph himself had to leave the country just then for a short visit back in Germany. He and Andrei Blumer, who joined the project as a specialist in rural development, hastily shaped their best argument for valley protection, so that Andrei could present their case to the mayor.

Zarnesti's mayor at the time was a man named Gheorghe Lupu, formerly an engineer in the bicycle factory before Romanian bicycles lost their tactical military appeal. Bright and unpretentious, his dark hair beginning to go gray, Mr. Lupu wore a black leather jacket at work, kept his office door open to drop-by callers, and described himself jokingly as a "cowboy mayor." About the problems of Zarnesti, though, he was serious. Tax revenues yielded only 10 percent of what they did before the revolution, he could tell you; the pulp mill had laid off two thousand people, the bicycle factory even more; the sewage system and the gas-supply network needed work; the roads too cried out for repair. There was little basis to assume that this harried man would muster much sympathy for protecting wolf habitat — notwithstanding the fact that his own name, Lupu, translates as "wolf." But would he be able, at least, to grasp the connection between large carnivores, open landscape, and tourism? It was a tense juncture for Christoph, having to absent himself while the whole Barsa Valley stood in jeopardy.

Just before leaving for Germany, he received a terse electronic message on his mobile phone. It was from Andrei, saying: "Lupu stopped everything." The mayor had moved to reverse the council's decision. Let the tourists eat and sleep in Zarnesti, he agreed, and pay their visits to the wild landscape as day-trippers. He had embraced the idea of zoning protection for the valley.

But to announce a policy of protection is one thing; real safety against the forces of change is another. Barbara and I get a noisy reminder of that difference, in the upper valley, during an excursion to set traps for her lynx study.

We're twenty-some miles above Zarnesti, where the Barsa road narrows to a single snowmobile trail. Barbara has driven her Ski-doo, loaded with custom-made leg-hold traps and other gear. I ride my skis at the end of a tow rope behind. In the fresh snow at trailside we've seen multiple sets of lynx prints, as well as varied signs of other animals — deep tracks from several red deer that came wallowing down off a slope, fox tracks, even one set from a restless bear that has interrupted its hibernation for a stroll. Late in the afternoon, just as Barbara finishes camouflaging her last trap, we hear the yowl of another snowmobile ascending the valley. At first I assume that it must be Christoph's. But as the machine throttles back, I see it's a large recreational Polaris, driven by a middle-aged stranger in a fur hat, with a woman on the seat behind him. Then I notice that Barbara has stiffened.

She exchanges a few sentences in Romanian with the stranger. He seems rather jovial; Barbara speaks curtly. The man swings his snowmobile around us and goes ripping on up the valley. When he's beyond earshot, which is instantly, Barbara explains what just transpired.

Claims he's from Brasov, she says. But he is not Romanian, to judge from his accent. Probably a wealthy Italian with a second home. When he heard what Barbara was doing — setting traps to catch lynx — he thought she meant trapping for pelts, and he acted snooty. When she added that it's for a radio-tracking study, he graced her with his patronizing and ignorant approval. Oh, you're doing wildlife research — okay. His ladyfriend, on the other hand, was worried. "She asked if it would be dangerous to continue, with all the lynx in here. Ya, it would," Barbara says caustically. "Keep out." The upper valley is closed to joy-riding traffic,

and those two have no business being here, Barbara explains. Unlimited motorized access, along with development sprawl and
other symptoms of the new liberty and affluence, are now a
damned sight more threatening to the lynx population — and the
wolves, and the bears — than fur trapping, judicious timbering,
or even the crude, spoliatory hunting once practiced by Nicolae
Ceausescu, with all his minions and helicopter pads.

Barbara has never before seen a recreational snowmobile in
Zarnesti, let alone up here. "Aaagh," she says, as the roar of the Polaris fades above us. "It all starts with one. There are so many rich
guys in Brasov now."

The following day, Christoph receives a disturbing piece of news by
mobile phone from Marius: Tsiganu has been shot.

The details are still blurry, but it seems that a couple of boar
hunters let fly at the wolf for no particular reason except his wolf-
hood. Probably they were poaching, since no gamekeeper was present, as mandated for a legitimate boar hunt. Tsiganu is wounded,
hard to say how badly, but still on his feet at last report. Marius, having heard the shots, came upon the hunters a few moments later.
Marius is still out there, Christoph tells me, following a trail of radio beeps and blood spoor through the wet snow. Before long he
will either find Tsiganu's fresh carcass or else run out of daylight
without knowing quite what's what.

A day passes. Still there's no definite news of Tsiganu. On the
morning of the second day, I set out tracking with Marius and two
project assistants.

We park the Dacia truck on a roadside above a village and begin
hoofing along a farm lane into the foothills. We follow a snow-covered trail on a climbing traverse between meadows, along wooded
gullies, beyond the last of the farmhouses and the last of the barking dogs, past two men hauling logs with a pair of oxen. Marius
moves briskly. He's a short, solid fellow with good wind and a long
stride. He cares about this animal — both about *Canis lupus* as a
denizen of the Romanian mountains, that is, and about Tsiganu
as an individual. But Marius is a homebred Romanian forestry
worker, not a foreign-trained biologist, and his attitude is com-
plexly grounded in local realities.

"Last year the wolf was killing for me two sheep," he says as we walk. "Because the shepherd was drunk. Was like an invitation to eat." Some farmers moan about such losses, Marius says, but what do they expect? That the wolf, which has lived as a predator in these mountains for thousands of years, should now transform itself into a vegetarian? As for hunters who would offhandedly kill a wolf for its fur, he can't comprehend them. "Also I am a hunter," he says. He shoots ducks, pheasants, wild boar, and in self-defense he wouldn't hesitate to kill a bear. But a wolf, no, never. It's much nicer simply to go out with his dogs, hike in the forest, and know that in this place the ancient animals are still present.

Two miles in, we pick up a signal from Tsiganu's collar. The bearing is south-southwest, toward a steep wooded valley that descends from a castle-shaped rock formation among the peaks above. Farther along, we get another signal on roughly the same line, and now the tempo of beeps indicates that Tsiganu is alive — at least barely alive, because he's moving. Here we split into two groups, for a better chance of crossing his trail. Marius and I continue the traverse until we find a single set of wolf tracks, then back-follow them up a slope. The tracks are deep, softened in outline by at least one afternoon's melting, and show no sign of blood. Yesterday? Or earlier, before the shooting? They might be Tsiganu's or not. If his, is the stride normal? Has his wound already clotted? Or is he lying near death with a slug lodged against his backbone, or in his lung, or in his jaw, while his packmates have gone on without him? Are these in fact his tracks, or some other wolf's? No way of knowing.

So we hike again toward the radio signal, post-holing our way through knee-deep crust. We round a bend that brings us into the valley below the castle-shaped peak. Here the radio signal gets stronger. We stare upward, scanning for movement. We see none.

Marius disconnects the directional antenna from the receiver. He listens again, using the antenna cable's nub like a stethoscope, trying to fine-focus the bearing. Again a strong signal. So we're close now. Maybe one hundred meters, Marius says. He tips back his head and offers a loud wolfish howl, a rather good imitation of a pack's contact call. We listen for response. There's a distant, dim echo of his voice coming off the mountain, followed by silence. We wait. Nothing. We turn away. I begin to fumble with my binoculars.

Then from up in the beeches comes a new sound. It's Tsiganu, the Gypsy carnivore, howling back.

SALMAN RUSHDIE

A Dream of Glorious Return

FROM *The New Yorker*

THURSDAY, APRIL 6: I have left India many times. The first time was when I was thirteen and went to boarding school in Rugby, England. My mother didn't want me to go but I said I did. I flew west excitedly in January 1961, not really knowing that I was taking a step that would change my life forever. A few years later, my father, without telling me, suddenly sold Windsor Villa, our family home in Bombay. The day I heard this, I felt an abyss open beneath my feet. I think that I never forgave my father for selling that house, and I'm sure that if he hadn't I would still be living in it. Since then the characters in my fiction have frequently flown west from India, but in novel after novel their author's imagination has returned to it. This, perhaps, is what it means to love a country: that its shape is also yours, the shape of the way you think and feel and dream. That you can never really leave.

Before the Partition massacres of 1947, my parents left Delhi and moved south, correctly calculating that there would be less trouble in secular, cosmopolitan Bombay. As a result, I grew up in that tolerant, broad-minded city whose particular quality — call it freedom — I've been trying to capture and celebrate ever since. *Midnight's Children,* which was published in 1981, was my first attempt at such literary land reclamation. Living in London, I wanted to get India back; and the delight with which Indian readers clasped the book to themselves, the passion with which they, in turn, claimed me, remains the most precious memory of my writing life.

In 1988, I was planning to buy myself a place in Bombay with the advance I'd received for my new novel. But that novel was *The Satanic Verses,* and after it was published the world changed for me, and I was no longer able to set foot in the country that has been my primary source of artistic inspiration. Whenever I made inquiries about getting a visa (although I was born an Indian national, I now have a British passport), word invariably came back that I would not be granted one. Nothing about my plague years, the dark decade that followed Ayatollah Khomeini's fatwa, has hurt more than this rift. I felt like a jilted lover, left alone with his unbearable love.

It has been a deep rift. India was the first country to ban *The Satanic Verses;* the book was proscribed without due process before it entered the country, by a weak Congress government led by Rajiv Gandhi, in a desperate, unsuccessful bid for Muslim votes. After that, it sometimes seemed as if the Indian authorities were determined to rub salt in the wound. And the ban on *The Satanic Verses* is, of course, still in place.

After the September 24, 1998, agreement between the British and the Iranian governments, which effectively set aside the Khomeini fatwa, things began to change for me in India too, and I was granted a five-year visa. At once there were threats from Muslim hard-liners like Imam Bukhari, of the Delhi Jama Masjid, and, more worryingly, some commentators told me not to visit India, because if I did so I might look like a pawn of the Hindu-nationalist Bharatiya Janata Party government, the BJP. I have never been a BJP man, but that wouldn't stop the party from using me for its own sectarian ends.

"Exile," I wrote in *The Satanic Verses,* "is a dream of glorious return." But the dream fades, the imagined return stops feeling glorious. The dreamer awakes. I almost gave up on India, almost believed the love affair was over for good. But not so. As it turns out, I'm about to leave for Delhi after a gap of twelve and a half years. My son Zafar, twenty, is coming with me. He hasn't been to India since he was three, and is very excited. Compared to me, however, he's the picture of coolness and calm.

Friday, April 7: The telephone rings. The Delhi police are extremely nervous about my impending arrival. Can I please avoid being spotted on the plane? My bald head is very recognizable; will I please wear a hat? My eyes are also easily identified; will I please wear sunglasses? Oh, and my beard, too, is a real giveaway; will I wear a scarf around that?

The temperature in India is close to a hundred degrees Fahrenheit, I point out: a scarf might prove a little warm.

Oh, but there are cotton scarves.

I'm going to India because things are better now and because if I don't go I'll never know if it's okay to go or not. I'm going because, in spite of everything that has happened between India and myself, the hook of love is in too deeply to pull out. Most of all, I'm going because Zafar asked to come with me. High time he was reintroduced to his other country.

So: I fly to Delhi, and nobody sees me do it. Here's the invisible man in his business-class seat. Here he is, watching the new Pedro Almodóvar movie on a little pop-up screen, while the plane flies over, er, Iran. Here's the invisible man sleep-masked and snoring.

I feel an urge to kiss the ground, or, rather, the blue rug in the airport "finger," but am embarrassed to do so beneath the watchful eyes of a small army of security guards. Leaving the rug unkissed, I move out of the terminal into the blazing, bone-dry Delhi heat, so different from the wet-towel humidity of my native Bombay. The hot day enfolds us like an embrace. We climb into a cramped, white Hindustan Ambassador, a car that is itself a blast from the past, the British Morris Oxford, long defunct in Britain, but alive and well here in this Indian translation. The Ambassador's air-conditioning system isn't working. I'm back.

Saturday, April 8: India rushes in from every direction, thrusting me into the middle of its unending argument, clamoring for my total attention. Buy Chilly cockroach traps! Drink Hello mineral water! SPEED THRILLS BUT KILLS! shout the hoardings. There are new kinds of message too. Enroll for Oracle 8i. Graduate with Java. And, as proof that the long protectionist years are over, Coca-Cola is back with a vengeance. When I was last here it was banned, leaving the field clear for the disgusting local imitations, Campa Cola and Thums Up. Now there's a red Coke ad every hundred yards or so. Coke's slogan of the moment is written in Hindi transliterated into roman script: Jo Chaho Ho Jaaye. Which could be translated, literally, as "Whatever you desire, let it come to pass."

HORN PLEASE demand the signs on the backs of a million

trucks blocking the road. All the other trucks, and cars, bikes, motor scooters, taxis, and phut-phut autorickshaws enthusiastically respond, welcoming Zafar and me with an energetic rendition of the traditional symphony of the Indian street.

Wait for Side! Sorry-Bye-Bye! Fatta Boy!

The news is just as cacophonous. Between India and Pakistan, as usual, acrimony reigns. Pakistan's ex–prime minister Nawaz Sharif has just been sentenced to life imprisonment after what looked very like a show trial stage-managed by the latest military strongman to seize power. India's army of vociferous commentators, linking this story to the unveiling by Pakistan of a new missile, warn darkly of the worsening relations between the two countries. *Plus ça change.*

I've been back only for an instant, and already everyone I talk to is regaling me with opinions on the new shape of Indian politics. If Bombay is India's New York — glamorous, glitzy, vulgar-chic, a merchant city, a movie city, a slum city, incredibly rich, hideously poor — then Delhi is its Washington. Politics is the only game in town. Nobody talks about anything else for very long.

Once, India's minorities looked for protection to the left-leaning Congress Party, then the country's only organized political machine. Now the disarray of the party — and its drift to the right — is everywhere apparent. Under the leadership of Sonia Gandhi, the once mighty machine languishes and rusts. People who have known Sonia for years urge me not to swallow the line that she was never interested in politics and allowed herself to be drafted into the leadership only because of her concern for the party. They paint a portrait of a woman completely seduced by power but unable to wield it, lacking the skill, charm, vision, indeed everything except the hunger for power itself. Around her fawn the courtiers of the Nehru-Gandhi dynasty, working to prevent the emergence of new leaders who just might have the freshness and will to revive the party's fortunes but who cannot be permitted to usurp the leadership role that, in the Sonia clique's view, belongs to her and her children alone.

I was last in India in August 1987, for the fortieth anniversary of Independence. I have never forgotten being at the Red Fort, in Old Delhi, and listening to Rajiv Gandhi delivering a stunningly tedious oration in broken schoolboy Hindi, while the audience simply and crushingly walked away. Now, here on television, is his widow, her Hindi even more broken than his, a woman convinced of her right to rule but convincing almost nobody except herself.

I remember another widow I met during that 1987 visit, a Sikh, Ravel Kaur, who had seen her husband and sons murdered before her eyes by gangs known to be led and organized by Congress people. Indira Gandhi had recently been assassinated by her Sikh bodyguards, and the whole Sikh community of Delhi was paying the price. The Rajiv Gandhi government prosecuted nobody for these murders, in spite of much hard evidence identifying many of the killers.

For my friend Vijay Shankardass, who had known Rajiv for years, those were disillusioning days. Vijay is one of the most distinguished attorneys in India, with a proud history of anticensorship victories to his name. He and his wife hid their Sikh neighbors in their own home to keep them safe. He went to see Rajiv to demand that something be done to stop the killings, and was deeply shocked by Rajiv's seeming indifference: "Salman, he was so calm." One of Rajiv's close aides, Arjun Das, was less placid. "*Saalón ko phoonk do,*" he snarled. "Blow the bastards away." Later he too was killed.

The Congress Party has strange bedfellows these days. Its decay can perhaps best be measured by the poor quality of its allies. In the state of Bihar, these include the bizarre political double act of Laloo Prasad Yadav and his wife, Rabri Devi. Some years ago, Laloo, then state chief minister, was implicated in the Fodder Scam, a swindle in which large amounts of public subsidies were claimed for the maintenance of cows that didn't actually exist. Laloo was jailed, but first managed to make his wife the chief minister, and blithely went on running the state by proxy from his prison cell.

Since then, he has been in and out of the clink (though never convicted). At present, he's inside, and his wife is at least technically still in the driver's seat, and another juicy corruption scandal is emerging. The tax authorities want to know how Laloo and Rabri manage to live in such high style (they have a particularly grand house) on the relatively humble salaries that even senior ministers in India pull down. Laloo and Rabri were, very loosely, the models for the wholly fictitious and wildly corrupt Bombay politicians Piloo and Golmatol Doodhwala in my novel *The Ground Beneath Her*

Feet. In the novel, Piloo, India's "Scambaba Deluxe," runs a scheme that involves claiming public subsidies for nonexistent goats.

Sunday, April 9: Zafar at twenty is a big, gentle young man who, unlike his father, keeps his emotions concealed. But he is a deeply feeling fellow, and is engaging with India seriously, attentively, beginning the process of making his own portrait of it, which may unlock in him an as yet unknown other self. At first he notices what first-time visitors notice: the poverty of the families living by the railway tracks in what look like trash cans and bin liners, the men holding hands in the street, the "terrible" quality of Indian MTV, and the "awful" Bollywood movies. We pass through the sprawling army cantonment, and he asks if the armed forces are as much of a political factor here as they are in neighboring Pakistan, and looks impressed when I tell him that the Indian army has never sought political power.

I can't tempt him into Indian national dress. I myself put on a cool, loose kurta-pajama outfit the moment I arrive, but Zafar is mutinous. "It's just not my style," he insists, preferring to stay in his young Londoner's uniform of T-shirt, cargo pants, and sneakers. (By the end of the trip, he is wearing the white pajamas but not the kurta; still, progress of a kind has been made.) Zafar has never read more than the first three chapters of *Midnight's Children*, in spite of its dedication ("For Zafar Rushdie who, contrary to all expectations, was born in the afternoon"). In fact, apart from *Haroun and the Sea of Stories* and the story collection *East, West*, he hasn't finished any of my books. The children of writers are often this way. They need their parents to be parents, not novelists. Zafar has always had a complete set of my books proudly on display in his room, but he reads Alex Garland and Bill Bryson, and I pretend not to care. Now, poor fellow, he's getting a crash course in my work as well as in my life. In the Red Fort after Partition, my aunt and uncle, like many Muslims, had to be protected by the army from the violence raging outside; a version of this appears in my novel *Shame*. And here, off Chandni Chowk, the bustling main street of Old Delhi, are the lanes winding into the old Muslim *mohallas* (or neighborhoods), where my parents lived before they moved to Bombay. It's also where Ahmed and Amina Sinai, the parents of the narrator of *Midnight's Children*, faced the gathering pre-

Independence storm. Zafar takes all this literary tourism in good part. Look, here at Purana Qila, the Old Fort supposedly built on the site of the legendary city of Indraprastha, is where Ahmed Sinai left a sack of money to appease a gang of arsonist blackmailers. Look, there are the monkeys who ripped up the sack and threw the money away. Look, here at the National Gallery of Modern Art are the paintings of Amrita Sher-Gil, the half-Indian, half-Hungarian artist who inspired the character of Aurora Zogoiby in *The Moor's Last Sigh* . . . Okay, enough, Dad, he plainly thinks but is too nice to say. Okay, I'll read them, this time I really will. (He probably won't.)

There are signs at the Red Fort advertising an evening son-et-lumière show. "If Mum was here," he says suddenly, "she'd insist on coming to that." Zafar's bright, beautiful mother, my first wife, Clarissa Luard, the Arts Council of England's highly esteemed senior literature officer, who was the guardian angel of young writers and little magazines, died of a recurrence of breast cancer last November, aged just fifty. Zafar and I had spent most of her final hours by her bedside. He is her only child.

"Well," I say, "she was here, you know." In 1974, Clarissa and I spent more than four months traveling around India, roughing it in cheap hotels and long-distance buses, using the advance I'd received for my first novel, *Grimus,* to finance the trip, and trying to stretch the money as far as it would go. Now I begin to make a point of telling Zafar what his mother thought of this or that — how much she liked the serenity of this spot, or the hubbub over there. What began as a little father-and-son expedition acquires an extra dimension.

I've always known that this first visit would be the trickiest. Don't overreach yourself, I thought. If it goes well, things should ease. The second visit? "Rushdie returns again" isn't much of a news story. And the third — "Oh, here he is once more" — barely sounds like news at all. In the long slog back to "normality," habituation, even boredom, has been a useful weapon. "I intend," I start telling people in India, "to bore India into submission." Things have improved in England and America, and I have grown unaccustomed to the problems of having to be protected. What's happening in India feels, in this regard, like entering a time warp and being taken back to the bad old early days of the Iranian attack.

My protection team couldn't be nicer or more efficient, but, gosh, there are a lot of them, and they are jumpy. In Old Delhi, where many Muslims live, they are especially on edge, particularly whenever, in spite of my cloak of invisibility, a member of the public commits the faux pas of recognizing me.

"Sir, there has been exposure! Exposure has occurred!" my protectors mourn.

"Sir, they have said the name, sir! The name has been spoken!"

"Sir, please, the hat!"

It's useless to point out that I do tend to get recognized a fair bit, because, well, I look like this and other people don't; or that, on every single "exposure," the reaction of the persons concerned has been friendly. My protectors have a nightmare scenario in their heads — rioting mobs, et cetera — and mere real life isn't enough to wipe it away. This has been one of the most frustrating aspects of the last few years. People — journalists, policemen, friends, strangers — all write scripts for me, and I get trapped inside those fantasies. What none of the scenarists ever seem to come up with is the possibility of a happy ending — one in which the problems I've faced are gradually overcome, and I resume the ordinary literary life, which is all I've ever wanted. Yet this, the wholly unanticipated story line, is what has actually happened. My biggest problem these days is waiting for everyone to let go of their nightmares and catch up with the facts.

I dine with the artist Vivan Sundaram and Geeta Kapur, at their home in the Shanti Niketan district of South Delhi. Vivan is a nephew of the painter Amrita Sher-Gil, and some of her best canvases are on the walls of his home, as is his own luminous portrait of Amrita and her family.

"So, do things feel different?" Vivan asks, and I say, Not as much as I thought they would. People don't change, the heart of the place is the same. But of course there are the obvious changes. The BJP in power. The new-technology boom that has given even more impetus and affluence to the Indian bourgeoisie.

Bill Clinton's visit to the subcontinent coincides with my own, and Geeta and Vivan portray the president's stay as a defining moment for the rich India that, since my last visit, has experienced exponential growth fueled by new technology. In America, 40 percent of all Silicon Valley start-ups are launched by people of Indian origin, and in India itself the new electronic age has created many fortunes. Clinton made much of these new technoboomers, and visited Hyderabad, one of the new boomtowns. For the Indian rich, his coming was both a validation and an apotheosis.

"You can't believe how they loved it," Geeta says. "So many people longing to bow down and say, Sir, sir, we just love America."

"India and the U.S. as the two great democracies," Vivan adds. "India and America as partners and equals. That was the idea, and it was said without any sense of irony at all."

The India that remains in thrall to religious-communalist sectarians of the most extreme and medievalist type; the India that's fighting something like a civil war in Kashmir; the India that cannot feed or educate or give proper medical care to its people; the India that can't provide its citizens with drinkable water; the India in which the absence of simple toilet facilities obliges millions of women to control their natural functions so that they can relieve themselves under cover of darkness — these Indias were not paraded before the president of the United States. Gung ho nuclear India, fat-cat entrepreneurial India, supernerd computer India, glam-rock high-life India, all pirouetted and twirled in the international media spotlight that accompanies the Leader of the Free World wherever he goes.

Monday, April 10: I learn that the head of the British Council in India, Colin Perchard, will not let me use the council's auditorium for a press conference at the end of the week. In addition, I was told that the British high commissioner, Sir Rob Young, was instructed by the Foreign Office to stay away from me — "not to come out of the stables." Robin Cook, the British foreign secretary, is arriving in India the day I am due to leave and, it would appear, is anxious not to be too closely associated with me. He is scheduled to travel to Iran soon, and naturally that trip must not be compromised.

Hansie Cronje, the captain of the South African cricket team and poster boy for the new South Africa, is being accused by the Indian police of having been involved, along with three of his teammates, in taking money from two Indian bookies to fix the results of one-day international games. Sensational news. The police claim to have transcripts of telephone conversations that leave no room for doubt. There are hints of a link to underworld crime-syndicate bosses like the notorious Dawood Ibrahim. People start speculating about this being the tip of an enormous iceberg. It's no secret that as the one-day version of the game has become a big money-spinner, and as such matches have proliferated, the interest of Far Eastern betting syndicates and bookmakers with underworld links has grown. But no cricket lover wants to believe that his heroes are jerks. Such chosen blindness is a form of corruption, too. "We treated them like gods," a fan says, "and they turned out to be crooks."

Within moments, the denials begin. Hansie is a gent, as clean as a whistle, as honest as the day is long. And why were Indian policemen bugging South African players' phones in the first place? And the voices on the tapes don't even sound South African. Cronje himself gives a press conference denying the charges, insisting that his teammates and his bank statements will confirm that he never tried to throw a match or received any cash for doing so. And behind all the backlash is what sounds, to Indian ears, suspiciously like racism. Commentators from the white cricket-playing countries have been the fastest out of the blocks, rubbishing the allegations, casting doubt on the professionalism and even the integrity of the Indian policemen investigating the case.

The officer in charge of my protection team is the kindly natured Akshey Kumar, who loves literature, can speak with knowledge about the work of Vikram Seth and Vikram Chandra, Rohinton Mistry and Arundhati Roy, and is proud of having two daughters at college in Boston, at Tufts. Kumar's friend K. K. Paul, New Delhi's joint commissioner of police, is running the Cronje investigation. He is a superb detective, says Kumar, and a man of great probity. What's more, South Africa being a friendly nation, the Indian authorities would never allow these accusations to be made public unless they're 110 percent convinced of the strength of the case that K. K. Paul and his team have built. Therefore, Kumar advises with great prescience, just wait and see.

We're off on a road trip to show the boy the sights: Jaipur, Fatehpur Sikri, Agra. For me, the road itself has always been the main attraction. There are more trucks than I remembered, many more, blar-

ing and lethal, often driving straight at us down the wrong side of
the carriageway. There are wrecks from head-on smashes every few
miles.

Look, Zafar, that is the shrine of a prominent Muslim saint; all
the truckers stop there and pray for luck, even the Hindus. Then
they get back into their cabs and take hideous risks with their lives,
and ours as well. Look, Zafar, that is a tractor-trolley loaded with
men. At election time, the *sarpanch,* or headman, of every village is
ordered to provide such trolleyloads for politicians' rallies. Alleg-
edly, for Sonia Gandhi ten tractor-trolleys per village is the require-
ment. Nobody would actually go to the rallies of their own free will.
Look, those are the polluting chimneys of brick kilns smoking in
the fields. Outside the city, the air is less filthy, but it still isn't clean.
But in Bombay between December and February, think of this, air-
craft often can't land or take off before 11:00 A.M. because of the
smog.

The New Age is here, all right. Zafar, if you could read Hindi
you'd see the New Age's new words being phonetically transliterated into that language's Devanagari script: Millennium tires. Oasis
Cellular. Modern's Chinese "Fastfood."

Behold, Zafar, the incomprehensible acronyms and abbrevia-
tions. What is a GIS? What is the HSIDC? One reveals a genuine
shift. You see it every hundred yards or so: STD/ISD PCO. PCO is
Public Call Office, and now anyone can pop into one of these little
booths, make calls to anywhere in India or, indeed, the world, and
pay on the way out. This is the genuine communications revolution
of India.

Zafar wants to learn Hindi and Urdu and come back without all
the paraphernalia that now surrounds us: without, to be blunt, me.
Good. He's got the bug. Once India bites you, you'll never be
cured.

In the roadside *dhabas* where we stop for refreshments, they're
talking about Hansie Cronje. Nobody is in any doubt that he is as
guilty as sin.

Bill Clinton visited the hilltop fortress-palace of Amber, outside
Jaipur, but his security people wouldn't allow him to indulge in the
famous local tourist treat. At the bottom of Amber's hill is a taxi
rank of elephants. You buy a ticket at the Office of Elephant Booking and then lurch uphill on the back of your rented pachyderm.

Where the president failed, Zafar and I succeed. I feel glad to know — in a moment of Schadenfreude — that somebody else's security was tighter and more restrictive than mine. Rajasthan is colorful. People wear colorful clothes and perform colorful dances and ride on colorful elephants to colorful ancient palaces, and these are things a president should know. He should also know that at a test site nearby, in Rajasthan's Thar Desert, Indian know-how has brought India into the nuclear age. Rajasthan is, therefore, the cradle of the new India that must be thought of as America's partner and equal. What was not drawn to Clinton's attention — because it has no place in either the colorful, touristic, elephant-taxi India or the new, thrusting, Internet-billionaire, entrepreneurial India that is currently being sold to the world — was that Rajasthan was dying of thirst, in the grip of one of the worst droughts for a century. Or that Prime Minister Atal Behari Vajpayee's appeal to the people of India to help fight the massive destruction wrought by the drought by making charitable contributions, "no matter how small," was absurd while the Indian government is spending a fortune on Rajasthan's other weapon of mass destruction.

It's hot: almost 110 degrees. The rains have failed for the last two years, and it's two months to the next monsoon. Wells are running dry, and villagers are being forced to drink dirty water, which gives them diarrhea, which causes dehydration, and so the vicious circle tightens its grip. As the gulf widens between the feast of the haves and the famine of the have-nots, the stability of the country must be more and more at risk. I have been smelling a difference in the air, and, reluctant as I am to put into words what isn't much more than an instinct, I do feel a greater volatility in people, a crackle of anger just below the surface, a shorter fuse.

Tuesday, April 11: At dinner last night, Zafar ate a bad shrimp. I blame myself. I should have known to remind him of the basic rules for travelers in India: always drink bottled water, make sure you see the seal on the bottle being broken in front of you, never eat salad (it won't have been washed in bottled water), never put ice in your drinks (it won't have been made with bottled water) . . . and never, never eat seafood unless you're by the sea. Zafar's desert shrimp knocked him flat. He has a sleepless night: vomiting, diarrhetic. This morning he looks terrible, and we have a long, hard journey ahead of us, on bumpy, difficult roads. Now he too needs to guard against dehydration. Unlike the villagers we're leaving behind, however, we have plenty of bottled water to drink, and proper medication. And, of course, we're leaving.

A day to grind through. Long, grueling journey to Agra, then back to Delhi. Zafar suffers but remains stoical. He's too weak to walk around the magnificent Fatehpur Sikri site, and only just manages to drag himself around the Taj, which he declares to be smaller than expected. I am very relieved when I can finally get him into a comfortable hotel bed.

I turn on the television news. Cronje has confessed.

Wednesday, April 12: I AM A CROOK!: CRONJE, says the banner headline in the morning paper. The erstwhile cricketing demigod has admitted to having feet of clay: he has "been dishonest," he has taken money, and now he has been fired from the South African captaincy and kicked off the national team. K. K. Paul and his men have been thoroughly vindicated.

The money Cronje took was paltry, as it turns out: a mere $8,200. Not much for a man's good name. Hansie Cronje's locker-room nickname — given him long before the present scandal — was Crime. As in crime doesn't pay. (He was notoriously stingy, the story goes, about buying a round of drinks.) Now, as the South African government moves toward agreeing to his extradition to stand trial in India, and his lawyers warn him to expect a jail term, he must have started thinking of that nickname as a prophecy.

I am impressed by the relative lack of triumphalism in the Indian response to Cronje's downfall. "What are we gloating over?" warns Siddharth Saxena in the *Hindustan Times:* meaning, Let's not be self-righteous about this. The bookmakers were Indians, after all, and in the revelations that should now begin to flood out we may learn that we're no angels, either. One of the bookies, Rajesh Kalra, is already under arrest, and a suspected middleman, the movie actor Kishan Kumar, will be arrested as soon as he gets out of the hospital, where he is being treated for a sudden heart problem.

Sometime in the 1920s, my paternal grandfather, Mohammed Din Khaliqi, a successful Delhi businessman, bought a hot-season retreat for his family, a modest stone cottage in the pretty little town of Solan, in the Simla Hills. He named it Anis Villa, after his only son, Anis Ahmed. That son, my father, who later took the surname Rushdie, after the Arab philosopher Ibn Rushd (Averroës), gifted the house to me on my twenty-first birthday. And eleven years ago the state government of Himachal Pradesh took it over without so much as a by-your-leave.

It isn't easy to seize a man's property in India, even for a state government. In order to get hold of Anis Villa, the local authorities falsely declared it to be "evacuee property." The law pertaining to evacuee property was devised after Partition to enable the state to take possession of homes left behind by individuals and families who had gone to Pakistan. This law did not apply to me. I was an Indian citizen until I became a British one by naturalization, and I have never held a Pakistani passport or been a resident of that country. Anis Villa had been wrongfully seized, and provably so.

Vijay Shankardass and I became close friends because of Solan. He took on the Himachal authorities on my behalf. The case took seven years, and we won. Both parts of this sentence are impressive. Seven years, by Indian standards, is incredibly fast. And to defeat a government, even when right is quite clearly on your side, takes some doing.

We regained possession of the Solan villa in November 1997. Since then the roof has been fixed, the house cleaned and painted, and one bathroom modernized. The electricity, plumbing, and telephone all work. In preparation for our visit, furniture and furnishings have been rented for a week from a local store, at the surreal cost, for a six-bedroom house, of $100. A caretaker and his family live on the premises. Solan has grown out of all recognition, but the villa's view of the hills remains clear and unspoiled.

Zafar is just a few weeks shy of his own twenty-first birthday. Going to Solan with him today closes a circle. It also discharges a responsibility I have long felt to the memory of my father, who died in 1987. You see, Abba, I have reclaimed our house. Four generations of our family, living and dead, can now forgather there. One day it will belong to Zafar and his little brother, Milan. In a family as uprooted and far-flung as ours, this little acre of continuity stands for a very great deal.

To get to Solan, you take a three-hour ride in an air-conditioned "chair car" on the Shatabdi Express from New Delhi to Le Corbusier's city of Chandigarh, the shared capital city of Punjab and Haryana. Then you drive for an hour and a half, up into the hills. At least, this is what you do if you're not me. The police do not want me to take the train. "Sir, exposure is too great." They are upset because someone at a hotel in Jaipur has blabbed to Reuters that I was there. Vijay has managed to squash the Reuters story for the moment, but the shield of invisibility is wearing thin. At Solan, as even the police accept, the cat will surely spring from the bag. It's where everyone expects me to go. The day before yesterday, the Indian state TV service Doordarshan sent a team up to Anis Villa to nose around and quiz Govind Ram, the caretaker, who stonewalled nobly. Once I'm actually there, however, the story will surely break.

One rather unattractive development: the police high-ups who telephone Akshey Kumar every five minutes to ask how things are going have developed the notion that the Jaipur leak was engineered by Vijay and myself. This germ of suspicion will shortly blossom into a full-blown disease. Zafar is feeling better, but I refuse to inflict what will be a seven-hour car journey on him. I put him on the train, lucky dog. I am to meet him at Chandigarh station with my inconspicuous "car-cade" of four black sedans.

There's another train leaving Delhi, the one that links the Indian capital and the city of Lahore, in Pakistan. However, I discover that the service is now at risk. Pakistan complains that India isn't providing its share of the rolling stock. India complains, rather more seriously, that Pakistan is using the train to smuggle drugs and counterfeit money into India.

Drugs are a huge issue, of course, but the counterfeit-money issue is also a big one. In Nepal these days, people are reluctant to accept Indian 500-rupee notes, because of the quantity of forgeries in circulation. Not long ago, a diplomat from the Pakistan High Commission in Delhi went to pay his young son's school fees, and used a mixture of genuine and funny money to do so. The boy was expelled, and although he was later reinstated, the link between the Pakistani government and the bad money had been clearly established.

I collect Zafar at Chandigarh, and as we go up into the hills my heart lifts. Mountains have a way of cheering up plains dwellers. The air freshens, tall conifers lean from steep slopes. As the sun sets, the lights of the first hill stations glow in the twilight above us. We pass a narrow-gauge railway train on its slow, picturesque way up to Shimla. For me this is the emotional high point of the trip, and I can see that Zafar too is moved. We stop at a *dhaba* near Solan for dinner, and the owner tells me how happy he is that I'm there, and someone runs up for an autograph. I ignore the worried expression on Akshey Kumar's face. Even though I've hardly ever been here in my life, and not at all since I was twelve years old, I feel that I'm home.

It's dark when we reach the villa. From the road, we have to climb down 122 steps to get to it. At the bottom, there's a little gate, and Vijay, also in a state of high feeling, formally welcomes me to the home he has won back for my family. The caretaker runs up and astonishes Zafar by stooping down to touch our feet. I am not a superstitious man, but I feel the presence at my shoulder of my grandfather, who died before I was born, and of my parents' younger selves. The sky is on fire with stars. I go into the back garden by myself. I need to be alone.

Thursday, April 13: I am woken at 5:00 A.M. by amplified music and chanting from a mandira, a Hindu temple, across the valley. I get dressed and walk around the house in the dawn light. With high-pitched pink roofs and little corner turrets, the house is more beautiful than I remembered, more beautiful than it looked in Vijay's photographs of it, and the view is as stunning as promised. It's a very strange feeling to walk around a house you don't know that somehow belongs to you. It takes awhile for us to grow into each other, the house and me, but by the time the others wake up it's mine. We spend most of the day mooching around the premises, sitting in the garden under the shade of big old conifers, eating Vijay's special scrambled eggs. I know now that the trip has been worthwhile: I know it from the expression on Zafar's face.

In the afternoon, we make an excursion to the next town, the former British summer capital. They called it Simla, but it's gone back to being Shimla. Vijay shows me the law courts where he fought for Anis Villa, and we go too to the former Viceregal Lodge, a big old pile that once staged the crucial pre-Independence Simla Conference of 1945 and now houses a research establishment called the Indian Institute of Advanced Studies.

Zafar walks gravely around the conference table, where the

shades of Gandhi, Nehru, and Jinnah are seated, but when we get outside again he asks, "Why is that stone lion still holding up an English flag?" The probable answer, I hypothesize, is that nobody noticed until he did. India has been independent for over half a century, but the flag of St. George is still up there on the roof.

The Institute of Advanced Studies is run by a local BJP wallah, and I do a little ducking and swerving to dodge him in the grounds. Alas, I mustn't fall into the trap of looking like the BJP's man. A handshake that would certainly be photographed is worth a little fancy footwork to avoid. Unlike V. S. Naipaul (who is also in India, I gather), I do not see the rise of Hindu nationalism as a great outpouring of India's creative spirit. I see it as the negation of the India I grew up in, as the triumph of sectarianism over secularism, of hatred over fellowship, of ugliness over love. It is true that Prime Minister Vajpayee has tried to lead his party in a more moderate direction, and that Vajpayee himself is surprisingly popular among Muslims, but his attempt to reshape his party in his own image has failed. The BJP is the political manifestation of the extremist Hindu movement the RSS (Rashtriya Swayamsevak Sangh), rather as Sinn Fein, in Northern Ireland, is the political offspring of the Provisional IRA. In order to change the BJP, Vajpayee would have to carry the leadership of the RSS with him. Regrettably, the opposite is happening. The relatively moderate RSS chief, Professor Rajendra Singh, has been ousted by a hard-liner, who has started warning Vajpayee to toe the RSS line.

The prime minister's options are limited. He could give in and unleash the dogs of religious strife. He could try doing what Indira Gandhi brilliantly carried off in 1969, when the kingmakers of the Congress tried to turn her into their puppet. (She was expelled from her own party, formed her own faction in the Congress, rallied MPs to her side, and later called a general election and destroyed the old guard at the polls.) Or, as seems most likely, he could soldier on until the next election and then stand down. At that point, the BJP's moderate mask will slip, the party will no longer be able to hold together the kind of broad-based coalition of the sort that currently underpins its power, and, given the shambles that the Congress Party is in, India will enter another phase of splintered, unstable governments. It's not a happy prediction, but it's what the probabilities suggest. And it's a good enough reason for keeping away from BJP apparatchiks, however low-level they may be.

My metamorphosis from observer to observed, from the Salman I know to the "Rushdie" I often barely recognize, continues apace. Rumors of my presence in India are everywhere. I am profoundly depressed to hear that a couple of Islamic organizations have vowed to make trouble, and trouble is news, and so maybe, I think, this will be seen as the meaning of my trip to India, which will be very, very sad, and bad indeed.

At dinner in Solan's Himani restaurant, I'm tucking into the spicy Indian version of Chinese food when I'm approached by a TV reporter called Agnihotri, who happens to be vacationing up here with his family. And there it is: he has his scoop and the story's out. Within moments, a local press reporter arrives and asks me a few friendly questions. None of this is very unexpected, but as a result of these chance encounters the jitteriness of the police escalates into a full-scale row.

Back at Anis Villa, Vijay receives a call on his cell phone from a police officer named Kulbir Krishan, in Delhi. Krishan is somewhere in the middle of the invisible chain of command of Delhi desk pilots, but what he says makes Vijay lose his composure for the first time in all the years of our friendship. He is almost trembling as he tells me, "We are accused of having called those journalists to the restaurant. This man says we have not been gentlemen, we have not kept our word, and we have, if you can believe the phrase, 'talked out of turn.' Finally the fellow says, 'There will be riots in Delhi tomorrow, and if we fire on the crowds and there are deaths, the blood will be on your heads.'"

I am horrified. It quickly becomes clear to me that there are two issues here. The first, and lesser, issue is that after a week of accepting all manner of limitations and security conditions we are being accused of dishonesty and bad faith. That is insulting and unjust, but it isn't, finally, dangerous. The second issue is a matter of life and death. If the Delhi police have become so trigger-happy that they are preparing to kill people, then they must be stopped before it's too late. No time now for niceties.

Zafar looks on, dazed, while I blow my stack at poor, decent Akshey Kumar (who is not at all to blame) and tell him that unless

Kulbir Krishan gets back on the phone right now, apologizes to Vijay and me personally, and assures me that there are no plans to murder anybody tomorrow, I will insist on our driving through the night back to New Delhi so that I can be waiting at Prime Minister Vajpayee's office door at dawn, to ask him to deal with the problem personally.

After a certain amount of this kind of raging — "I'll go to the British high commissioner! I'll call a press conference! I'll write a newspaper article!" — the hapless Kulbir does call back to speak of "misunderstandings," and promises that there will be no shootings or deaths.

"If I spoke out of context," he memorably concludes, "then I am very sorry indeed." I burst out laughing at the sheer absurdity of this formulation and put down the phone. But I do not sleep well. The meaning of this entire journey will be defined by what happens in the next two days, and even though I believe that the police are overreacting, I can't be sure. Delhi is their town, and me, I'm Rip van Winkle.

Friday, April 14: We leave Solan at dawn and drive Zafar and Vijay to Chandigarh station. (I am going all the way by road.) Zafar is recovering from the shrimp attack, but Vijay looks worn out, frazzled. He repeats several times that he has never been spoken to so rudely, and doesn't propose to let the matter rest. I can see that he's had it with the police, with all the traveling, and probably with me. Tomorrow night, I tell him, all this will be over and you can go back to being a lawyer and not think about Salman Rushdie and his problems anymore. He laughs weakly and gets on the train. I am traveling to Delhi at the invitation of the organizers of the Commonwealth Writers Prize, and today is their banquet. But I'm not thinking about the prize. All the way back to Delhi, I'm wondering whose instincts will prove the sharper: mine or my protectors'. How will my return-of-the-native trip end: happily or badly? I'll soon know.

At half past twelve I'm closeted in a meeting with R. S. Gupta, the special commissioner in charge of security for the whole city of Delhi. He is a calm, forceful man, used to getting his way. He paints a dark picture. A Muslim politician, Shoaib Iqbal, plans to go to Friday midday prayers at the city's most important mosque, the Jama

Masjid, in Old Delhi, and there get support for a demonstration against me, and against the Indian government for allowing me to enter the country. The congregation will be in five figures, and if the mosque's imam — it's Bukhari — supports the call to demonstrate, the numbers could be huge and bring the city to a standstill. "We are negotiating with them," Gupta says, "to keep the numbers small and the event peaceful. Maybe we will succeed."

After a couple of hours of high-tension waiting, during which I am effectively confined to quarters — "sir, no movements, please" — the news is good. Only about two hundred people have marched (and two hundred marchers, in India, is a number smaller than zero), and it has all gone off without a hitch. "Fortunately," Mr. Gupta tells me, "we have been able to manage it."

What really happened in Delhi today? It is one of the characteristics of security forces everywhere in the world to try to have it both ways. Had there been mass demonstrations, they would have said, "You see, all our nervousness has been amply justified." But there were no such marches, and so I'm told, "We were able to prevent the trouble because of our foresight and skill." Maybe so. But it might also be that for the vast majority of Indian Muslims the controversy over *The Satanic Verses* is old hat now, and in spite of the efforts of the politician and the imam (both of whom made blood-and-thunder speeches) nobody could really be bothered to march. Oh, there's a novelist in town to go to a dinner? What's his name? Rushdie? So what?

It's a hot day in Delhi, and there's a hot wind blowing. A dust storm rages across the city. As we all take in the news that the only storm today is meteorologically induced, we can finally begin to relax. The script in people's heads is being rewritten. The foretold ending has not come to pass. What happens instead is extraordinary, and, for Zafar and me, an event of immense emotional impact, far exceeding in its force even the tumultuous reception of *Midnight's Children*, almost twenty years ago. What bursts out is not violence but joy.

At a quarter to eight in the evening, Zafar and I walk into the Commonwealth Prize reception at the Oberoi Hotel, and from that moment until we leave India the celebrations never stop. Journalists and photographers surround us, their faces wreathed in most unjournalistic smiles. Friends burst through the media wall to embrace us. The actor Roshan Seth, recently recovered from serious heart problems, hugs me and says, "Look at us, yaar, we're both supposed to be dead but still going strong." The eminent columnist Amita Malik, a friend of my family's from the old days in Bombay, quickly gets over her embarrassment at mistaking Zafar for my bodyguard and reminisces wonderfully about the past, praising my father's wit, his quick gift for repartee, and telling tales of my favorite uncle, Hameed, who died too young, too long ago. One of the great English-language Indian novelists, Nayantara Sahgal, clasps my hands and whispers, "Welcome home." I look around and there's Zafar being interviewed for television and speaking fluently and touchingly about his own happiness at being here. My heart overflows.

Saturday, April 15: In all my conversations with the press, I've tried to avoid reopening old wounds, to tell Indian Muslims that I am not and have never been their enemy, and to stress that I'm in India to mend broken links and to begin, so to speak, a new chapter. Now the media agrees. "Let's turn a page," the *Asian Age* says. Dileep Padgaonkar, of the *Times of India,* will put it more movingly the day after I leave: "He is reconciled with India, and India with him. . . . Something sublime has happened to him which should enable him to continue to mesmerise us with his yarns. He has returned to where his heart has always been. He has returned home." In the *Hindustan Times,* there is an editorial headed "Reconsider the Ban." This sentiment is echoed right across the media. The *Times of India* finds an Islamic scholar, as well as other intellectuals, supporting an end to the ban. On the electronic media, opinion polls run 75 percent in favor of allowing *The Satanic Verses* to be freely published in India at long last.

Vijay throws a farewell party for me. And there's a surprise: my two actress aunts, Uzra Butt and her sister Zohra Segal, are there, with my cousin Kiran Segal, Zohra's daughter and one of the country's foremost teachers of the Odissi school of Indian classical dancing. This is the zany wing of the family, sharp of tongue and mischievous of eye. Uzra and Zohra are the grand old ladies of the Indian theater, and we were all in love with Kiran at one time or another. Kiran lived with her mother in an apartment in Hampstead for a time in the 1960s, and when I was at boarding school at Rugby I sometimes spent vacations in their spare bedroom, next to Kiran's bedroom door, on which there was a large, admonitory skull-and-crossbones sign. I now discover that Vijay and Roshan Seth stayed in the same spare room in the same period. All three of us would look wistfully at the skull and crossbones, and none of us ever got past it.

"I haven't seen you dance for years," I say to Kiran.

"Come back soon," she says. "Then I'll dance."

EDWARD W. SAID

Paradise Lost

FROM *Travel & Leisure*

FOR THOSE OF US who were children in the Middle East during
World War II, the Lebanese mountains — but not Beirut, the capital — were an almost inevitable summer destination. This was especially true for residents of the urban al-Mashriq, or Arab east,
whose large cities such as Cairo, Baghdad, Damascus, Jerusalem —
and shortly after World War II, such newly prosperous Gulf towns
as Jeddah and Kuwait — were intolerably hot in June, July, and August. For the solicitous and sufficiently well off parents of growing
children, the empty months required a mountain or seaside so-
journ.

From today's perspective, those summer holidays seem very long
indeed, with the private (in most instances missionary or colonial)
schools pretty much closed from early June till the beginning of
October. Since there were no camps or organized summer activities for children, it was taken for granted that the family should
leave the sweltering, dusty metropolis for a cool, distant place.
Many middle- and upper-class Lebanese families would also seek
out a congenial place for their children to escape Beirut's oppres-
sively humid heat. They, too, were part of the summer community
that flourished for a while and is still remembered by many with a
nostalgia that has had little to nourish it since the Lebanese civil
war ended in 1990.

It was in 1943 that a Lebanese mountain village called Dhour el
Shweir became our summer home. Dhour was my parents' choice
because some of my mother's relatives originated there, and it

seemed like a logical destination for us as a family living intermittently in Jerusalem and Cairo. But there were several other, similar Lebanese villages and their hotels that attracted visitors from the Middle East, drawn to the prospect of comfort and coolness well before Greece, Italy, and France were holiday destinations. Indeed, Lebanon was the generic backdrop for many of the rustic quasi-alpine settings that were de rigueur in Arabic films of the time whenever the plot called for a honeymoon. The country had been reduced emblematically to its mountain resorts, and Beirut, later to become a worldwide symbol for horrendous violence, was scarcely mentioned and rarely so much as seen.

I vividly recall that Dhour's landscape was dominated by the Grand Hotel Kassouf, a fortresslike structure near the end of the single winding road built by the French along the spine of two mountains, five thousand feet straight up and slightly to the north of the capital. This road, with its massive red-roofed houses, small hotels, and a few scattered shops on both sides, made up the long, stringy town that stretched for about two miles and overlooked Beirut from the east. We spent that first summer at the Kassouf, and then rented houses all over Dhour every year after. But for Dhour's residents, the hotel was the great social pinnacle of the village, just far enough away from the little shopping area and most of the summer rentals to represent a sophisticated, somewhat remote aerie that set it apart from the not always convincing rusticity of Dhour. Many families would return to Dhour year after year for the pure and usually dry mountain air, the misty afternoons and evenings, and the compelling views of the surrounding mountains, with Beirut's white houses and its blue bay shimmering in the sunset like a dream city without inhabitants.

In my young consciousness, the Kassouf was part of a constellation of mountain *grands hôtels* that we occasionally visited on the "outings" that my father planned for us as a family. This group of destinations included the Park and the Printania Palace hotels in nearby Brummana and, just a little farther away, down that town's southern slope, the Grand Hotel in Beit Mery, a small adjoining village. If the resort was near enough to Dhour we would go there for tea or lunch. The distant hotels were usually reserved for rest stops on the way back from some remote waterfall or spring that my parents thought would be amusing for us to sit at for a while.

The grandest of all the grand hotels in this category was in the small town of Sofar, about four hours away and across several stony valleys from Dhour. Aside from its hotel and its social eminence, Sofar's distinction was, first, that the French ambassador's summer residence was there, and, second, that the tiny rail station could be seen from the hotel terrace: It was the only one of its kind I knew in the mountains. That it was on the Damascus-Beirut line with incredibly steep inclines and many hairpin curves gave it an added mystique. Feeling (and probably looking) rather bedraggled and dusty, we would stop at the Grand Hotel Sofar for tea after having lunch at the neighboring Hammana's Shaghour Spring (or mountain rift, with its small cascade of water) and sit awkwardly in the elegant garden surrounded by all sorts of meticulously dressed, distinguished guests among whom my parents would point out an Egyptian pasha or two, a former Syrian cabinet minister, a super-wealthy Iraqi industrialist, a Jewish department store owner.

Down the Sofar road we usually stopped again for ice cream at Tanios's in Aley, or after visiting our Cairo friends the Dirliks in the town of Bhamdun, we would order sandwiches from a café adjacent to the town's Hôtel Ambassadeur. Different though each of these places was, they made up a core that basically gave Lebanon its prestige as a *station d'estivage,* and which — along with its splendid peaches, figs, mulberries, and plums, its legions of white-jacketed waiters with names like Édouard, Georges, Joseph, Pierre, and Nicola, its promenades, boutiques, pine forests, and steeply inclined roads — made Lebanon unique in the Arab world.

This part of Lebanon was essentially French in tone and vocabulary, full of *thés dansants,* table d'hôtes, matinées, *numéros,* and the like, replicas of an original none of us would see until much later in Europe. These little islands of imported gentility were among the nicer and certainly the more innocent legacies of the French political hold on Syria and Lebanon that originated with the Sykes-Picot Agreement of 1916, which divided what was one large Ottoman province into several new states under either British or French tutelage. Syria and Lebanon, with long histories of Gallic interest and intervention, went to France while Britain took Palestine, Jordan, Iraq, and most of the Gulf.

I don't think it's an irrelevant political comment to say that much of the trouble that has beset this region in the seventy-five subsequent years has had a great deal to do with the imperial policy of divide and later quit. New states that were formed when the British and the French departed, competing national majorities and minorities, and very different ideas about identity and alignment in the Cold War — to say nothing of meddling outside powers, various military coups, and wildly incompatible perceptions of what was in effect a common history — produced a highly combustible mix that left no life unchanged. The main change for the worse, I think, has been to isolate communities from one another. In the Lebanon of old, Jews, Armenians, and Greeks from Syria, Egypt, Palestine, Lebanon, and Iraq, as well as Christians of all denominations from those countries, plus of course Muslims (both Sunni and Shia) from all the Arab nations (as well as Cyprus, Afghanistan, and Iran) would sit at dinner together, shop, go for walks, frequent the same hotels and cafés — all without a second thought. For my generation that kind of polyglot mixing was the natural condition of being a Levantine, not the sullen segregation and the ideological narrowness that defeated our world in the end and reigns over the Middle East today.

Certainly the Lebanon of quasi-French summer resorts and grand hotels has changed beyond recognition. Whatever else it is, this change isn't for the better, even though it is enough to say that the privilege, to say nothing of the often purely fictitious world of summer leisure on which that world depended and from which its structures were borrowed, was very precarious. What amazes me now is how readily those of us who knew that world accepted it and its customs, which in retrospect seem confected out of literature and films, especially in the grand hotels that were so central to the system of summertime and rarefied tourism.

Waiters were always male, uniformed, deferential; they used non-Arabic words like *merci* and *monsieur* without embarrassment; the female staff was also uniformed, only did the rooms, said very little. The tone and the sound of the Grand Hotel Sofar or of the Kassouf was hushed and understated, almost whispered, and dress codes required, demanded, an ample wardrobe of suits, evening wear, tasteful little dresses for the girls, gray shorts, white shirts, and single-color ties for the boys. Shoes were glisteningly shined, and sandals for the children were to be seen only before noon, always with socks. The very idea of sports clothes (except for impeccably white tennis outfits) such as the canvas shoes, colored T-shirts, jeans of today, had not even been dreamed of. Chairs and tables were for politely sitting at tea or playing games such as snakes and ladders, pick-up sticks, Monopoly; cards were frowned on, as were rough games of any kind.

One couldn't just have a meal whenever one felt like it. There were appointed sittings, tables, waiters, and of course set menus, all of them designed for endurance rather than speed. An afternoon siesta was mandatory. Phones were rare, and the radio was for BBC news broadcasts only. An Armenian violinist and pianist were regularly in evidence for weekend meals, often accompanied by an accordionist, the convenient substitute for winds and brasses. If you wanted to you could recognize in all this something of Proust's Balbec (minus the sea) or, strangely transmuted into something quite different but arguably the same, the château setting of Marcel Carné's 1945 film *Les Enfants du Paradis*.

The hotels themselves were large establishments, some with as many as seventy-five rooms, several dining rooms, a banquet hall, gaming and billiard rooms, and, because of the mountain setting, immense terraces with colorful umbrellas, metal tables, and wicker chairs interspersed with languorously extended deck chairs. Size was everywhere used to impress, if not awe, the visitor. In the Kassouf, for example, an enormously long and steep staircase swept up from the driveway into the front terrace and reception area: It was like something out of Hollywood's Technicolor version of *The Three Musketeers*. Sofar's Grand Hotel had two majestic staircases just inside the entrance; they appeared to dare you (if you weren't a guest) to mount them. On the occasion of a big event like a wedding reception, a floor show — usually made up of a celebrated magician, medium, and singer — or a banquet, the huge hulk of the Beit Mery Grand Hotel would be thrown open almost recklessly, one felt, its great terraces, eating areas, salons, exposed to public view as if to say, *Isn't all this so much grander, so unlike anything you've seen anywhere before?*

The remarkable thing about all the grand hotels was that they were only passably comfortable and not at all luxurious. Compared with today's notion of comfort — telephones, electronic equipment, superabundant bathrooms, fancy furniture, thick towels, room service — the Lebanese summer palaces were actually austere. Water was always a problem, so bathrooms were both scarce and quite minimal. You couldn't take a bath, so half the rooms were equipped only with a basin and a toilet, perhaps a shower, plus all the necessities for a sponge bath. Menus varied from a Lebanese dish such as stuffed zucchini and grape leaves one night to an international (and rather tough) roast lamb with potatoes the next. Hotel furniture was of the rudimentary summer category: pine cabinets and tables, steel-frame beds, wicker chairs, and large brown or burgundy wool or velvet sofas and armchairs. Overhead lights, direct and brutally bright, were everywhere. Soft, indirect lighting was unknown. And that was about it, so far as décor and atmosphere were concerned. It was the appearance, location, and reputation of the hotels that gave them their status, not what was in them.

Faster cars allied with rapid, easy plane travel and the idea of a quick weekend was what first began to erode the grand hotels' haughty glamour. Air-conditioning completed the process. If you didn't need to be in one of them for a minimum of six weeks — they were terribly hard to get to, and that was an essential aspect of their hauteur — and if you could go to Cyprus, then later Greece, Italy, Turkey, in a few hours and if, most important of all, distance and social status were no longer the domain of a few people, there weren't many customers left to spend an unexciting period of time at sleepy places like Sofar or Dhour. Why leave the city at all if the heat could be held at bay by refrigerated air, or forgotten in a more and more varied array of fashionable beaches and yachts? I doubt that with the advent of television, for instance, the sedate, cloistered world of perennial regulars could have survived. The region's numerous political upheavals also slowly drained the old hotels of their relaxed and cosmopolitan clientele.

A more cruel fate than television and air-conditioning overtook Lebanon's mountain resorts in 1975 — civil war. In Beirut, for instance, the ponderously big seafront hotels like the Phoenicia and the Holiday Inn, built during the 1960s and 1970s oil boom, were ideal locations for artillery posts set up by the strenuously competing factions, and choice targets as well, none sadder than the legendary St. Georges Hotel, Beirut's most distinguished hostelry (now being rebuilt). By the end of the seventies and the early eighties, after seven to nine years of furious shelling that engulfed first the city, then the mountains, the Kassouf was knocked out, as well as the Grand Hotel Sofar; and then the big palaces of Aley, Bhamdoun, Beit Mery, and Brummana were either gutted or made uninhabitable. The summer mountains became refuges for city people fleeing the Israeli invasion of 1982 as well as the 1985 war of the Palestinian refugee camps and General Awn's random bombing of the city a few years later, or they became outposts of one or another military force.

Dhour today is still a Syrian army redoubt, most of its bombed-out houses still unrepaired and unpeopled, the great old Kassouf a sprawling shambles of what it once was, the noble front staircase crumbling and useless, a pathetic reminder of great days all but forgotten under the indifferent sun. The big hotels and houses of Aley, Bhamdoun, and Souk el Gharb were demolished in the fighting, their cavernously empty interiors turned into barracks or arms depots. So far as I can tell no faction refrained from this pointless vandalism. To the fighters themselves a place like the Grand Hotel Kassouf could have meant nothing except temporary protection or a target; to the warlords these summer castles were convenient stopping places for the armed forces who, like so many minor employees, were paid to do a messy job. Certainly none of these people had any memory of what once had been.

The Lebanese civil war ended officially a decade ago. Under the premiership of Rafik Hariri, a Croesus-like Lebanese contractor who made his endless supply of money in Saudi Arabia and ran the country between 1992 and 1998, rebuilding began — but it was a rebuilding unlike any other. Central Beirut, completely ravaged during the war, was redesigned as a spanking oversized postmodern commercial headquarters for the region, startlingly unlike the beehive of small buildings and narrow casbah streets that had stood there for centuries. A few luxury apartments were built and a souk or two restored, though not before a public outcry about the threat to the mainly Roman and Phoenician archaeological remains forced a change in the original plans. There was much regret expressed about the passing of old Beirut with surprisingly little said about the disappeared mountain resorts, which have been left in ruins like the old Kassouf, or — much more disturbing —

buried under a heap of new, unplanned, unzoned, unrestricted housing and commercial areas that have completely defaced, indeed massacred, the physical setting for which Lebanon had once been famous. Lebanon's wealthy have retreated to new gated summer colonies like Faqra in the north or to overseas pleasure palaces in Super Cannes and Marbella, leaving the exhausted middle class in frantic search of a foothold outside Beirut.

The result in once placid, leafy places like Brummana and Beit Mery is garishly dreadful. (Dhour and Sofar are still largely barren and unrebuilt.) The old hotels have simply disappeared. The once quiet and largely pedestrian streets have become horn-blaring single-lane nightmares with cars at a standstill for long periods at a stretch. Village grocers and butchers who lived off the summer trade from beneath white canvas awnings have given way to a mishmash of shops with multicultural signs that scream at you: Henny Penny, Cheyenne Western Store, Nokia, Pretty Woman, Edelweiss Tapis-Antiquités, Speedy-Foto, Super Superette, Better Clothing, Bonny Shoes & Socks. And dozens upon dozens of restaurants and fast-food stalls, each of them completely and surprisingly appetizing. (One mustn't forget that Beirut's branch of McDonald's has valet parking and is no ordinary hamburger joint.)

The sedate old Printania Palace Hotel in Brummana, damaged during the war, still stands but is now obscured by a fancy modern hotel with the same name, clearly designed with the Hyatt and Inter-Continental trade in mind. At the other end of town, the Park Hotel — in its day a smaller, more refined, and exclusive hotel that rivaled its Sofar and Dhour counterparts while lacking their monumental presence — has also disappeared, as has most of the little hill overlooking the valley on which it perched. An enormous multilevel condo project has come into being, ten times too big for the site, grotesquely misnamed the Grand Hills Village. Made of mountain stone and not quite ready for its prospective tenants as I drove by in early July, it seemed to have been dragged out of a Bela Lugosi–meets–Wyatt Earp movie, with perhaps equally confusing results. The Grand Hotel Beit Mery has been replaced by a tastefully modern hotel, the Bustan.

The Grand Hotel in Sofar still stands — somber, bombed out, ragged, and yet a quietly dignified, even majestic, ruin. The terraces and gardens on its northern and southern sides are a riot of bramble and charred building fragments. In a distant corner of the northern garden is a large shack; inside the hotel, nestled beneath the dark arches that were still standing on one side, I found several half-gutted cars, basically chassis without tires or interiors. It was impossible to tell whether they were being repaired or had been put there pending further deconstruction. As a pair of open-faced young men approached me from a corner of the untended garden, I tried to disarm them. "I used to come here many years ago. Do you live here?" I asked, nodding toward the shack. They were immediately friendly, even welcoming. Their father had been the customer service manager, but as the hotel was damaged and the owners had no money to pay employees, the old man had been given the right to live on the property and shelter his family from the ongoing war. He had since died, however, and as there seemed no prospect of the tourist industry reviving, his sons had gone into the car repair business. What had been a temporary abode had become a permanent one, though at a vast social remove from its original purpose.

Last summer I managed to traverse the eastern Mediterranean littoral from Tripoli and Beirut in the north to Port Said and Alexandria in the south. Gone was the graceful arc of pleasant ports, citrus groves, fishing villages, small beachfront resorts. In its place was an almost continuous wall of concrete. Polluted water was everywhere, and commercialized seafront properties, all of them (and regardless of whether in Israel or an Arab country) the result of unrestricted development that seemed to be battling for a foothold at the water's edge and beyond. In each country the reasons for the new ugliness were different. Yet this wave of crowded and decidedly aggressive construction had effectively throttled what had once been a welcoming environment, relatively small in scale, that E. M. Forster had contrasted favorably with the overwhelming vastness of India. All that had changed.

In Lebanon, the summer mountain peaks that seemed like a last outpost of rest and natural pleasure were erased during the civil war — itself a symptom of the tenuousness and fragility of the social fabric that had once given Lebanon its unique blend of individuality and collective anarchy — leaving behind nothing very lasting or attractive. In its scramble to reemerge as a regional financial and cultural center, Lebanon has become a frantic new place, beset with overcrowding and a floundering economy, in addition to the region's political volatility. Relatively unencumbered by puritanical laws, it remains the Arab world's most exciting country, but, except for its immensely energetic citizens, its mountains are minus a summer vocation.

BOB SHACOCHIS

Something Wild in the Blood

FROM *Men's Journal*

HURRICANE DEBBY had broken up, humbled by shearing winds
into a tropical depression, trailing a steady, bracing suck of breeze
that stretched east from Cuba all the way back to the Turks and
Caicos Islands, where, on Providenciales, a young islander in swim
trunks helped me lug a mountain of gear from my Turtle Cove hotel to his pickup truck. I asked the driver if he was the boatman too,
and he said yes, he was Captain Newman Gray.

"Good. You can tell me where we're going."

"East Bay Cay."

Twenty years ago, when I first came to Providenciales aboard the
South Wind, a derelict ninety-eight-foot tramp freighter captained
by Tay Maltsberger and his wife, Linda, the forty-nine Turks and
Caicos were tiny, arid, sunbaked, and mostly useless outposts of the
British Crown, still virgin turf for sportsmen, drug-runners, and
real estate pioneers.

Now I was looking out the window of Captain Newman's truck at
the resorts and casinos crowding Grace Bay, remembering when
there was nothing on its austere sweep of beach, when Providenciales did not have a jetport or a store, only an islander-run
rice-and-peas shop at its dusty main crossroads and a warehouse
stocked with booze, frozen steaks, and a thin collection of building
supplies. Nobody was around on the bay then except my wife and
me and Tay and Linda. We'd swim from shore to a nearby reef
and spear lobsters, perform ballet with eagle rays and sea turtles,
and slowly retreat from the tiger shark, as big as a sports car, that
regularly prowled the formation. At the end of the day, we'd walk

carefully back through the thorny island scrub to where Tay and Linda had anchored themselves and were attempting an unlikely enterprise for professional seafarers: Provo's first nursery and landscaping business.

"I know that place," I said to Newman, pointing to the new parking lot and retail office of Sunshine Nursery. I told him there had been a time on Provo when everybody — whites and blacks, and the West Indians especially — knew and loved the couple who started that nursery. But the captain had never heard of my friends the Maltsbergers and made only the smallest grunt of acknowledgment. My memories were beside the point to young Newman, who had migrated from his home on North Caicos to Providenciales to take advantage of the recent economic boom. I was simply the latest job, an American who wanted to be dropped for ten days on some ideal island, the only criterion being that the place have no people, no nothing, except flora under which I could escape the sun.

Within an hour we were aboard the captain's twenty-four-foot cat-hulled reef cruiser, flying toward East Bay Cay, a skinny sidecar that hugs North Caicos's windward side, separated from the mother island by a half-mile-wide channel. I had provisioned myself modestly with rice, beans, fresh vegetables, onions, and limes for conch salad, beer, a bottle of rum. Otherwise I planned to fish and dive for my food, which is what one does, happily, on a deserted island in these latitudes.

Captain Newman jutted out his chin to direct my attention to a narrow cut, which I could not yet demarcate, behind a glistening bar mouth between the big island and the cay. "This is the road in," he announced, pointing to a slight taint of turquoise indicating deeper water — perhaps six inches deeper.

We came aground about a hundred feet off a rocky point, the terminus of the shaded white-sand beach I had been watching unwind for twenty minutes. We waded the gear ashore through transparent water, the two of us together hauling the heavy coolers and my main duffel bag, and finally it was done. I saluted the captain goodbye and then turned my back on him and (I hoped) every other human being on the planet for the next ten days.

As his boat receded into the distance, I pulled a celebratory beer from my cooler and sat down to engage myself in what could have been a most illumining conversation about the liberties we finesse for ourselves, but my mind went stone blank with euphoria and I could only stare at the opulence of color — the blue of jewels, eyes, ice, glass — and the glowing white towers of late-summer cumulus clouds queuing across the wind-tossed horizon.

I was alone, as sooner or later we are all meant to be.

Texas, three days earlier. More than a few years had passed since I'd last bunked with Captain Tay, and this was by far the largest space we had shared: an expansive bed in a dim apartment annexed to the house in San Antonio that had once been his father's and was now his son's.

The captain's one-room apartment had the ambience of an exhibit in some provincial museum — the Explorer's Room — its walls hung with crossed spears, shark jaws, barnacled fragments of sunken ships, intricately carved wooden paddles, yellowed newspaper clippings, and glossy photographs of adventure.

I opened my eyes to stare at the ceiling, the morning sunlight a radiant border around the two makeshift curtains pinned over the windows, and finally called the old captain's name. No answer, and when I nudged him, no response. Captain Tay was a self-proclaimed dying man, an arthritic and half-blind silverback awaiting winter in his bone-strewn lair, and I thought, *Well, that's it for him.* Apparently he had slipped away in the night, fulfilling his chosen destiny by dying in the same bed his wife, Linda, had died in thirteen years earlier.

The night before, the captain had shown me a sketch on a legal pad: the outlines of a human body, front and back, with twenty-eight red X's drawing the viewer's attention to a catalog of the physical indignities Tay had suffered over the years: stitches, concussions, animal bites, punctures, cracked ribs, broken bones, and a shrapnel wound he had sustained from a mortar round in the jungles of Colombia while tagging along with his blood brother, a commander in the National Police, on a 1973 raid against guerrillas. Not indicated on the drawing were the recent, less visible assaults: a bad heart, diabetes, clogged lungs, an exhausted spirit. He had also handed me — one of his designated undertakers — his self-composed obituary, the last line of which read, "He will be buried at sea in the Turks and Caicos," and his desire was that the burial take place over the *South Wind,* the ship his wife's ashes had been scattered over in 1987. As I was leaving for the archipelago after my stopover in San Antonio, I thought it was damned decent of the captain to die with my convenience in mind.

But when I came out of the bathroom a few minutes later, Lazarus was sitting up, pawing the nightstand for his glasses and cigarettes. He was already dressed, because he'd slept with his clothes on. As far as I know he had always done so, ready to leap up at a moment's notice into the god-awful fray.

"I thought you were dead."

"Any day now," said the captain with a spark in his hazel eyes, lying back down to smoke, his shoulders and head propped up with stale pillows. He'd been lying there for six or seven years, a veteran recluse, the lone survivor of all that he had loved, shipwrecked here on this rumpled king-sized mattress.

I offered him a respite from the soul-heavy inertia of his retirement, as I'd done annually since he had hunkered down. "Come with me, Tay. Ten days on an uninhabited island. The sort of thing you and Linda used to love. What the hell are you doing lounging around here, waiting to croak?"

This was a bit more irreverence than the captain was accustomed to, and I could hear the growl forming in his throat. "I'm seventy-one years old, I'm an alcoholic, my legs are going out, I've buried all my lovers, and I've done everything a man can do down there where you're going," he barked. "Get it through your head: I want to die."

I tried to imagine him as he had been four decades earlier: a thirty-one-year-old man carrying a briefcase and umbrella, dressed in a Brooks Brothers suit, stepping aboard the commuter train in Westport, Connecticut, riding to Manhattan in the glummest of moods, believing he had traded his "real" life for a halfhearted commitment to virtues that read like a checklist of the American Dream — social status, upward mobility, material comfort — but were somehow entering his system tilted, knocking him off balance. He had married Barbara Rolf, a lithe, sensual blonde from the Ford Modeling Agency, a woman whose face was radiating from the covers of *Life* and *Paris Match* and who had borne him a son named Mark. Tay was natty, lean, dashingly handsome, husband of one of the world's original supermodels, and the father of a towheaded three-year-old boy — all this, and yet he was still a despondent man riding a commuter train from Westport into the city. It wasn't another company job he was hunting for, but a resurrection, some kind of a life in which he could breathe freely again.

He had had that freedom, had pursued it with Hemingwayesque flair — Golden Gloves boxer, three years with the Eleventh Airborne Division during the Korean War, the big man on campus at the University of the Americas in Mexico City, twice elected student-body president. In Mexico City, he had operated his own gymnasium, teaching boxing, judo, bodybuilding. Exciting opportunities had knocked relentlessly at his door. While doing graduate work in industrial psychology, he had led a group of scientists into unexplored regions of British Guiana, Venezuela, and Brazil. There was something wild in his blood that wasn't going to be tamed, no matter how much he muffled it beneath button-down oxfords and dry martinis. Being Texan was likely part of it, he figured. His family had come to Texas just before the Alamo fell, and his great-grandfather had been a civilian scout for the Mormons on their trek to Utah. On both sides, his family lines were heavily saturated with footloose visionaries and hell-raisers and uncontainable spirits.

Stepping off that train in Manhattan, he crossed the platform and caught the next train back to Connecticut. Off came the suit, the briefcase landed in the trash, and he hired on as first mate on a sailboat out of Westport that carried tourists around Long Island Sound. And then he was gone.

"All right, come die in the islands," I told him. "Save me the sorrow of carrying you back there in an urn."

"I'm not moving," the captain snapped, but then he shifted himself upright and his voice became sonorous with care. "You have a good knife?" he asked. "Something that will hold an edge?" He eased up off the bed to rummage around in his moldy piles of gear. "Here, take this knife. I want you to have it."

Ever since I had met Tay and Linda in Colombia in the early seventies — I was fresh out of college, a twenty-two-year-old tadpole who had decided to see the world — the Maltsbergers had seemed intent on teaching me how to take care of myself. I took the knife, just as three months earlier I'd reluctantly taken the pistol he'd been trying to give me for years.

"Any advice, Captain?"

"Keep your matches dry."

Then I held him — this man who had taught me the vocabulary of freedom, schooled me in how it could be seized and harvested and lost, who had made his world so big and then made it as small as you can have it outside a coffin — and said goodbye to him. For all that, I could see that his inner world had never really changed, and that for those of high spirit, a life wish can at times bear a terrifying resemblance to a death wish, and a certain degree of metaphysical disorientation is bound to seep into the program. It was only that the seep had become a flood. You could walk on its banks all day long, throwing lines into the current, but the captain was indifferent to rescue, not dissatisfied with being swept along toward a promise he had made to Linda decades ago:

I will not leave you alone in the sea.

It was January 1971. Meteorologists call the type of storm that slammed into Tay and Linda in the Bay of Biscay, off the northern coast of Spain, an extratropical Atlantic cyclone — an out-of-season, out-of-place hurricane. Trapped in the storm's cataclysmic center, the ten people aboard their boat, the *Sea Raven,* watched in awe and horror for seventy-two hours as the fury doubled and then tripled in intensity. Their efforts to reach port were cruelly defeated by straight-on winds, with the tops of the massive waves humping green over the bow. Force 6 became Force 8 became Force 10. The mainsail blew out, and the captain, unable to steer, ordered the crew to chop the mizzen sail off its mast to bring the ship under control. The pummeling wind and pounding swells vibrated the caulking out of the boards beneath the engine housing, and the ship lost power.

They issued a Mayday, but the answer from the Spanish navy only increased their sense of helplessness and doom. They were going to have to wait in line; ships were in desperate straits throughout the bay, and resources were fully deployed and floundering. Not far from the *Sea Raven*'s position, a tanker's castle toppled into the water, taking sixteen men with it. Thirty people were rescued off an American freighter that was going down nearby. A boat put out from the port of La Coruña to respond to the *Raven*'s Mayday but had to turn back, heavily damaged. Linda watched the water rise up the hatchway steps as the *Raven* sank lower and lower into the colossal waves.

One summer night eight years before, she'd pulled up in front of Slug's Saloon, an infamous bar and jazz club in Greenwich Village, in a green Porsche coupe. Linda Johnson, a bony doctoral candidate in experimental psychology at NYU, was working in the lab at Albert Einstein College of Medicine. She also was a girl who'd been stuck too long in the convent of her education, and she was beelining from Mary Washington College to Manhattan, the center of the universe, partying like nobody's business and collecting so many speeding tickets in the city that she'd have to sell her beautiful car. She took a seat at the bar at Slug's, where Tay, back after a year in the islands, was running the food concession.

Glamourwise, Linda was the antithesis of Barbara Rolf. She was a big-toothed, stringy-haired blonde who talked with a cornpone drawl and a skeptically raised eyebrow. The daughter of a Virginia state senator, she looked like an egghead, her blue eyes blinking behind thick kitty-cat glasses she was always terrified of losing. What Tay saw when he came out of the kitchen that night was . . . brains, an irresistible, exotic quality, given the women he'd been dating. They talked just long enough to recognize themselves in each other: two dreamers in a barely subdued fever of restlessness, possessed with a great need to be on the move away from an ordinary life. She showed up the next night at a party at his loft, and they started seeing each other. She had finally connected with the man who would open the door to the controlling passion of her life: the ocean. When her mother suddenly died in 1965 and left her $20,000 and a Volkswagen, she and Tay hit the road.

"I have left New York — it's true," Linda crowed to a childhood friend four months later in a letter sent from Isla Mujeres, off the coast of the Yucatán. "With only two chapters left to write on my dissertation, eye to eye with a goal that has teased me through sixteen, seventeen, eighteen years of training, I pulled the reins on my job, my Ph.D., my career, all for a little taste of fantasy. After cooping up my spirit for so long in stiff-paged textbooks and overcrowded seminars, when it finally broke free it shook my whole foundation, like waking up with a dream intact, or falling through a keyhole you never thought existed. . . ." She promised her friends and family that she'd be back in several months, but that would never happen. Her jaunt, her waking dream, her infatuation with the questing beast, would last for almost twenty years.

And what exactly was that trip? A very old story, a myth, the type of tale humans have been telling one another for thousands of years: two enchanted lovers, a magical boat called the *Bon Voyage,* harrowing misadventures, a pot of gold — in this case sunken galleons in Cartagena Bay, off the coast of Colombia. They'd been together for five years when in the autumn of 1968 Tay got word that his ex-wife, Barbara, was dying of leukemia; back in the States, ten-year-old Mark needed him. By this time, Linda had fallen in love with Tay to the extent that she could no longer imagine a life without him, and their next few months were a whirlwind of sorrow and happiness: They were married in November, Barbara was dead by January, and before the winter was out, Tay and Linda and Mark were living together in Dallas, where a network of friends had helped Tay secure a job as foreman of a highway construction crew. But as soon as the three of them reached a level of comfort as a family, the shared lust for adventure churned back into focus. Their recurring dream: to get a bigger, better sailboat and return to Colombia. Linda took classes with the Coast Guard and earned her license as a full navigator, Tay began to cultivate investors, and together they constructed a castle in the air called Sea Raven Enterprises, printed stationery and business cards (CHARTER SERVICE — SEAFARIS — UNDERWATER PHOTOGRAPHY — SALVAGE — CRUISING — MOVIES — TREASURE), and sold shares of stock.

Linda had found the *Sea Raven* in Denmark, frozen solid into a fjord: a 99-ton, 110-foot, gaff-rigged-topsail ketch, a classic Baltic trader built in 1920, as beautiful as any ship ever put to sail. She purchased it for $13,000, and soon Tay and Mark followed her to the Danish coast. The three of them lived on the ship at first, out on the ice; then, when the harbor began to thaw, they set up house in a nearby shipyard and hauled the boat to dry dock for a year of extensive refurbishing.

And then, having sent Mark back to his grandparents in Texas and having welcomed aboard as their captain a former Dutch naval officer named Jaap Stengs, his movie-actress girlfriend (who had never been to sea before), and a crew of six free spirits, they were finally setting sail across the Atlantic, passing first through the Bay of Biscay.

By the fourth day of the storm, the *Sea Raven* was drifting aimlessly in sixty-foot seas and Force 12 winds. The ship's main pumps had ceased to function, and two hundred tons of water had risen four feet above the bilge line. The nearness of death was like a dull pressure somewhere behind the freezing weight of Linda's adrenaline-wracked fatigue, and it translated into a specific dread, which she expressed to Tay: With the *Raven* about to go under, Linda feared they would be separated, and she couldn't bear the terrifying thought of being alone in the sea. Prodding her up the slopes of panic was the image of being tossed around — alone and drowning, with her eyeglasses slapped from her face by the waves, cruelly blinded at the one moment of clear vision. How could she swim to Tay, her one hope for survival, if she couldn't even see him? He calmed her nerves as best he could by roping her to him with an umbilical cord of sheet line. Come what may, he promised, they'd be together.

They waited for the ship to sink or for help to arrive, whichever came first. At last out of the howling gloom a Spanish tanker appeared. With superhuman effort a line was made fast, and the *Raven* was towed into the harbor of Gijón, where, according to the official record of the Spanish port authority, "after having moored the *Raven* and put new pumps on board, Captain Jaap Stengs burst out weeping and was not to be calmed down within fifteen minutes. Then he fell asleep."

For five months Tay and Linda remained in Gijón, overseeing the repairs to the storm-mauled ship, but back in Texas the corporation Tay had started was imploding, riddled by infighting and embezzlement. The Maltsbergers' shipyard account was suddenly cut off. To lose a ship in a hurricane was no injustice, but to lose a ship to crooks and double-crossers was an unbearable betrayal.

There's a Jimi Hendrix lyric that poses what perhaps is the only question worth asking: *Are you prepared to be free?* Not free from responsibility, necessarily, but free from external oppression and internal fear. In everyone's life, it seems, there is a season in which this question is addressed or withdrawn, one's habits changed or calcified, one's dreams realized or rejected.

When I was coming of age in the 1960s, in the suburbs of Washington, D.C., my mother took to calling me, disapprovingly, a wandering Jew, implying that I was infected by some disease of waywardness that had the potential to undermine my future and land me in serious trouble. When I graduated from college in the spring of 1973, the gate finally opened on the mystique of other places, other cultures, *otherness* itself, and four months later, instead of securing an entry-level position in my expected career as a journalist, I boarded a flight from Miami to South America. My mother's suspicion was confirmed: At age twenty-two, I was declaring myself a type of hobo, falling from middle-class life into a pit of daily uncertainty.

Flying toward the San Andrés archipelago in the southwestern Caribbean, the cheapest destination available that was technically in Latin America, I was unaware that there were other people like me, people who might think of their urge to travel as an acceptable characteristic of a bona fide lifestyle. Romantics, to be sure; fools, possibly; escapists, probably. Dreamers who pursued irregular but nonetheless intrepid dreams of dubious value to the social order, their minds flaring with extravagant narratives. That's who Tay and Linda were, the first adults I befriended who had decided to step off the well-marked path and keep going.

"I surge into the waves of time, fascinated by the billowing soul of man," Linda wrote a few days before she died, composing her own epilogue. "What imponderable excess baggage we travel with on this trip bound for old bones and flaccid skin. Why ever let it be boring?"

I was grateful for the way she lived; she was the boldest person I ever knew. A life of bravery begins almost by default when you first find yourself oppressed by a low and unforgiving threshold for being bored. The only deliverance for the neurotic, the explorer, and the traveler alike is to throw himself off a cliff into the boiling waters of crisis. And then, to the best of his ability, to have fun.

"You know what's funny about our adventures all those years?" Tay mused as we lay back down together in his bed, smoking cigarettes and watching the Weather Channel play a mindless loop of Hurricane Debby footage. "We never had any money."

A friend, hearing in the Maltsbergers' sad tale a raw need to move beyond the agony of the *Sea Raven,* mentioned he knew an old gringo in Colombia who had a gold mine high up in the Andes and was looking for help. Never especially pragmatic until they were already immersed in challenge or folly, Tay and Linda went off to live in a bone-chilling tamped-earth hut at 11,500 feet, above the jungles of Bucaramanga. Tay and the old man struggled to refine a process for filtering gold out of the large heaps of tailings left centuries earlier by the Spanish conquistadors. They collected seven or eight ounces a week, but it wasn't enough.

After a year and a half the Maltsbergers packed their sea chests and descended the mountains all the way to the coast and beyond, to the San Andrés archipelago, where they had previously chartered out the *Bon Voyage*. This time, they homesteaded on remote Isla de Providencia, its barrier reefs dotted with the seduction of shipwrecks and the promise of treasure. On the edge of Providencia's central town they rented a two-story clapboard building called Lookout House and opened a four-table restaurant, the only thing they knew to do to make a living while they engaged in their treasure hunt. Mark, by then fourteen years old, joined them; he was being home-schooled by Linda and living like a kid in the Swiss Family Robinson, every day a boyhood novel of adventures.

The first time I met them I was a customer in their restaurant, having sat next to one of their partners in fantasy, Howard Kahn, a diving instructor from Chicago, on the flight from Miami to San Andrés. After a fabulous dinner of baked red snapper, Linda offered us drinks on the house and sat down with us, her only customers. I had planned to stay on Providencia for a week, but before the month was out Howard and I had rented a house together down the beach. Soon I was strapping scuba tanks on my back to claw through the ballast stones of the wrecks that Kahn and the Maltsbergers were working, inconceivably, by hand, the salvage operation ill-equipped for recovering anything more noteworthy than a few copper nails and coral-encrusted potsherds lying half-exposed on the bottom. At dinner each evening, Tay and Linda would open their mouths and it was like popping the cork on a magnum of rich stories. A year passed before I tore myself away.

Lookout House was sold out from under them, and they moved to Bottom House, in the poorest village on the island, sent Mark back to family and to public school in Texas, and lived on the beach in a hut they nailed together out of hatch covers from a shipwrecked freighter. One day a pre-cartel entrepreneur plying the trade routes between Colombia and Florida sailed his sloop into the island, and the Maltsbergers sailed away with him to the Bahamas, passing through the Turks and Caicos, which looked to Tay and Linda like their kind of archipelago.

On Grand Turk, they opened a restaurant, only to have the newly elected government fire the sole airline that brought tourists to the island. They took to the sea again, with Tay as captain and Linda as first mate of the *Blue Cloud*, a five-hundred-ton freighter that sailed from South Florida to ports throughout the northern Caribbean. But after a year of offering themselves up to every petty bureaucrat in every customs house on the trade routes — imagine bringing a shipload of anything into the wharves of Port-au-Prince and you get the picture — they bought a few acres of scrubland on Providenciales and jumped ship, their long love affair with life on the sea having ripened and burst. I think they meant to start another restaurant on Provo, not a nursery, but they inherited a truckload of pots and potting soil from a bankrupt hotel and that was that. In their fifties, the Maltsbergers finally retired their quest for gold, more emblematic than real anyway, and returned to the fold of property-owning, tax-paying citizens.

My wife and I visited Tay and Linda in Provo whenever we found the time and money, and the last time the four of us drove the road between town and Sunshine Nursery, we stumbled out of the bar at Turtle Cove into the star-smeared island midnight. As we walked toward the nursery's mufflerless old Chevy pickup, Linda tripped on a rock — the roads were unpaved then — and in falling to her hands and knees she lost her glasses, which we promptly found and placed back on her face. The four of us squeezed into the timeworn cab of the truck, Linda behind the wheel. "My God," she exclaimed a few hundred yards down the road, "Bob, you're going to have to drive." She slammed on the brakes. "Tay," she said fiercely in her molasses twang, "I've drunk myself blind. I can't see a fucking thing."

In the morning we solved the mystery of Linda's sudden blindness: When she tripped coming out of the bar, the lenses had popped out of their frames, and they were still there in the dirt when Tay drove back to look for them. But on the road that night, her worst fear had finally materialized: She had lost her precious sight, the ability to see the world. She and I had climbed out of the truck to trade places in total blackness, not a light to be seen anywhere but from a canopy of diamond-bright stars above, with one big one blazing down as we passed each other around the front of the Chevy.

"Goddamn," she said. "I may be blind, but I saw *that*. Beautiful."

Seven years earlier, after a radical mastectomy, the doctors had given Linda six months to live, and she had lit into them, calling them frauds and swearing she would prove them and their voodoo wrong. She and Tay had been captaining the *Blue Cloud* then, and Linda had started visiting an experimental cancer-treatment center in Freeport and injecting herself daily with a controversial immunological serum she carried everywhere in a dry-ice-filled thermos. Her cancer had been in remission ever since, but she could sense it was coming back, and it wasn't very long after that night together on the road that they would sell the nursery, which was prospering as the island developed, and Tay would take Linda to the States to die. He brought her ashes back to spread them over the wreck of the *South Wind,* which had proved so unseaworthy that it had been sunk by its owner, a Provo entrepreneur, off the reefs of the island, to be enjoyed forever after by scuba divers.

After the star fell and we started down the road again, Linda, staring blankly into the darkness, surprised us by asking whether we believed in life after death. If there was life after death, Linda wisecracked, Tay had better watch out: Her ghost would come achaperoning his liaisons with other women.

But there would never be other women, because grief too is blindness, sight fading inward toward memory, and the captain was too heartsick ever to care to begin again.

"Last chance, Tay. You coming with me?"

No, he wasn't, not today.

On East Bay Cay I savored the exquisite waste of time, time that other people were using to prosper in the world, time forged by others into progress and still others into dreams. I dove for lobster and conch, speared snapper, fly-fished for barracuda just for the violence of the hookup. Down in the sand I walked for miles, beachcombing in a daze. I scribbled dry observations in my journal as if it were a ship's log, and I slept soundly every night, lulled by the constant noise of nature: the far-off thunder of waves on the reef, the constant hiss and flutter of wind, the lap of shorebreak. For ten days I did precisely what I wanted: I read. Great books have made me unemployable; I can't pick one up without completely shutting down my life. In this respect Linda's influence continues to inform my days, for it was she who introduced me to Gabriel García Márquez, she who gave me my first copies of Peter Matthiessen's *Far Tortuga,* Joshua Slocum's *Sailing Alone on the World,* Graham Greene's *The Comedians.*

I knew what I was doing here on this far-off island — I knew how to take care of myself, how to enjoy myself — but I couldn't quite explain to myself why I had come, what I was looking for. Perhaps it was only a rehearsal for my final voyage with the captain. Or maybe it was an act akin to a transmission overhaul, lubricating the machinery damaged by life's inevitable grinding down of the romantic dream.

I thought of Captain Tay, back there on the king-sized island of his isolation, about his influence on how I'd lived my life, and about how I might measure the difference between us. Technically, at least, we were two of the most cut-loose people on earth: Americans, white males, sometimes penniless but possessed of the skills and tenacity that would always stick enough money in our pockets to get by, with a powerful and abiding sense of self-reliance and self-sufficiency. We were doing what suited us and what often made us happy. But Tay's obstinate disconnection from a world he had formerly possessed with such ferocious energy had unsettled me. Perhaps I saw myself doing just that: disconnecting. What is it that finally conquers your appetite for the world? Fear? Exhaustion? The formerly wild places now sardined with stockbrokers on tour? Paralyzing nostalgia for the way it was? Age and health? Self-pity?

The epiphany of my relationship with Tay and Linda Maltsberger, the revelation that had become as clear and guiding as the North Star, still struck me as the larger truth: Whatever your resources, the world was yours to the exact degree to which you summoned the fortitude and faith to step away from convention and orthodoxy and invent your own life. Tay and Linda knew better than most that there's never a good reason to make your world small.

*

An image presents itself from aboard the *South Wind,* an abominable vessel with a history as a drug-runner, eventually rehabilitated to run fuel between Provo and the Dominican Republic. In 1980, her owner coaxed the Maltsbergers into bringing the freighter down from a Florida boatyard. They hired me on as ship's carpenter to enclose the toilet on the stern of the boat — Linda never did get much privacy in her life with Tay — and to help them deliver the *South Wind* to Provo.

On the fourth day out we entered an armada of vicious squalls in the channel off the Exuma Cays. At midnight I took the helm from Tay, and for the next three wretched hours I fought alone in the darkness to keep the ship on course, waves breaking over the bow and foaming down the deck, lightning strikes erupting on all sides, white rain pelting horizontally into the windshield. Toward the end of my watch Linda awoke, stepped over to the radar screen, and proclaimed that she didn't know where we were, but from the looks of it I had steered too far west and we were about to crash into unseen rocks. Terrified, I changed course twenty degrees, and Linda, storm sibyl, as always so transcendently composed, walked out into the tempest. Sometimes I had to shake my head clear to see her properly. Her physical self, her sense of style — the clothes, the cut of her lank hair, the clunky eyeglasses — seemed so retrograde, so bolted down to the Camelot sixties, as if she still was and always would be some bookish chick from NYU who couldn't quite finish her dissertation on the urban insane.

After the ship's mechanic crawled up out of the engine room to relieve me at the wheel, I went looking for Linda and found her back at the stern. The worst of the storm had passed, and she stood in the cone of illumination under the pole that held our running light, her body swarmed by hundreds of shrieking birds that had sought refuge with us, swirling like snowflakes past the fingertips of her outstretched arms, landing on her shoulders, her head. It seemed for a moment they might carry her away. There was a look of extreme delight on her rain-streaked face, and she turned toward me and nodded as if to say, *How marvelous! How miraculous!* And then she retreated back inside to chart our position and bring us men safely through the night.

THOMAS SWICK

Croatian Rock

FROM *South Florida Sun-Sentinel*

Split: Croatian Pop

DARKNESS FELL as I entered Split. An unknown quantity now cloaked in shadow. The airport shuttle — a huge sightseeing bus carrying me and another guy — loped past twinkling sheets of socialist housing before dipping into leafy confines halved by immemorial walls. Bare bulbs under awnings illuminated the playlet of a night market, and then a tenebrous opening of water appeared.

We pulled into a space at the edge. I gave the driver the name of my hotel — Bellevue, pronouncing it, as an old Croatian hand had coached me, "Bellevie" — and he pointed at the other end of the harbor. I rolled my bag into the dimness of a palm-lined promenade, passing pensioners, families, grills pyramided with blackened ears of corn.

The hotel — thin neon lettering and Venetian windows — occupied the front of a boarded-up square. It bespoke, even at night, a history of better days. On the first landing a timeless tableau — two dusty potted plants and the letters R E C E P C I J A coupled with a slightly askew arrow — transported me back to communist Poland.

I climbed the last steps with trepidation. I had called a month earlier to make a reservation, and a deep, lethargic voice at the other end had responded: "Just give me your name and dat will be dat."

The man at the reception desk took in my name, and then we performed the old-fashioned exchange of passport for room key. I couldn't tell if this was the result of a written record or a chronic availability of rooms.

Mine had a bathroom light that took fifteen seconds to illumine. When it did, I found that the maid had left a dirty mop in the tub. On closer inspection, I discovered it was a spot where the enamel had worn off. I walked past the two single beds, a thin white sheet folded barrackslike at each foot, and opened the window. And in rushed the smell of the sea, and the sounds of the music festival directly below.

There is nothing like Croatian pop for getting the jet-lagged travel writer out of his room. I fled the vicinity, weaving my way through slippery stone streets that opened eventually into a smoothed stone square. Shuttered stone houses faced off across from a crenellated round tower.

I slid through more right-angled alleys that deposited me into a hallucination: a sunken square hemmed in by antiquities. The delicate remains of a colonnade filigreed one side, and the skeletal façade of a temple, now buttressed by brick, classically filled in the back. (And, above this weighty space, rose an illuminated campanile.) Spotlights dramatized the age-blackened columns, giving the scene a crumbling magnificence, while the café tables spread across the peristyle provided a jarring contemporary note. So that welded onto the indoor-outdoor motif — niches and statuary under the stars — was the even more compelling one of ancient and modern: teenagers flirting on ruinous walls; couples drinking in the shadow of the gods. It was like stumbling upon a cocktail party in the Roman forum.

I had found my way into Diocletian's palace. The guidebooks all told of this marvel: a massive edifice built at the edge of the sea by the retired Roman emperor. Diocletian had had an impressive career: born of slaves in nearby Salona, the capital of Roman Dalmatia, he so distinguished himself as a soldier that he eventually rose to the rank of emperor. Calling it quits at the beginning of the fourth century, after a robust persecution of Christians, he returned to his homeland with the desire to grow cabbages. Swords into plowshares.

Yet his final residence belied any delusions of simplicity. It was less a palace than a small walled city. (Covering nine and a half acres, it takes up, on contemporary maps, half of Split's old town.) The façade alone contained fifty Doric columns. Within the gated borders were not only imperial suites but temples, streets, public buildings, baths, courtyards, galleries, a garrison, a domed vestibule, and a mausoleum, which housed Diocletian's tomb for nearly two centuries (before his body mysteriously disappeared) and which, in a sweet revenge, was turned into the town cathedral.

On a somewhat distant shore, architectural splendors. It is said that the Georgian parts of London, Bath, and Bristol were inspired in part by the drawings Scottish architect Robert Adam returned with after a visit to Split in 1757.

But what really distinguishes the complex today is not its size or its symmetries but its fantastic utilitarianism. It is not just that people now gather where Praetorian Guards once strolled, but that they live here. In what must stand as one of the world's, if not first, at least most spectacular instances of adaptive reuse, the citizens of Split blithely built their dwellings within the palace. They grafted their humble residences onto the walls and filled in the arcades with bedroom windows. Just as weeds sprout among ruins in other lands, here it's houses. (It is almost as if, after the Cultural Revolution, the Chinese had erected apartment blocks in the Forbidden City.) In the coming days I would stroll the grounds shaking my head in wonderment at the curtained front doors next to erstwhile temples, the soccer balls sailing past toppled pillars. I could not walk along the waterfront promenade without staring up in amazement at the stately columns embedded in the condo façade, and occasionally bookending sagging lines of wash.

But now I needed to sleep. Back at the Bellevue, a new receptionist rose for my room number.

"Dwiescie dwanascie," I told him.

"What godforsaken language is that?"

"Polish," I said. "I thought it might work."

"Nothing ventured, nothing gained."

I tried a simpler way, number-by-number: *"Dwa jeden dwa."*

"We are very proud of you," he said sarcastically, reaching for the key to 212.

The waiters in the dining room wore embroidered vests that reminded me of the wallpaper in the corridor. If I drank coffee, I would have thought it strange to have the cup delivered by someone not wearing a black T-shirt. Tea seemed to work better with the wardrobe.

After breakfast the palace always beckoned (you never really tired of the juxtapositions), but one morning I headed off in the opposite direction, through Veli Varos. This neighborhood of twisting lanes and chock-a-block houses is regarded as the proving ground for the city's humor. (The writer Miljenko Smoje had grown up here, and the TV series based on his stories, *Our Little Town*, became the most popular comedy show in Croatia.)

I climbed winding alleys that carried familiar Mediterranean echoes — Spain, Greece, Italy, Turkey — but held something slightly off-kilter, an indefinable otherness, a Croatianness, I assumed. And it wasn't just the architecture. Locals passed — men often in shorts and sandals — and I greeted them with good morning (*"Dobro jutro"*) to no effect. I took it personally, but then noticed that they were equally aloof with each other. In this sunny picturesqueness, a grim introversion.

This was disheartening because I had seen Veli Varos (the very name makes you smile) as my last hope. Downtown, simply trying to get basic tourist information (not daring to hope for some deeper insight), I had found most personal encounters unpleasant. It ranged from the sullen indifference of shop assistants to the brusque, unsmiling replies of the ferry representatives to the hostile glare of the harridan occupying, of all things, the city tourist office (out of which I staggered like a schoolboy after a run-in with the principal). There were a few exceptions: the man in the fabric shop who walked me several blocks to my elusive restaurant; the woman in the grocery store who found a bruise on my orange and went and got me another. But even these acts were performed with a hardened helpfulness. One morning I woke up in my hotel room and thought for a brief instant (as I have in very few places in the world): I don't want to go out there again.

I walked back down the hill, and then along the sea, pondering civic mindsets. The war, no doubt, had played a part, as had the crippling economy. (The government of the late president Franjo Tudjman had lifted millions of dollars out of the country, which now was experiencing 25 percent unemployment.) But what disconcerted outsiders was that while the moodiness was all too apparent, its sources weren't. The city showed no signs of wartime devastation (the fighting, of which Split saw little, ended in 1995) and it contained no real pockets of poverty. Even the most identifiable mark of idleness — young men filling cafés in midafternoon —

had an untroubling, *dolce vita* cast. People were struggling more than suffering, and struggle is a private, invisible process.

And the struggle, perhaps, was not just with the present. In 1993, in *Granta* magazine, the writer Michael Ignatieff described a visit to Jasenovac, fifty miles east of the Croatian capital of Zagreb. This was the concentration camp where, during World War II, 40,000 Serbs, Jews, Gypsies, and Croatian Communists were murdered. That is the Croatian estimate; independent researchers put the number closer to 250,000.

"When Croatia declared its independence in 1990," Ignatieff wrote, "it made one central mistake, one that may have put the new state on the road to war: it failed to disavow publicly its fascist past, to disassociate itself from the Ustashe state and what it did at Jasenovac." Had it done this, he suggested, "the local Serb leaders would have had difficulty persuading their Serb followers that the new Croatia was the fascist Ustashe come again."

He went on to write: "The wartime Ustashe state was Croatia's first experience of being an independent nation. It has proved impossible for Croatian nationalists to disavow that nationhood, even if it was also a fascist one. Instead, they evade the issue. They dismiss tales of Ustashe atrocity as Serbian propaganda; they airbrush atrocity into crime by playing statistical sleight of hand with the numbers who died."

I found a walkway down by the water, which led me past rocky inlets and leathery bodies. Matrons spilled from bikinis, their pendulous breasts and life-preserver stomachs warming unapologetically in the sun. I wondered what the widow in black walking in front of me was thinking until she removed her blouse to reveal the top of a two-piece. People took to the water with a naturalness that reminded me of Australia — where swimming appears to be less a recreation than a basic human need — but that here, in this Catholic land, seemed to have a deeper, almost sacramental quality. The morning dip as spiritual cleansing.

"Ours is a lost generation," Sonja said almost sunnily. She sat with her math book in a courtyard of the palace, a pretty woman with a clean face and dull teeth and the long legs that seem the happy prerogative of the Dalmatian female. I had stopped by her sign advertising portraits and asked why the young women selling souvenirs in the passageway were so listless.

"It's the end of the season," she had said, laughing. "They don't have to be nice anymore."

It was a joke. "There's a word — *fiaka:* It means laziness, and it's used to describe the feeling in Split."

There were also problems with drugs. "It's a big drug city," she said. "We have drugs and football. Two extremes."

"And a pop music festival," I said.

"I don't listen to that music. You hear one song, and all the other songs sound just like it."

Sonja had spent the war in London, where many of her friends still lived, where she had first gotten up the courage to sketch people's faces in public. And she was moving soon to Zagreb, to resume her studies, this time in computers.

"I wish I could study what the Greeks did," she said. "Mathematics, philosophy, music. The highest things." But not, clearly, the stuff for interrupted students of a struggling young nation.

I asked if she would miss her hometown: the sun, the sea, the quality of the light.

"It's nice to be nostalgic about Split," she mused. "Because it means you're somewhere else."

Parishioners filed down the steps of the Franciscan church on Trg Gaje Bulata. With its box shape and square columns, it had looked the first time I passed it like a socialist ministry, but now, after Saturday-night Mass, it reverted to form. The congregation thickened at the doorway and seemed to flow back into the fresco behind the altar.

It filled the wall: The risen Christ looming above a long green land sprinkled not with trees and houses but with hundreds of people in regional dress. Some of the figures stood cluelessly, arms akimbo in black vests; others strode daintily with drooping heads, while a bull, a lion, and an eagle flew symbolically above. In the morning I had seen the sharp-nosed figures of the sculptor Ivan Mestrovic — "there is something very distinctive about Mestrovic's faces," Sonja had told me — and been awed by the power of his art. Yet this strange vision of Ivan Dulcic was, in its soberly whimsical piety, even more moving.

The Bellevue was still being besieged by pop. It was, I had concluded, the hotel where Rebecca West had stayed while researching her classic book on Yugoslavia, *Black Lamb and Grey Falcon*. In one of the chapters on Split, she describes looking out her window at three men talking in the square, and her husband's observation that "these people are profoundly different from us. They are not at all sentimental, but they are extremely poetic." I was glad she wasn't here for the music festival.

The handsome, white-haired receptionist greeted me in English. Vladimir had spent twelve years in Australia, where he'd gone in the fifties to avoid military service. "I didn't want to carry a rifle around for three years. And it was very hard-line here then. We sang songs to Stalin and Tito, about how they were going to rule the world."

He returned in the seventies, when a general amnesty was declared. I told him that he lived in a beautiful city. He gave a noncommittal shrug.

"It was built by the Romans. We don't have much regard for our antiquities. There's a place not far from here — Salona — with an amphitheater, ruins. In any other country it would be protected by a fence and they would charge people to see it. Here there are sheep and goats wandering about."

He agreed that the city had a problem with drugs, but insisted it hadn't led to crime. "This is one of the safest places in the world. We don't have muggings, robberies, holdups — it's not in our tradition. I work here all night by myself, and I leave the door open downstairs."

A haggard woman appeared and unleashed a pitiful whine, which Vladimir countered with gruff, helpless appeals. I thought perhaps she rented rooms from her home and had a business bone to pick; then Vladimir turned to me and said, "This woman is complaining about the condition of her room. But there is nothing I can do. I told her: When the state runs a hotel, it's already a bad situation. When that state is Croatia, it's catastrophic."

The tone turned more sedate, and the woman retreated. Vladimir explained to me that for about four years, two-thirds of the Bellevue had been occupied by refugees. "All the hotels had refugees. They'll have to do millions of dollars of renovations. The way those people treat property. They were from rural areas; many had never been in a hotel before."

I asked what part of the country they came from.

"Many from the northeast. Did you ever hear of a place called Vukovar?"

I nodded gravely.

"I was brought up to believe that everyone is the same," Vladimir said. "I am not racist. But the brutality that the Serbs have shown, the utter barbarity."

He went on talking, about the "madman" Milosevic, the old Serbian desire to rule all of Yugoslavia. "They say wherever there is a Serb living, that is Serbia. Which is preposterous. Their military is one of the largest in Europe. Before the breakup, eighty-five percent of the officers in the Yugoslav army were Serbs. They didn't want to give up power."

He scoffed at demands that Croatian war criminals stand trial. "That's like calling the Allies to answer for bombing Dresden."

His was a perfectly clear, undoubting, one-sided view, which I didn't challenge, partly out of deference to the first Croat who'd opened up to me, and partly out of an already (after only three days) profound sense of futility.

Upstairs, the sounds of Croatian pop filled my room. I turned on the TV in hopes of drowning it out, and got a station that was broadcasting the festival. It was a strange sensation: hearing from the tube the same cloying music that was coming through my window. And then switching it off, and finding it still going strong. The sheet was too thin to block it out, so I tried the pillow, with little success. But even as I moaned, I knew I was getting a valuable lesson in the meaning of the word *inescapable*.

Hvar: A Life in Stone

I stood on the top deck of the *Petar Hektorovic* overlooking Split on a brilliant fall morning. For three days I had gazed at these gleaming white ferries until the word JADROLINIJA — the company name emblazoned on the side in giant blue letters — became in my mind a synonym for escape. It had something to do with Split, but also with a personal restlessness. On almost every trip I take I am reminded of the perceptiveness of the man who wrote that his two favorite things in the world were arriving in a new city and then leaving that city.

Three backpackers stretched out on benches with a heavy weariness. The city laid out beneath us was to them just a faceless way station on their progress toward another. But maybe not. Perhaps they were the exhausted Hvar chess team coming back from a weekend competition in Zagreb. The thing about being a traveler is that you just don't know.

I turned back to the city, so suddenly likable from the deck of a ship. A young woman came and stood to my left. Normally I would have hesitated to speak, but a long weekend of solitary wandering had made me recklessly bold. I didn't even wait to come up with something clever.

"Nice view."

"Yes, it's pretty," she said softly. "But I didn't like the city. The people were very sad."

She had a stern attractiveness and a clear-eyed gaze. Her long, straight brown hair and her flowery ankle-length dress gave her an air of hippie puritanism. Her accent was vaguely German.

"I'm from Switzerland," she said. "Near Basel. I arrived here by bus yesterday. It took twenty hours, but it was better than flying."

She'd been to Hvar a few months earlier. "It's such a beautiful island. In the summer you smell lavender everywhere."

I asked about hotels in the town of Hvar; as usual, I hadn't made a reservation. "I'm staying at a friend's house, but I don't think it will be a problem now that the season is over."

The engines began rumbling, and we inched away from the pier. "I guess the war had an effect on people's moods here," I said. "Perhaps on the islands they're more removed."

"Yes, a little I think. But my friend never wants to talk about the war. He had family in Sarajevo."

A male. When she had mentioned the house, I had pictured a villa overlooking the sea. Now I imagined a tall, dark Adonis, a black lock of hair bouncing over his forehead. Hvar is sometimes called Croatia's St. Tropez.

I asked what she did in Switzerland.

"I paint and write — poetry and small stories."

"So you're going to Hvar for inspiration?" I was still hopelessly curious.

"It's more than that," she said thoughtfully. "I need to decide what I'm going to do. And I'm pregnant, so that changes things."

We stood in silence for a while, and then she said: "If you don't mind, I'm going to sit down. I'm starting to feel a little . . ."

I remained at the railing, marveling at the variety of fates these ferries carry. They seem so obvious, taking tourists to their vacations and islanders to their jobs. But there were breaches, anomalies, intertwined futures in the balance. Planted into the frivolous and the mundane was a subversive element of responsibility and beatitude.

As we entered the harbor of Stari Grad, she came over and said her friend would give me a ride into Hvar. Then she added: "But please don't say anything about my pregnancy. He doesn't know yet."

He was waiting on the dock, a short, stocky man with a bulbous nose and a shocking mane of unkempt hair. He threw out his arms for a sporting hug, before kissing her decorously on each cheek. His surprise at seeing me seemed completely lost in a still percolating astonishment at seeing her.

We piled into a car with a shaved head at the wheel. "You have good trip?" her friend asked, turning around in the passenger seat. When she said yes, he turned back to continue a conversation with the driver.

The interior filled with oblivious Croatian. We drove past cool forests of pine as the men in front engaged in animated discussion. I felt so bad for the woman that I couldn't bring myself to look at her. I thought about kicking the passenger seat just to get the dumb father to turn around.

At last a development appeared on a hill. We rolled down a bumpy street and stopped in front of a half-finished house. Construction equipment littered the dirt yard.

"We get out here," the man said, now turning to me. "My friend take you to town." I thanked him for the ride, and said goodbye to the woman. Then I watched them walk, one after the other, into a hefty privacy.

Hvar half cups its harbor in oatmeal tones. A cozy spill of sun-warmed stone around a shimmery liquid center. Fishing skiffs bob and sleek sailboats nuzzle, their white masts dwarfing the regimental palms. The scent of lavender rises from vendors' vials and, in stepped alleys, Slavic susurrations echo. A walkway winds out along the harbor, past the fifteenth-century Franciscan monastery and the circle of bikinied schoolgirls batting a ball over transparent water.

Cafés sprinkle the waterfront promenade and amble into the cathedral square. A Venetian arsenal hugs a corner, its top floor housing Croatia's first theater, one of the oldest in Europe. It sends a note of real artifice into the prevailing atmosphere of suspected theatricality, bolstered by the last-minute appearance, high atop the hill, of an ancient citadel.

The extras filling the stage in late September are mostly bargain-hunting easterners — Poles, Czechs, Slovaks, Hungarians, with a handful of Brits, Italians, and Germans. They stroll the promenade and study the blackboard menus (an endlessly repeated chorus of fish and spaghetti frutti di mare). They walk out along the sea path and throw down beach towels on unclaimed rocks, the Germans sometimes shedding every stitch of clothing in the conquest. Imagine the Little Mermaid grown up and flabby.

In the evening, concerts enliven the monastery courtyard — a touring Czech choir, a pianist from Zagreb — after which people quietly make their way back along the water (so close they can stoop and touch it), the lights of the town dancing helplessly on the surface.

Hvar, at least at the end of the season, has the feel of a languid idyll. It appears as that rare thing: an exquisite place devoid of pretension. It is like something out of the pre-attitudinal age. The occasional native indifference is the result not of disdain but an ingrained fatalism (the malaise of a people with a long history of being ruled by others, and then Communists). The teenager sitting on the wall outside the monastery alerts you to a darker side: warring mafias, rumbles at the discos. "Hvar is a cross between Sicily and Jamaica," he says in excellent English, and you are struck not so much by the harshness of his imagery as by the worldliness.

Hvar is the belle of the island of the same name, while the venerable statesman is Stari Grad. It horseshoes its own less crystalline harbor with houses that are somehow not quite as spruce. But what it lacks in charm it makes up for in character. For it was here, around 385 B.C., that Greeks from Paros first settled, calling the place Pharos. (Which the arriving Slavs pronounced as Hvar.) And it was here that the Renaissance poet Petar Hektorovic lived and wrote. His narrative poem *Fishing and Fishermen's Conversations* was probably the first in a still-kicking line of philosopher-angler books (though titles have improved with time), and as such was hailed for its originality and its role in helping break down the destructive barrier, through its sympathetic portrayal of two fishermen, between aristocrat and commoner.

> Outwardly they seem but simple folk,
> Yet inwardly they have a wondrous wisdom.

Just up from the harbor his house — Tvrdalj — still stands, with its famous fishpond and inscriptions in Latin: How beautiful Faith and Truth are! Alas, the days flow by like waves and do not return. And, above the entrance to the lavatory: Know what you are, and then how can you be proud?

I visited the house on a sunny Tuesday morning, and then walked through quiet stone streets narrowed by ancient stone houses. In a stone square I found a stone stairway, at the top of which stood the door to Maja's.

"We were just talking about you the other day," she said, having recovered admirably from the shock of my presence. She looked unchanged from the Fourth of July picnic in Victoria Park (our only previous meeting): long thin arms and thick head of hair, the Israeli boyfriend still smoking in the background.

It was a little past noon and they had just gotten up (the life of an artist). The apartment had a makeshift air, as some of their belongings had not yet arrived from Miami, where they had spent the last year. And they had just bought a house, which they would show me. But first we must stop at the Lampedusa Café.

"This is where we come every day for our coffee," Maja said, pointing to the terrace along the waterfront.

A friend was waiting: a large man with a bald head grinning peacefully from behind lozenge-shaped shades. He wore the loose white clothing and the three-day beard of a man of leisure.

"Aldo works in the cultural center," Maja said as we took our seats. "He can tell you everything about Hvar. The only problem is, he doesn't speak English." So she interpreted, starting with the Greeks, then the Romans and Byzantines, the grand entrance of the Slavs in the eighth century, followed by the Venetians and the period of Austro-Hungarian rule. Even our café had a story: Its name was taken from the island south of Sicily where, in the late 1800s, many men from Stari Grad went to fish and, in a few cases, settle.

Recent history was less remarkable. "Nothing happened here

during the war," Maja said. "Two or three times a month the Yugo-slav army blockaded the harbor, so we couldn't go to the mainland. Their planes flew over the island regularly. Once they destroyed the two planes that took tourists on little sightseeing tours. That made people really mad."

I asked what she thought about the elections in Yugoslavia, then five days away.

"Nobody here is paying much attention."

Two young women came over to say hello. Mira was an athletic-looking blonde who spoke English like a Dutchwoman; Ivana was short and fashionably bespectacled, frizzy brown hair falling onto a skimpy mauve dress. She sounded 100 percent American.

"I just graduated from NYU," she said, "with a degree in archae-ology and art history."

We all walked to see Mira's new house. She was an artist who had moved here from Zagreb. How she had bought it, I hadn't a clue.

"This is the street where they found a mosaic," Ivana said.

"It's a shame it's covered up," I said.

"That's the best way to preserve it," said Maja.

"What I'd like to see them do is unearth it again and put a Plexi-glas cover atop it," said Ivana. "But of course there's no money for that."

Mira's house stood at the corner of Srednja Kola and Vagon, two glorified passageways seemingly carved out of stone. "Srednja Kola used to be the main street," Ivana said, "because the Riva [water-front promenade] was too windy. Now people meet on the Riva, but it's not as nice as in Hvar. There the water is so clear it just invites you to jump in. Here we have a sewage problem — a few people have already gotten sick. They're trying to do something about it."

We entered a dusty darkness. The first floor had no windows; by the light from the open door we could make out a vast cavity in the front room, its bottom a jigsaw of mostly intact mosaic.

"I was just cleaning it this morning," Mira said. "I'm going to live upstairs and turn this room into a gallery. What I'd love to do is put pillows around and have people come and sit, just like in Roman times. Make it a kind of meeting place for artists."

Then she said casually: "The Greek street's in the next room." And moving through the doorway, with help from Aldo's cigarette lighter, we saw the large squares of cut stones purposefully placed. This was the first house I'd ever seen in which not just the décor but the era changed from room to room.

"There are many more finds in this neighborhood," Aldo said through Maja.

"Yeah!" cried Ivana. "My sister just bought the house next door!"

"You know what I missed in Miami?" Maja said. "Stones."

We were outside again, navigating a maze of oatmeal walls with green and brown shutters. The remark carried a little of the mystification of the pet rock craze (I can see missing your language, or even the particular blue of the water), but the more I thought about it, the more sense it made. Here stone walls enclose rock-strewn fields outside of stone villages. Along the sea, stone houses sit above stone steps leading down to beaches jagged with boulders. In missing stones Maja was missing her world.

We were nearing Tvrdalj. "Did you see the fishpond?" Ivana asked me. "The story was that whenever a fish died, Hektorovic didn't eat it, instead he buried it. They do that today."

In the cultural center, housed in an old sea captain's house, we found more artifacts, here under glass and informatively labeled. Aldo went into his office and returned with a paperback.

"For you," he said in English, handing it to me. It was a copy, in Croatian and English, of *Fishing and Fishermen's Conversations*.

"I was editor," he said proudly.

On the way to Maja's new house, we stopped at St. John's Church and examined more mosaics. To show us the fine acoustics, Maja sang a few lines of "Ave Maria." I asked why, in such a small town, there were seven Catholic churches. (Earlier I'd seen St. Lucija, with its poignant stone relief of the resurrected Christ above the doorway.)

"They're dedicated to different saints," Maja said. "Saint Nikola, for example, is the saint for sailors and travelers. Most of them are only open a few times a year, like for the saint's day."

"Are young people religious here?" I asked.

"A lot of them believe in God, but they don't like organized religion." Though Ivana said she had gone to Rome in August to participate in World Youth Day.

Down the street stood Maja's house, catty-corner from St. Stephen's Church. Its Venetian campanile filled the bedroom window.

"The bells start ringing at six in the morning," said Maja.

In the garden, Aldo picked almonds and figs from the trees. "We also have tangerines, lemons, plums," said Maja. "We're going to fix the place up and then rent it out."

But not this afternoon. A visitor had arrived, from far away. The figs were ripe, and lusciously sweet. And the days flow by like waves and do not return.

"This is a terrible car for Hvar," said Maja, as her boyfriend negotiated the narrow lane in his ancient Mercedes. She sat in the back seat with Vanda, another artist who had joined us for a ride after the others had drifted off. I thought if Hektorovic were around today, his great work would be titled *Art and Artists' Conversations.*

"I know something special about the island," said Vanda, who had been silent, searching for something with which to impress me. "The Easter procession. There are five villages that people walk to, one after another. When they get to a church, they sing in an indescribable way. It is like crying."

"There's a local men's choir," Maja said, "that put out a CD called *Following the Cross.* They're famous all over the world now."

We passed a truck packed tight with grapes; a sweet viscidity filled the air.

"Wine is one of the major industries on the island," Maja said, "along with olives and lavender."

It was almost dark when we got back to Stari Grad. After a drink at Café Antika — "We usually sit outside on the benches and watch people go by" — we walked a few yards to Jurin Podrum.

"This is where everybody gathers in winter," said Maja, taking a seat at a corner table. "It's run by Aldo's brother." A rustic simplicity: stone walls, wooden roof beams, two small flags (Croatian and American), and a snapshot of a man with a maniacal expression. "That's the cook," Maja said with satisfaction.

We ordered: salad, fish, grilled squid, red and white *bevanda* (wine mixed with water). Then I asked Maja what it was like here in winter.

"There is so much time in twenty-four hours you can't realize it. But it's good for contact with nature. You go for walks and you find wild asparagus, wild cabbage. It's more interesting to spend hours collecting than to buy. And in winter we drink young wine."

I asked if she took the ferry into Split very often. "No. You don't go to Split with only one reason. You need five reasons to go to Split. There are people on the island who have never been to Split. They know nothing outside the island."

A rotund man with a mustache entered. "He has a popcorn concession during the summer," Maja told me. "Last weekend he said: 'That's it. I'm on vacation.' He's on vacation till next season."

"People here live very simply," the boyfriend said. "They get by with only the basics."

Our salads arrived, beautiful presentations of tomatoes, lettuce, arugula. Maja picked a leaf out of hers. "This is a weed. It's what you find growing in walls. Hey, Vlad, what's this doing in my salad?"

"I wanted to remind you of your new house."

Aldo and his wife sauntered in, taking the table next to ours, followed by Mira and her boyfriend. Then the man I had met in the morning in the yard of St. Lucija. It was like a tourist edition of *This Is Your Life*.

When the entrées arrived, Maja said: "My fish is delicious. The head is full of white meat, and I don't usually eat the head."

She and her boyfriend insisted on paying, and driving me back to Hvar, though I said I'd be happy to take the bus. No, they said, it would give them an excuse to visit the town.

"Hvar is big business now," Maja said. "It attracts some people who are not so nice."

I asked about the shooting the other week, which the teenager at the monastery had told me about.

"That was very unusual. And it had to do with mafia," she said. "It doesn't affect other people."

We found a café on the waterfront just down from my hotel. Almost immediately, a young woman stopped to talk to Maja.

"I used to be in a rock group," she said, after the woman had gone. I wouldn't have imagined her in any other kind. "It was called Gego's Band — Gego was a nickname of the leader. I played electric guitar. And we had one hit, 'Mama, I'm Crazy.' It was the number-one song the summer of ninety-four. Every station played it, and every island wanted us to come play. We would take boats to the islands, and all these people would come along. Many of them were drunk even before they got on the boat.

"On the mainland was war. Here was crazy time. I think it's always like that — you need balance. In America during the Vietnam War you had the hippies."

I asked if it was possible to get a copy of "Mama, I'm Crazy," and Maja said no, even she didn't have one. The recording had somehow disappeared from the earth. Which was a shame, for it would have gone nicely with my Hektorovic.

PATRICK SYMMES

Miraculous Fishing

FROM *Harper's Magazine*

BOMB DOGS would stop around my hotel in the capital every few nights. Usually it was a pair of handsome German shepherds, eager warriors who padded through the lobby, dreaming of biscuits and sniffing for cordite. The hotel was located in Bogotá's red-tiled neighborhood of La Candelaria, where the Street of Sighs passes that of Hope, and because it was just two blocks from Colombia's congress there were always men in the bar who needed protection. I waited out these nocturnal sweeps in a little plaza across the street, buying plastic cups of *aromática*, a tea made of lemongrass, honey, and lime juice. This keeps you warm in a city set at 8,500 feet, where the wet, penetrating fog is almost perpetual.

On my left was the house where Colombia's first president, Simón Bolívar, survived an assassination attempt thanks to his mistress. She tossed him from a second-floor window, followed by his sword, and then his pants, and she stalled the conspirators for a few precious seconds. Meanwhile the father of his country sprinted up this very street, retreating into the night with the last tatters of Colombian idealism clutched to his privates.

While the dogs sniffed each car in front of the hotel, there was time to discuss the news of the week with the *aromática* vendor: a nun had killed another nun a few blocks from here, then chopped the body into pieces and burned them.

Americans usually don't wander the streets of Bogotá at night. When a lame-duck President Clinton came to Colombia last August, he avoided the capital entirely for the safer precincts of Cartagena, on the Caribbean coast. Clinton was shepherded through his eight-hour visit by 5,500 Colombian troops and 350 U.S. agents, with four frigates and eighteen patrol boats standing by. He pronounced his support for Colombian democracy in the form of a billion-dollar "anti-drug" aid package that came with as many as five hundred military trainers and sixty helicopters attached. Reflecting the relative strength of aerospace lobbyists and their captive congressional delegations, that $400 million fleet is divided between Texas-made Huey troop transports, à la Vietnam, and Connecticut-made Black Hawk gunships, à la the Gulf War. This aid, Clinton vowed, would accomplish what every previous initiative in the drug war has failed to do: reduce the supply of drugs in America while increasing their price.

This venerable logic was torpedoed only a week later, when police discovered that Colombian drug smugglers were building a sophisticated double-hulled submarine that could slip two hundred tons of cocaine right under the keels of American policy. The Colombian guerrillas who benefit from the drug trade are also, already, adapting to America's thoughtless intervention in a messy civil war that kills some 3,500 people a year. They have been fighting for decades, under different names, in different parts of the countryside. Today there is the ELN, which has about five thousand men and is often called "Cuban-inspired" in the U.S. media. But the real threat is the much larger guerrilla army called FARC, which now earns about $250 million each year from taxing the cocaine business. After almost forty years of unsuccessful warfare, FARC is suddenly flush with cash, weapons, and recruits. It has 17,000 soldiers, has kicked the government out of huge swaths of territory, and has come within thirty miles of Bogotá twice. FARC has already announced that it will match the increased American aid by the simple project of kidnapping more Colombians for ransom. The escalation of the war will generate hundreds of thousands of new refugees, while driving many of them into the arms of our enemies. Colombia produced 570 tons of cocaine in 1999, almost 70 percent of the world's supply. But if, to some small degree, the Clinton plan succeeds here, then drug production will simply balloon elsewhere, as already happened after drug war successes in Peru and Bolivia. All these omens of failure have been duly noted in the *New York Times* and in the halls of Congress, but we sleepwalk steadily forward, driven by the needs of helicopter manufacturers and pothead politicians eager for bona fides in a moral crusade.

The drug war now enters into the relentless logic of escalation.

Helicopters need crews and mechanics, who in turn need trainers; trainers need guards; when guards die, more guards are needed. This is always how it starts. Colombia isn't Vietnam in 1965; it is closer to Vietnam in 1955, when America's wise men offered military aid, not civil reform, and shipped ammunition, not electoral monitors. The course of action we set now will close off future options and lead, inexorably, to next year's events, and then those of the year after that. We have tactics without strategy and short-term goals without any endgame. This is the exact scenario for failure described by Barbara Tuchman in *The March of Folly*, her pioneering work on policy disasters across the centuries. Like British generals in 1776, or American generals in 1966, we have fatally misunderstood the nature of the enemy we are fighting.

It was my intention, arriving on April Fools' Day, to find the guerrillas and gauge their intentions and capabilities against the eight-hour rhetoric of Washington. But as a pathfinder on this march of folly, I was off to a poor start. Sitting in the plaza on different nights, sipping lemongrass while the dogs lingered curiously over tires, I would watch for the city below, always hoping the fog would lift long enough to show me something, to give me a landmark or a point of reference. On some nights the cloud base would rise up, just a few hundred feet, and I could glimpse the sprawling capital, with remote streetlights marking the dark avenues as they ran out toward the slums. There was a hint of distance, of scale and perspective, of the three great Andean ranges that splinter this country into inaccessible valleys and centuries of solitude, but after only a moment the fog would drop down again like a cloak.

I never did see the mountain peak located right behind the hotel. Not even once.

You might think it difficult or even dangerous to study the wily and elusive Latin American guerrilla in his natural environment, but all you need to do is take a regularly scheduled flight into southern Colombia, and then hire the taxi driver who shouts, "Do you want to meet the guerrillas? I can take you there."

Indeed he can. Within minutes of landing, I am deposited in a small cement office on the plaza of a flat Amazonian town in the heart of a 17,000-square-mile chunk of terrain that belongs to FARC, the Revolutionary Armed Forces of Colombia. The government has actually ceded this land to the guerrillas, partly as a peace gesture, partly in recognition of the reality that FARC has controlled most of this area since the late 1960s. Known officially as the Zone of Disarmament, and unofficially as FARClandia, this sanctuary is the size of Switzerland. FARC is equally gigantic, equipped with the latest small arms and a decent supply of (homemade) artillery; the rebels are rumored to have surface-to-air missiles and even a couple of helicopters. They have been fighting continually since 1964; their top commander, known as Sureshot (alias "Manuel Marulanda Vélez," born Pedro Antonio Marín), has been leading one guerrilla group or another in this terrain since 1956. Apparently Sureshot hasn't been to a city for three decades.

The cement office on the town plaza is inhabited by several guerrillas dripping with weapons and is run by a silent female guerrilla in camouflage pants and a spotless white T-shirt. I tell her that I want to ask guerrilla leaders how they will fight this U.S. escalation, and whether they would ever surrender their de facto control over cocaine production. She makes no overt promise of help. The government and FARC are about to embark on another round of delicate peace negotiations, and things are "hot," the usual Colombian euphemism for any form of difficulty. Messages will be passed, she concedes, but action itself is too much to promise. Instead, she sits me in front of a VCR and plays a tape of some guerrillas dancing salsa. Then there's another tape of the guerrillas cooking and cleaning up, building an oven, and standing around in the jungle. Then she puts in another tape, this one of some FARC music videos. The singer is a guerrilla named Juan, who became popular around the campfires and now has his own music videos. Quite a few of them, in fact: I am forced to watch half an hour of Juan, strutting in the jungle with his actual platoon dancing behind him, a dozen men and women in green uniforms, their rocket launchers swiveling back and forth, the heavy M60 machine guns never slowing down the boogie, the bullets and grenades jiggling and bouncing in time with Juan's lip-synching of his own songs.

The peace talks are supposed to take place at something called the Peace Table, which is located near a village called The Wells (Los Pozos), deep in southern FARClandia. The discussions don't start for several days, but the leading *comandantes* are already out there, so I decide to take things into my own hands. I find the same cabbie — a shifty veteran who looks like he would die if he told the truth — and we depart at first light. I'm confident the journey is safe, if only because so many have been down this road before. Following the example of Colombian business leaders, both Richard Grasso, CEO of the New York Stock Exchange, and James Kimsey, cofounder of AOL, have journeyed to FARClandia to meet guerrilla leaders and open their eyes to the miracles of capitalism. On the other hand, both these men had invitations. The road expires right outside town, and we bounce along a track of mud and gravel in a gray fog that seems to have followed me from Bogotá.

Trees loom out of the distance, but not many. The jungle here has been clear-cut for cattle. I'm looking over the fields when I feel the cabbie tense up and move his foot back and forth between the gas and the brake without touching either. We are coasting.

On the other side of the road, just visible through the dense mist, are about fifty FARC guerrillas, standing in two loose platoons. Their uniforms are all solid green and neatly matched. Their black webbing looks brand-new. The Galil rifles — Israeli guns, used by all sides in this war — are clean. The guerrillas have plenty of grenades and ammo. They are all wearing machetes in elaborately tooled sheaths. Colombians don't fight without machetes.

"That's the Monkey," the cabdriver says, and finally makes up his mind to accelerate. I look back and catch a glimpse of a portly officer, facing the troops, gesturing with his right hand as he addresses them. The Monkey (alias "El Mono Jojoy," born Jorge Briceño) is FARC's top military strategist, notorious for his dislike of foreigners. Last year he conspired with his brother, a dim-witted field commander, in the execution of three Americans who were caught wandering in a FARC zone. ("Three gringos die," he complained later, "and it turns into a major brouhaha.")

We bounce deeper into the fog.

There is no peace table. There is only a huge, open-sided shed that is empty. This peace shed is well and freshly built, with lights, a cement floor, rooms off the back filled with chairs, and an air-conditioned communications center. Also three satellite dishes. And bags of ice-cold water. But no table. The shed is quiet when I wander up from The Wells at breakfast. A few guerrillas walk out of the surrounding trees, ignoring me. A guerrilla with a clipboard finally adds my name to some list, but I am condemned to wait all morning for an interview. I kill time by strolling up and down the only road, watching the occasional cowboy with a machete canter past. The guerrilla guarding the front gate of the peace shed watches me go up and down for a full hour.

"Can you speak?" he says at last. *Sí*, I tell him. I go to the fence, and he leans on one post while I lean on another. It is cloudy, humid, and still. He looks at my notebook. "You can read?" he asks. I nod yes. "Did you go to a school?" *Sí*. "Did you pay hundreds of pesos to learn Spanish?" Two hundred pesos would be about ten cents. Yes, I nod.

He entertains both of us with stories about jaguar hunting, and then he "does" the accents of the different Colombian provinces. "In Santander they say _____," he informs me, "and the *paisa* say _____, and in Putumayo, whoo, they talk funny, they say _____." I can't even hear the differences, but I laugh because he is enjoying it so much. He's just a kid. His name is Sebastian. He is illiterate, was raised right here in Caquetá province, and has never traveled anywhere except on patrol. He has been a fighter for "a few years."

Like the American drug czar, the Bogotá government claims that the guerrillas are succeeding because they are rich and that the average guerrilla is motivated by a generous paycheck. Our helicopters are supposed to help separate the guerrillas from the source of that money, the drugs. Then both guerrillas and drugs will atrophy. I ask Sebastian how much he is paid.

"Nothing," he says, gently. "We are here *en conciencia*. Otherwise the government would say we are *burguesa*. Here we receive all the necessities: food, clothes, everything. We study. We get the analysis. We learn about the classes and so on, the oligarchy and so on." He tries to talk about politics and "the analysis" but gets lost in the abstract language. Finally he retreats to a concrete idea. "There are little old ladies who don't have anything at all," he says, "and so we want to end that. I'm going to speak slowly now, so that you can understand. We act out of conscience. We want the petroleum, the minerals, and the land to be for everyone."

I look at Sebastian's feet. He's wearing a pair of new rubber farm boots. They aren't even scuffed yet. For many peasant recruits, their first pair of shoes is the pair FARC hands them. The government soldiers they shoot at are the only government employees they've ever seen. "Food, clothes, everything," covers a lot of ground in Colombia, where the revolution is fueled by a per capita GDP of just $6,200 and farmland is concentrated in fewer hands every year. A chance to help old ladies. Land for everyone. Why not?

Eventually Sebastian speaks again: "What do you think of this land?" he says. "Is it more beautiful in your country? Are there mountains, like here?" And again: "Is everything the same? Are the trees just like this? Is everything green like this?"

"Do people wear the same clothes?" he says. "Is everything just the same?"

At last, I am called to my interview. Comandante Simon Trinidad is, within the formal hierarchy of FARC, only the number-two commander of the Caribbean Block, which in turn governs the combat actions of various smaller guerrilla "fronts" along the distant coast. But the real power structure of FARC has emerged during the two-year-long prenegotiation with the government over possible future peace negotiations. Trinidad is one of the seven guerrilla negotiators known as "the Thematics": they negotiate which "themes" can be negotiated at later negotiations. The Thematics are the public faces of FARC, younger and more presentable than the tottering Sureshot, who grumbles about making journalists "pay" for their "lies" about FARC. Indeed, in 1999 FARC commandos kidnapped one TV commentator who criticized them, and five Colombian journalists were assassinated in the last six months, mostly by right-wing elements who shared Sureshot's distaste for criticism. Trinidad is dressed in worn camouflage from his ankles to his floppy hat, and he lays a loaded Galil on the table, next to a vase of flowers. He has a stereotypically big salt-and-pepper mustache and is, like me, sweating bullets in the stuffy concrete room.

We start with his résumé, which is in no way typical of FARC, except in the ways that matter. Born to an upper-class family on the coast, Trinidad attended prestigious prep schools, graduated from university, and was a navy officer, a landowner, and a professor of economics. He also spent ten years as manager at Colombia's Banco Comercial, which is, he assures me with quiet dignity, "affiliated with Chase Manhattan." Trinidad's own transition from banker to guerrilla began when he protested the way land on the coast was concentrated in the hands of a few powerful landowners, men from his own class.

"I said publicly, to friends and at the university, that we needed land reform. This turned me into an enemy of the powerful people on the coast, and they attempted to assassinate me. They did assassinate my friends: lawyers, doctors, health workers. This is when I dedicated myself to fighting. I could have gone into exile, but I didn't want to do that. I'm forty-nine years old. I have sixteen years as a guerrilla."

Sureshot's war predates the Cuban revolution, and his relationship with Fidel is notoriously frosty. Trinidad also seems to disregard the hemisphere's leading socialist utopia. The Cuban guerrillas were victorious after only two years in the field, he explains, while the more patient FARC has had decades of war to solidify its revolutionary character before coming to power.

He has a loaded Galil lying on the table, so I don't challenge his defeat-is-victory logic. Instead I ask him where FARC gets its rifles.

"From all parts," he says, laughing and tapping the stock of the Galil. "From the U.S., Germany, Switzerland, Russia. All parts. Arms dealing is the best business in the world, after drugs. States do it, mafias do it."

It has been alleged that FARC earns $500 million a year, mostly from "war taxes" on the drug trade, but also from the practice known here as miraculous fishing, after a popular children's game in which prizes are pulled at random from a barrel: the guerrillas grab random groups of people at roadblocks or church services, perform credit checks via radio, and keep anyone with a healthy bank account. Kidnapping, I remind him, is the number-one complaint against the guerrillas.

"Somebody has to finance this war," Trinidad replies, "and the rich are going to pay." The guerrillas are not involved in drugs, he insists; they simply protect peasant coca farmers, because they are peasant farmers, and then tax large businesses, regardless of what they sell. "It is a financial strategy," the banker-guerrilla explains. "A tax. We are financing the war. Where do the arms come from? The food? We have to pay for the medicine, clothes, medical bills, the lawyers for our imprisoned guerrillas, their education."

The guerrillas are "by principle Communists" but also "patriots"

and "nationalists" who "want peace" and a "new economic model."
He talks about a "new economy" and a "new political regime that
opens space for others" and a "new state" and a "new structure for
the armed forces" and a "new system of justice" and a "new model
of social society." Colombia also needs a new road and communications infrastructure, a new crop-substitution program, a new anticorruption culture, and a new distribution of land, water, mineral,
and other rights, not just in some places but in every part of the
country.

This speech is finally interrupted by the guerrilla spokesmodel
in her white T-shirt. She comes in holding a note Simon Trinidad
has written; she can't understand it. He looks at the note.

"*Trinidadtres a* 'otmail dot com," he says.

"'otmail?"

"Hotmail," he says, pronouncing it properly in English, with the
breathy H. "Hotmail dot com." She stares at him. "Hotmail dot
com!" he says again. Finally he has to go outside for a minute and
explain the e-mail address to someone himself; then he comes back
in and apologizes. Good help is hard to find.

I ask him what impact U.S. military and financial aid will have on
Colombia's 40 million people. "If your neighbor's house is on fire,"
he replies at once, "you shouldn't throw gasoline on it. This will increase the horror of the war. A modern war — like in Yugoslavia,
with helicopters and airplanes — can destroy bridges and buildings, factories and so on, but not us guerrillas. We will spread out to
all parts of the country. We will fight the war of mobile guerrillas, as
Che Guevara taught. Today, here; tomorrow, there. It will general-
ize the war. You are going to bring the war to all Colombia. However, misery will continue."

He watches me for a while and then says, "Write that down. The
struggle will continue. Hunger and misery will continue."

I'm still having trouble catching up with the list of all the new
things Colombia needs, and he watches my notebook like a hawk.

"Write that down!" he says again. "Misery continues! Write that
down!"

While I am interviewing Simon Trinidad, a peace delegation of
Pentecostal Christians is in another room, slinging scripture at the
glad-handing guerrilla spokesman Raúl Reyes. (Reyes is notorious

for declaring, between stints as the FARC man in Costa Rica, Mexico, and Sweden, that he was tired of living "in the mountains.") The Pentecostals finish before I do and swipe my cabdriver. I sprint after the taxi — the only one for twenty miles — but it flees over a ridge, sagging with Bibles, and I am left to walk. I stroll into the hamlet of The Wells, with its twenty-three tin-roofed shacks. There are a pair of fly-infested cantinas along the main street. Shortly after a man tells me it never rains during the day, it begins to pour. I spend two hours sitting in one of the cantinas, drinking coffee, watching the rain, and waiting for any kind of transport. There are no taxis; one bus comes by, so packed that men are literally hanging from the sides, and the driver refuses to take me. Once in a while a pickup truck comes through, never headed the right way. The rain stops, mostly.

A five-year-old boy from the village watches me sit there. He's patient and charming. "I have paint on my shirt," he finally offers. Yup — bright orange paint. I notice a bit more in his hair. I look around. The whole village is bright. All twenty-three shacks are bright orange. The cantina is bright orange. The entire street is painted in hydraulic reds and oranges. I push a fingernail into a yellow fence post. The paint is soft. Only the fronts of the twenty-three shacks have been painted. It is a Potemkin village.

"When did they paint everything?" I ask the boy.

"Yesterday!" he shouts. "Yay!"

I don't know why I am surprised when a couple of guerrillas walk in for lunch and within seconds spot themselves on the restaurant's television set. They are watching a long news report about FARC, broadcast from the capital but filmed just up the hill at the peace shed and beamed from those convenient dishes. "There you are again," one guerrilla says to the other, grinning. Then the same report shows a long interview with Comandante Simon Trinidad, talking about the need for new things. On camera, the mustache works.

Eventually I talk my way onto a cattle truck heading toward the big town with the airport. There are already a driver and three assistants in the cab, all older men with filthy, ripped clothes and hands like slabs of burned beef. I sit amid a tangle of legs as we haul nine gray oxen through guerrilla country at ten miles an hour. After ninety minutes we pass a large house with twenty or thirty guerrillas lolling around. Some are sitting on the porch, others are standing on the wet grass, others are sleeping in the backs of three big, covered trucks.

"Look at those drunkards," the driver says. "They are sleeping it off."

"Look at those trucks," the man on my right says. He whistles under his breath: "They have everything."

FARC has scared some order into the region, but the local schools still have no desks, and people in the towns bitch about the guerrillas openly. Posters criticizing FARC are up in some homes I saw. And more people wear the green ribbon that symbolizes Colombia's burgeoning peace movement, known by its simple, nondenominational slogan: NO MAS.

The guerrillas return the favor. Flush with money, FARC doesn't depend on the peasants and doesn't need the towns. It isn't really a guerrilla army, and it isn't building models of anything in FARClandia, nor is it disarming in the Zone of Disarmament. The rebels just rest and train here, and then move off in their nice trucks to fight somewhere else.

Twenty minutes along, the cattle truck makes a sudden turn left. They have to drop off the oxen not in town, as I had assumed, but far outside. It will mean a delay of an hour or two. Impatiently, I decide to walk the last two miles and jump down. The men wish me luck, and the truck rumbles off.

I'm a hundred yards down the dirt road when I notice something on a barbed-wire fence: a standard-issue FARC uniform. It's wet. I stop to look at it and then hear laughter. Over the course of a minute, I notice, scattered in the distant trees, the following things in the following order: a camouflage pup tent; a rifle; a path; a FARC guerrilla smoking a cigarette; another camouflage tent, set on a sleeping platform with mosquito netting; another guerrilla; another tent; another rifle; another path; a curl of smoke from a cooking fire hidden deeper in the jungle.

It's a FARC forward camp: a blocking force laid across the main road between the town, with its airport, and the FARC leadership near The Wells. I walk slowly down the exact middle of the road, hoping to seem either innocent or invisible, but it descends toward a creek, and when I get to the bottom I have to cross a bridge. I can see a checkpoint a hundred yards on the other side of the bridge. There are three sentries standing there, facing away. Out in the middle of the bridge I can hear the laughter, clearly, and I look up-stream. Thirty or so FARC guerrillas are bathing in the creek. Their rifles are leaning on trees, and guerrillas are plunging in and out of the water. There are at least six women soldiers among them. Like the men, they have stripped down to their underwear and are soap-ing up in the creek amid gales of laughter, splashing, and flirting.

I stand in the middle of the bridge for a long time, watching the strong men and handsome women. These are the Monkey's troops, the same ones I saw in the mist this morning. Lurking in the zone of denial, well equipped with music videos and mosquito netting, they resemble the hard-working staff of an IPO primed for the big pop. They have 17,000 soldiers and are growing. FARC talks about a long-range plan, about needing twice as many fighters with air power before the final assault on Bogotá. Even if the peace shed produces a treaty, some people won't accept that. The Monkey and his brother won't disarm. They will take their own troops, and the hard-liners, and the hungry peasant kids like Sebastian, and they will regroup and keep fighting. They know what happens to guer-rillas who run for office in Colombia: after FARC formed the Patri-otic Union Party in the 1980s more than 3,500 of their candidates and campaign workers were assassinated. For the hard-liners, peace looks more dangerous than war.

I'm hypnotized by the sight of a darkly beautiful guerrilla rinsing her hair in the creek. She squeezes it out, dips it again, squeezes and dips, as if she could do this for just as long as she wants, as if the world would pause while gravity slowly pulled the water from around her legs, drained it down the muddy creek, into the Caguán River, and then into the Amazon, and finally, one day, into the Atlantic beyond.

There's a whistle, and it's not a wolf whistle. It's the sentry in charge of the roadblock. "You!" he barks, and gestures me up the hill.

There are two female guerrillas on duty as well; the male sentry is shorter than either woman. "Who are you?" he demands. A jour-nalist, I tell him, stuttering badly. I don't remember exactly what he says; he just yells at me. I'm sweating badly, stuttering worse, and I can't for the life of me recall the name of the town where I just was. This is panic.

"What town?" he shouts when I can't remember. "You are lying!"

He makes me angry. Suddenly I can speak Spanish again. I begin talking, a steady stream of complete nonsense about how I'm on my way to interview his commander right now and I had better not . be late. I hand him an ancient photocopy of my passport and keep talking. I'm interviewing the Monkey in thirty minutes; I rattle off the names of different commanders, anything I can think of to keep him busy.

Meanwhile a pickup truck pulls into the roadblock, and the female guerrillas look over the passengers, check the driver's papers, and then lower the chain to let it pass. I'm still talking, describing my close friendship with the Monkey and my upcoming book about Simon Trinidad, but I catch the driver's eye, hopeful, and he nods. Without ever ceasing to talk I step up into the bed of the truck, and the driver suddenly hits the gas, hard. We roll over the resting chain, sprint down the hill, and are out of sight. The whole episode is over in ninety seconds.

The last thing I see is the short guerrilla standing in the middle of the road, watching us disappear, the faded photocopy in one hand, the rifle in the other.

The appearance of sunshine in Bogotá is a rare event, considered news in the local papers and fiction in the works of García Márquez. I return through a haze to the Street of Sighs, dodging some war refugees in the same little plaza on my way into the hotel.

Maybe it is the altitude, or maybe the damp Andean chill, or maybe something else, but immediately on arrival a fever lashes through my body, confining me to bed. I shiver for two days and watch the peace negotiations on live television. Peace activists, union organizers, crackpots, students, and a government delegation all arrive at The Wells, and the Thematics take the stage in the peace shed. Different civilians get five minutes each to propose schemes for rebuilding Colombia — the construction of a huge new city from scratch in the deep jungle; or guaranteed employment for everyone; or the proper use of parapsychology; or nationalizing all the industries, all the farmland, and all the water, oil, minerals, and TV stations — but nobody is listening to anybody else. It is a dialogue of the deaf, a spectacle without substance. Simon Trinidad sits gravely on the platform in the shed, nodding like a branch manager, thanking people, asking them to keep it to five minutes. At one point, the aged Sureshot staggers in, dressed for golf and looking like he couldn't scratch a barn with a bazooka. He listens for ten minutes, and then staggers back out to shouts of "Viva!"

On the second day in the hotel room, still sweating, I catch a short news item about some mothers who have taken over a local church. Colombia has the worst kidnapping rate in the world, and the mothers are demanding the release of their sons. I jot down the name of the church, eat two aspirin, and ride a taxi into a vast, poor neighborhood on the outskirts of the city. Beggars chase me into the sanctuary, where I find about sixty of the mothers. They are very poor women from small towns and farmlands around Colombia. Each wears a shirt or a placard with a photo of her son, his name, and when and where he was taken hostage. It doesn't matter why he was taken hostage, or by whom. Most of the boys were Colombian army draftees captured by FARC in battle, but there are also mothers of boys who are being held by the ELN guerrillas, by the right-wing death squads, or by criminal syndicates, which kidnap people and then sell the captives to any group that needs ransom money. The mothers have bedrolls, plastic jugs of water, and cheap aluminum pots filled with rice. They've decorated the place with signs addressed to MR. PRESIDENT or GENTLEMEN OF THE GOVERNMENT or DEAR SURESHOT, always pleading for the release of their sons and an end to the endless war.

I'm in the church for hours, sitting on the floor, talking with the women, photographing their brown, weathered faces, the full panorama of Latin American despair hidden in every set of eyes. They hunch over transistor radios, tuned to the negotiations in the peace shed, wondering if Simon Trinidad or anyone will say the word *amnesty*. Each of these women has a hope: Maybe my son will come home soon. Maybe he will escape this nightmare.

I start thinking about the roadblock while I'm in there, and eventually I have to leave, because I start sobbing. Or maybe it is the faces of these women. Or maybe it is the fever, breaking.

The next day I notice an item buried on page six of a Bogotá paper: "Northeast Remains Cut Off." Guerrillas from Colombia's other major group, the ELN, have isolated three towns in the northeast flatlands by "flying" the nearest bridges. (This is the Colombian ex-

pression for blowing them up.) The most threatened of the three is
an oil center on the Magdalena River called Sandbanks (Barranca-
bermeja). ELN troops have cut all the roads into Sandbanks and
even closed the river to traffic by firing on relief boats. The city is already packed with war refugees — the population has doubled to
300,000 in the last few years — and with prices rising, residents are
starting to hoard food.

"The only manner of entering or leaving Sandbanks is by air
travel," the paper says. In the morning I buy a ticket and fly in.

"You've come to sun yourself?" the taxi driver from the airport
asks. Sandbanks is famous for its relentless sunshine, but as we go
through the town the hazy overcast is complete. At the weedy central plaza I jump out to investigate a large solar clock. As I suspected, it is no time at all here.

Sandbanks doesn't look like a city under siege. There are crowds
of people; shoeshine boys are blazing away; the stores are open. I'm
left at a dismal hotel overlooking the Magdalena and the seedy waterfront. The river is Colombia's Mississippi, once a commercial
and poetic artery in national life, now a deadly morass of twisting
channels, sandbars, eroding banks, and wrecks. García Márquez
called the river "a swamp with no beginning or end," only "an illusion of memory."

A more prosaic fluid — oil — now rules the region. Sandbanks
is dominated by a vast refinery, and greasy smoke billows from
three huge venting towers topped by balls of flame. These flares
burn all day against the gray sky, like false suns. At night their glow
is visible even in the surrounding guerrilla encampments.

In the morning I receive a briefing from Colonel Jaime Martínez, the national police commander responsible for defending
Sandbanks itself. "Only half the city is ours," he begins, spreading
out a map in his second-floor office and sending for coffee that
never appears. Although the national police are actually part of
the Defense Ministry, equipped with automatic rifles and armored
trucks, and received half of the $300 million the United States sent
to Colombia last year, the colonel's 1,000 men still can't venture
into most of Sandbanks's poorer neighborhoods. The streets there
are controlled by some 400 ELN urban guerrillas. Right outside
the city, 2,000 Colombian soldiers — part of the army's 135,000-

man force — are facing four other ELN *frentes,* totaling 800 men, and FARC also has about 1,200 fighters in the region. There is an obscure third group of guerrillas, the Maoist EPL, which has "only" 500 men and which fights in a loose battlefield alliance with the ELN. And there are also about 1,000 right-wing paramilitaries wandering the zone at night, conducting a dirty war of assassinations, orchestrated and financed by right-wing landowners and drug traffickers.

FARC guards about 100,000 acres of coca in zones across the river, Martínez says, but the ELN doesn't tax or protect the drug business, preferring kidnapping for profit. The paramilitaries themselves are involved in drugs, though. Everyone attacks the oil infrastructure in the region, blowing up pipelines, stealing gasoline for profit (about 60,000 gallons a day), and kidnapping oil workers for ransom. "Oil attracts the guerrillas, who need a way to finance their war, which attracts paramilitaries," Martínez tells me. "At any moment here, there are about three thousand men fighting one another with lead." Assassinations are constant. "We just had two Sunday," he says. Everything wrong with Colombia is wrong with Sandbanks. The terrain here is a single, swirling battlefield where distinctions among players, plans, and policy goals will be impossible. I ask the colonel what will happen when the United States sends sixty helicopters to aid the Colombian military in its fight.

"Personally, I'm very pessimistic," he replies, "because we haven't won this war in twenty years. The money would be better spent on social programs. On highways. Schools. Jobs. Small businesses. On employment and technology for the countryside. Economic opportunity can defeat the guerrillas. But a military program will increase deaths, increase war, increase civilian displacements, and not bring up peace." The colonel's office is spotless, a gesture of order against the chaos beyond. There is not a single paper in either his IN or OUT tray. I can see my unshaven face in the shine of his desk. "You could send two hundred helicopters and that wouldn't do it," he finally says. On the way out, I realize that he is wearing his watch upside down.

My phone rings at 7:01 A.M. two mornings later. "There's someone at the front desk for you," the receptionist tells me. I throw on

some clothes and go out. It is a man I can only call the Contact.*
We have had several frustrating conversations, vague chats about
"political actors" and "persons with knowledge of the situation." I
think we are maybe going to have a cup of coffee and another
pointless talk, but he looks at me and just says, "Get your cameras."

We march out of the front door, around the block, and behind
the hotel, where I am introduced to a man in a white shirt. We
shake hands. "You are late," he says, and sets off into a slum. The
Contact and I follow, trailing thirty feet behind. A disused path
leads down to the river. The man in the white shirt clambers down
to the waterline, whistles, and then comes back up. I buy a thimble
of coffee with the Contact's money — I've forgotten my wallet —
and then a canoe pulls up. It is made of brightly painted planks,
twenty-three feet long and three feet wide, with no seats. This is the
classic *yonsin,* misnamed long ago for the Johnson brand of outboard motors that powered the first of these fast canoes.

As I climb in, the man in the white shirt says, "You may have to
spend the night." I've been awake for fifteen minutes, so all I can
think of to ask is, "With whom?" *"La guerrilla,"* he replies, and the
canoe pulls away, leaving the man in the white shirt on the bank.

The Boatman shakes my hand and gestures for me to sit in front.
We shoot down the Magdalena at twenty miles an hour, spray flying, the skinny boat dashing behind vast islands and then rejoining
the main channel. After an hour we turn up a broad *quebrada,* or
side branch, and then race through an endless series of sweeping bends, leaning into the turns and accelerating in the straight-
aways.

The early morning sun lights us for five minutes — the sun! —
just as we approach a riverside checkpoint sometimes manned by
Colombian marines. The Boatman tells me that we are on a bird-
watching expedition. Do I understand that? I do. I turn the phrase
"expedición ecológica" around in my mouth, but the government post
is abandoned, and we roar past. Then the sun rises behind the
clouds again, and we turn into yet another side branch of the side
branch. We swing steadily through an ever tighter series of horseshoe bends, the river folding back on itself. We slow and get quiet.
There are more agonizing hidden bends, muddy banks that look

---

* I have also changed some compass bearings.

like ambush posts, and an endless wall of green. It is already hot, and impossible to see much in any direction.

I am let off at a bump in the bank. A little path leads up to a clearing ringed by a high green wall of trees and vines. As instructed, I walk into the clearing, sit down, and then the *yonsin* leaves. I swat at insects for half an hour and finally build a tiny grass fire for the smoke. This doesn't scare off a single mosquito. There is lots of time to think about bad movies set in the jungle, and then about García Márquez, lingering in his cancer ward, composing lists of all the things that Fidel Castro absolutely never told him. In *The General in His Labyrinth,* Márquez warned against loitering like this on the banks of the Magdalena: "There were men roaming that desolate place," he wrote, "who were as big as ceiba trees and had the crests and claws of roosters."

Fifteen more minutes and I hear a rustle, and then look over to see a forehead. It turns into a head, and then a camouflage uniform, and then five more uniforms. The six men step out of the brush. They aren't as tall as ceiba trees, and their claws are Galils and AK-47s. They come right over to me, pretending to be relaxed. The first thing they do is shake my hand, one by one, and then stamp out the grass fire.

The guerrillas are in camouflage, with worn webbing that holds radios, rifle grenades, and spare clips. Some of them have shoulder boards in ELN red and black, which is a relief: I wouldn't want to run into the wrong set of guerrillas out here. They are all wearing battered leather combat boots and have small green towels draped over one shoulder, which they use to swat at bugs. They leave one man to watch me, and go back into the jungle again. For the next two hours the mosquitoes are on me like NATO on Belgrade, and the guerrillas have clearly picked their dumbest soldier to guard me, fully aware that I will not get one single word out of him. Finally the other five guerrillas reappear.

One of them — a vaguely amused twenty-eight-year-old, who is tall by local standards — searches my camera bag. He has two radios and a codebook, and I finally realize he is the leader. I explain that I am a journalist, that he may have received a message I was coming, that I want to ask about American poli——

"Yes," he interrupts. "We had a very nice woman from the *Washington Pist* one time."

"*Post,*" I blurt out. I can't stop myself. "The *Washington Post.*"

"*Pist?*" he asks.

"*Post.*"

"Yes, the *Post.* She never sent me the article she wrote. Why do you suppose that is?"

He pats me down carefully, then tells me his real name, but later insists that I forget it. I have to refer to him by his war name, which is Comandante Diego. He is the commander of the ELN's *frente sur oriental,* one of four in the Middle Magdalena, and is currently orchestrating the siege of Sandbanks.

We get in another *yonsin,* sitting on the gunwales and packed tightly together, knees interlocked for stability in the tippy canoe. I look down, avoiding their eyes, and study the interspersed pattern of legs: camo, denim, camo, denim, camo. The canoe motors upriver, through smaller bends, and we pick up a second *yonsin* with two more guerrillas. All the men are silent. I'm thinking about the extremely small possibility (the *im*possibility, really, if you consider odds and chances and geography) that a new Black Hawk gunship is patrolling over this area. Six choppers — state-of-the-art machines, bristling with rocket pods, miniguns, and other tools for fighting drugs — have been delivered to Colonel Martínez's National Police.

Maybe one of these lethal machines is going to stumble overhead, by chance, and the pilot is going to look down and see two canoes filled with guerrillas. Despite the U.S. pretense of "only" getting involved in fighting drugs, there is only one battlefield in Colombia, and the pilot is not going to pause to see if we are ELN guerrillas or FARC guerrillas, or to inquire whether we take drug money, or to ask if that is a civilian on board. He's just going to lean over the cyclo, drop the ship down fast, and press a button. Sooner or later, in one spot or another, a piece of the American drug war will come hurtling out of the sky looking for these men.

Around noon, we pull into the bank, camouflage the *yonsins,* and hike in single file through the forest.

The secret jungle hideout is first betrayed, as are all guerrilla camps, by the amount of laundry hanging around. After spotting a T-shirt and then a pair of socks, I walk on a bit and notice a pig and a few chickens. Finally, we come to a grove of wild plantain trees, with a handful of people loitering in the cool yellow shade. The guerrillas have assembled a few crude stools from logs, but this isn't the summer-camp lifestyle of FARC. FARC tents have mosquito netting; the ELN tents are just black plastic sheets draped over ropes. The ELN kitchen tent looks deadly; FARC has brick ovens for baking fresh bread.

And instead of FARC's guerrilla girls in wet panties, I find a few men in sweat-soaked camouflage uniforms, somebody's girlfriend with a baby, and another 500,000 mosquitoes. There are only a half dozen fighters waiting in the camp. Each of them comes over and shakes the hand of the *comandante,* and his men, and then my hand too.

Diego fetches a thermos of coffee, and we settle into the command tent and light two mosquito coils. I rest on a log; he sits on a battered camp chair. There are a couple of plywood tables holding the laptop, printer, TV, and VCR without which no guerrilla encampment is complete. Everything is run off a big truck battery, but later I hear a small generator rumbling in the bushes. We sip the piping-hot coffee.

"The worst enemy of the Colombian people is the oligarchy," Comandante Diego announces, *sip,* "and then second worst is the *burguesía* of the United States, which tries to keep them in power."

He tells me about the founding of the ELN in July 1964 — a few days before I was born — and how four decades without victory have actually helped them, allowing the ELN to become "well consolidated, politically. This is a very consolidated project."

Diego talks for an hour about the oligarchy and about Colombia's grave crisis of disequality; about the need for schools, health clinics, employment, crop-substitution programs, agricultural-support programs, and infrastructure of all kinds; about the lack of "space" within Colombian politics, the way reformers have been subject to assassination ever since Bolívar sprinted up the Street of Sighs; about the need for a new justice system, a new economy, a new military, a new social order, a grand political discussion involving all sectors of the society, and land redistribution in all parts of the country, not just some. Despite what the media say, they don't care much for Cuba. ("You have to respect Fidel, though," Diego offers. "That *hijo de puta* can work. He's like Yimmy Carter.") They are Colombian nationalists and Colombian patriots seeking a Colombian socialism. They see the drug war as thin cover for a U.S. takeover of Colombia and will fight us every way possible.

This all sounds a little familiar. I ask him how the ELN differs from FARC. "We are not very different," he immediately replies. "Not ideologically. The plans are really similar. It is more a difference in style."

By "style" he is referring to the fact that FARC protects coca plantations and taxes cocaine-processing plants. The ELN has mostly left the drug business, but for now they fund their war with "detentions," or what most Colombians call kidnapping. The ELN took 695 of the 2,945 people kidnapped in Colombia last year, including a seventy-three-year-old peasant they kept in a hole in the ground for thirty days. They'd hoped to make $150 from him. "We are the most accused of kidnapping," Diego acknowledges, "but we don't kidnap. We detain people within the political-economic context of the war." I confess that I can't see the difference. "The difference," he replies, a touch angry, "is who makes a profit. We just detain people. If they pay voluntarily then we don't detain them!"

Outside the tent, there is a maze of paths through a cloudy quagmire dotted with self-sustaining encampments of rage. There will be no peace here either. Diego doesn't even pretend this will end soon. They support a peace process, he says, but in the next breath he admits that he feels a "military-political" victory for the ELN is certain. They look forward to a confrontation with the United States, to drawing Americans into a disastrous battle. "We call it the final war," he says. "It could last five, ten, or twenty years."

A patrol stumbles in. Exhausted men appear one by one, their uniforms just dark stains of sweat. The leader is a strong, light-skinned black man who comes into camp laughing. Everyone calls him the Witchdoctor for some reason. The last guerrilla is a girl, perhaps seventeen, with a long braid, a Galil, and a look of nausea on her face. All the incoming guerrillas shake my hand, then go around the camp shaking everyone else's hand. I watch the girl prop her rifle on a tree, slowly undo the braid in her hair, and then walk stiffly around the camp, shaking the necessary hands. She looks me in the eye when it is my turn, and the meaning of the ritual becomes clear in the instant we touch hands: There aren't a lot of places in Latin America where she would receive the respect she has earned here. For all their madness, the guerrillas — both

FARC and ELN — are socially progressive organizations, shaped by the egalitarian necessities of the battlefield, and open in ways that the rest of Colombia's deeply conservative society has never been.

The patrol has captured one prisoner, an adorable gray puppy that comes trailing into camp after ten more minutes. Everyone groans. There are already too many dogs in camp. They eat too much and give away the position by barking. The rules of war are ruthless, but nobody has the heart to tie the poor creature into a bag and throw it in the river. The puppy settles into the mud and starts gnawing on a boot.

There weren't any dogs in the FARC camps.

By midafternoon I am one huge welt of bites and have run out of questions. Like FARC, the ELN is obsessed with media relations, and I am forced to watch a half-hour demonstration of close-order marching and drilling by the guerrillas. The chants, the snapping to attention, the red and black flags, the fetish for insignia, are all meant to show that the guerrillas are a legitimate army with discipline. I sit and watch, unsure how marching in lockstep could be useful in jungle warfare. The Witchdoctor apparently feels the same way: He mutters jokes to his comrades as Diego makes them snap, swivel, and sweat in the heat. At the end, he encourages the chorus line to join him in the theme song from the movie *Car Wash*.

We're all laughing when the shot rings out.

Humans and dogs react the same: total silence and stillness. The blast was deep and serious, definitely a high-powered rifle, but it was also quite far away. Across the camp, the guerrillas stand motionless, their eyes unfocused, their ears tuned to the jungle. After ninety seconds, Diego finally speaks. "A hunter," he says. "Yes, a hunter." Dogs and people begin to move again, but slowly, warily.

An hour later the Boatman reappears, stepping out of the bushes without fanfare. This is good: I've delivered myself into the hands of one of Colombia's worst kidnappers, and my home has never seemed farther away. Around 5:00 in the afternoon I hear distant thunder, and the first drops land after thirty minutes. The Boatman suddenly rises and nods at me.

Eight of us return to the river, led by the *comandante*. The Boatman and I shake everyone's hand, then climb into the *yonsin*. We aren't five minutes downstream when the storm attacks. This is a lashing, fat tropical rain at dusk, and exactly what he was waiting for: It is safer to move under the cloak of rain, when the air above and the river below are empty. We sprint downstream, hurling ourselves into a downpour so dense that the Boatman cannot see where he is going.

Over the course of an hour, sweeping through ever wider bends, the creek opens into a branch, which becomes a tributary, which becomes the Magdalena. It doesn't seem possible, but the rain actually increases as we turn upstream. I haven't consumed anything in twenty-four hours except two thimbles of coffee, so I sit upright and rip mouthfuls of water from the sky.

At the last moment of the day, the sun drops again below the clouds, and a powerful belt of yellow light passes flat across the dark landscape. I can't see the sun — I can't see a hundred yards on either side of the river — but the light is there, a yellow band across the rain, and then it throws up a smooth rainbow.

The Boatman times it perfectly. We drift into Sandbanks just after dark, the oily flares of the refinery guiding us in, and he leaves me on the bank. Standing once again among the living, we realize that we cannot go forward, nor can we go back. America must not head down the jungle paths our congressmen and helicopter companies have chosen. Only the slow, painful labor of renovating both our societies — economic development, political reform, drug-treatment programs — can begin to lift the fog enveloping us. But tonight, as darkness settles over the black silt beach of Sandbanks, the only light is the dim orange glow cast down on us by the hissing torches of the refinery flares. The Boatman shakes my hand, pushes the *yonsin* back into the current, and drifts away. I stand there, watching him turn the nose of the *yonsin* downstream and then putter into the dark one last time.

JEFFREY TAYLER

Back in the USSR?

FROM *Harper's Magazine*

I'M FLYING from Moscow to Minsk on Belavia (the Belarusian national airline) aboard a twin-prop Antonov 24, a wobbly sixty-pas-
senger steel crate whose blighted upholstery and bony seats incline
me to lean forward and peer out the window. As we lurch and sput-
ter westward beneath the clouds, the most conspicuous geographic
characteristic I detect about Belarus, spread out below, is its lack of
conspicuous geographic characteristics. Not a single river, mountain range, depression, or eminence presents a natural border with
Russia or the other surrounding countries. Belarus is flat, covered
with a mosaic of forest, peat bog, and swamp; crisscrossed by rivers
that, for the most part, originate and terminate beyond its fron-
tiers; traversed by highways running south from the Baltic republics to Ukraine and east from Western Europe into Russia. When
the stewardess asks us to buckle up for landing, her language at
first sounds like some sort of rural Russian dialect; Belarusian resembles Russian enough to be largely comprehensible to Russian
speakers. After we touch down, I catch a trolley bus plastered with
toothpaste advertisements in Russian for the quick ride downtown
through rows of the same five-story Khrushchev-era cinder-block
apartment buildings one might see in Omsk or Tomsk.

The similarities between Belarus and Russia extend far beyond
linguistic kinship or even what seven decades of shared Soviet
history can explain. With the exception of a republic killed off by
the Bolsheviks in its infancy, the territory of present-day Belarus
had, until 1991, never supported an independent Belarusian state.
From the sixth century on, the land belonged to the domain of the

Eastern Slavs, pagan tribes of fur traders, farmers, and honey merchants who spoke Old Russian. In the ninth century its princes fell under the suzerainty of Kievan Rus, the state from which Russians, Ukrainians, and Belarusians were to evolve. Prince Vladimir of Kiev's acceptance of Christianity from the Byzantine Greeks in the tenth century launched the Eastern Slavs on a path that, after the Great Schism of 1054, would lead them to isolation from Western Europe — and to a fractious but essentially familial association with one another.

The absence of natural borders made Belarus vulnerable to incursions from its neighbors. After the Mongols sacked Kievan Rus in the thirteenth century, Lithuania moved in from the north and incorporated Belarusian territories. In 1569 Lithuania united with Poland. During the era of Catholic Lithuanian-Polish rule, Belarusians achieved a semblance of national identity based on Orthodox Christianity, language (Belarusian began evolving out of Old Russian), and folk culture. In the eighteenth century the Russian empire took over Poland, violently supplanting Belarusian culture with its own in the process. It was thus natural that Belarus, pacified and for the most part Russified, ended up a founding republic of the Soviet Union. Yet in 1991 Belarusian nationalism helped sunder that union, and Belarus became a sovereign state.

A longtime student of Soviet and Russian history, for the past seven years I have lived in Moscow and have followed recent events in Belarus with puzzlement. Since 1996 Belarusian president Alexander Lukashenko has been pounding on the Kremlin gates demanding reunification with Russia, and union treaties, however vague, have been signed, with little substantial protest from either people. In view of the Russian-Soviet legacy to Belarus (which includes the Chernobyl meltdown that irradiated a quarter of its land, Stalinist purges that killed hundreds of thousands, a moribund economy, and more than a century of czarist oppression), to say nothing of Russia's quagmire economy, what could account for the Belarusians' acquiescence, so soon after independence, to a proposed merger with their historical oppressor? Belarusian friends of mine in Moscow have praised Lukashenko and described a quiet life at home, free of the market chaos and anarchy of Russia, words that do not jibe with press reports that demonize the president and blame him for a curtailing of civil liberties that recalls the Soviet days.

I have come to Belarus to travel the land and find out what is going on.

As I walk the broad sidewalk flanking Fransyska Skaryny Avenue, the eight-lane thoroughfare that sweeps across central Minsk, it takes me no time at all to perceive how Minsk differs from Moscow: streets are immaculate, kiosks are few and well kept, cars stop obligingly when pedestrians enter a crosswalk, militiamen do not extort bribes from passersby, and signs are in Belarusian (even though Russian is the native language of more than 80 percent of Belarusians, including Lukashenko). Other differences do not flatter the city: a shortage of gasoline keeps the streets nearly empty of traffic, and people queue for sausage in fetid, state-owned shops that would have been privatized and renovated long ago in Russia.

Skaryny Avenue runs into October Square, a vast plateau of stone on whose northern reaches stands a half-finished behemoth of granite and glass — the future national palace of culture. Next to the palace, fifteen-foot-high steel letters rise atop a building and proclaim, in Russian, MAY THE HEROIC DEED OF THE PEOPLE LIVE THROUGHOUT THE CENTURIES. (The reference is to the Soviet victory in World War II, which killed one out of four Belarusians and razed the city.) The expanses of Minsk call to mind the steppes of Russia; standing in mid-square, I feel I'm offered up to a boundless sky, diminished by the massive granite palace and humbled by notions of heroes and sacrifice and immense tragedy. I am, in sum, infused with the spirit of a national mythology far grander than anything that this Kansas-sized country of 10.5 million people would have concocted on its own. The mythology is that of the Soviet Union, of deified proletarians and the righteousness of their cause, of the inevitable worldwide victory of Communism. It was Soviet architects, after all, who, following World War II, turned the rubble of what was once a provincial town into the major industrial hub of the western USSR, constructing defense plants and auto factories, widening streets for May Day parades, erecting apartment blocks for hundreds of thousands of mostly Russian laborers arriving from the east.

With *perestroika*, the myths were officially discarded, and a new, specifically Belarusian nationalism arose, deriving in part from revelations concerning the local death tolls of Stalin's purges and the Soviet government's cover-up of the Chernobyl disaster, and in part from enthusiasm for the prosperity that, it was assumed, would naturally follow upon the introduction of a free market. A prominent physicist, Stanislav Shushkevich, served as Belarus's first head of state, but the Communist-dominated Supreme Soviet stymied his efforts at economic reform and pushed the country back into the Russian embrace. Almost as soon as it arose, Belarusian statehood found itself threatened, and the pull of the past, the grandeur of the myths, regained the ascendancy.

On ORT, a Russian television channel also transmitted in Belarus, President Lukashenko is giving an interview. His habit of combing his thinning brown hair across his broad bald pate has turned him into the butt of jokes among the post-Soviet intelligentsia, and the mix of Russian, Belarusian, and Soviet bureaucratese he often uses makes him sound buffoonish ("like a manure slinger or tractor driver who ended up president," as one Russian friend of mine put it). An energetic hockey player, tall and wide-shouldered, and a youthful forty-five, Lukashenko cuts an imposing figure; his he-man image wins him popularity, especially with rural and elderly Belarusians, who admire strength above all in a leader. Perhaps in the West he would not impress, but this is the former Soviet Union, where rulers are compared with the dithering and dazed Yeltsin. Lukashenko's supporters have nicknamed him *Batka* — Dad.

Dad is angry (he often is before the cameras). When the interviewer brings up an imprisoned opposition leader, Lukashenko asserts that the man is in jail for embezzlement and if he returns the stolen funds, he will be released; as for Lukashenko, he's acting for the good of the people, both Russian and Belarusian. If he succeeds in his quest for union, yes, he would be prepared to give up some of his powers.*

Lukashenko's angry tone reflects the mood of a majority of Belarusians. Who, save swindlers and crooks, wouldn't be angry in the former Soviet Union? A former collective farm boss, Lukashenko was elected on an anticorruption platform of "market so-

---

* His local powers, that is. A few weeks later he would again express his willingness to assume the vice presidency of the unified state. As leader of Belarus, Lukashenko commands one of the less significant countries of Europe. If Belarus unites with Russia, he becomes co-ruler of a vast, if crumbling, megastate that can, if nothing else, inspire fear across the globe.

cialism," which was supposed to permit his citizens, dispirited by falling living standards and the rise of bandit capitalism, to enjoy the financial security they knew in the Soviet past and to taste the sweets of the free market, but which, in fact, denied them both, amounting to government meddling in the private sector, continued subsidies for the state sector, a halt to privatization (only 10 percent of the economy had been privatized), and the imposition of price controls. In 1996 he held a referendum, regarded by the Belarusian opposition and Western governments as flawed and unconstitutional, that granted him exceptional powers and an additional two uncontested years in office as well as authorized him to seek union with Russia. Lukashenko and Yeltsin have since signed a series of confederation treaties (the most recent of which was on December 8, 1999, exactly eight years after Belarus and other former Soviet states gained their independence from Russia) designed to create a single state within the next decade; a common customs zone has already been established, and border controls have been abolished. The treaties are intentionally vague but do signal that both countries are pulling away from the West. Lukashenko violently suppressed the demonstrations that his economic measures and unionization efforts incited among young, Western-oriented Belarusians, drove opposition leaders abroad or imprisoned them,* closed down opposition newspapers, and has even proposed five-year prison sentences for anyone who publicly insults him. The word *dissident,* no longer in use in Russia, has regained currency in Belarus.

Despite economic stagnation and political repression, Lukashenko's popularity appears to hold steady. Unionization has antagonized the intelligentsia, but it has the support of rural and elderly Belarusians who never accepted the nationalism of the *perestroika* era and whose self-esteem might be raised by returning to the fold of an internationally feared, if domestically chaotic, Russia. Among former Soviet rulers, Lukashenko has been alone in his courtship of Moscow: protective of their new powers, the last thing other ex-USSR honchos want is closer ties with Russia. If Luka-

---

* In the last year, four opposition leaders have simply disappeared: Tamara Vinnikova, former chairwoman of the central bank; Yuri Zahkarenko, the former interior minister; and, in September, leading dissident Victor Gonchar and publisher Anatoly Krasovsky.

shenko's union happens, it will set a precedent that could threaten the stability of countries with large ethnic Russian populations, such as Ukraine and Kazakhstan. In any event, the spectacle of a *compos mentis*, if poorly coiffed, democratically elected national leader striving to strip his electorate of its sovereignty is bizarre and unsettling. Lukashenko has often said that if he pulls off this union, he will go down in history for it. No doubt he is right.

Inevitably, the thought of union between Belarus and Russia evokes the two peoples' recent, shared past — and its horrors. The next morning I decide to visit the memorial to the victims of Stalin's purges in Kurapaty Forest just north of Minsk. Discovery of these mass graves played a crucial role in igniting Belarusian separatism during the *perestroika* era.

My driver, Dmitry Varivonchik, is a flaxen-haired, burly fellow in his early thirties, a trained engineer who left his job at a state enterprise seven years ago for the private sector when the latter was flourishing. As we shoot down Minsk's lightly trafficked lanes in his minivan, he tells me he now earns the equivalent of $100 a month — a king's salary by local standards — driving for a foreign company that brokers the sale of coal from Russia to Eastern Europe and moonlighting by using the company vehicle for trips like this one. A year ago, before the Russian economic collapse and the steep devaluation of the Belarusian ruble, he was making three times as much. The union is not on his mind; making ends meet is.

The two-lane road leads us through lonely stretches of forest. We pull onto the shoulder and halt. Horseflies harry us as we make our way through drizzling rain down a steep path into a pine grove echoing with the songs of thrushes and the pattering of raindrops. A few yards in stands a wooden cross engraved with the words: IN MEMORY OF THE VICTIMS OF THE MASS REPRESSION OF 1937–1941. I glance around. Shadows throughout the grove resolve themselves into crosses; the farther in you look, the more crosses you see. Here lie the bodies of tens of thousands of Belarusians (estimates run from 30,000 to 900,000) who were executed by the Soviet authorities on trumped-up charges of treason, espionage, economic sabotage, bourgeois nationalism, anti-Soviet agitation, and so forth.

Since the days of the Mongols, there have been state-orchestrated massacres of innocents in Russian lands. Visits to sites like this occasion little distress among former Soviets, though the massacres tend to repeat themselves, and no generation feels safe — a twin gene for fear and apathy must characterize the DNA of Eastern Slavs. Dmitry shifts his weight from one foot to the other, then lights a cigarette. "You know, my grandfather was a warehouse manager in a village near here. The local *osobist*" — secret police agent — "accused him of economic sabotage. He was due to be shot the next morning. But during the night that same *osobist* was accused of treason and executed, and my grandfather survived."

I ask Dmitry if the Kurapaty memorial means anything to him. He shrugs. "We Belarusians are used to being occupied by one people or another. We're a tolerant people — we've had to learn tolerance — and we wouldn't have done such a thing ourselves. Our tolerance has been our undoing, in fact. But I don't have time to think about it. I have a wife and a daughter to feed."

The rain picks up, and we head back to the van.

The next morning I climb aboard the *elektrichka*, or electric train, for Orsha, a city of 130,000 straddling the confluence of the Dnieper and Orshitsa rivers, 125 miles northeast of Minsk near the Russian border. A friend of mine in Moscow has given me the address of her parents, Victor and Galina Shcherbo.

The *elektrichka* creaks its way through a softly contoured countryside of birch forest and fields, many of which lie fallow, belonging to defunct state and collective farms. Around these *izby* spread welltended produce plots; when peasants farm for themselves, they farm well. Peasant boys, tanned and barefoot, ride horse-drawn carts over mud roads bearing not a single tire imprint. At village stations bronzed men and hale women wearing track suits and leather shoes board the train, their fingernails caked with soil, their forearms rippling with muscles as they drag along the sacks of beets and potatoes that they will sell in Orsha's market. Ahead of me, in a summer frock, sits a teenage girl, chewing sunflower seeds and spitting out the husks, her face wan with boredom, her delicate features still perceptible through a patina of country dirt. Farther on, a shirtless young man leans against the vestibule wall, swaying from vodka and drooping his head. As the car fills with people, a scent of sweat and booze pervades the air.

Orsha's history, like that of much of Belarus, amounts to a chronicle of trespass and adventitious devastation. It lies on the route that the Varangians (the Viking founders of Kievan Rus) traveled from the Baltic to the Black Sea. The Lithuanians fortified the town against incursions from Russia. Peter the Great stopped here during his war against the Swedes (which brought much collateral ruin to Belarus). Napoleon burned the city to the ground in 1812. During World War II, Orsha saw heavy fighting and was almost completely destroyed.

Today the rebuilt city straddles a junction of rusting rail lines and has a reputation as a gathering place for those disenfranchised by the collapse of the Soviet empire. Still dominated in spirit by its four Soviet-era prisons, Orsha is also known as a stopover for transients, as a warren for gangs of youths who do drugs and prey on those passing through, and as the home of merchants from the Russian Caucasus living desperate lives *sans papiers,* trading fruits and vegetables or engaging in crime.

Four hours after departing from Minsk, the *elektrichka* stops in front of Orsha Station. With its shacks and cinder-block hovels and smashed windows, Orsha has the look of a town where the mill has gone under and the people have given up. I ride the bus to the town center in the company of drunks and take a room in the one hotel.

That evening Victor and Galina meet me at the hotel entrance and usher me to their Audi. They work as engineers for Orsha's main employer, the state-owned flax-processing plant. Both are middle-aged. Victor is swarthy, with something of the Romany in him. "He's a Gypsy!" says Galina, pinching his forearm playfully. "I am not!" Victor barks. He clears his throat and changes the subject. "Welcome. Please excuse us. For us simple people, an American is like a Martian," he says with a nervous laugh as he steers out into Orsha's traffic-free lanes.

Their apartment, on the ninth floor of a concrete block, is appointed with the best of Soviet furniture, and its shelves are stocked with Pushkin, Turgenev, Tolstoy. Their two teenage daughters are languidly watching Russian television. Victor, after apologizing at length for the humbleness of his home, pulls a bottle of vodka out of a cupboard, and Galina bears from the kitchen a tray with a half-dozen plates of cheese, tongue, salted fish, and fresh cucumbers.

We toast to our new friendship and dig in. I remark that the daughters are watching Russian, not Belarusian, television.

"Yes. You see, it was really tough in the beginning, after 1991. Shushkevich changed the school language to Belarusian, and our daughters began doing badly. But then Lukashenko came and switched the language back. How could we be expected to change languages, and why? We're Belarusian, but our language is Russian. We watch the news from Russia. Everything here comes from Russia."

It's humid, and mosquitoes dance in the blue glow of the television. As we talk, I become aware of a certain distance, a half-ashamed wariness, such as I encountered in Russian homes during the Soviet years. But the vodka flows and so does our conversation.

"Our president won't allow the chaos they have over in Russia," Victor explains. "We don't want sudden change. He's done a lot of good for this town. He issued a decree that kept our plant from going under, and he visited and made sure it was implemented."

Galina brings out the meat and potatoes. Victor's face flushes with vodka. "Who wanted the Soviet Union to break up?" he asks. "Only the leaders. The common man was left with nothing. Look at Belarus. We're really the same as the Kursk region in Russia. Why should we be independent? Why?"

We talk on, the evening never really cools off, the mosquitoes multiply. The daughters drift off to bed, and Galina and Victor bring up the stability of a past the girls would never know: the Brezhnev years. I would like to know their opinion of Solzhenitsyn, who was persecuted and exiled by Brezhnev, I want to ask about the prisons and Orsha's reputation for violence, but I sense that I should hang back. In the Russia of today, everyone slams the government, but here I feel as though a critical word would elicit gasps and stunned silence and a look over the shoulder to see who might have overheard.

"Lukashenko assures us of regular salaries," Victor says, filling a pause with a loyal utterance. Just across the border is Russia, where salaries are not paid. Suddenly a salary in hand, however small, seems like a grant from a benevolent czar, and we should be grateful for it, receiving it with bows as we genuflect away from the throne. Do the benevolent czar's unionist strivings appear illogical? The question doesn't arise: Subjects don't question the czar, whom they trust to provide for them and set things right.

Later they walk me to my hotel, down streets dark due to "power conservation measures." Victor asks me to pardon him for not driving me back: his supply of gasoline, bought through connections from black-market traders, is running low. On that note we part.

For Victor and Galina, middle-aged folk with paying jobs and comforting memories of the Soviet years, Orsha might be bearable, but how do the young find it? Another friend of mine, Natasha Kiselyova, left the town when she was eighteen to study accounting at an institute in Moscow, where we met. For seven years after receiving her diploma, she worked in a foreign company there and never mentioned Orsha to me. After my evening with Victor and Galina, I find out Natasha has returned for a visit. I call her, and we agree to meet.

She and I stand in the entranceway of the Beryozka Café, since there are no seats available inside. Sipping a screwdriver, she appears comfortable in a faded denim dress and canvas shoes. She is tanned and looks fresher and healthier than she ever did in Moscow. She has married an Italian and moved to Italy. Orsha, she says, is a place to which she returns to see her parents and nothing more. "There are four prisons here. Whoever can get out of this town gets out. Imagine what a future a young woman would have here! Imagine! The men drink themselves to ruin or they're criminals or bums."

Soon the music dies and the lights come on: The Beryozka is closing. The crowd of revelers floods outside, a neighbor of Natasha's I will call Ira among them. (Like others I talked to, Ira asked that I not use her real name.) The two exchange startled greetings, and we are introduced. Ira's moon face is friendly, her eyes are a bright blue, and her long feathered hair bounces off her bare shoulders. She is eighteen. It's clear that Friday night and its partying mean a lot to her: She's dressed in a black evening gown and high heels, on which she totters.

We march out into the night. "There's this club — the Tri Limona [Three Lemons]. It's the only place that stays open after twelve. Let's go there!" Ira says.

We fall in with the rowdy crowd and set off into the dark lanes running between *izby*. In a park on the bank of the Dnieper, behind a looming statue of Lenin, we find the Tri Limona, a single-room, garage-sized brick house with a bar and a wall of illuminated mirrored shelves supporting a dozen brands of vodka, cognac, and whiskey. We take a seat at a booth. Bullnecked men dance to Russian pop and perform scissor motions with their fingers à la John Travolta, their shaved heads spewing sweat as they shimmy; ashes flutter from the cigarettes in the hands of their dates, who pirouette and twirl in the yellow light.

We order pizza and a carafe of Finlandia vodka. There's nothing to do here in Orsha, Ira says. She's just finished school and is waiting for a sign of what the future holds for her. Natasha tells us about her life in Europe and about Sai Baba, India's "incarnation of God," and suggests that I write a story about him. For Ira this is all incredible. She opens her eyes wide at the talk of India and Italy and Moscow.

A glass is smashed on the floor. Then another. At the next table sit three youths, whose olive complexions and roughshod Russian suggest the Caucasus as their provenance. Maybe they are Chechens, maybe Ingushetians. With Zorba-like élan, seized by the music, the one nearest us grabs another glass and smashes it. When the waitress runs over, he hurls a fistful of rubles at her and shouts, "I'll break what I want and I'll pay, whore!"

He gets up, steps over to our table, and extends his hand to Ira. "Miss! Please dance with me!" She declines. He pauses, then returns to his table.

"Khatchiki! I can't stand them!" Ira says.

"Shsh!" hisses Natasha. *Khatchiki* is offensive slang for people from the Caucasus.

At the next song he smashes his empty vodka bottle, hurls more money toward the bar, and in seconds is standing at our table, swaying and holding out his hand.

"Girl, dance with me!"

"No thanks," Ira says, shrinking from his hand. "Really, I'm very tired."

"I said dance!" He wobbles toward her.

"Look," I say to the intruder, as I stand up, "she's tired and doesn't want to dance. She —"

Natasha grabs my arm and starts pushing me out of the booth, whispering, "Let's go! Oh, please, let's get out of here!" Ira jumps up and shoves past him, and we exit into the humid night.

The door slams behind us. The three youths have set out after us. The dance aficionado seizes my shoulder and puts his arm around my neck, but his buddies hang back. His voice slurs with vodka but his grip is sober. "*Bratok* [Brother], listen to me. Who the hell do you think you are, telling me who I can dance with?"

I gently remove his arm and affect a calm demeanor, a friendly tone, as I have done in the past with aggressive drunks in Russia, but my heart starts pounding like a gong, and blood surges in my temples. "Listen, maybe we've all had a bit too much to drink. We should part friends and go home. It's late."

His comrades take up positions beside me; they are readying themselves to grab my arms so that he can slug me at will. Natasha and Ira stand back, wringing their hands.

He lurches into my face. "So who the fuck do you think you are, telling me to leave this bitch alone? Huh?"

He strikes out, aiming for my eye, but I pull away in time and his fist misses me. Again he locks his arm around my neck; again I push him back. His friends stay at my sides, but they don't attack. We jostle, a hairbreadth from fisticuffs.

"Oh, Jeff! Jeff!" Natasha screams.

"*Dzhe* — what did she call you?"

"Jeff." I'm as nonplused as he is by the sudden indication of my foreignness. "That's my name."

He steps back. One of his buddies hands me my passport, which unbeknownst to me had dropped from my pocket during our scuffle, then leads the belligerent away.

"Oh, my God!" Natasha exclaims. She and Ira check me for wounds. My shirtsleeve has suffered, torn at the shoulder; my left eye is slightly blackened, grazed by his forearm.

We start off down the path through the park, heading for the statue of Lenin, listening to every sound behind us, but we're alone, and remain alone, all the way to their neighborhood. Natasha and Ira say that the aggressor and his buddies are probably melon vendors (now is the season), living in Orsha without residence permits, paying the militia bribes when they run into trouble or taking beatings from them if they're broke. A desperate and uncertain life, to be sure, but preferable to staying at home in the Caucasus, where there may be war and there is certainly poverty. On learning my nationality, they might have foreseen serious consequences with the militia had they touched me. Or maybe an American — an enemy, they would reason, of Russia, the nemesis of the Caucasus — would deserve an automatic pardon.

I won't ever find out, but suddenly I understand why Natasha never spoke to me of her hometown, I see why she left it, and I feel a rush of pity for Ira, teetering along on her high heels, suppressing sobs, and trying to keep up. For Ira, if she stays, life here will be long and full of grief and drunks and trauma.

A hundred miles northwest of Orsha, high on the wooded and windblown banks of the Dzvina River, the grand white belfries of Polatsk's eleventh-century St. Sophia Cathedral rise into a cerulean sky, the leaf green of their domes harmonizing with the hues of the birches beneath. The day of my arrival barefoot boys are fishing in the shallows, and young men are rowing their dates across expanses of shimmering, sun-dappled water. The roads are empty of cars; as usual, there is no gas. Fresh wind, birches, a pacific river — the impression is one of peace eternal.

The impression is deceptive. Polatsk first appears in regional chronicles in the year 862, when it was the center of a princedom aspiring to rival Kiev and Novgorod. Later Russia and Lithuania fought over the town repeatedly until Catherine the Great acquired it during the First Partition of Poland in 1772. Napoleon's invasion of Russia began nearby, and destruction was widespread during both world wars. Time and time again war has visited Polatsk and leveled it. The cathedrals on its banks are restorations.

I have come to Polatsk for the third of July — World War II Liberation Day for Belarus. At noon a parade is scheduled to take place in the town center, starting from the columned façade of my hotel. Lamppost loudspeakers pipe Soviet war songs into the sun-drenched air. But there are few celebrants, perhaps no more people than would be out and about on any mild Saturday afternoon.

Suddenly there is a bugle blast, and, with heroic music blaring from every corner, fifty or so veterans in their seventies, besuited and bemedaled, set off down Marx Avenue, followed by blasé recruits fifty years younger carrying a red flag emblazoned with FOR OUR SOVIET MOTHERLAND and a hammer and sickle. A single tank chugs along behind, fouling the air with its exhaust. At Lenin Square they halt for fist-waving addresses from the mayor and various veterans: "We must unite with our brethren in great Russia. . . . Clinton began World War III in Yugoslavia. . . . Belarus is next in line for NATO aggression. . . . Woe upon those in the West who dare to dream of conquering great Russia. . . . More unity with

brotherly Russia!" These veterans are among the most fervent supporters of Lukashenko, the generation that remembers war and
hunger and slaughter, those for whom a baton of sausage in hand
and peace at home prove a ruler's legitimacy.

The voices resound. Children fidget. Families begin breaking
away, and soon the veterans and city officials are shouting to a couple dozen citizens too polite to leave.

Later, on Skaryny Square, during the violet summer dusk, a con-
cert is held. Police in camouflage fatigues stand in rows to one side.
After an introduction containing no words about war, Yugoslavia,
union, or politics, a young Russian-language band pounds out a
mix of Westernized Russian pop songs, country-and-western tunes,
and rock-and-roll hits for a crowd of baggy-trousered teens for
whom Soviet power and the heroic deeds of fifty years ago can be
little more than ballads, banners, and the stories of old people.

It says much about the state of the Belarusian economy that President Lukashenko foresees its salvation in a union with Russia. (In
one respect he is right: union would permit Belarus, which has few
natural resources aside from peat, access to Russian oil and gas.)
Encouraging statistics presented by the Belarusian government —
a per annum growth rate of 8 percent, a 13 percent increase in industrial output, a 3 percent unemployment rate — bear no relation to the queues for food that have reappeared across the country, the chronic shortages of gasoline, the pensions and salaries
averaging the equivalent of $10 and $50 a month, respectively, and
the dying private sector. Private businesses survive now only if they
operate under the protection of Lukashenko's elite. The KGB and
tax authorities harass those who don't, closing down and even jail-
ing unconnected entrepreneurs.

The crash of the interim national currency, the Belarusian ruble
(a.k.a. the *zaychik,* or bunny, on account of the furry little rabbit
depicted hopping across now-extinct one-ruble notes), has been
among the most conspicuous failures of Lukashenko's market socialism. Plans to introduce a permanent national currency, the
taler, have been shelved since Lukashenko's ascension to power.
The Belarusian ruble, which in 1993 traded at the state rate of 699
to the dollar, hit 25,964 by December 1997. By the time of my trip
in July 1999, $1 bought 300,000 rubles. Three-digit inflation keeps
pace with the devaluation, making it senseless for Belarusians to

keep savings in anything but cash U.S. dollars. (As in Russia, Belarusians do not trust banks, preferring to keep their funds under the mattress.) Legally acquiring dollars, however, is next to impossible: Exchange bureaus don't sell them, choosing to retain or dispose of them on the black market at rates 50 percent higher. As in Soviet times, the black market has become the only option for most Belarusians looking to safeguard their savings from inflation, though penalties for "illegal currency transactions" — the purchase of hard currency from other than state-licensed exchange bureaus — range from heavy fines to arrest, and always involve confiscation of the money.

Lukashenko's proposed union would do away with this bunny money and reestablish the Russian ruble — a dubious achievement by any measure. Yet the union treaty stipulates that Belarusian monetary policy would remain in his hands and that the Belarusian central bank would retain the right to print Russian rubles, both of which measures raise fears of inflation among Russian politicians who are knowledgeable about economics.

From Polatsk, by way of Minsk, I have arrived in Hrodna (Grodno), in westernmost Belarus. Even by Belarusian standards, Hrodna has suffered a high number of overlords. Starting in 1772, the city bounced from Poland to Russia, from Russia to Germany, and then back to Poland. Hrodna would have remained in Poland had it not been for a secret codicil to the nonaggression pact signed by Stalin and Hitler in 1939 that returned it to the Soviet fold.

Hrodna's tidy streets and courteous inhabitants manifest the liberalism that developed during its prewar years as a part of the West. But the Hrodna region did not submit quietly to Soviet rule. For a decade after the Second World War, armed bands of Belarusian independence fighters harried the Soviet authorities, hindering the collectivization of agriculture and the spread of Soviet power. Hrodna remains a city of dubious and divided allegiances.

My guide to the city is a local historian in her thirties whom I will call Svetlana. Trilingual (she speaks Russian, Belarusian, and Polish, though she's most at ease in Russian), Svetlana talks with pride of her affinity to Poland and her research trips to France. She is Orthodox; European culture and the study of history are her passions.

After touring the city center, Svetlana and I hike out along the

Neman River and follow a dirt path through a grove until we arrive at a dark rectangular brick structure — the twelfth-century Orthodox Church of Saints Boris and Gleb, the second-oldest building in Belarus. It is locked. A young man in black and white approaches with keys in hand and opens the door for us. "Oh, *Batyushka* [Father], we're lucky you came," Svetlana says. "Please meet our guest from America!"

The priest sets his eyes on me; they are icy blue. A crest of flaxen hair rises above his jutting brow; his mouth is grim. Looking away, he motions us inside.

The church's interior has been restored and has a modern, unappealing look. Svetlana explains the iconostasis to me. The priest, who has been following me with his eyes, interrupts her. "America, you say? Your planes did a good job bombing Orthodox monasteries in Kosovo."

Yes, I say, some missiles did land on monasteries and —

Svetlana interrupts curtly: "You know, religion and politics should be separate. Maybe a church isn't the right place to talk about war."

"So I don't have the right to express my opinion?" The *batyushka* cocks his head. "Who can speak the truth now? Look at Russian television. It's run by Jews. Even in Russia you can't speak the truth."

"Oh, I see. Let me ask you a purely Russian question — are you Jewish?" Svetlana's question is really a barb at his anti-Semitism.

The *batyushka* frowns. "Who betrayed Jesus? The Jews."

"Who was Jesus himself? A Jew!"

"That's absurd. That is blasphemy. That was only his earthly manifestation."

The priest's eyes burn. Svetlana's face reddens, her cheeks tense. She looks away, then abruptly turns back to him. "You should try and understand other people's points of view, to find a compromise."

"In religion, as in philosophy, compromise amounts to heresy. There is only one truth."

"I would prefer to have no convictions rather than extremist convictions. Our country has suffered so much at the hands of those who know the Truth. Look at what the Communists did to us. The most dangerous thing is extremism."

"The most dangerous thing is to have no convictions," the *bat-yushka* answers. His voice is steady, but a pogrom hatred flashes from his eyes. "You must have the right convictions. You must follow the one Truth."

This debate is not between two people but between two worldviews: the Eastern absolutism of Moscow as the Third Rome, with its Holy Truth and its God-appointed executor; and the Western-derived pluralism of the intelligentsia. His is the doctrine of state power; hers, the ideology that would wrest that power from him. Reconciliation is impossible.

The priest has to close up and asks us to leave. When we step outside, Svetlana is trembling. The *batyushka* leaves us at the gate. As his parting shot he remarks that Belarus should never have given up its nuclear weapons.

A priest advocating nuclear weapons! When Svetlana calms down she surmises that he is an agent. "His Russian sounded peasant — the KGB has an easy time winning over peasants. This is Hrodna, which the Soviets had a tough time pacifying, and the intelligentsia attends this church. The KGB knows this, and they want to keep an eye on us."

Plausible conjecture. The Belarusian Orthodox Church* is not autocephalous; it answers to the Moscow Patriarchy, and the Russian Orthodox Church has always acted as an organ of the state, whether czarist, Soviet, or post-Soviet. Absolutism in religion and politics has distinguished Russian polity since the rise of Muscovy. Throughout the Russian and Soviet empires God and caesar were one, with God's sacerdotalists often serving as caesar's agents. Suspicions that some priests were hiding secret police epaulets under their cassocks were confirmed when, after the fall of the Soviet Union, many high-ranking Orthodox clergymen were exposed as members of the KGB.

Our talk of the KGB leads us to the subject of union, and I ask what future Svetlana sees for herself if Belarus and Russia unite. "In

---

* Hoping to bring their Orthodox population under tighter spiritual and political control, Belarus's Catholic Lithuanian and Polish overlords created the Uniate Church, which recognized the primacy of the Pope but allowed adherents to worship with Eastern rites. For a time, the Uniate faith spread, but when Belarus returned to Russian rule, it was persecuted and largely wiped out. Today some 70 percent of Belarusians are Orthodox, and 20 percent are Catholic.

the eighteenth and nineteenth centuries there were huge revolts against Moscow after it took over Belarus. I wouldn't exclude such an outcome today."

"So would you be prepared to fight for independence?"

"Oh, well . . . really, we've been too beaten down to think of fighting . . . we're used to foreign rule . . . but maybe someone here would protest, somewhere."

NO ONE HAS BEEN FORGOTTEN — NOTHING HAS BEEN FORGOTTEN asserts the bold lettering over the memorial to the 128 citizens of the village of Papsuyevka who lost their lives during World War II.

The memorial lies. There is no one left to forget and nothing left to be forgotten. Papsuyevka, near Vetka in southeastern Belarus, is only ninety miles north of Chernobyl. When the reactor melted down in 1986, Papsuyevka was doused in radiation that exceeded forty curies per square kilometer, which rendered it uninhabitable for decades. In 1991 the Soviet government finally evacuated and resettled Papsuyevka's 108 families and marked the road through the town with a sign reading RADIATION! ENTRY FORBIDDEN!

The horrific effects of Chernobyl have been thoroughly documented, and it would be easy to imagine that human history in the region ended with the meltdown. But while visiting an exhibition of Old Believer icons in Vetka, I heard rumors that people were still living in the radioactive zones. Short trips to the area supposedly do no harm, so I hired a van and a guide and set out to investigate.

Next to the memorial a statue of a defiant Red Army soldier stands enwrapped in creepers descending from the trees. Farther on, a bust of Lenin glares vigilantly into the steely noon light above a decrepit Board of Honor (a glass case in which the portraits of model Communist villagers were once displayed). The wind rises, whishing through the collapsed roofs and glassless windows of the houses at my back. My guide, whom I will call Anna, picks her way toward me through the rubbish. She swats at the dragonflies and other bugs whirling around us. "These are turn-of-the-century houses. What a pity they had to be abandoned. Houses die quickly without human care."

We jump into Anna's minivan and speed off down the road through the scrub forest and weed-choked fields of the contaminated zone. In places the earth is sandy, and miniature dunes edge

onto the tarmac. Just beyond another RADIATION! ENTRY FOR-
BIDDEN! sign cluster a few *izby*, and in front of them, on a bench,
sits a middle-aged couple. Their eyes, bleary, vaguely ornery, fall
on us.

As we slow to a halt alongside them, they straighten up. Another
man, his ears cocked in our direction, feels his way toward us along
the side of the house, his eyes rolling white: He is blind. A gnarled
old woman, looking like a troll in a tattered track suit, emerges to
peer at us from a doorway.

Anna says to me, "This is Bartalameyevka. It was evacuated."

"Who are you and what do you want?" the man on the bench demands.

We jump out, and Anna introduces us. "Oh!" he exclaims. "We
thought you might be marauders! Marauders are the only ones
who come out here. They come from Vetka and rob the houses
[residents were prohibited from taking their belongings with them
during the evacuation]. They killed one of our neighbors recently.
Bashed his head in to steal a calf." Marauders, not neglect, he says,
reduced the houses in Papsuyevka to ruins.

A dust twister spins past, peppering our eyes.

"Why have you stayed on?" I ask.

The wife answers. "We saved up all our lives to build this house.
Do you think we were going to let the state drive us out? That's the
way things are here in the Soviet Union — you build something,
then the state steals it from you. No sir, we refused to move, even
though they cut off our electricity and gas and water." Her lips part
to show steel teeth.

"Anyway," the old man says, "in ninety-one the state evacuated
the families to Vetka, which is almost as radioactive as here. What
good would it have done us to move there?"

There is no defiance in their words, only resignation.

While we talk, twisters roil the sand and insects crawl all over us,
enmeshing themselves in our sweat. The radiation comes to mind,
and what these people must have lived through, and the resignation that roots them to this wasteland of bugs and gamma rays,
holding out against marauders. We take our leave and climb into
the minivan for the ride back to Vetka, here and there coming
upon other villages with their scatterings of radiation homestead-
ers, who dart behind their doors and hide, taking us for marauders.

This seems to be a metaphorically apt way to end a tour of

Belarus. Belarusians are holding out on their trespassed home-steads, in their historical camp, occupying themselves with personal survival, and they have little energy left for matters of state or sovereignty. The spheres of culture and political tradition arising from the eleventh-century split between the Eastern Orthodox and Western churches persist today. The passivity instilled by foreign rule and religion-sanctioned autocracy, combined with the terror-bred nihilism born of the Stalin decades and the conservatism deriving from just-tolerable economic straits, ensure that Belarus will remain in the Russian domain, whether or not the two states unify and regardless of how most Belarusians feel about union; few associate personal disapproval of policies with the need to take collective action.

Although Lukashenko and his elite stand to gain from the union, they are not the cause of Belarus's statehood dilemma but opportunists exploiting it, for nihilism and passivity create a vacuum that tyrants and their schemes fill. And if union is consecrated, the terms hardly matter for either party. Russia is vast, and adding one more impoverished province, one more realm of neglect, will probably have no negative effect on Russia economically and at the same time will provide it with buffer territory along the borders with new NATO countries. Belarusians will again make do with satrapy status, reacquiring, in exchange for their freedom, a mythology not their own. They have not created or sustained a national idea that could counter it. They could not have: Russification has slain their culture; it has turned them into the Buffer People.

We reach the hovels dotting the fields around Vetka. Maybe during Belarus's march back into the embrace of Russia, I think, chance and evolution will impose change where none was striven for, and Belarus will halt and stand up for itself. But this notion resembles a fantasy, a fantasy as realizable as the national myths of its boundless eastern neighbor.

MARCEL THEROUX

The Very, Very, Very Big Chill

FROM *Travel & Leisure*

WHEN I FINALLY got to the coldest town on earth, the first person I met had a frozen fish tucked into one of his felt boots. He was swaying slightly in the headlights of our truck, which had broken down two hundred yards short of our final destination.

"Hey," he said, "have you got a bottle for me?" His vodka breath rose up in clouds of ice crystals. It was then that I noticed the fish. He pulled it out of his boot and gave me a welcoming wave with it. *"Pokushaite!"* he cried — "Have something to eat!" The fish was a foot and a half long and as solid as an iron bar.

It was past midnight. By local standards, we were enjoying balmy February weather — just a few degrees shy of forty below, Fahrenheit.

Verkhoyansk, in the republic of Sakha, northeastern Siberia, has the dubious distinction of being the coldest inhabited place on the planet. It's not considered chilly here until the thermometer has dipped to about sixty below. And the record, set in 1892 and celebrated on the town's most famous landmark — a monument called the Pole of Cold — is minus-ninety degrees.

I'd come to Russia with a cameraman, a soundman, and a television director to make a program for the Discovery Channel about traveling through Siberia in winter. Three weeks earlier we had flown from Moscow to the Siberian city of Irkutsk. We'd filmed on Lake Baikal and in the Buddhist republic of Buryatia before flying north to Yakutsk, where we began our journey to Verkhoyansk. For ten days we would travel by truck and reindeer sleigh through unmarked snowfields and along frozen rivers, spending nights with reindeer herders in isolated winter cabins.

Siberians are fond of telling you that there's no road, just a direction, and on the way to Verkhoyansk this was often literally true. The truck drivers had to read the pattern of the snowdrifts to see where we could safely drive. We often got stuck — hence the need for two vehicles. One night both of them sank and froze fast in the thin ice of the river Nyura. Eight of us spent a sleepless night in the back of one truck, jostling for positions farthest from the wood-burning stove that was welded to the floor. Inside we were sweating and restless. Outside it was fifty below.

As we made our way into Russia's northern regions, the temperature dropped further and the fur hats grew bigger and bigger. When I'd arrived in Moscow, the local men were wearing small hats perched on top of their heads; the earflaps seemed purely decorative — throughout Russia it's considered effeminate for a man to put his flaps down if the temperature is above minus-twenty. By the time I reached Yakutsk, a city built entirely on permafrost, women and men alike wore giant fox-fur bonnets that reminded me of the most outlandish 1970s Afros. Finally, in the villages around Verkhoyansk, I saw people whose faces bore the physical scars — burns around the mouth and cheeks — of a lifetime of intense cold.

The man with the fish had ruby cheeks and the genial glow of a benign drunk. Seeing him made me think of the taxi driver in Moscow who had advised me to drink a glass of vodka every hour or so when I reached Sakha, "whenever you start feeling ill." When I tried to explain that alcohol gives an illusory feeling of warmth and actually speeds up heat loss, he looked at me as though I'd suggested we lower our earflaps.

I politely refused the man's offer of food. Thin slices of raw frozen fish — *stroganina* — are tasty dipped in salt, but I wasn't sure how long this one had been tucked into his boot. The last thing I wanted was extra visits to a dark and drafty Siberian outhouse.

But the fish-man didn't give up easily. Our guide, Anatoly, had mischievously told him we were carrying cases of neat alcohol in the truck: *spirt,* the tipple of Russia's poorest. The fish-man offered to put two of us up in his house. I told him we already had a place to stay. He shook my hand several times and disappeared into the darkness.

Imagine the set of a spaghetti western erected in the Arctic Circle, and you have some idea of what Verkhoyansk looks like. Cossacks founded the village in 1638 as they moved east in search of fur pelts; parts of it retain the ramshackle charm of a frontier town. Low wooden buildings line the streets, which seem all the wider because there are no cars: some two thousand people live here, but the only vehicles I saw were ours. Most of our time in Verkhoyansk was spent trying to scrape together enough petrol to get us to the airport.

Until the 1980s, Verkhoyansk was a tin- and gold-mining center, but today its residents survive through their own resourcefulness. Our hosts, for one, kept cows, and a frozen haunch of moose was stashed beneath their porch.

People in Sakha eat a lot of frozen food. Frozen raw fish, frozen raw reindeer meat, frozen patties of whipped cream and blueberries, and frozen patties of raw pony liver are all regional specialties. Milk is sold at the market in frozen chunks, and in smaller villages the winter water supply is stacked by each house in huge frozen blocks like outsized pieces of pale blue Turkish delight.

Frozen pony-liver patties turned up on our breakfast table the first morning. Curious, but too squeamish to try it myself, I told Nigel the cameraman that it was whipped cream and strawberries. As soon as he bit into one, he spat it out like a hot coal and swore at me. I asked what it tasted like. "Blood," he said, with a murderous look in his eye.

Local people told me that at minus-sixty and below, a dense fog settles in the streets, and pedestrians leave recognizable outlines bored into the mist behind them. A drunkard's tunnel will meander and then end abruptly over a prone body. At minus-seventy-two, the vapor in your breath freezes instantly and makes a tinkling sound called "the whisper of angels."

In fact, the temperature never fell past sixty below during the month I was in Siberia. People here agree with experts on climate change: Every year the winters are getting warmer. School is canceled whenever the temperature slips into the negative sixties; this used to happen for weeks at a time, but now only a few school days are missed each year. Even so, I learned to distinguish different levels of extreme cold as we traveled northward.

My nose was one reliable gauge: at zero degrees, it crackled when I breathed as the hair in my nostrils froze; twenty degrees colder, and it would stream and then freeze. At minus-forty, an apple froze solid in my hand when I paused too long between bites. Plastic becomes rock-hard within seconds. The soundman's wire cables froze into absurd shapes. The resin grips on my Extremities mittens became sharp and rigid like plastic hatchets. When I retreated indoors, Edward Scissorhands turned into Mr. Magoo as a thick layer of ice formed on my glasses. I would stumble around blindly in the dim lamplight, trying not to trip over discarded footwear or collide with the woodstove. It took me a week to realize that the sore on the bridge of my nose was a frost burn caused by the metal frame of my spectacles.

One compensation for the intense cold is a landscape as beautiful as any I've ever seen. The countryside around Verkhoyansk is wooded, not at all bleak. During the day, the low sun painted everything with golden light and long blue shadows. The trees, trimmed with ice, became elaborate glass sculptures. When the wind blew, the air sparkled with snow crystals. It was too cold for anything to smell of much — even the outhouses. And the snow itself acted as an acoustic blanket, throwing every sound into sharp relief: the squeaking of boots or hooves, the bells on a reindeer's harness, the soft crump of snow thrown aside by a shovel. Just below the Arctic Circle, I saw the northern lights for the first time: luminous green gauze curtains blowing around in outer space.

The Russian word for Siberia, *Sibir,* comes from Mongolian Altai and means "sleeping land." The woods and rivers and mountains did seem to be in suspended animation. I was reminded of the impenetrable forest around Sleeping Beauty's castle, where everything is frozen at the moment she pricks her finger: the waves sculpted into the rivers, the autumn berries iced onto the bushes, a skinned wolf carcass frozen into an unspeakable shape outside a reindeer herder's hut.

Anatoly, our anthropologist guide, was himself born into a family of Even reindeer herders. The Even were nomads until they were collectivized by the Soviets in the 1920s and 1930s and moved into villages. They live hard lives, ignored by the regional and national governments, which are far more interested in the land beneath them (Sakha holds diamond reserves as vast as South Africa's).

Anatoly bears an open grudge against the European civilization that has so disrupted the Even's traditional life. He enjoyed subjecting me to funny and unsettling lectures about my personal responsibility for the destruction of Even culture. He also liked to point out the shortcomings of our high-tech apparel. He laughed at our bulky Canadian boots. "Pure European approach!" he snorted. "Below minus-forty, you will freeze. We should just take a match and set fire to them now." He warned me that if I insisted on wearing my North Face hat instead of a fur one, an archaeologist would be digging me out of the permafrost in a thousand years' time like a woolly mammoth.

On his own feet, Anatoly wore *unty*, made from reindeer leg fur, and hardly larger than a regular shoe. When we traveled by reindeer sleigh, I borrowed fur clothes from the herders: *unty*, trousers made from wolverine, snow-sheep mittens, a reindeer jacket. These were not only warmer than my other clothes but stayed quiet and flexible, and the smell of the fur seemed to put the reindeer at ease. (Nigel the cameraman, rustling around in artificial fibers and big boots, kept startling the animals, who would get all tangled up in their harnesses as they leaped to avoid him.) At the end of the day, the fur clothes were placed in a sack and left outside. Warmth and damp destroy them. Yet after a night at forty below, they were never cold to the touch when I put them on in the morning.

While few in the West have heard of the Even, everyone knows one word of their language. *Shaman* is the Even term for a traditional spirit healer. Its etymology is uncertain — it may mean "one who knows" — but the word has been internationalized, passing into various languages from Russian ethnography. During long hours in our overheated truck, Anatoly told me stories about the Even shamans, celebrated by his people as the most powerful shamans of all. According to Anatoly, not only were most Western scientific discoveries preempted by the shamans, but it was also commonplace for Even shamans to visit the moon.

Anatoly told me all this with a smile on his face, but his stories correspond to a belief in Siberia that when Neil Armstrong landed on the moon, he was met by an old Russian wise man called Ivanov. It would be interesting to ask Armstrong about this. In particular, I'd like to know whether Ivanov had a frozen fish in his boot.

BRAD WETZLER

Is Just Like Amerika!

FROM *Outside*

IF IT'S TRUE that you are what you eat, then I am a big, greasy kielbasa. I brought this on myself: For the past week I have been camping with a dedicated band of carnivores who favor canned meat and an alarming variety of sausages. We're deep in the Brdy Hills, a rolling patch of beech forest as charming as a dream, about thirty miles south of Prague in the Czech Republic. The air is full of the smell of honeysuckle, the buzzing of bees, the chirruping of bluebirds, and the sizzling of meat. The only human tracks within sight are our own.

But this is a curious bunch. There is Jerry, the frequently drunk prankster who gets his kicks hiding pinecones in our sleeping bags. He whispers that his real name is Vladimir but tramps are supposed to go by their tramping names. Which is why "Jerry" is tattooed in boldface on his right forearm. George, a starry-eyed guitar player, can do a rendition of "This Land Is Your Land" in Czech that would make anyone homesick for the hills of central Bohemia. Ace is a private in the Czech army who always wears a Daniel Boone–style coonskin cap; he sucked down too much rum last night and, while dancing to George's intoxicating music, fell into the fire. Lucky for him, Sheriff Tom was still sober enough to pull him out. A one-armed bear of a man, Sheriff Tom is, at forty-five, the oldest hobo, and he happens to own the biggest bowie knife, making him the logical choice to be the group's chief law-enforcement officer.

They are also a slovenly bunch. Empty sausage casings litter our campsite. Dirty clothes hang from branches. Camping gear — knapsacks, tarps, cooking kits — is strewn about like leftovers from a yard sale. The tramps themselves lounge in the dirt, sleeping, smoking, singing songs, telling stories . . . and eating meat. So far this week we've feasted on pork, beef, pork-beef sausage, ham steak, chicken, herring, sardines, smoked oysters, and plain old grilled meat, a gluey pink mush that comes in a can labeled "Grilled Meat." It's dinnertime on my fifth day with this group, and I've had enough — but that's only my opinion. Sheriff Tom insists that I keep up with my compatriots. He catches me sneaking away from the campfire and blocks my path, brandishing a bright red, footlong salami in his one good hand. He's staring directly into my eyes.

"Very . . . special . . . sausage," he says in deliberate, broken, heavily accented English. "You . . . will . . . enjoy . . . very much."

I ask what's in it. Sheriff Tom casts his gaze skyward, as if scanning the animal-cracker-shaped clouds to find the poor beast from which this sausage was rendered. "How you say . . ." Sheriff Tom says, sounding flustered. "I don't know. It is big, with hooves. Please. Eat!"

He hands me the sausage and motions for me to try it. Hesitant, I oblige, biting into the pasty gristle and rolling it around in my mouth. Then I make myself swallow.

"I know! I know!" Sheriff Tom suddenly blurts out as the sausage slides down my gullet. "It goes, '*Neighhhhhh!*'"

The men I'm traveling with call themselves the Red Monkey Gang. They're a proud part of a nationwide movement called tramping, or *vandr* in Czech. As the name suggests, tramping is a takeoff on hoboing — the act of drifting from place to place by train or on foot. Real hoboing had its heyday during the Great Depression in the United States, when an estimated 1.5 million people lived on the loose. Most came to their vocation involuntarily, driven to the road by poverty and desperation. Nonetheless, hoboes, like tramps, acquired a reputation for their carefree way of life, their predilection for booze, and a canon of whimsical folk songs and stories.

The Czech species of tramp, or *vandrak,* has the happy-go-lucky, alcohol-soaked aspects of the lifestyle down cold. But these are not bona fide, full-time tramps. The Czechs are dilettante vagrants: Recalling the lore of tramping, they embark on excursions in which they merely *pretend* to be down-and-out wastrels. Nor do they follow the hobo tradition with any commitment to verisimilitude; America's wide-open spaces have inspired many Czech "tramps" to dress up as cowboys or Indians or, just as bizarrely, World War II GIs. On weekends and during vacations, thousands of them hop trains (paying their fare rather than stowing away in boxcars), camp out under the stars, or rendezvous in the hills and at festivals, all the while singing Czech and American folk tunes. Most are middle-class working men with homes and families, though it's not uncommon to see women marching into the woods, too. Come Sunday night, everybody climbs on the train and goes back to his day job.

Sounds like a pretty good life to me. So a few months back I flew to the Czech Republic and on a balmy Friday afternoon took a cab straight from Prague's Ruzyne Airport to Smichov Station, a.k.a. Tramp Central. There were tramps everywhere, relaxing on the ground, drinking in the station pub, strumming guitars. I bought a southbound ticket to the central Bohemian village of Revnice, which, I'd been told, was a jumping-off point for a lot of hobo outings. I boarded one of the shiny aluminum cars and, imitating the weekend tramps already on board, slumped on the floor with my backpack. "Ahoy," the other tramps said to me, using the traditional tramp greeting. (No one seems to know how ersatz hoboes in the landlocked Czech Republic came to address each other as British sailors.) "Ahoy," I returned, and each one grasped my hand in the thumb-gripping, soul-style tramp handshake. We passed around a bottle of rum until Revnice, where I detrained.

Waiting at a bus stop just outside the station was a group of eight men wearing camouflage: tramps, I surmised. They introduced themselves as the Red Monkey Gang, welcomed me with handshakes and high-fives, and waved me on board the bus to Halouny. After five minutes, the bus let us off in a tiny hamlet consisting of a dozen or so stone houses with red tile roofs.

We shouldered our backpacks and set out up a steep hill in the direction of some thick green woods. The sun was beginning to set, and I was concerned that we'd be making camp in the dark. But having spent the better part of a day in the cramped middle seat of a 747, I relished the exercise and camaraderie of a group hike. In-country for only a few hours and here I was, trampin' with tramps!

After about fifty paces, though, Sheriff Tom motioned for me to remove my pack and pointed at a dilapidated stone building with a leaning porch in front and a stinky outhouse in back. This was the Red Monkey Pub — U Cerveneho Paviana — the terminus, it turned out, of our hike. We entered and drank cold pilsner until 1:00 A.M., closing time, after which we set up camp in a small clearing behind the building. We spread our sleeping bags on the ground, crawled in, and woke up at noon, just in time for the pub to open.

For the next five days our routine was basic: Sleep till 11:00 or so in the morning, skulk over to the pub for our noonday beer, pick wild mushrooms and blueberries, and hike. In the evenings we'd dine on sausage, drink rum, smoke cigars, and stare into the fire while George serenaded us with Czech versions of country-and-western songs.

Which brings us up to Saturday night and Sheriff Tom, who's holding me up with his sausage. I choke the entire thing down under duress while he watches, and then live with the consequences for the rest of the evening, sitting in a dyspeptic drowse beneath an incandescent full moon while George sings "King of the Road," "Hobo Bill's Last Ride," "Wabash Cannonball," and "Alaska, I Love You."

I'm still wide awake at 1:10 A.M., lying by the fire in my mummy bag, listening to Sheriff Tom's semidrunken snoring and trying to calm my aching stomach, when I hear a scream.

"*Kanec!*" somebody yells. It's Jerry the prankster, only now he seems in earnest. He trips over himself, lunging in my direction. "*Kanec!*" he shouts again.

I can hear grunting and heavy breathing, not all of it coming from my fellow tramps, who are frantically trying to free themselves from their sleeping bags. Suddenly a squadron of feral pigs crashes through the brush in single file. One, two, three, four, five. Noses to the ground, they begin to vacuum the campsite of its rubbish, eating sausage casings, residue in empty Spam cans, even dirty socks. Their beady eyes, glinting in flashlight beams, give them the look of crazed beasts from hell, and their razor-sharp tusks could rip flesh from bone. But then one pauses next to my backpack and I get a sense of proportion: These pigs are no bigger than Yorkshire terriers. Indignant, if more than a little relieved, I squirm out of my sleeping bag and prepare to defend our camp with honor.

Fortunately, I don't have to. The raid lasts less than a minute. Before anybody gets hurt, the pigs scurry off into the dark — presumably in the direction of another, even more slovenly, tramp site. The Red Monkeys saunter back to bed. When I crawl into my bag, a sharp object pricks my thigh and I grope after it: pinecone. I look over at Jerry, who is sitting up, grinning.

Tramp. Vagabond. Vag. Bum. Stew Bum. Profesh. Bindle Stiff. Alki Stiff. Roadie-Kid. Hobo. The wandering soul has countless names, many of them suggestive of sloth and indolence. The hobo (the term possibly a bastardization of a nineteenth-century vagrant's greeting, "Ho, beau!") is, one might say, prone to go long stretches without showering and unapologetic about his heavy smoking and drinking. He rides from city to city, from job to job — and sometimes he rides just for the peripatetic hell of it, gathering with fellow tramps in train yards and sleeping under bridges, outraging the local constabulary. Jack London, who as a youth spent eight months hoboing in 1894, wrote that the life of the road "entices romantic and unruly boys, who venture along its dangerous ways in search of fortune or in a rash attempt to escape parental discipline. It seizes with relentless grip the unfortunate who drifts with, or struggles against, the tide of human affairs."

Even in postwar America, nostalgia and wanderlust kept tramp wanna-bes hopping boxcars. Nostalgia eventually outweighed wanderlust, though, and tramping fully evolved into an idiosyncratic pastime, with aficionados in hobowear gathering like Civil War reenactors to sing the old songs of the road and swap pork-and-bean recipes. In keeping with the times, those who struggle against the tide of human affairs now have a support group: the 5,800-member National Hobo Association, which has a Web site (www.hobo.org), a magazine called *The Hobo Times* ($25 a year), and annual gatherings. The most recent conclave was in July in Elko, Nevada, where tramps spread out their bedrolls at a fairgrounds that, according to hobo.org, offered "electric power, showers and change rooms, and night lighting."

Unlike the Americans, however, the Czechs never really tramped out of necessity. From its start in the 1920s, it was a hobby — an amusing interpretation of American hoboes and cowpokes. Marko Cermak, an outdoors writer and the unofficial historian of tramping in the Czech Republic, says the first tramps were lone-wolf types who headed for the hills after watching movie cowboys like Tom Mix and "Bronco Billy" Anderson battle Indians and herd cattle on the open range. These early Czech tramps would dress like cowboys, ride the trains to the edge of town, and sleep out under the stars "cowboy style," as Cermak calls it. It was a time when Europeans were developing an obsession with all things western through the novels of turn-of-the-century German writer Karl May, who never set foot in the American West but wrote of the high mesas and howling coyotes with a Prussian commitment to authenticity.

Taking a more laid-back approach to the western mania than their neighbors the Germans, who began organizing cowboy conventions and staging mock shoot-outs, the Czechs mixed up stories of hoboes and cowboys-and-Indians into a happy stew and called it tramping. Teams of dozens, sometimes hundreds, of Czech hoboes and cowboys established elaborate camps in the hills, where they elected sheriffs to keep order. (Some camps survive to this day, with cabins proudly named El Passo [*sic*], Jack London, Tacoma, and Cimarron.)

Over time, several factions formed. Some tramps, especially those with an ecological bent, began imitating the Indians they saw in American movies, dressing in elaborate costumes, carving totem poles, tanning hides with cow brains, and erecting tepees. Others specialized in canoe tramping, lugging their vessels onto trains and riding to their favorite rivers and lakes. After World War II, American movies inspired yet another vogue, one that is still prevalent today: the GI tramp. GIs dress in camouflage army fatigues (to blend in with nature, they say), black army boots, and dog tags.

To make any sense of all this — to form a rational connection between army-surplus getup, pub-oriented camping, and the Czech version of the "cowboy life" — you must put yourself in a bohemian frame of mind. The word *bohemian*, with all its boozy, shiftless, rules-be-damned connotations, was born in this very region of Czechoslovakia — Bohemia, which comprises half the nation. Gypsies, otherwise known as Roma, or *Cikani* in Czech, have long been a significant minority here. (They make up 0.3 percent of the population today.) When Gypsies trekked beyond Bohemia into France during the fifteenth century, the French dubbed them Bohemians, and *gypsy* and *bohemian* became more or less synonymous. Bohemianism aside, the Czech Republic consumes more beer per capita than any other nation on earth — almost twice as much as the United States. This only helps make the country more fertile for tramping. In fact, the national anthem is fittingly titled "Where Is My Home?"

Even the Nazis and Communists couldn't keep the tramps down. Tramping groups were active in the underground resistance after Germany invaded Czechoslovakia in 1939; some who worked in munitions factories employed their prankster skills in the cause of freedom by mislabeling boxes so that German troops on the front lines got the wrong-sized bullets. When the Reds took over in 1948, the apparatchiks felt sufficiently threatened by tramps to spy on the larger camps and break some of them up. Unsupervised assembly was outlawed — which, of course, only made tramping more attractive to the bohemian soul. In his 1990 book *Disturbing the Peace*, Czech president Vaclav Havel recalled the role a group of tramps played when Russian tanks rolled into a small town north of Prague called Liberec in 1968, at the end of the Prague Spring. Led by a young man called "The Pastor," the tramps took down all the street signs overnight to confuse the Russians. Another "poignant scene" involved the group standing guard at the town hall and singing the Bee Gees hit "Massachusetts." Havel writes: "I saw the whole thing in a special light, because I still had fresh memories of crowds of similar young people in the East Village in New York, singing the same song, but without the tanks in the background."

While disparate tramping groups went on to hold illegal rock concerts in the seventies and eighties, and in some cases went to jail for their provocative displays of affection for Western pop culture, tramping didn't face a real threat to its ethos until shortly after the Velvet Revolution in 1989. By the time the Czechs and Slovaks had parted ways, in 1992, the Czech Republic was already knee-deep in its attempts to graft a Western capitalistic head onto a moribund Eastern Bloc economic body. The transformation worked, for the most part, but it's had a sullying effect on tramping. Tramps who once scorned communism began to cast a yearning eye toward Western-style yuppiedom. Though hordes still tramp, the new economy has inspired careerism among many would-be hoboes.

"Now everybody wants to make money," the bartender at the Red Monkey Pub told me. "They work long hours and don't have time to spend their weekends in the woods. They take vacations abroad. I think, too, that there is nothing to rebel against now." Up until the Velvet Revolution, she explained, tramps fancied themselves on the outside of society. "Of course," she said, brightening, "the young tramps, the seventeen-year-olds, rebel against capitalism now. So hopefully tramping won't disappear forever."

One hopes the bartender is right — that democracy, like Nazism and communism before it, will fail to take the bohemian out of the Bohemians.

I've grown tired of the Red Monkey Gang — bless their souls — and their slothful ways. On the morning of the sixth day, a pack of chipper, clean-cut tramps marches up to the pub, where we're seated on the front porch, and I quickly invite myself to join them. But saying goodbye to the boys is not easy. Sheriff Tom, I'm certain, has never had a more faithful sausage-eating mate.

"Why no more drink *pivo* with us?" he asks, gesticulating with his pilsner. "No like us?"

"Yes. Yes," I say. "I like you."

"No like our sausage?"

Well, now he's getting warmer. I mumble that my bum knee requires constant movement and move out. The new crew includes a couple of fresh-faced college students; a lanky young woman; a bony English-speaking thirtysomething; and a hirsute middle-aged man. A hundred yards down the trail I look back — I shouldn't, but I do — and there is the Red Monkey Gang, waving a forlorn goodbye.

After a few minutes we stop, and the tramps introduce themselves. The two college kids are called Little Pid and Pad; it's never quite clear what "Pid" stands for, but "Pad" is Czech slang for "he who falls down a lot." Rita is Pad's girlfriend. The bilingual guy is the only one willing to give his real name: Pavel Bem, a talkative psychiatrist who's also the mayor of one of Prague's fifteen boroughs. His nickname, Strevo, translates as "he who acts with extreme intentions." The leader, a six-foot-two bruiser with a thick beard, is simply Big Pid.

We grip thumbs, toast one another with the requisite shot of rum, and set off hiking down a potholed dirt road. Soon the road becomes a single rutted track in a green tunnel of clattering branches. It's late morning, but the farther we walk, the darker the woods get. The group plans to hike ten miles to Kytin, on the eastern slope of the Brdy Hills, and then head for Brdsky Kempy, "Valley of Brdy Camps," a narrow, heavily wooded canyon that isn't on any of my maps but, I'm reliably informed, was home to some of the earliest tramp camps, dating back to the 1920s.

Hiking with this new gang is like competing in a speed-walking contest. All five are former participants in the Czech scouting movement, and over the years they've spent a lot of time tramping in the Brdy Hills. Like most, they've perfected the art of traveling light. Each wears a small, threadbare green knapsack in which he or she carries a fluffy cotton sleeping bag, a cooking pot, a spoon, and ingredients for a few meals.

The path meanders between woods and fallow fields where quail and grouse flutter. According to a historical map of the Brdy Hills, during the thirties and forties, the most famous group in these parts was the Beer Volunteer Workers, a pack of about 150 tramps who wandered around dressed like American cowboys, carrying genuine Colt .45s. Their badge was a Boy Scout fleur-de-lis with a glass of beer in the center. The gang dwindled during the fifties, though, due to Communist harassment.

Strevo himself suffered under the regime; he was once jailed for two days without being told why. "You can't understand unless you've lived under a totalitarian government," he says. "You begin to question what the truth is. I think that's why Czechs are very outdoor-oriented. The TVs and radios constantly played propaganda. We had to get away from it. At least out here in the woods you could find some truth."

After three hours of hiking we come upon a fire ring nestled beneath a forty-foot rock face and a twisting rivulet. It's one of the early tramp sites. The wet air drenches my socks and shirt, and giant ferns bow down in the mist. "We are here," Big Pid says, taking the pack off his back.

We set our things down and begin gathering logs for a fire. I help the group string a tarp between two trees in case of rain and then unsheath my nylon tent. I hardly have the first stake in the ground before Big Pid motions for me to stop. "There are no tents in tramping," he lectures, shaking his black beard. "You must see the stars." This didn't come up with the Red Monkeys, but then, I was never sober enough to try to put up a tent. I slide it back in its sleeve, but Big Pid isn't done yet. "And there are no gas stoves, fancy backpacks, and none of those PowerBars." He glares at my carbo stash. "We will show you real tramping food."

I thought I'd already seen real tramping food. Since we got to the campsite, we've been eating sausage and washing it down with rum. But sausage is just an appetizer for this crew. As Big Pid speaks, I watch him pull an entire roasted chicken out of his backpack, followed by an assortment of vegetables. He dismembers the bird and mixes up a stew over the open fire. The other tramps prepare meals in their own pots — everything from noodles to chicken casserole. Then, one at a time, each pot is set in the middle of the campsite. We stand in a circle and take turns bending down and spooning out a bite. For about an hour, the six of us share dinner and compliment the chefs. The evening's entertainment is a traditional tramping game: Standing nose to nose, we try to knock each other off balance. Big Pid, naturally, goes undefeated. Then we sprawl on the ground, light cigars, and pass a flask. As the fire dies down, a cuckoo fills the forest with its unmistakable call. *Cuckoo. Cuckoo. Cuckoo. Cuckoo. Cuckoo.* Five cuckoos. "Bad news," Strevo says. "According to the cuckoo bird you have only five years left to live."

That's not very heartening, I say.

"If it's any consolation," he replies cheerfully, "we only have five years, too."

What? Do I look like I was in the Party?" exclaims a thin man dressed in beads and buckskin, with blue streaks of war paint on his face. His name is Jiri Kohout. I seem to have offended him by asking whether he'd been a Communist.

My search for tramps has taken a side trip into terra incognita. I have rented a minivan and, accompanied by my nineteen-year-old translator, Hana Kozakova, have driven to the small city of Plzen, about sixty miles west of Prague, in search of the more settled, rendezvous-oriented, cowboy-and-Indian side of tramping. A rodeo is taking place here, and I've been told I might find Indians. A good tip, as it turns out: Within five minutes I bump into Jiri and his tribe next to the funnel cake booth. His wife, Gabriela, son, Jarda, and daughter, Nikolka, are dressed up like Lakota Sioux. I ask if he would be so kind as to take me back to his tepee for a short pow-wow, and we walk down a sidewalk to a small patch of grass outside the rodeo arena. There, next to his car with bumper stickers that read I LIKE AMERICAN INDIAN POWWOWS and AMERICAN IN-DIAN HOBBYIST, are two tepees, outfitted with colorful blankets and animal-skin rugs.

The Kohouts are here at the rodeo to perform a prayer dance at halftime. It would be nice if they did a stop-the-rain dance. It's pouring, putting a damper on the rodeo. A few moments ago a Czech cowboy slipped in the muck and was gored by a bull. He's not badly injured, but the ambulance siren is ruining any sense of authenticity. Meanwhile, water is blowing in through the tepee's door, drenching the tom-toms and blankets. Making the situation worse — at least from where I sit — is Jiri's sidekick, a pale, burly, Indian-loving friend who is wearing chaps sans underwear. He's in-advertently mooning the group while he tries to close the tepee flap, eliciting groans from Jiri's son, a sixteen-year-old who is chill-ing in Indian garb and a pair of Oakley sunglasses.

Oblivious to the commotion, Jiri launches into his story as if it were ancient cosmology. "Tramps and Indians were together at the beginning," he says wistfully, relating his thoughts through Hana. "But then something happened. Tramps became very dirty and smelly. And all that drinking was unsatisfactory to me. Indians aren't dirty. They are clean and smooth."

I notice that the Kohouts certainly are. Their blond hair is tightly braided, and their outfits are crisply pressed.

Jiri continues: He started dressing as an Indian thirty years ago, when, as a young man, he witnessed the horrible way in which Indi-ans were treated in American westerns. "I knew then that Indians were my people," he explains. Already a veteran GI-style tramp, he began to wear Indian garb on outings. Soon he was erecting tepees in the woods, where he and his family spent weekends and holi-days, living "the simple life" the way the Indians did. He beaded belts and purses for sale at Czech rodeos and other western-themed occasions. And he got himself a booking agent. Yes, he says, he's been to the States once, but he prefers being an Indian in the Czech Republic. "It's very good here," he says. "There are no snakes in Czech. It's much fewer dangers here."

I ask if being a Central European Indian opens him up for ridicule. "Yes, people joke about me being a blond Indian," he admits. He lights a cigarette and takes a deep, contemplative drag. "But I just stand proud. I give them no pleasure in teasing me."

As I prepare to leave, the Indians begin talking among themselves. Jiri looks concerned and takes me by the arm. "You understand, don't you," he asks, "that I am not a real Indian?"

What is this thing called the Wild West? John Wayne hunting Apaches? A faded denim jacket from the Don Imus catalog? Those who live there are forced to separate fact from myth. But in the Czech Republic, the myth remains untainted by reality. Czech tramps choose among happy clichés — footloose hobo, Marlboro Man, noble savage, GI Joe — celebrating wide-open America and throwing out the details. When I tell my new cowboy and Indian friends that I am from Santa Fe, New Mexico, the heart of Indian country, most of them seem to care not at all. They are more interested in showing me their new plastic pistol or horseshoe belt buckle.

Nonetheless, I don my armadillo bolo tie and head to the stark suburban neighborhood of Vestec u Prahy on the south side of Prague. There, in the middle of a cornfield, just beyond a row of housing projects, sits a weather-beaten ghost town called Westec City. Part theme park, part banquet center, Westec City represents the big-business side of Czech tramping; it pulls the ethos out of the woods and half-bakes it, hosting western-style barbecues and rodeos for corporate clients.

Tonight the partyers are from the Czech division of Microsoft. Cowgirls in cleavage-revealing western garb hand each guest a black cowboy hat and a mint julep at the door. Black-hatted executives and programmers line Main Street, a row of buildings labeled SALOON, UNDERTAKER, and POST OFFICE. As the sun sets behind the neighboring housing blocks, a tinny loudspeaker blasts the spaghetti-western theme song from *The Good, the Bad, and the Ugly,* and shutters creak in the wind.

A heat wave has descended on Central Europe, so I decide to wet my whistle with a drink in the Westec Saloon, hoping, as I've been promised, that I'll hear some good live music. Cowboys belly up to the bar, drinking the local brew. Faded wallpaper, round card tables, and a mounted deer's head make me feel like I've stepped into a scene from Kenny Rogers's *The Gambler.* A man in a cowboy hat is standing onstage, singing sad-sounding country-and-western songs in Czech, accompanied by a boom box. "What kind of music you got here?" I ask.

"Both kinds," says the barkeep. "Country and disco."

Through the window, I watch a man practice for the calf-roping event by tossing his lariat over anybody who passes by. I go outside and introduce myself. He tells me his name is Jaroslav Krchov, but his cowboy friends call him Dick. "That's spelled D-y-k," he says. Dyk, thirty-three, has the callused hands of a cowboy. He sports a tattoo of his horse, Black-and-White, on his right arm. We arrange to meet the next day at the garage where he works as an auto mechanic and then drive out to his "ranch" on the outskirts of Prague.

When I pick him up in my minivan with Hana, Dyk seems a more subdued, blue-jumpsuited version of the gregarious cowboy I met at Westec City. We wind through narrow streets on the way to his house, past pubs and parks full of kids, and I ask him if anything is wrong. "I must tell you," he blurts. "My ranch is not like your ranches in the U.S. It is a very small ranch."

Five minutes later we are at the road's end, on a hill overlooking a busy expressway. "This is home," Dyk says, gesturing to a small, red-brick bungalow with a vegetable garden for a front yard. Behind it is a fence made of a few stakes and some twine. Four horses stand in stalls beside a pasture the size of a putting green.

Dyk walks over to his faithful Black-and-White, who is standing in the shade of a cherry tree. Wrapping his arms around the horse's neck, he recalls the first time he saw *The Treasure of the Sierra Madre* — the movie that made him, at age nineteen, a cowboy. Inspired, he found time apart from his mechanic's job to ride horses at a stable near his parents' home northwest of Prague and experiment with saddle repair. Over the next fourteen years he built the stable behind his house, converted a delivery truck into a horse trailer, and began driving to rodeos in the Czech Republic and Germany. He spends a third of his $388 monthly salary on hay and oats, but his appearances at Westec City are for love, not money. Once a year he rides in the Czech Pony Express, in which horsemen race from town to town across the country, carrying real mail. He looks out across his quarter-acre spread and tells me that he plans to move his family to a bigger place farther from the city, with more space to practice his calf-roping and barrel racing. Capitalism has been good to Dyk and his clan. "It's much easier to be a cowboy these days," he says. "We no longer have to hide our cowboyness."

With my work finished and my pores oozing sausage grease, I find my way back to the train station at Revnice, where I first entered the Brdy Hills. It's a Sunday night, and homebound tramps are everywhere, in the station bar, sleeping on benches, strumming guitars, or nuzzling with sweethearts. Everyone looks half-dead: It's a scene from *Night of the Living Hoboes*. Tomorrow the tramps will return to their jobs as clerks, mechanics, psychiatrists, and mayors.

For a brief but glorious time, I've lain myself down in the bohemian heart of camping. My extreme-sports-loving friends back in the States spend thousands on high-tech gear and strenuous expeditions that cannot possibly deliver the degree of comfort I got lying on the ground twenty yards from a pub. At every step my beer glass was full, my belly had meat, and my cigar was lit. Soap? Razor? I don't need no stinking razor. I've found the real, world-preserving wildness celebrated by that Yankee bohemian, Henry David Thoreau — the wildness not of place, but of what he called "foresters and outlaws." This is camping: eating junk, getting dirty, misbehaving. I've gone native: This boy is a tramp.

The train pulls into the station. I climb aboard and once again sprawl on the floor. As we pull out, the car begins to shake and clank in a satisfying rhythm. I'm just drifting off to sleep when a man dressed in ripped jeans and a torn army jacket, accompanied by a mangy dog with a metal muzzle, plops down next to me. He pulls an envelope full of tobacco out of his pocket and offers to roll me a cigarette. I decline, but look closer. Though I probably appear rather disgusting myself, this man looks much worse. He has clearly been on the road a long time, a lot longer than a couple weeks. Wait a minute, I think — here's a *real* hobo.

He pulls out a stainless steel hip flask and offers me a swig. I take a long pull, wipe my mouth with the back of my hand.

"Dekuji," I say in thanks.

Realizing from my accent that I'm an American, he sits up, grabs his guitar, and begins to play: "This land is your land, this land is my land, from South Moravia to North Bohemia . . ."

It's time to go home.

JASON WILSON

Dining Out in Iceland

FROM *The North American Review*

I AM SURROUNDED by Vikings. I'm standing in the kitchen of a restaurant called Fjörukráin, in one of Reykjavík's ever-growing suburbs called Hafnarfjördur. Jóhannes Bjarnason, the restaurant's owner, and his waitstaff ready themselves for the night in full Viking costume: leather, thick fur, helmets, shields, armor. Fjörukráin's dark interior consists of exposed wooden rafters, while various horns and animal pelts, including a full-sized stuffed polar bear, line the walls. Patrons sit at long wooden tables and benches. At each place setting sits a paper Viking hat and a shot glass made out of sheep's horn. Fjörukráin's brochure shows a Viking waiter placing a diner in a headlock.

One of the Vikings, a white-bearded man named Haukur Halldórsson, who wears thick glasses and a fur vest and smokes a pipe, guides me through the restaurant and shows off hand-painted Old Norse runes he's spent six years translating. "*Blót* was a sacrifice to the pagan gods," Haukur says, in explanation of one rune.

Tonight is the first night of the ancient Viking month of Thorri, named for the winter god, which runs from late January through late February. Thorri on the old pagan calendar traditionally marked the coldest, most brutal months in what was already a brutal place to live. Icelanders are not people who've had an easy time of things, and from the ninth century until just after World War II, they lived a harsh existence as a neglected Norwegian, and then Danish, colony on a cold, remote, volcanic island, with little fertile ground, few trees. It's hard to imagine now, seeing all the new, modernist, almost Lego-like office and apartment buildings in

Reykjavík, but for many centuries, Icelanders lived in houses made of turf and mud.

The reason I've come to Iceland in the dead of winter is to experience *Thorrablót,* the pagan feast in Viking culture given in honor of Thorri. It's full of drinking, songs written to Thorri, and traditional Icelandic food. The custom of *Thorrablót* actually lay dormant for many years, but was resurrected in the late nineteenth century during the Icelanders' struggle to gain independence from Denmark. Icelandic students in Copenhagen used the pagan feast as a symbol of their basic difference with the European colonizer. *Thorrablót* in modern Iceland, then, can be seen as a show of nationalist pride. It caught on and, since the middle of this century, each town, family, and organization has celebrated its own *Thorrablót.*

What I will soon be eating for *Thorrablót* — the *Thorramatur,* or traditional "Thorri-food" — seems to be culled from the pages of the medieval sagas. I've already received a glimpse earlier today, courtesy of the newspaper's front page, which featured a photo of a man grinning widely and pointing to his grocer's selection of *Thorramatur.* Nothing could prepare me, however, for what it looks like in person. I stand in Fjörukráin's kitchen and watch sous-chef Ingi Gudjonsson prepare for tonight's feast: the food frankly frightens the hell out of me.

"In the middle of the winter, every part of the animal had to be used," Ingi says as he carries a wooden platter full of food for Thorri, the *Thorrabakki,* into the dining room. Ingi lays the three-foot *Thorrabakki* under a dim light in the cavernous Viking hall and demonstrates just how much of an animal can actually be eaten.

Immediately I notice the *svid,* or sheep head, lying smack in the center, eyeing me. Ingi dips a flatbread pancake into a dish of *svidasulta,* or sheep-head jelly. "This is sort of like pâté," he says, "but I don't like the word *pâté* because it's too fancy."

Next Ingi points out the *pungar,* ram's testicles, and chuckles. The testicles are all mashed together into a pasty white mass and then sliced. You can still make out the ovals. After that we taste the *pungavefjur,* which is the testicles wrapped in loin of lamb. Then come two types of *slátur,* literally translated as "slaughter." Two choices here: *blódmör* (blood pudding) and *lifrapylsa* (liver pudding), both of which are mashed up and cooked in the sheep's stomach. They are sliced and laid out like salami. I taste a pinkish piece of meat called *hangikjöt,* which afterward I'm told is lamb that's been smoked in sheep's dung.

Ingi hands me a piece of *hardfiskur,* or dried fish jerky, smothered in warm butter. I tap the table with the tough white strip, then nearly pull my teeth out of my head trying to bite off a piece. I'll let W. H. Auden's report on *hardfiskur* in his *Letters from Iceland* stand for me: "The tougher kind tastes like toenails, and the softer kind like the skin off the soles of one's feet."

Finally I'm introduced to the centerpiece, the king hors d'oeuvre, of *Thorrablót* — the *hákarl.* Literally translated as "rotten shark," *hákarl* is Greenlandic shark that has been buried in the ground for several months, left to decompose, then dug up, cubed, and served cold. The smell emanating from the little bowl holding these grayish white, somewhat congealed cubes is enough to make me step back from the *Thorrabakki.* "People eat this like candy," Ingi says, and pops one in his mouth with a smile. I wince for him. Maybe later, I say when he offers one.

Most of the *Thorramatur* gives off a smell similar to milk that's three weeks gone bad. This is because the meat has been preserved in *mysa,* which is similar to whey, but different. *Mysa* is an extremely sour byproduct of Icelandic *skyr,* which is sort of a low-fat yogurt. *Skyr* is delicious. *Mysa,* however, is basically the same thing as the disgusting urine-colored liquid that floats on the top of your yogurt when you first peel it open. Imagine for a moment plopping bits of sheep's intestine into that sour liquid and then, several months later, eating it. Apparently this was the only way the Vikings were able to preserve their food. Now it's tradition.

"I've really never seen a written recipe for this stuff. It just moves on from person to person," Ingi says, adding that there are some regional variations, including pickled seal flippers in more rural areas, or rotten eider duck eggs near Lake Myvatn.

Later my Icelandic friends Eirikur and Addy will tell me that the young people think *Thorramatur* is just horrible. "They hate it," Eirikur and Addy say. "We tell our kids, well, you just have to eat one bite, then you can have something else. Then the next year we make them take two bites." Eventually the children like it, which is important to their parents. "Growing up, this was never a big deal for us," they say. "We would eat this food throughout the year. I would say until about 1980, Icelanders only ate traditional foods."

This, of course, has long ceased to be the case. Walk through downtown Reykjavík, and you'll find all manner of foreign restaurants, with names like Asia Palace, Samurai, Amigo's, Pasta Basta, the Dubliner, or the once unthinkable One Woman Vegetarian Restaurant. Then, of course, there are the inevitable Pizza Hut, McDonald's, and Subway.

After Ingi's demonstration, Haukur joins us in Fjörukráin's dining room, with sheep heads in hand. He offers me a head and a knife and begins to explain how to eat the poor thing. I'm told to grab the head in my left hand and take a knife in the right. The sheep head glares up at me. First, Haukur says, carve out the eyeball. "Be careful not to eat the pupil, though, or you'll go blind." Second, he tells me to carve off the ear. "But throw away the cartilage, or you'll go deaf." Then he says to discard the nose. "Sheep notoriously contract colds." Finally he tells me just to dig in, jaw, cheek, tongue — wherever. "In the old days, we had to eat everything except the shit," he says. "And even the shit we used to cook the meat."

After I finish chewing the leathery meat, I notice a few traditional items missing from the *Thorrabakki*. I know from my guidebook, for instance, that puffin — the cute little seabird with the big eyes that looks like a penguin wearing a colorful toucan's beak — is an Icelandic favorite. I ask Ingi why there's no puffin meat prepared, and he just shrugs. "Oh, puffin's nothing special. We always eat puffin. Puffin is just everyday food."

Then, rather delicately, keeping in mind the environmental battles of the last decade, I inquire about whale meat. Ingi and Haukur glance uncomfortably at each other. "Ah, whale is beautiful food," Haukur says with a mouth full of sheep head. "But Greenpeace, they have ruined everything."

Ingi explains that pickled whale blubber was until recently a *Thorrablót* tradition — and perennially since the worldwide whaling ban, prowhaling supporters become most vocal during Thorri. In the weeks before I arrived, a grocery store chain called Noatún attempted to import whale blubber from Norway in preparation for this year's *Thorrablót*. It's been nearly a decade since the Icelanders were able to get their hands on good whale blubber, and

Júlíus Jónsson, Noatún's owner, had the support of the Icelandic government to bring in one hundred tons to be pickled and sold. But the Norwegians, for fear of sparking international antiwhaling tensions, eventually refused to export the delicacy.

"Whale is more precious than gold," Ingi says. "I really wish we had some."

From this moment forward, know that I am an eater of whale meat. On a quiet night when a thick layer of snow blankets the sidewalks and roofs of Reykjavík's primary-colored houses, I sit in the candle-lit dining room of Thrir Frakkar, one of the city's finest restaurants, where I've now sliced into my second bite of a juicy whale steak, served in a pepper sauce.

My dining companion tonight is Ína, the Herring Girl, an icy-blue-eyed, nineteen-year-old daughter of Iceland who's also never eaten whale meat before tonight. She gingerly cuts the meat and tentatively eyes what's on her fork before she pops the first piece into her mouth. Our brows remain furrowed as we chew the meat over and over before swallowing.

Thrir Frakkar, everyone says, is the only place in town where you can find whale on the menu. It's served two ways, both as steak and "in the Japanese style," which our waitress tells us means raw. The price for the steak: more than $25 per plate. Though I shouldn't be, I'm shocked that whale is a red meat and has no taste of the sea at all. It's served rather on the rare side, and a little bit too bloody for me. There is an odd, sharp, and tangy aftertaste that is not entirely pleasant, yet I cannot say I feel any differently after eating whale than I have after eating ostrich, emu, buffalo, reindeer, rabbit, venison, or any of the more common warm-blooded animals that have appeared on my plate at one time or another.

As a side dish, the Herring Girl and I order puffin. The strong, gamy meat comes served in dark strips, glazed with a honey mustard sauce. Puffin tastes like a cross between duck and calf liver. We scarf it down with red wine.

The cozy dining room stands half filled, and judging from the fanny packs and heavy winter coats, it's safe to say most of the diners are tourists. I eavesdrop; nearly half of the people order whale, just like us. Two white-haired gentlemen, obviously Americans, probably southerners from the Carolinas, sit down at the table next to us and address each other as "y'all." "Where do y'all think they keep all the old people in Reykjavík?" one asks the other. The Herring Girl — who can quote *Austin Powers* in four languages ("Shall we shag now or shag later?") — doubles over laughing at what she calls the gentlemen's "hilarious" southern accent. "Half of this restaurant is speaking English," she says. I gently point out that she is too. "Well," she says, "at least I don't have a horrible accent like that."

I call Ína the "Herring Girl" because I met her during the previous summer in a northern fishing village called Siglufjördur. There she worked, in fisherwoman's costume, at the local Herring Museum, a nostalgic monument to the profitable early-twentieth-century herring runs on which the Icelandic economy was built. But thirty years ago the herring "simply failed to show up" (or more precisely were overfished). Siglufjördur is a herring boomtown gone bust. Ína took me hiking above the fjord and picked purple wildflowers. We climbed to a waterfall and drank from water so cold it burned. Ína's grandmother invited me for coffee and cakes. While we drank coffee in the midnight sun, Ína told me her parents had moved away from Siglufjördur to Mosfellsbær, one of Reykjavík's sprawling new suburbs. Ína's grandmother told me she didn't want her little Herring Girl to follow suit. Towns like Siglufjördur, she said, are losing too many bright young people. Ína rolled her eyes and said that she wanted to get a job in a big hotel. That was six months ago. Now, as Ína and I dine on whale steaks at Thrir Frakkar, she's already begun applying for summer work in the capital.

When Ína and I finish dinner, I ask our waitress what species of whale meat we've just eaten. Is it minke or humpback or orca? She can't say, exactly. I ask where Thrir Frakkar gets its whale meat — what with hunting whales being illegal at the moment and everything.

"Oh, this is old meat," she replies, with a puckish grin. "It's from 1989. We have it in deep freeze."

"Really?" I ask. "It must be a pretty big freezer. You must have an awful lot stored up."

"Oh no, only two or three more years' worth," she says. "After that, there's no more left."

After dinner, the Herring Girl and I trudge past the clean, stark

Hallgrímskirkja church and the statue of Leif Eirikson, "Discoverer of America," then up to the huge geothermal tanks that provide ecofriendly energy for the entire city. From high atop the tanks, the symmetrical streets and identical, perfectly rectangular apartment buildings make Iceland's capital city look like a child's toy built only yesterday. It is only 9:00, though the sun set more than six hours ago. It will not rise again until after 10:00 A.M. tomorrow.

As we wander back downtown, the Herring Girl explains that it's not by choice that she's never eaten whale meat before tonight. Others in her family have certainly eaten whale at one time or another. It just so happens that this Herring Girl grew up during a period of history when Iceland was forced to stop its traditional whale hunts by the larger nations — the ones whose literature includes books like *Moby-Dick,* the ones who initially hunted whales to near-extinction. That was the same period when environmentalists sank part of Iceland's whaling fleet in protest. Faced with boycotts and embargoes, and then after several years of killing at least one hundred whales annually "for scientific purposes," Iceland stopped whaling altogether in 1989. So for more than half of Ína's life, whale meat, once an Icelandic birthright, has been illegal and next-to-impossible to obtain.

By the time I arrive in Reykjavík, support for whaling has peaked. More than 80 percent of all Icelanders surveyed in a recent Gallup poll say they support a repeal of the whaling ban — the highest level of support in a decade. Underlying this support is the belief that some whale populations, such as minke whales, have sufficiently recovered and can now be harvested. Many Icelanders also believe, with sketchy scientific proof, that whales are beginning to eat into their nation's fish stocks.

If Iceland resumes whaling, most of us know how the story will play out. Nations such as Britain and Germany and the United States will respond by threatening to boycott Icelandic fish. The international press will predict financial ruin for Iceland's enviable economy, since fish accounts for 75 percent of its exports. But whaling in Iceland has never really had anything to do with economics. "Whaling is an emotional issue," says Margrét Bjorgulf-dóttir, a journalist with the English-language *Iceland Review.* "The whaling issue is sort of like the pro-choice/pro-life argument in the United States."

The Icelanders bristle at being lectured to by environmentalists. This attitude becomes evident whenever, and with whomever, I happen to bring up the topic of whales. "You're not a member of Greenpeace, are you?" they ask. My friend Eirikur once explained how his family lived for several years in Madison, Wisconsin, and how Greenpeace had come into his daughter's fourth-grade class to speak about whaling. Greenpeace, Eirikur says, told the nine-year-olds that the Norwegians and the Japanese and the Icelanders were the evil countries who killed whales. "My daughter looked around at all the children in the classroom staring at her. 'Don't look at me,' she said, nearly in tears. 'I didn't do it.'"

More than anything else, Icelanders will assert their sovereignty. "Being an independent, autonomous nation, we are entitled to utilize our national resources," says Einar Gudfinnson, a parliamentarian from Iceland's remote West Fjörds. "People in this country see it as our right to hunt whale."

And when the Icelanders assert their sovereignty, they traditionally threaten to sever ties with NATO and shut down the military base at Keflavík, where the 5,000 mainly American servicemen stationed there present an imposing presence in a nation of only 270,000 people.

But what most complicates and exacerbates any discussion about whaling these days is the fact that Keiko, the famed orca whale and star of the 1992 movie *Free Willy*, now resides in Iceland.

You've seen the movie, you know the story: Willy lands in captivity. Impossibly cute kid befriends Willy. After much weeping and hand-wringing, Willy is finally released back into the wild. Everyone goes home happy. The only problem: After the movie was released, people discovered that the real Willy was actually an orca with skin lesions. Its name was Keiko and it lived in a Mexican amusement park. A public outcry ensued: Warner Brothers, Mattel Toys, the Humane Society, cell-phone billionaire Craig McCaw, and countless others donated millions to form the Free Willy Keiko Foundation to save the whale — and to make certain that life can be just like the movies.

In September, after several rehabilitation years at the Oregon Coast Aquarium, a U.S. Air Force cargo plane airlifted Keiko to Heimaey, in Iceland's Westmen Islands. Now, after twenty-two years in captivity, Keiko will be trained in his native North Atlantic waters on how to live once again as a wild animal. Schoolchildren in the United States can log on to Keiko's very own Web site and follow his progress. "You Americans are insane," said Gunnar, who ran the guesthouse where I lived during the summer. "You love killer whales, the most vicious animal in the sea."

Icelanders' opinions on Keiko vary. Many children with banners and flags came to greet the whale when he arrived. Some old fishermen suggested to the news media that Keiko be ground up into meatballs and served to the starving people in Somalia. Nearly everyone scratches his head in bewilderment. Perhaps most importantly, about half the population believes Keiko's presence will make it much more difficult for the Icelanders to ever resume whaling.

Over and over, when the topic of whaling is raised, I hear comparisons between *Thorrablót* and Thanksgiving. "Imagine," says a taxi driver named Jóhannes, "if we saved a turkey and brought him to the United States and told you, you couldn't kill it, because we're going to keep him in a cage and then release him into the wild. To us, it's the same. It's no big thing, you know, for Icelanders to eat whales."

On this silent winter night, however, the whaling issue seems merely to simmer, like lava beneath the city's frozen pond. The Herring Girl and I take a taxi down Tjarnargata, the street next to the pond, with boxed houses of bright green and red and royal blue. We pass a small theater where once I watched an English-language documentary about the history of Iceland. Besides re-enactments of bloody Viking battles, here is what I gleaned from that film: Iceland is "the world's smallest superpower" and Icelanders agree that "to be caught between the past and the future is a good place to be."

It's around 2:00 A.M. and I'm standing in an über-chic club called Astro listening to a girl with dyed black hair begin crying for the third time tonight. "You don't understand what it's like to live here in this country," she sobs. Her name is Brynja, and in between more sobs and shots of vodka she tells me about how she worked as a nanny in the United States last year. And how she loved the fact that she could go to New York every weekend and listen to hip-hop music. "Nobody understands me here," she says. "Nobody understands hip-hop culture here."

Do I also need to tell you Brynja is really drunk? Well, let's just say everyone in Astro is really drunk. Here's how the tourist publication *Around Reykjavík* summarizes the city's nightlife: "Two things to keep in mind: Bars get crowded and Icelanders get drunk."

I tell Brynja that over the summer I'd attended a party at Astro thrown to celebrate the August issue of *Playboy,* which featured a special "Women of Iceland" pictorial spread. That Playboy party was quite obviously a major social event, the place to be seen, and a line of Reykjavíkites snaked around the block. Not just men, either. Inside, free champagne, chocolate-covered strawberries, and pigs-in-a-blanket circulated. Fake orange-skinned tans abounded, as did frost-colored lipstick, as well as several knee-length coats and tiny, tiny dresses. A guy lounged near me in a khaki suit with *CHiPs*-style shades and a fake, pencil-thin mustache. Copies of the August issue of *Playboy* were passed around like family albums. Everyone, young or old, male or female, commented politely on how nice the girls looked.

Páll Óskar og Casino, the hottest band in Iceland, played such treats as "Do You Know the Way to San Jose," "Up, Up, and Away," "Witchita Lineman," and a bring-the-house-down version of "Hava Nagila." I staked a spot near the bar where I could see the head table, where the dozen or so "Women of Iceland" sat. I imagined that a table full of Playboy bunnies would, at most, be sharing a plate of lettuce. These women, however, chowed down on big hunks of lamb. One of the women, tucked precariously in a handkerchief-sized dress, nearly decapitated me as she refilled her dessert plate.

For the next several weeks, the August issue of *Playboy* would be a major topic of discussion, seemingly a source of national pride. The on-line *Daily News from Iceland* declared the photo spread "extremely tasteful." In a gas station the day after the party, I watched a middle-aged woman snag the last copy, look both ways after paying for it, then slide the shrink-wrapped magazine into her black bag.

Now, only six months later, Brynja tells me there's been a definite backlash to the "Women of Iceland" spread. "After that *Playboy* article was published, all these foreign men came here thinking Icelandic girls will go to bed with anyone. It's just so untrue."

On the third floor of a drab office building overlooking Reykjavík's harbor, hangs a sign on a door announcing the existence of something called the Elfschool. During a summer visit, I had spoken at length with the headmaster here, a man named Magnus Skarp- hedinsson, who claims to be an expert on the elves and other hid- den people, or *huldufólk,* that are believed to inhabit Iceland. The Elfschool is taught in English and Swedish and German, and fur- nished with small classroom desks. The bookshelves in Magnus's office are lined with plastic garden gnomes and books on UFOs, clairvoyancy, and life after death.

When I return to Iceland during Thorri, I speak with Magnus again. He reminds me that once, in 1986, he was named "the most unpopular man in Iceland" by the state-owned radio station. This title, however, was not won through his work with the Elfschool. Magnus says that back in the 1980s, he led a tiny protest group of Icelandic antiwhaling activists.

At that time the Icelandic government, under the threat of eco- nomic sanctions, rallied its people to dutifully eat more whale meat. Newspapers published photos of the prime minister and his cabinet enjoying blubber and passing on family recipes. It was a dangerous time for an antiwhaling vegetarian like Magnus. "I was looked upon as a traitor," he says. "People in this country thought I and my friends were just crazy liberals who had no touch with reality."

Even today, Magnus blames foreign environmental groups like Greenpeace and Sea Shepherd Conservation Society for strength- ening support for whaling among the proud, nationalist Iceland- ers. "Greenpeace came here and screwed everything up. They came with great arrogance and behaved like colonizers. They came here and told Icelanders how to act, how to behave. They took no steps to understand the Icelandic people. They never listened to the Icelandic environmentalists," he says. "Icelanders really looked upon Greenpeace as a postponed part of the American imperial- ism. Or a prolonged colonialism toward Iceland."

Meanwhile, as the whaling issue gains steam during Thorri, an- other controversy appears in the Reykjavík newspapers — this one over an alleged "elf stone." Road engineers, in preparation for road improvements, would like to demolish a large boulder which juts up beside the Vesturlandsvegur highway, the major artery from Iceland's north and west regions into the capital. Many Icelanders believe that elves or hidden people, *huldufólk,* live in this rock. And therefore, they believe it should be left undisturbed.

Helgi Hallgrímsson, a director of Iceland's Public Roads Administration, is quoted in the daily *Morganbladid* as saying, "Some people believe there is a colony of elves or something similar in the stone . . . We try to take people's feelings into consideration as far as possible and in this case we do not think it will be too expensive or difficult to achieve." The *Morganbladid* devotes a whole page to the issue.

It is not uncommon throughout Iceland to find roads that suddenly narrow or curve, simply because they pass what is believed to be an elf dwelling. Icelanders believe bad things will happen if a road crew attempts to smash or move such an elf stone. The last time the boulder beside the Vesturlandsvegur highway was moved, in 1970, the bulldozer cut through a water pipeline for a nearby fish farm, causing thousands of dollars in damage. The bulldozer driver was convinced the elves caused this accident.

Several months before, in the summer daylight, I'd driven with Magnus to the outskirts of the capital to check out the elf stone in question. As we stood on a moss-covered field in the shadow of snowcapped Mount Esja and cars whizzed by, a group of young men rode past on Icelandic ponies, pointing at Magnus and laughing. "There are no hidden people in that rock!" yelled one of them. Magnus just smiled. "Many of the people in Reykjavík, in the city, just don't want to believe in hidden people," he said. "But look, they still plan the roadwork around them."

Magnus claims to have recorded more than three hundred interviews with Icelanders who've had contact with hidden people, claims he looks deep into these people's eyes and he believes they are telling the truth. "But this is vanishing," Magnus concedes. "I don't know the reason, but the hidden people are vanishing. If you had asked one hundred years ago, fifty years ago, 'Do you believe in the hidden people,' most Icelanders would say they did. Not now. I know that the hidden people are much more afraid of the humans than they once were. They say the humans' arrogance toward nature is much worse, that nothing is sacred anymore."

He relates the story of an old man, who as a child was taken in the night from his bed by the hidden people into the cliffs above his family's farmhouse. Inside the rocks, he was fed pancakes and dark nuts and glasses of milk and was told he was a good little boy because he did not throw rocks at the cliffs. After several hours they returned him to his bed before morning, and he never saw them again. That, Magnus says, would have been a common encounter among older Icelanders.

"But there are so few Icelanders who live in the countryside anymore. Now everybody lives in towns and cities," he says. "You can't see hidden people in the city."

My friend Eirikur, a statistician, has no time for crazy, irrational people like Magnus who believe in such things as elves and hidden people and saving whales. While I am sitting at his kitchen table on the cold night before *Thorrablót*, over wine and pasta, Eirikur jokes about elves. "They once reported that nearly seventy-five percent of Icelanders believed in elves, but I don't believe it," he says. "I would be surprised if even half of the people believed in elves."

I look around the table at his wife, Addy, and their friend Sonja. "I believe in elves," Addy says with a smile.

"I believe in elves," says Sonja. Her tone is a serious one. "After my grandmother died, we found her diary, and in it she wrote about how an elf-woman once asked her to babysit for an elf-child. That was when she was ten years old, and she never spoke a word of it to us during her whole life. So I know it is true."

"Well," Addy says to Eirikur. "That's two-thirds of the Icelanders at this table who believe in elves."

Eirikur yells into the next room, where their eighteen-year-old daughter is getting ready for a night out. "Andrea," he says, "do you believe in elves?"

"Noooo," says Andrea, laughing on her way out the door.

I'm flying to the West Fjörds, the northwesternmost claw of Iceland. My destination is a town called Bolungarvík, population one thousand, where I have been invited to a *Thorrablót*. My friends in Reykjavík, none of whom have ever been to Bolungarvík, keep teasing me, saying that I'll be stuck there a week. To watch out for avalanches. To watch out for drunk fishermen.

A man named Rúnar picks me up at the airport and we make the twenty-minute drive to Bolungarvík. On one side of the road is sheer cliff stretching down into the Atlantic. The other side is lined with nets and then the slope of a mountain. "A few years ago, two people died on this road in an avalanche," Rúnar says.

Rúnar drops me off at a guesthouse, and after I settle in, I wander the noiseless streets of Bolungarvík, past the harbor filled with ice chunks. The snow is piled high beside the sidewalk as I head to the town's swimming pool. I soak in a natural outdoor hot pot, and the sun sets over the town and the little church's lights come on. Towns similar to Bolungarvík exist all over Iceland, though many villages have even less to offer. Some are little more than a bunch of metal houses, a post office, and a lonely Esso station — the kind of place where one can buy near beer or wool caps or pickled herring or Prince Polo candy bars or the biography of Yasser Arafat or rent *Ernest Goes to Camp*. Every weekend night in these towns the same scene unfolds: a slow line of teenagers in cars cruise up and down the main strip, past the harbor, past the school, past the soccer field, past the café and the bakery, then turn around with a view of a mountain, then back again. Every night the same. These are the kids you've seen earlier hanging out at the Esso station, eating french fries, while all around them, through the picture windows, the rocky, empty countryside rolls on for miles and miles.

But tonight is different. *Thorrablót* is the biggest, most important event of the year in Bolungarvík and — with the journalistic exception of me — the only people allowed to attend are married couples from the town. At the restaurant below my room, the man behind the bar says this is the busiest takeout night of the year. "All the parents are going to the *Thorrablót* tonight, so the kids are all ordering pizzas," he says.

I'm soon retrieved by my hosts: Anna, who is the headmistress of the elementary school, and her husband, Kristjan, who works at the town sports center. Anna is dressed in the traditional Icelandic costume: a long black skirt with a colorful apron tied at the waist. Anna's apron happens to be a red, yellow, and blue plaid, but each woman's is different. A scarf matching the apron is tied over a white shirt and black jacket. On her head, she wears a small black cap with a tassel. Some of the other women at the party will wear a slightly different costume, with a gold-embroidered black bodice over a white shirt. Kristjan wears the dapper men's version, which is a dark suit and vest with nine pairs of buttons up the front, and underneath a white high-collared shirt, a white scarf, and a simple silver clasp under the neck holding the scarf in place.

I tell Anna that some of my friends in Reykjavík have never been to the West Fjörds, and the schoolteacher launches into a lesson. "There's a whole generation of young people who have no connection at all with the country," she says. "They don't realize where the money comes from."

Anna tells me that she is originally from Reykjavík, but moved here because this is where her husband's family lives. "In the city, you buy yourself entertainment. Here, you have to make it up yourself," she says.

Each year, I'm told, eleven different townswomen are selected to organize and entertain at the *Thorrablót*. Anna, this year, has been selected. When Anna, Kristjan, and I arrive at a big hall called Víkurbær, where the feast will take place, several of these eleven women are smoking and drinking shots of schnapps in the kitchen.

Soon, all the lights in Víkurbær are shut off. Three hundred townspeople begin to file into the hall. All the men sit at one side of the long tables, and the women at the other. I sit with Kristjan and his friends Solrún and Jónas. They, like everyone else, have brought their own *Thorrabakki*, and their own booze. I'm told that many of the people here sit in the same seats at every *Thorrablót*. The couple next to us has been coming here for thirty-one years. Of course, as people die and new couples marry, the crowd changes, but they all have to obey the same bylaws. "I heard one time a young couple came here and they brought chicken. And some older people who saw them said, 'Hey, that's against the rules!'" Solrún says.

A bowl of *hákarl*, the rotten shark cubes, is broken open. As are frozen bottles of brennivín, a schnapps made with potato and caraway that's the Icelandic national drink. Its nickname is Black Death. "You must try the shark," says Kristjan, who pours me a shot of brennivín.

There's no turning back now. With a toothpick, I stab at a cube of *hákarl*. I close my eyes, because even in the bowl I can smell how bad it's going to be, and pop the cube into my mouth. How do I begin to describe the putrid taste? The feeling of biting through rubbery layers of skin? A sensation not unlike a rush of ammonia flies up my sinuses, and I gasp for breath. I quickly wash the rancid meat down my throat with a shot of brennivín, which itself burns like kerosene all the way down my esophagus. The entire table is watching me, chuckling and elbowing one another. Over the course of dinner Kristjan, to my amazement, will nibble no fewer than a dozen pieces of the rotten shark, many without a chaser.

We eat the *Thorramatur* with small pocketknives and our hands. All the favorites are here: the sheep's head, the testicles, the meat smoked in dung. Solrún says I must break the jawbone of the sheep's head into three pieces to ensure that my children will speak. I tear at the *hardfiskur* like an animal. "People claim that the West Fjörds has the best *hardfiskur* in Iceland," Solrún says. I'm pre-occupied with drinking more beer and more brennivín and more whiskey to wash the sour taste of the *mysa* out of my mouth. For dessert, Solrún produces a *skyr* cake made with crowberries that also helps.

Throughout dinner, the eleven townswomen perform a play, a satire about events in Bolungarvík during the past year. In the first scene, they are all dressed in blond wigs and dresses, poking fun at a girls' singing group that visited from Reykjavík. Apparently, the teenage girls attended a local dance and ended up getting really drunk, and some of them missed their plane home the next morning. The girls appear in scenes throughout the play — visiting the local museum, meeting the mayor. In another scene, the chain-smoking queen of Denmark is spoofed. There are plenty of jokes about fishing quotas and local politicians. It gets personal in a way that only a small-town play can. In one skit they parody a men's aerobics class. During the class, one man's cell phone begins ringing — something that really happened to one of the townsmen in church one Sunday. "I remember when this happened," Solrún says. "I was sitting right behind him in church."

In between skits, the entire room opens songbooks and boldly sings:

> To drink, to drink
> We wake every man to drink.
> The king of bad weather, Thorri, is here,
> He's cold and angry as hell at our country.
> With sacrifice, with sacrifice
> We need to calm him down.
>
> To peace, to peace
> We salute Thorri, cheers.
> We sacrifice for a good year and good fishing!
> We clink, we clink
> And make merry our life and soul.

By the end of dinner, we will sing nearly all of the twenty-two songs in the book.

After dinner and the play, all three hundred people are asked to leave the building for an hour or so while the eleven women and their husbands prepare the Víkurbær for a dance. I go with Jónas and Solrún and three other couples to the home of Halldór and Gudrún. This intermezzo party, I'm told, is also an annual event for these couples. "Tomorrow," says one man, "we will gather with our children to eat the leftovers of the *Thorramatur.*" Halldór maintains a radar tower for the NATO base high above Bolungarvík, something he needs a snowmobile to accomplish. "When the U.S. decides to make war in the Persian Gulf, we have to be prepared all the way up here," he says. Halldór points out fishing antiques in the restored house, including an interesting little pair of shoes made out of fish skins. I'm told that distance used to be measured in how many pairs of fish shoes a person would wear out — a "ten-fish-shoe walk" to the next town, for instance.

After an hour or so of continued drinking, all three hundred people return through the cold to the hall. As we return, our little group passes a huge fish factory at the center of town. "I hear now that Greenpeace wants to limit cod fishing," Halldór says. "If they take away the cod, we are finished as a town."

Back at the hall, the serious drinking begins — the beer and brennivín flow freely. On the dance floor, I join a line of men holding hands who circle around the women. When we stop, everyone has to dance with the person who's standing in front of him. I'm the lucky dog the first time around. I get to dance with the most beautiful girl at the ball, another icy-blue-eyed daughter of Iceland, and the only person who appears to be under thirty. At the end of the dance, she giggles and demurely says, *"Takk fyrir."*

Near 4:00 A.M. Some of the men have brought out snuff tobacco and inhale it into their nostrils. I pass when offered. I fall into conversation with Einar Gudfinnson, a parliamentarian who sponsors a pending resolution to lift Iceland's ban on whaling. I tell him that I too am an eater of whale meat and we speak briefly about Keiko. "To the group you see tonight," Einar says, "the babysitting of a whale looks very silly. To a nation of fishermen it all looks a little strange.

"But," Einar adds, "tonight is not a night to talk politics." With that, we join the line of dancers for a final round.

Einar promises to give me a lift to the airport in the morning so I can catch my 11:00 A.M. flight. But when I wake at my guesthouse at 10:00 and go downstairs, the place is dark and all the doors are locked. Einar is nowhere to be found. Neither is anybody else in town, for that matter. I run across the street to a pay phone, but it's broken. Now I start to panic — I don't want to get stranded out here. I wander until I see a single light in a building along the dock. Inside, a lone fisherman stands baiting his line, watching the sun rise over the harbor. He wipes the fish guts off his hands and passes me his cell phone. As I call for a taxi, I can still smell the fish on the receiver.

Back in Reykjavík, I show a friend, Hjalti, some photos I shot of *Thorrablót* in Bolungarvík. He stops at one photo of all the people in traditional costumes, at the long tables, singing old songs. Hjalti points at the photo and frowns. "You know," he says, "fifty years ago, they wouldn't have needed songbooks."

Over coffee at one of Reykjavík's trendy cafés, Hjalti asks me: "Do you know the whale that I'd like to eat? If I had the chance, I would boil Keiko and eat him for *Thorrablót*. Oh, my stomach is growling just thinking about it."

I decide to fly out to Heimaey and check out old Keiko for my-self. The flight is delayed two hours because of hurricane-force winds, which doesn't surprise me, because I've already been told there's a good chance I'll be stranded on Heimaey for a day or two because of severe North Atlantic weather. When I finally arrive at around 10:00 A.M., the weather clears and a brilliant sun rises, setting the snowy volcanic mountains against a fiery orange and purple sky.

Though it's an island one hundred kilometers from Reykjavík, Heimaey, with a population of five thousand, is one of Iceland's most productive fishing ports. Stark rows of weathered, corrugated metal houses line the streets. After hitching a ride with a carpenter in his van, I hike up to the lava field on the east side of town. The snow-encrusted lava here is the remains of an eruption in 1973, the same one John McPhee chronicled in his book *The Control of Nature*. Icelanders believe they were able to stop the molten lava from destroying the town of Heimaey by cooling it with high-pow-ered fire hoses. Many geologists around the world believe this is complete hogwash.

As I'm walking up to a spot that overlooks Heimaey's bay, I see four people in bright yellow snowsuits fussing with a large video camera and tripod, beside what is obviously a rental car. "Excuse me," I say. "Can you tell me where I can find Keiko?" One of the yel-low snowsuits, a tall man with glasses, points down toward the bay. In a cove, surrounded by rocks, I can make out the sea pen, but even with binoculars Keiko would be just a black speck. "Is that as close as you can get?" I ask.

"That's about it," he says, and then adds a bit haughtily: "We're shooting a piece for NBC News. We're going out on a boat later with the Free Willy Foundation people." At that, the yellow snow-suits jump into their rental car and drive off.

I follow the car, on foot, down to the docks, where the yellow snowsuits are now joined by two bearded orange snowsuits. These, I presume, are the Free Willy people. They are loading a large boat. I introduce myself and ask if I can tag along. "Afraid not," says one of the orange snowsuits.

I smile. "Come on," I say. "I don't take up much room."

"How did you even find out we were here?" he asks, and I'm im-mediately reminded of Keiko's vigilant around-the-clock security and fear that this man can tell I am indeed an eater of whale meat, and thus a threat to Keiko's well-being.

The orange snowsuit tells me to call a man named Hallur, an Ice-lander who works for a public relations firm in Reykjavík. I trudge back toward the town center, to the local tourist office so I can use the telephone. "This is a science project, this is not tourism," Hallur says over the phone. "We're trying to dehumanize the ani-mal, you see, so we have to be careful about how many people visit him." Dehumanize the animal? Aren't people regularly referring to this animal on a first-name basis?

"Is the animal going to know if there's seven people on the boat instead of six?" I ask. Hallur chuckles uneasily. "Come on," I say, "it's not like I have a harpoon in my bag." Hallur chuckles uneasily again. He agrees to set up another time to visit Keiko — but not un-til after he checks out my credentials.

When I hang up the phone, I see a skinny teenage girl, perhaps sixteen — with, of course, straight blond hair and icy blue eyes — has been listening to all this, and when she realizes where I'm from, she says, "I want to live in the United States. I went to summer school at Harvard but I didn't like it because the people were snobby. But I loved Disney World. And I definitely want to go to California because that's where my favorite band, No Doubt, lives. My school is going to Halifax this year, and I'm going to take a train to visit Boston again. I'm going to get a tattoo."

"Can't you get a tattoo in Iceland?" I ask.

"Sure," she admits, "but it's cooler to say you got it in the United States."

"What kind of tattoo are you going to get?" I ask the girl.

"A snowflake. And that's pretty funny too, because I hate the snow."

Before I head back to the airport, I stop at an Esso station and, along with a half-dozen teenagers, I eat another Icelandic favorite — *pylsur med öllu*, or "a hot dog with the works." The weather remains clear as my flight later ascends above the barren volcanic cliffs of Heimaey, battered by the North Atlantic. How long, I wonder, can a rock like Heimaey contain a girl who yearns to have an American tattoo artist draw a snowflake on her rear end? The plane banks high above Keiko's sea pen, and then soars across the deep blue ocean, where the wild orcas live. Beyond the sea, the rugged coast of Iceland can barely contain its gigantic glaciers. As we approach Reykjavík, an utterly blank, utterly vast whiteness surrounds the city and its suburbs.

Hallur eventually faxes a release form to my hotel, stating, "You must include a letter from your editor or news director on your news organization's letterhead verifying you are working on a story." He adds, "The whaling issue certainly is big in Iceland. But we don't want to be involved in the whaling issue."

Exactly six weeks from the day I leave Iceland, an overwhelming majority in the Althing, Iceland's thousand-year-old parliament, votes to repeal the decade-old ban on whaling. Though the government still has to sell the idea to the international community, several fishing fleets say they are ready to resume whale hunts as soon as next summer. When the international press reports Iceland's intention to resume whaling, and predicts doom for the Icelandic

economy, the *Times* of London writes: "Every Icelander recalls with
a shudder the disappearance of the herring stocks in 1967, when
overfishing wiped out the livelihood of whole towns and coastal
settlements. Thousands were unemployed, hundreds emigrated."
When I read this article, I think about towns like Bolungarvík,
stuck between an avalanche zone and an unforgiving sea. I think of
Ína the Herring Girl, of the fact that there are very few herring
girls left, and that even fewer have ever tasted the meat of a whale.

Though many will insist that Keiko's return to Iceland and the
vote to resume whaling have nothing to do with each other, it certainly isn't all coincidence. Ironically, the Keiko Foundation's con-
servationist efforts may end up being the last straw, the catalyst that
brings a return to whaling in the North Atlantic. Iceland's vote to
resume whaling is, in many ways, a vote against the onslaught of
American values and desires that many Icelanders fear permeates
and will eventually strangle their own ancient culture. Viewed
through this lens, the vote may seem a wholly sane and reasonable
response.

On my last day in Reykjavík, Hjalti and I walk the slushy midafternoon streets, while Hjalti rants on and on against Keiko and America. Just before he wanders away into the silent, gray afternoon, he
shouts for all to hear: "People need to see what it's really like here
in Iceland. They should see the cold and the rain and the darkness.
And the drinking. And the fornication. We Icelanders are moving
toward international nothingness! We should be drinking more
brennivín! We should be eating more fish! We should be eating
more whale!"

Beyond Siberia

FROM *Condé Nast Traveler*

THERE ARE TWO surprising things about reindeer, aside from their wholesale lack of red noses. The first is that their antlers, when new, feel very soft and are covered with thick fur. The second is that if you ride them expecting them to be like your basic horse, they will promptly and inevitably collapse under you. Or at least they will if burdened by the 210 pounds that I consider my fighting weight.

I discovered these curious facts in a moment of surprise and brief but bearable pain in a larch forest recently, on the far eastern Russian island that Anton Chekhov once declared was the absolute worst place, the ghastliest dump, in the world. Yet despite the brief deer-related drama, I have to say that the island didn't actually seem a bad place at all. It was a brilliantly sunny afternoon, with a warm breeze blowing off the Pacific. There were two rare sea eagles perched on a branch nearby (I had it in mind that I might ride over to look at them, but the reindeer had other plans). The deer's herdsman was a splendid-looking man who was a member of an exotic tribe called the Nivkhy but who nonetheless had once been Russia's cross-country ski champion, and when Rudolph did eventually toss me off his back, I tumbled onto a carpet of moss and blueberries that provided a softer landing than any equine trauma I can remember.

My dignity suffered, but nothing else, and once I had remounted and been instructed that you sit on a reindeer's shoulders, not over his waist, we trotted off quite briskly and happily into the woods. Sea eagles are evidently birds that bore easily, because they were gone by the time the deer and I trotted up to their tree. But otherwise — with the herdsman giving me handfuls of blueberries and strawberries every so often, and then reaching over with a flask of cloudberry-flavored vodka — it seemed a pretty idyllic afternoon.

My reason for recounting this small adventure is to make the point that once in a while, travel can be an extraordinarily redemptive experience. Normally it is quite the opposite: You go somewhere that is touted as being magnificent, delightful, spectacular, or whatever, and it turns out to be a disaster. But once in a while the reverse happens: You fetch up somewhere that has a reputation for being dreadful, and it turns out that you have a stunning experience and leave thinking that the place truly is the stuff that dreams are made on. It has to be a place that has bad, bad karma, and you have to adore it for being so.

It has to be, in other words, a place much like the island where I rode the collapsing reindeer: the far eastern Russian hellhole that was, Sakhalin. "I have been to Ceylon," wrote Chekhov, "and it is paradise. And I have been to Sakhalin Island, and it is utter hell."

The famous first line of the epilogue to *Crime and Punishment* reads: "Siberia. On the bank of a wide and desolate river stands a town; in the town there is a fortress; in the fortress, a prison." Siberia is a cheerless place, a land of the ruined palings of czarist prison camps and Stalinist gulags, a land of perpetual frost, amply deserving of its fearful reputation. Not for nothing is Siberia called the "Land Beyond the Sun."

But Sakhalin Island lies beyond even this. It is two thousand miles beyond Siberia's hugely wide eastern frontier river, the Lena; one thousand from the Amur and Black Dragon rivers and the border of bleak Manchuria; way beyond the terminus of the Trans-Siberian Railway. Sakhalin is referred to as the island at the end of the world, and people shudder when they hear that you're going there. "Sakhalin?" said a Muscovite, peering at me queerly. "Rather you than me."

It is an elongate island, six hundred miles from tip to toe. It looms like some vast sea monster behind the eternal fog banks: low, scrubby hills, coal-streaked cliffs, the ruins of czarist forts, and the almost equally ruined but newly built border-guard stations of today, with whirling radars and armed sentries to keep people out where once they kept people in.

The island has been known, above all, for its prisons. This is where, from 1875 onward, the tyrant-emperors of St. Petersburg sent the most incorrigible flotsam of society, the persistent murderers, the spies, the morally deformed, and the officially mutilated. Tens of thousands of Russian prisoners, deemed vile enough to send well beyond Siberia, ended up on Sakhalin, faraway and forgotten — a melancholy situation that drew the young and then unknown playwright Chekhov to the island, as a journalist, to write a book that exposed the excesses of torture and brutality and gave him the kind of Muscovite fame and confidence he needed. His digs remain — the wooden house a small museum, rarely visited.

The Russians came east to an island that was far from deserted, however. As with the Britons who came to New South Wales, so the Russians in Sakhalin displaced thousands of their own aboriginals — Aleut hunters and herders, scores of the hairy Ainu (whose womenfolk painted bright blue mustaches on their faces and thought themselves not at all unusual-looking), the fish-skin-wearing Ulti and Evenki, and the salmon-worshiping Nivkhy, all of whom had for centuries clung to a precarious existence on the island. And they all grumbled mightily at their displacement then, and they still do today, a constant background threnody.

Exile remained a dominant force in twentieth-century Sakhalin, too. Beria sent his traitors there in the early Bolshevik days, Stalin his enemies in the thirties, Brezhnev those whom the state considered useless — right up to the seventies. And world politics intruded as well: The island seesawed between the competing suzerainties of Russia and Japan — the latter, since Sakhalin is a geological extension of Hokkaido, believing it has some right to claim the island as its own.

First the island was all Japanese, then it was shared, then it was Russian, then divided half-and-half with a latitude line down the center, separating the frosty imperium of St. Petersburg from that of Tokyo. And finally, following a decision made in 1945 at faraway Yalta, it became all Russian once again, as it is today. But tens of thousands of Koreans, stateless slave-workers for the Japanese, were forbidden by the Communist Russians to return home, and they remain there still, Russian-speaking and sullen, roundly and endlessly cursing their lot.

Add to this potent mix of gloom the discovery of coal (and consequent environmental ruin in places) and then huge quantities of oil (with the same results threatened), the breakdown of communism, the growing influence of the Mafia, and the collapse of the ruble. . . . A deeply bad karma hangs over Sakhalin.

And yet . . . And yet . . . I have been there twice now. I have spent a total of about one month on the island, and together with almost all other Westerners who make a habit of going there (of whom there are an ever-increasing number, mainly from Texas and Louisiana, now that Russia is allowing Americans to exploit her island oil), I find myself becoming helplessly enchanted with the place. It turns out to be unutterably beautiful; its people are as friendly as any one can find; and perhaps best of all, though Sakhalin is easy enough to reach by air or sea, virtually no one goes there. It is, in short, a splendid secret, its treasures protected by the cloak of its vile repute.

The reindeer day was a classic of its kind. Deep berry-rich woodlands, kindly deer herders living in tents made of skin, huskies as guardians of the camp, tiny lakes, freshwater streams, cups of strong tea brewed over a birch-twig fire — and the talk of this tall, rangy cross-country skier. Though a Nivkhy tribal, he had taken a degree in anthropology thirty years ago and then had decided to leave city life and spend the rest of his years driving reindeer across the Russian tundra. He is one of the happiest and most remarkable men I have ever met.

But there were other days of equal joy. I once went with a boatman out toward a sandbar that separates the Sea of Okhotsk from the river estuary near Nogliki, in the north of the island. There is always a two-mile patch of dense fog to negotiate, and the skiff had to steer blindly through the mudbanks, following a course of small trees that have been stuck into the flats as markers. Once you're through, the sandbar is a place of wind and wild grasses and dozens of small wooden dachas, from which families venture out to fish for salmon — which they hang out to dry in the gales and then smoke and sell for about 50 cents a fish. To stand on the sand in the teeth of an Okhotsk gale, to drink a beer and eat fresh-smoked salmon dipped in fresh-pressed seal oil — it is an experience, once again, like few others.

A Nivkhy family took me in for a couple of days and fed me roast reindeer and salmon caviar and newly churned butter and homemade bread and fresh lingonberry jam. And vodka, of course, rasp-berry- and blaeberry- and blueberry-flavored and flowing end-lessly, to the point of forgetfulness.

But perhaps the best day of all was when a group of us decided to walk from Yuzhno-Sakhalinsk to the four-thousand-foot summit of Mount Chekhov. We rose at dawn, strode through long, muddy lanes, up a narrow path through forests of birch and Japanese bam-boo, then ever upward, to where the trees gave way to low grasses and rocky plains alive with wildflowers. We made the summit after four long hours, and ate caviar and salmon and drank beer, and watched while the girls collected berries and then made blini over the fire.

Lena, who had come as my interpreter, was a small, pretty woman whose husband was an oceanographer. She was fiercely na-tionalistic and kept telling me how much greater Russia still was than America could ever be.

And on the day we reached the summit of Mount Chekhov and looked over at Mount Pushkin, a mile off to the east, and over at the wild, wild Sea of Okhotsk and the still blue waters down toward Japan, and talked about the enormous impact all the newfound oil was about to have on the island, Lena rose to her full five feet and, with immense pride, spread her arms at this astonishing panorama and said simply: "Watch out, West! Russian bear is leaving its den!"

And while I still do not quite believe her, I am glad she said it and that there is pride and optimism and beauty to be found, and shared, in a place that Russia's greatest playwright once thought of as hell but which clearly isn't anymore.

Contributors' Notes

Notable Travel Writing of 2000

Contributors' Notes

Scott Anderson is a journalist and novelist who lives — at least some of the time — in New York. A contributing editor at *Harper's Magazine,* he also writes frequently for the *New York Times Magazine* and *Esquire,* usually on foreign, war-related themes. His most recent books are *Triage,* a novel, and *The Man Who Tried to Save the World,* a nonfiction investigation into the mysterious disappearance of an American relief worker in Chechnya.

Russell Banks is the author of thirteen books of fiction, including the novels *Continental Drift, Rule of the Bone,* and *Cloudsplitter,* and four collections of short stories, most recently *The Angel on the Roof: New and Selected Stories.* Two of his novels, *The Sweet Hereafter* and *Affliction,* were made into award-winning motion pictures. His work has received numerous awards and has been widely translated and anthologized. He is a member of the American Academy of Arts and Letters and is the president of the International Parliament of Writers. He lives in upstate New York with his wife, the poet Chase Twichell.

Tim Cahill was one of *Outside*'s founding editors. He is currently a contributing editor at *Men's Journal.* His books include *A Wolverine Is Eating My Leg, Jaguars Ripped My Flesh, Pecked to Death by Ducks,* and *Pass the Butterworms: Remote Journeys Oddly Rendered.* Most recently, he wrote the text for *Dolphins,* published by the National Geographic Society. He is the coauthor of the IMAX film *Everest* as well as the coauthor of the Academy Award–nominated documentary *The Living Sea.*

Philip Caputo is the author of eight books, including *A Rumor of War, Horn of Africa* (a finalist in 1981 for the National Book Award), and, most recently, *The Voyage.* He rewrote a film adaptation of *A Rumor of War,* which aired in 1980 as a four-hour miniseries on CBS, and wrote the screenplay for the film *Distant Thunder,* released in 1988 by Paramount. Caputo is a former reporter and foreign correspondent for the *Chicago Tribune,* and won both the Pulitzer Prize, for investigative journalism in 1972, and the Overseas Press Club Award in 1973. His articles and essays have appeared in the *New York Times,* the *Washington Post,* the *Boston Globe,* the *Los Angeles Times, Esquire, George, Men's Journal, National Geographic Adventure,* and many others. Caputo served in the U.S. Marine Corps from 1964 to 1967. He currently lives in Connecticut.

Andrew Cockburn, raised in County Cork, Ireland, and a resident of Washington, D.C., for the past fifteen years, is the author of numerous articles, books, and documentary films. His travel reportage, mostly for *Condé Nast Traveler* and *National Geographic,* includes writing on Burma, Moscow, Shanghai, Yemen, Libya, Mexico, Hong Kong, Tibet, and Connemara, Ireland.

Gretel Ehrlich was born in California and educated at Bennington College and UCLA film school. She was a filmmaker until 1978, when she began writing full-time. She has published three books of poems; a book of short stories; two books of narrative essays, including *The Solace of Open Spaces;* a novel, *Heart Mountain;* a novella for young adults, *A Blizzard Year;* a biography of John Muir, *Nature's Visionary;* and two memoirs. *A Match to the Heart* concerns her recovery from being struck by lightning, and *Questions of Heaven* follows a journey through the mountains of western China. *This Cold Heaven,* just published, is a nonfiction narrative about Inuit life in northern Greenland written over a period of seven years. Ehrlich's work has been widely anthologized, including *The Best Essays of the Century.* Her work has appeared in *Harper's Magazine, The Atlantic Monthly,* the *New York Times, Time,* and *Life,* among many others. She is a recipient of an NEA Writing Fellowship, a Whiting Award, a Guggenheim Fellowship, a Bellagio Fellowship (with Martha Clarke), and a Harold D. Vercell Award from the American Academy of Arts and Letters. She was a rancher in Wyoming for seventeen years and now divides her time between California and Wyoming.

Michael Finkel is a contributing writer to the *New York Times Magazine* and *National Geographic Adventure* and is the author of *Alpine Circus,* a book of wintertime travels. He runs a very small chicken operation in western Montana, and co-owns a taxicab in Port-au-Prince, Haiti.

Ian Frazier writes essays and longer works of nonfiction. His books include *Great Plains, Family, Coyote v. Acme,* and *On the Rez.* He lives in New Jersey.

Peter Hessler is a native of Columbia, Missouri, and has degrees in English from Princeton and Oxford. In 1996, he went to China's Sichuan province as a Peace Corps volunteer. There he taught English and American literature at a teachers college in Fuling, a small city on the Yangtze River. His memoir from that experience, *River Town: Two Years on the Yangtze,* was recently published. He is currently based in Beijing, where he contributes to *The New Yorker, National Geographic,* the *Boston Globe, The Wall Street Journal,* and other magazines and newspapers.

Pico Iyer is the author of six books, including *Video Night in Kathmandu, The Lady and the Monk,* and, most recently, a journey into the nature of modern travel and of a world on the move, *The Global Soul.* He lives somewhere between Japan and California.

Kathleen Lee is a writer and frequent traveler to Asia, and other parts of the world. Her collection of short stories, *Before the Afterlife,* will be published in 2002. She keeps a post office box in Santa Fe, New Mexico.

Janet Malcolm's previous books are *Diana and Nikon: Essays on Photography, Psychoanalysis: The Impossible Profession, In the Freud Archives, The Journalist and the Murderer, The Purloined Clinic: Selected Writings, The Silent Woman: Sylvia Plath and Ted Hughes,* and *The Crime of Sheila McGough.* She lives in New York with her husband, Gardner Botsford.

Lawrence Millman is the author of nine books, including *Our Like Will Not Be There Again, Hero Jesse, A Kayak Full of Ghosts, Last Places, An Evening Among Headhunters,* and — most recently — *Northern Latitudes.* He writes for *Smithsonian, National Geographic, The Atlantic Monthly, Islands,* and numerous other magazines. He is a fellow of the Explorers Club and has a mountain named after him in East Greenland. When not on the road, he makes his home in Cambridge, Massachusetts.

Susan Minot is the author of *Monkeys, Lust & Other Stories, Folly,* and most recently, *Evening.* She wrote the screenplay for Bernardo Bertolucci's film *Stealing Beauty.* Her next books will be a novella, *Rapture,* and a collection of poems. The author would like to dedicate "This We Came to Know Afterward" to Simon Dolan, the Simon in the story, who was tragically killed in a motorcycle accident in Cape Town in November 2000. "The story is dedicated to the great spirit in him."

Susan Orlean has been a staff writer at *The New Yorker* since 1992. She is also the author of three books, *Saturday Night* (1990), *The Orchid Thief* (1999), and *The Bullfighter Checks Her Makeup* (2001). She has worked as a reporter in Portland, Oregon, and in Boston, and now lives in New York City. She has contributed to *Rolling Stone, Esquire, Vogue, Outside, Travel & Leisure,* and *Condé Nast Traveler.* She prefers the aisle seat.

David Quammen is the author of *The Song of the Dodo* and eight other books of nonfiction and fiction. For fifteen years he was a columnist for *Outside,* and twice received the National Magazine Award for his science essays and other work there. In 1996 he received an Academy Award in literature from the American Academy of Arts and Letters. Quammen lives in Montana and travels frequently on assignment to jungles and swamps. His most recent book is *The Boilerplate Rhino.*

Salman Rushdie is the author of eight novels, including *Fury, Midnight's Children* (for which he won the Booker Prize and the "Booker of Bookers"), *Shame, The Satanic Verses, The Moor's Last Sigh,* and *The Ground Beneath Her Feet.* His books have been translated into thirty-seven languages.

Edward W. Said is University Professor of English and Comparative Literature at Columbia University. He is the author of twenty books, including *Orientalism* (nominated for a National Book Critics Circle Award), *Culture and Imperialism, The End of the Peace Process,* and *Out of Place,* a memoir, winner of the 2000 New Yorker Award for Nonfiction. He lives in New York City.

Bob Shacochis's collection of stories *Easy in the Islands* received the 1985 National Book Award for first fiction, and his first novel, *Swimming in the Volcano,* was a finalist for the 1993 National Book Award. Among his many other honors and awards are the American Academy of Arts and Letters Rome Prize, a James Michener Award, and a grant from the National Endowment for the Arts. Currently a contributing editor for *Outside* and *Harper's Magazine,* he has been a *GQ* columnist and writer for numerous other national publications. He is also the author of a second collection of stories, *The Next New World;* a collection of essays on food and love, *Domesticity;* and, most recently, a nonfiction work on Haiti, *The Immaculate Invasion.* He lives in Florida and New Mexico.

Thomas Swick is the travel editor of the *South Florida Sun-Sentinel.* His work has appeared in *The American Scholar, The Oxford American, The North American Review,* and *Ploughshares,* as well as a number of other publications. He is the author of the travel memoir *Unquiet Days: At Home in Poland.*

Patrick Symmes is a foreign correspondent for *Harper's Magazine* and *Outside*. His book *Chasing Che* describes crossing South America by motorcycle, retracing the journeys of the guerrilla leader Che Guevara.

Jeffrey Tayler is a frequent contributor to *The Atlantic Monthly, Harper's Magazine,* and Salon.com, and a regular commentator on National Public Radio's *All Things Considered.* His work has also appeared in *Condé Nast Traveler* and *Spin.* His first book, *Siberian Dawn,* was published in 1999 and nominated for the Pacific Rim Book Prize; his second book, *Facing the Congo,* appeared in 2000, and was selected by the *New York Times* as a Notable Travel Book of the Year. Two of his travel essays were chosen for *The Best American Travel Writing 2000.*

Marcel Theroux was born in Kampala, Uganda, in 1968 and was educated at Cambridge and Yale. A Russian speaker, he has traveled widely in the republics of the former Soviet Union and made a number of documentaries about the region for British and American television. The *New York Times* called his first novel, *A Stranger in the Earth,* "sprightly and charming." His second, *The Confessions of Mycroft Holmes,* was published in 2001.

Brad Wetzler is a contributing editor of *Outside.* He writes regularly for that magazine and other publications, and his assignments have taken him to such far-ranging places as the Amazon, Greenland, India, Russia, and the Czech Republic, not to mention L.A.'s murky, milk-warm reservoirs, where Sow Belly, the world's largest largemouth bass, is presumed to dwell. His work has appeared in the *New York Times Magazine,* the *New York Times Book Review, GQ, Men's Journal,* and *Wired,* and he was the author of a nationally syndicated adventure-travel column. He lives in Santa Fe.

Jason Wilson is the series editor of *Best American Travel Writing.* He has written for the *Washington Post Magazine, Condé Nast Traveler, Saveur, Travel & Leisure,* Salon.com, *Maxim,* and other magazines and newspapers. Wilson is currently at work on a memoir about his travels in Iceland, where a cookbook writer has named a dessert after him.

Simon Winchester, a former geologist, is currently researching a book on the eruption of the Indonesian volcano Krakatoa in August 1883. Among his recent books are the best-selling *Professor and the Madman* and *The Map That Changed the World.* Simon Winchester, who is British, divides his time between a village in upstate New York and an island in the Scottish Hebrides.

Notable Travel Writing of 2000

SELECTED BY JASON WILSON

SCOTT ANDERSON
The Last Penal Colony. *Esquire,* May.

TARA BAHRAMPOUR
Georgian Revival. *Travel & Leisure,* July.
MELISSA BIGGS BRADLEY
Far and Away. *Town & Country,* January.
TOM BISSELL
Mars: The Final Frontier. *Men's Journal,* November.
EUGENIA BONE
A Good Hunt. *Gourmet,* November.
TED BOTHA
Miles from Nowhere. *Islands,* March.
TIM BROOKES
Rediscovering America. *National Geographic,* January.
BILL BRYSON
The (Seriously, Truly, Very) Fatal Shore. *Outside,* June.

TIM CAHILL
The Most Dangerous Friend in the World. *Men's Journal,* November.
CAROLYNN CARREÑO
Looking for Guillermo. *Saveur,* July/August.
DENNIS CASS
Let's Go: Silicon Valley. *Harper's Magazine,* July.
EDIE CLARK
Early Stage: First Foliage in Aroostook County. *Yankee,* September.
TOM CLYNES
Hip Deep in Dreamtime. *National Geographic Adventure,* September/October.

WILLIAM DALRYMPLE
Antigua. *Islands,* March.

BILL DONAHUE
  Pilgrim at Johnson Creek. *DoubleTake,* Spring.
BEVERLY DONOFRIO
  The Sacred and the Mundane. *Washington Post Magazine,* September 24.

LESLIE EPSTEIN
  Pictures at an Extermination. *Harper's Magazine,* September.
JEFFREY EUGENIDES
  A Writer's Berlin. *Food & Wine,* December.

MICHAEL FINKEL
  Crazy in the Congo. *National Geographic Adventure,* March/April.

TIM GAUTREAUX
  Perfect Strangers on a Train. *Oxford American,* April.
ADAM GOODHEART
  Passages and Promenades. *Civilization,* August/September.
CYNTHIA GORNEY
  Balinese Lessons. *Washington Post Magazine,* September 24.
LAURIE GOUGH
  Naxos Nights. *Salon Travel,* March 11.
CHARLES GRAEBER
  Train Through Hell. *GQ,* November.

MIMI HARRISON
  Seen in a New Light. *National Geographic Traveler,* July/August.
TONY HENDRA
  Pamplona por los Numeros. *Men's Journal,* June.
PETER HESSLER
  Hamlet Meets Mao. *The New Yorker,* November 13.
  A Rat in My Soup. *The New Yorker,* July 24.
JACK HITT
  The Billion-Dollar Shack. *New York Times Magazine,* December 10.

PICO IYER
  A Room of My Own. *Condé Nast Traveler,* March.

DAVID B. JENKINS
  See Rock City. *Preservation,* April.
DENIS JOHNSON
  The Small Boys Unit. *Harper's Magazine,* October.
  Wing-Tips in the Mire. *Outside,* June.
ERICA JONG
  Out of Time. *Travel & Leisure,* January.

BARBARA KINGSOLVER AND STEVEN HOPP
  Seeing Scarlet. *Audubon*, September/October.

MARK LEYNER
  We'll Always Have Iqaluit. *Travel & Leisure*, November.
PETER JON LINDBERG
  Behind the Scenes on Singapore Airlines. *Travel & Leisure*, August.
  My Life as a Cosmonaut. *Travel & Leisure*, January.

BUCKY McMAHON
  Percival Gordon, King of the Howlers. *Esquire*, November.
JAMES McMANUS
  Trekking the City of Light. *Harper's Magazine*, April.
JONATHAN MILES
  Forgotten Ocean. *Travelocity*, November/December.
  Piranha Mañana. *Escape*, January.
VIRGINIA MORELL
  The Blue Nile. *National Geographic*, December.

DARRELL NICHOLSON
  Theater of the Soul. *Escape*, January.

SUSAN ORLEAN
  A Place Called Midland. *The New Yorker*, October 16 and 23.
LAWRENCE OSBORNE
  La Vida Mexicana. *Condé Nast Traveler*, April.

ROBERT YOUNG PELTON
  Under the Hammer. *Blue*, April/May.
TONY PERROTTET
  A Mythical Playground in the Mediterranean. *Islands*, April.
ROLF POTTS
  Backpackers Ball at the Sultan Hotel. *Salon Travel*, March 13.
  Dancing at the Blood Festival. *Salon Travel*, May 9.
  My Beirut Hostage Crisis. *Salon Travel*, June 6.

DAVID RAKOFF
  Land of Rising Fun. *Condé Nast Traveler*, June.
CHRISTOPHER REYNOLDS
  Slovenia's Quiet Beauty. *Los Angeles Times*, June 4.
ALAN RICHMAN
  Food Noir. *GQ*, December.
  Pete Jones Is a Man Among Pigs. *GQ*, November.
TIM ROGERS
  Honeymoon Deviant. *Travelocity*, November/December.

PAUL SALOPEK
  Pilgrimage Through the Sierra Madres. *National Geographic,* June.
KENNETH SHERMAN
  Void and Voice: Notes from Poland. *Creative Nonfiction,* Issue 14.
FLOYD SKLOOT
  A Wild Place. *Southwest Review,* Volume 85, Number 1.
JANE SMILEY
  Oaxaca: Baroque Jewel in a Pre-Hispanic Setting. *The Sophisticated Traveler,*
  May 14.
MATTHEW STEVENSON
  Vacationing in Croatia. *The American Scholar,* Summer.
MARTHA STEWART
  Martha Stewart Leaving. *New York Times Magazine,* April 9.
GWEN STRAUSS
  A French Love Affair. *New England Review,* Spring.
ROBERT STRAUSS
  My Road to Nowhere. *Stanford Magazine,* May/June.
PATRICK SYMMES
  Sheikhs and Freaks. *Outside,* September.

JEFFREY TAYLER
  White Nights in Siberia. *The Atlantic Monthly,* December.
PAUL THEROUX
  Getting Out There. *Islands,* July/August.
JONATHAN TOURTELLOT
  The Tourism Wars. *National Geographic Traveler,* October.
CALVIN TRILLIN
  Seeking Ceviche. *Gourmet,* August.

BILL VAUGHN
  "Survive This!" *Outside,* July.
WILLIAM VOLLMANN
  Across the Divide. *The New Yorker,* May 15.

ANTHONY WALTON
  Views from a Bench Above the Sea. *Preservation,* July/August.
SARA WHEELER
  Morocco: A Vision of Green Oases and Golden Sands. *The Sophisticated Traveler,*
  November 19.
CHRISTIAN WIMAN
  Milton in Guatemala. *The Threepenny Review,* Winter.

THE B·E·S·T AMERICAN SERIES™

THE BEST AMERICAN SHORT STORIES 2001
Barbara Kingsolver, guest editor · Katrina Kenison, series editor

0-395-92689-0 CL $27.50 / 0-395-92688-2 PA $13.00
0-618-07404-X CASS $25.00 / 0-618-15564-3 CD $35.00

THE BEST AMERICAN TRAVEL WRITING 2001
Paul Theroux, guest editor · Jason Wilson, series editor

0-618-11877-2 CL $27.50 / 0-618-11878-0 PA $13.00
0-618-15567-8 CASS $25.00 / 0-618-15568-6 CD $35.00

THE BEST AMERICAN MYSTERY STORIES 2001
Lawrence Block, guest editor · Otto Penzler, series editor

0-618-12492-6 CL $27.50 / 0-618-12491-8 PA $13.00
0-618-15565-1 CASS $25.00 / 0-618-15566-X CD $35.00

THE BEST AMERICAN ESSAYS 2001
Kathleen Norris, guest editor · Robert Atwan, series editor

0-618-15358-6 CL $27.50 / 0-618-04931-2 PA $13.00

THE BEST AMERICAN SPORTS WRITING 2001
Bud Collins, guest editor · Glenn Stout, series editor

0-618-08625-0 CL $27.50 / 0-618-08626-9 PA $13.00

THE BEST AMERICAN SCIENCE AND NATURE WRITING 2001
Edward O. Wilson, guest editor · Burkhard Bilger, series editor

0-618-08296-4 CL $27.50 / 0-618-15359-4 PA $13.00

THE BEST AMERICAN RECIPES 2001–2002
Fran McCullough, series editor · Foreword by Marcus Samuelsson

0-618-12810-7 CL $26.00

HOUGHTON MIFFLIN COMPANY / www.houghtonmifflinbooks.com